W9-AGC-338

HANDBOOK
OF VOCATIONAL
SPECIAL NEEDS
EDUCATION

Second Edition

Edited by
Gary D. Meers, Ed.D.

Associate Professor
Vocational Special Needs Teacher Education
University of Nebraska
Lincoln, Nebraska

AN ASPEN PUBLICATION
Aspen Publishers, Inc.
Rockville, Maryland
Royal Tunbridge Wells
1987

Library of Congress Cataloging-in-Publication Data

Handbook of vocational special needs education.

"An Aspen publication."
Includes bibliographies and index.
1. Handicapped children—Education—United States.
2. Socially handicapped children—Education—United
States. 3. Vocational education—United States.
4. Education, Cooperative—United States. 5. Vocational
education—Law and legislation—United States. I. Meers,
Gary D.
LC4019.H36   1987   371.9   87-17576
ISBN: 0-87189-868-3

The first edition of the book was entitled *Handbook of Special Vocational Needs Education*

Editorial Services: Carolyn Ormes

Library of Congress Catalog Card Number: 87-17576
ISBN: 0-87189-868-3

Printed in the United States of America

1 2 3 4 5

To All Special Needs Students

Contents

Preface xi

Acknowledgments xiii

Contributors xv

Part I   —INTRODUCTION AND FOUNDATION OF
          VOCATIONAL SPECIAL NEEDS PROGRAMS 1

Chapter   1—An Introduction to Vocational Special Needs Education .. 3
          Gary D. Meers, Ed.D.

          A Profile of Change 4
          The Youth To Be Served 7
          Historical Perspective 10
          Program Descriptions 17
          Delivery of Services 25
          Conclusion 26

Chapter   2—The Impact of Federal Legislation on Vocational
          Special Needs Programming 29
          John D. Bies, Ph.D.

          Foundations for Federal Legislation 30
          Rehabilitation Legislation 31
          Social Action Legislation 35
          Educational Legislation 39
          Summary 43

**Chapter   3—Identification and Assessment of Disadvantaged
            Students** **47**
Jerry L. Wircenski, Ph.D.

Characteristics of the Disadvantaged 47
Identification of Disadvantaged Learners in Vocational
    Education 53
Identification and Assessment of Disadvantaged Learners ... 62
Summary 73

**Chapter   4—Identification and Characteristics of Handicapped
            Students** **81**
Stanley F. Vasa, Ed.D., and Allen L. Steckelberg, M.Ed.

Identification of the Handicapped 82
Incidence of Handicapping Conditions 85
Review of Handicapping Conditions 87

**Part II   —VOCATIONAL SPECIAL NEEDS PROGRAM
            DEVELOPMENT AND IMPLEMENTATION** **113**

**Chapter   5—Designing Vocational Programs for Special Needs
            Individuals** **115**
Lynda L. West, Ph.D.

Program Delivery 116
Professional Development 120
Curriculum Development 125
Transition Programs 128
Program Evaluation 133
Summary 135

**Chapter   6—The Modification of Curriculum and Instruction:
            Catalysts for Equity** **137**
Stephen White, M.Ed.

A Conceptual Framework for Curriculum Modification 138
Content Modification 140
Modification of Tools and Equipment 146
The Special Needs of Targeted Groups 147
A Conceptual Framework for Instructional Practices 150
Direct Instruction 152
Program Guidelines 157
Implications for Administrators 158
Summary 160

**Chapter 7—Cooperative Work Experience Programs for Students
with Vocational Special Needs** **165**
David Kingsbury, Ed.D.

Types of Cooperative Education Placement Programs 165
Characteristics of Cooperative Vocational Education 168
Component Functions of Cooperative Programs 168
The Role of the Teacher-Coordinator 169
Training Site Location and Development 172
Uses of Vocational Cooperative Education Training Sites ... 175
The Placement Process: Matching the Student to the
    Training Site 177
Training Process Administration 181
Classroom Instruction in a Cooperative Work
    Experience Program 184
Coordination of Instruction in the Cooperative
    Vocational Program 196
The Follow-up and Transition of the Special Needs Student ... 197
Summary 198

**Chapter 8—Identification and Utilization of Support Services in
Serving Vocational Special Needs Students** **201**
Susan B. Asselin, Ph.D.

Diversity of Vocational Special Needs 202
Support Services 204
Cooperation and Coordination 208
Summary 211

Chapter 9—Vocational Assessment: The Evolving Role **213**
Carole A. Veir, Ed.D.

Defining Vocational Assessment 213
Types of Assessment 219
Multidisciplinary Teams 232
The Assessment Process 238
Summary 253

**PART III—VOCATIONAL SPECIAL NEEDS SUPPORT
SERVICES** **257**

Chapter 10—Career Education for Special Needs Youth **259**
Ronald J. Anderson, Ph.D., and Marlene I. Strathe, Ph.D.

Definition 259
Career Development Theory 260

Career Development Models 263
Career Education Curriculum 264
Summary 272

Chapter 11—Generalizable Skills Instruction 275
James P. Greenan, Ph.D.

Curriculum 276
Implementation 279
Evaluation 307
Summary 311

Chapter 12—Transition from School to Work and Community 315
Ronald J. Anderson, Ph.D., and
Marlene I. Strathe, Ph.D.

Transition Models 316
Organizational Support 318
School Responsibilities for Transition 319
Community Agency Responsibilities 320
Organizational and Administrative Considerations 321
Interface between Education and Human Service 324
Interface Issues 325
Personnel 326
Outcomes 326
Summary 327

Chapter 13—Postsecondary Institutions and Support Systems
for Special Needs Learners in Vocational
Education Programs 331
James M. Brown, Ph.D., and Paul M. Retish, Ph.D.

Secondary Vocational Education Programs 332
Institutions Offering Postsecondary Vocational
Education Programs 332
Support Services and Service Providers 338
Adapting to Future Changes 341
Review 342

Chapter 14—The Role of Parents in the Education of
Vocational Special Needs Youth 345
Stanley F. Vasa, Ed.D., and
Allen L. Steckelberg, M.Ed.

Assumptions about Parents 346
Purposes of Parent Educational Programs 347
Program Delivery Models 348
Program Evaluation 353

**Chapter 15—The Administrators Role in Vocational Special
Needs Programs** 355
Rosemary F. Kolde, Ed.D.

The Role of the Administrator 355
Philosophy and Policy 357
Provision of Services 357
Participating School District Relationships and
Responsibilities 359
Quality Programming 360
Job Placement 362
Community Resources 363
Summary 364

Appendix A—Additional Special Needs Resources 367

Books 367
Films 369

Appendix B—Glossary of Special Needs Terms 371

Index 387

Preface

This volume was written to fill a void that currently exists in the literature dealing with special needs programming for disadvantaged and handicapped students. This book is intended to serve as an information base from which teachers, administrators, and other involved individuals can make informed decisions concerning programming for special needs students.

This book can be used in a variety of settings ranging from graduate and undergraduate classrooms to inservice settings. Researchers and consultants will find it very helpful because of the historical perspectives and programmatic sections that are presented. School administrators will find it helpful in the establishment of vocational special needs programs because of the program organization and designs that are described.

The book is divided into three main parts, each of the latter two building upon the part preceding it.

Part I deals with the foundation of vocational special needs programs. Chapter 1 profiles the students of today, gives a historical perspective, and provides an introduction to vocational special needs programming. Chapter 2 describes the federal legislation that impacts upon special needs students, programs, and educational personnel. Chapters 3 and 4 describe the students that are being served.

Part II serves as a base for program development and implementation. Chapter 5 deals with designing vocational programs for special needs individuals. Chapter 6 contains curriculum modification techniques. Chapter 7 covers the critical area of work experience and cooperative placement programs. Chapter 8 focuses on the provision of support services for special needs youth. Chapter 9 deals with vocational assessment and its role in special needs programs.

Part III contains information about career education, transition, postsecondary opportunities, and administration of special needs programs. Chapter 10 outlines the components of a career education program. Chapter 11 identifies the transferable skills that special needs students can use in their everyday lives. Chapter 12 deals with the transition process from school to work and community living. Chapter 13 covers postsecondary opportunities for special needs youth. Chapter 14 identifies the role of parents and advocates in supporting special needs youth in vocational training. The last chapter, Chapter 15, discusses the administrator's role in the establishment and conduct of special needs programs.

Gary D. Meers, Ed.D.
August, 1987

Acknowledgments

As with any major undertaking, the end is attended by a sense of relief and accomplishment. Relief is felt because no longer do deadlines have to be met, nor rough copies read and revised. The feeling of accomplishment occurs because a wide range of thoughts, theories, and strategies have been brought together from a diverse group of authors into one whole. This alone gives cause for celebration.

I would like to thank all of the authors for their willingness to work within tight deadlines without becoming disturbed at my insistence that we meet those deadlines. Their ultimate reward for the sacrifices they made during the time of writing will be in the better programming for special needs students that hopefully will be achieved throughout the United States.

I, together with all of the authors, thank the special needs students we have had over the years. They have helped us to grow both as educators and human beings. They are unnamed, yet their faces, personalities, and dreams are with us always.

A special thanks goes to the team at Aspen Publishers, Inc.—Margaret Quinlan, Martha Sasser, and others—who provided essential help to the authors. They backed this endeavor and assisted at each step so that a dream could become a reality.

An expression of gratitude must be made in memory of Curt Whitesel. Curt devoted his life to securing the services of the best authors he could find. His belief in quality led him to search out and work with authors that had never published, were unsure of their abilities, and were puzzled as to how to proceed. Through his encouragement and support, these authors have developed into a group of contributors that are adding to the growth of quality literature in the field of special needs education. His memory serves to drive us to even better work, because all of us want his memory to continue to stand for excellence.

Contributors

Ronald J. Anderson, Ph.D.
Associate Professor
Department of Special Education
University of Northern Iowa
Cedar Falls, Iowa

Susan B. Asselin, Ph.D.
Assistant Professor
Vocational Special Needs
Virginia Polytechnic Institute and State
University
Blacksburg, Virginia

John D. Bies, Ph.D.
Human Resources and Management
Development Consultant
Germantown, Tennessee

James M. Brown, Ph.D.
Associate Professor
Vocational Technical Education
University of Minnesota
St. Paul, Minnesota

James P. Greenan, Ph.D.
Associate Professor and Chairman
Vocational Education
Purdue University
West Lafayette, Indiana

David E. Kingsbury, Ed.D.
Professor
Vocational Education
Bemidji State University
Bemidji, Minnesota

Rosemary F. Kolde, Ed.D.
Associate Superintendent
Greak Oaks Vocational School District
Cincinnati, Ohio

Gary D. Meers, Ed.D.
Associate Professor
Vocational Special Needs Teacher Education
University of Nebraska
Lincoln, Nebraska

Paul M. Retish, Ph.D.
Professor
Division of Special Education
College of Education
University of Iowa
Iowa City, Iowa

Allen L. Steckelberg, M.Ed.
Instructor
Department of Special Education and
Communication Disorders
University of Nebraska
Lincoln, Nebraska

Marlene I. Strathe, Ph.D.
  Professor of Education Psychology
  University of Northern Iowa
  Cedar Falls, Iowa

Stanley F. Vasa, Ed.D.
  Professor
  Department of Special Education and
    Communication Disorders
  University of Nebraska
  Lincoln, Nebraska

Carole A. Veir, Ed.D.
  Assistant Professor
  Director, Mid-Management/Supervision
    Certification Programs
  Department of Educational Administration
  The University of Texas at Austin
  Austin, Texas

Lynda L. West, Ph.D.
  Associate Professor
  Special Education and Practical Arts
  Vocational-Technical Education
  University of Missouri
  Columbia, Missouri

Stephen White, M.Ed.
  Coordinator
  The Great Falls Transition Project
  Great Falls Public School
  Great Falls, Montana

Jerry L. Wircenski, Ph.D.
  Professor
  Trade and Industrial Education
  North Texas State University
  Denton, Texas

Part I

Introduction and Foundation of Vocational Special Needs Programs

Chapter 1

An Introduction to Vocational Special Needs Education

Gary D. Meers, Ed.D.

Every fall, a human mass migration occurs that rivals any animal migration. This migration occurs when the school doors open and the educational process gets underway for another year. Among parents are those purchasing new clothes, school supplies, and colorful lunchboxes to prepare their sons and daughters for that very important first day of kindergarten. There are tears shed, pictures taken, and good-byes uttered as entrance is made for the first time into that large and often overwhelming structure called school.

Going with these small children are the hopes and dreams of the parents, who want only the very best for their children. They base their hopes upon the fact that in the United States every child is entitled to a quality education. The first day in kindergarten is the beginning of an educational experience that will transform a scared child of 5 or 6 into an 18-year-old young adult with a high school diploma.

Ideally, this educational experience would occur slowly and sequentially, so that the parents and students could see their hopes and dreams being realized. Provisions would be made by the school for the unique needs of each student, and every school day would provide for instructional growth. Both the school and the student would be aware of and receptive to their educational rights and responsibilities. The student would come every day to learn, and the teachers would be prepared every day to teach; and thus education would be exciting and rewarding for everyone.

The problem with this ideal is that life is simply not like that. Each fall approximately 3.6 million children start the educational process in the United States. The current profile for entering students includes the following facts:[1]

- One out of four will come from a poverty level home.
- Fourteen percent will become teenage mothers.
- Fifteen percent will be handicapped.
- Fifteen percent will have limited English proficiency.

- Fourteen percent will be children of unmarried parents.
- Forty percent will have their home broken before they are eighteen.
- Ten percent will have parents who are illiterate.
- Thirty-three percent will be latch key children.
- Thirty percent will not complete high school.

Not even touched on are other societal factors such as chemical dependency and suicide; data about these are almost impossible to secure because of the complexity of the problems.

Teachers, especially those who teach special needs students, quickly realize that in order to effectively instruct their students, they are going to have to develop different strategies and methodologies than those traditionally used. A student carrying a heavy burden of concern for a bad home situation requires a different approach from that required for a student with no serious problems and with maximal parental support.

No matter what environmental background they come from or disability they possess, all children in the educational system of the United States have a right to a quality educational program that will meet their individual needs. To meet these needs, comprehensive and specific programming is required that will allow participation in programs that previously have been closed to or nonexistent for special needs students.

This book focuses on the development of delivery systems for special needs students enrolled in vocational programs. In order to develop a comprehensive series of delivery systems, a user of this book must possess an adequate understanding of the terminology and purposes of vocational special needs programming. This chapter includes an account of current population shifts in the United States, profiles of students, a historical perspective, definitions of terms, and a description of programs that are designed to serve special needs students.

A PROFILE OF CHANGE

In order to understand the challenges facing special needs students and their teachers, the reader must be made aware of some of the changes that the United States is undergoing. These changes include general population shifts, school population shifts, and emerging labor market needs.

General Population Shifts

Americans are having babies at a rate less than the rate of replacement. In 1957, at the height of the baby boom, American women were having children at a rate of 3.7 per lifetime. Today the rate is 1.8, well below the 2.1 rate that demographers say is necessary for one generation to replace itself with another of equal size.

The average age of the United States population is just over 30 years. Currently, one out of ten Americans (11.6 percent) is 65 or older and this percentage is increasing each year. By 2030, one out of five Americans (21.1 percent) will be 65 or older.

The nation's population will continue to grow in spite of low birthrates as a result both of the elderly living longer and of increased legal and illegal immigration. By the year 2020, the population will be 265 million, with most growth being among minority groups.

Family structure will continue to change. Currently, 14 million children are in single-parent homes. Nine out of ten of these children live in a home headed by a female. The family situation of these 14 million children is indicated by the following:[2]

- Sixteen percent of these children have mothers who are under 25 and 3.5 percent have teenage mothers.
- Thirty-six percent have mothers who did not complete high school.
- Fifty percent have mothers who are unemployed or not in the labor force.
- Twenty-four percent were born out of wedlock.
- Sixty-two percent of such families have annual incomes under $10,000.
- Forty-two percent of such families live in inner cities.

These data suggest that as America turns gray and families restructure, there will be increased pressure and competition for social services. Schools are funded on local tax bases and by levies voted for by residents. A dilemma may well arise in the near future. As a result of increased costs of services and a higher proportion of citizens living on fixed incomes, the issue of limited services versus limited dollars will become sharper. Adults vote, children can't. The taxpayer revolts likely to occur in the future will put the interests of the latter in jeopardy, and consequently they must be carefully guarded.

School Population Shifts

Schools will be challenged on several fronts as the composition of their student population changes.

Children now constitute the poorest segment of society, having replaced the aged in the past ten years. There are approximately 13.8 million children under 18 who live in families with annual incomes below the poverty line for a family of four. They are coming to school carrying the effects of economic disadvantagement.

Students continue to push dropout rates higher and higher. The national dropout rate is 30 percent, and in a number of large urban areas the dropout rate is 50 percent. Increased dropout rates are occurring at a time when states are expanding their graduation and promotion requirements as a part of a national school reform movement. As of 1986, very few states had made any accommodation within their standards to help students who did not achieve the new goals. Only time will tell if dropout rates will level out or continue to rise, perhaps with the national rate approaching 50 percent.

The number of students coming from homes where English is not the primary language will increase. Many of these students will be first-generation immigrants, so they will be adjusting not only to a new language, but to a new culture.

Teachers will become a rarer commodity, especially in the area of vocational and special education. There are now 2.1 million teachers, with the average age being 42. By 1992, one-half of these teachers will resign, retire, or die, leaving many classrooms vacant because no teachers can be found. By 1993, there will be an annual need for 211,000 elementary and secondary teachers, while schools of education will be graduating only 133,000 teachers, leaving about a 37 percent shortage.[3]

With the development of the national educational reform movement, there has been increased scrutiny of teacher preparation, and observers of education are stating that there is an even more acute shortage of *qualified* teachers. In many cases, qualified teachers are the first to leave teaching, citing inadequate preparation, poor pay, and poor working conditions as the main reasons for their departure. A major question now facing education is how to recruit, train, and retain quality teachers, especially those who will work with special needs students.

Emerging Labor Markets

Over the past few years, because of the large supply of teenagers, business and educational institutions that depend on a steady supply of young people could afford to adopt a ''throwaway'' attitude about potential employees and students. Those days are coming to an end.

The population of 18- to 24-year-olds reached an all-time high of 30.4 million in 1980. During the next 15 years, this group is expected to decline by more than 7 million, causing a shortage of beginning workers. By 1995, the military, in order to maintain its present level of manpower, will need to attract 55 percent of all eligible 18-year-olds. Short-term, high-turnover employers will have to offer new incentives for employment or increase dramatically starting wages.

The emerging jobs are going to offer many new employment opportunities for special needs students. Table 1-1 shows where the growth in jobs is going to be.

Table 1-1 Largest Number of New Jobs

Occupation	Growth in Employment, 1978–1990 (in thousands)
Janitors and sextons	671.2
Nurse's aides and orderlies	594.0
Sales clerks	590.7
Cashiers	545.5
Waiters/waitresses	531.9
General clerks (office)	529.8
Professional nurses	515.8
Food preparation and service workers (fast food)	491.9
Secretaries	487.8
Truck drivers	437.6

Source: *Monthly Labor Review,* February 1986.

This table includes only one occupation, professional nursing, that requires a college degree; the others require only vocational or onsite training. The jobs are within occupation areas that have long offered employment opportunities for special needs youth. It is imperative that schools offering vocational training be cognizant of these emerging employment opportunities and develop training programs within these areas.

Much concern has been expressed about technology moving so rapidly that special needs individuals will lose employment opportunities because of their lack of "high tech" skills. This concern is one that can easily be laid to rest by considering the state of technology in every area from recreation to business. Thermometers are digital and activate a buzzer when the temperature has been taken. Fast food restaurants use cash registers with product symbols; the worker just hits the symbol for a particular item and the price is automatically entered and displayed. Grocery store checkers now move the products across a laser reader and the prices are entered. Cash registers display the amount of change to be returned. And the technology parade goes on. . . .

It should be obvious that technological development allows us all to be users of high-technology equipment without being concerned about how it was developed or how it works. On the other hand, the strictly high-technology industries are not providing the large number of employment opportunities that many forecasted. By 1995, high-technology industries will provide only 6.6 percent of all jobs and fewer than 4 percent of these workers will be actually involved in high tech work. Yet 90 percent of all workers will be using some form of high technology to do their jobs. The point is that special needs students need to learn how to make high-tech products work for them and not be intimidated by the flashing lights, digital readouts, or buzzing signals.

With the coming labor shortage resulting from low birth rates, the higher percentage of women in the workplace, and the greying of America, the future is one of promise for special needs students. A nation needs a labor resource pool from which it can draw, and the special needs population composed of disadvantaged and handicapped individuals is one of the most readily available.

THE YOUTH TO BE SERVED

There are two terms commonly used to identify special needs students enrolled in vocational programs: *disadvantaged* and *handicapped*. The following sections attempt to define these terms.

The Disadvantaged

The disadvantaged are persons (other than handicapped persons) who "(1) have academic or economic disadvantages, and (2) require special services, assistance, or programs in order to enable them to succeed in vocational education programs."[4]

The disadvantaged are divided into two major categories: academic and economic. A person is academically disadvantaged if that person (1) "lacks reading and writing skills," (2) "lacks mathematical skills," or (3) "performs below grade level."[5] A person is economically disadvantaged if (1) "family income is at or below national poverty level,'' (2) the ''participant or parent(s) or guardian of the participant is unemployed,'' (3) the ''participant or parent(s) of participant is recipient of public assistance,'' or (4) the ''participant is institutionalized or under state guardianship.''[6]

The above legislative definition (from Public Law 94-482) sets forth the technical aspects of an adequate definition of the disadvantaged. However, from an educational perspective, there are many other influencing factors that must be noted when defining the disadvantaged.

A disadvantaged student may have many personal problems that present themselves as barriers to successful completion of vocational training. The home situation may be such that the parents or guardian of the student has no expressed interest in the student's schooling. Whatever the student does at school is O.K. If the student does not go to school, that is O.K., too.

Another critical barrier to school success is the student's attitude. It has been said that 90 percent of success is in having the proper attitude. In many situations, this saying holds true. The disadvantaged student, after repeated failures at the elementary school level, moves to a junior high or middle school level only to encounter more of the same. By failing over and over again, the student's attitude changes from one of hope to one of despair. In getting to this point of hopelessness, the student generally will have moved through four stages of failure: disinterest, disillusionment, disassociation, and disenfranchisement.

Disinterested youth are those who cannot see any subject, topic, or activity within the school setting as being beneficial to them. Social studies is perceived as the study of bygone eras with no relevance to the present. English is a waste of time, because everyone knows how to talk. Other school subjects are perceived as having the same irrelevance, and disinterested students look for some other setting where their interests can be focused. These outside interests often bring the students into direct conflict with teachers and other school officials. The home settings, for one reason or another, are unable to capitalize on the students' interests, and thus the disinterest grows.

Out of this disinterest grows disillusionment. School is viewed only as a place to socialize with friends and to kill some time each day. Nothing of practical use occurs at school, and the groundwork is laid for the next stage: disassociation.

After repeated failures, conflicts with authority figures, and painful disappointments, troubled students disassociate themselves from the formal school setting. This disassociation may happen at any age, though it occurs most often between the ages of 14 and 16. In many states, the legal age for quitting school is 16, but it is a well-known fact that one can quit school at any time with minimal consequences. This knowledge enables students to work through the disassociation process more quickly, because there are no real restrictions on their actions.

After the students have become disassociated from the formal setting, they find themselves in a very uncomfortable position. They now have no identification with a school, yet they have not made a commitment to a career. They are caught between youth and adulthood without the benefit of the options available in either. They are seeking to be independent of their parents but do not have the resources available to make the complete break and become self-sufficient. They are, in a sense, floating between levels of maturity. They are disenfranchised, in that they have no person in whom they can place their confidence.

These young people have irregular school attendance, poor grades, conflicts with teachers, discipline problems (both at school and with the police), and difficult home situations. They are looking for some program or person that will involve them in a meaningful life-directing way. Their negative attitudes reflect their life experiences.

The above profile should serve to introduce the reader to some of the general characteristics of the disadvantaged student. Chapter 3 discusses the disadvantaged student in much greater detail.

> The handicapped are those individuals who have been evaluated appropriately as being mentally retarded, hard of hearing, deaf, speech impaired, visually handicapped, seriously emotionally disturbed, orthopedically impaired, other health impaired, deaf-blind, multi-handicapped, or as having specific learning disabilities, who because of those impairments need special education and related services.[7]

The Handicapped

The above legislative definition (from Public Law 94-142) sets forth the technical categories of the formal definition of handicapped individuals who are to be served. In order to become familiar, on an introductory level, with the handicapped and their problems, one must explore the barriers they commonly face. The barriers that generally arise when the handicapped—or the disabled, as many individuals prefer to be called—seek specialized educational services are physical, psychological, and social.

The physical barriers are those that stand in the way of a disabled person who seeks admittance to a particular location. Section 504 of the Rehabilitation Act of 1973 (Public Law 93-112) specifies that the handicapped shall not be denied access to public-use facilities due to physical barriers. The American National Standards Institute provides accessibility standards both for new construction and for remodeling existing structures. At present, not all of the barriers faced by the physically disabled have been removed, nor will they be in the very near future. But major progress has been made. There is now greater access to public transportation, such as buses, planes, and trains; there are curb cuts on major pedestrian thoroughfares; and there is greater building accessibility to public-use facilities. Much effort is being expended to ensure that the remaining physical barriers are removed as rapidly as possible so that the disabled will be able to participate in whatever activities they choose.

The removal of physical barriers is very important to those handicapped youth who seek access to vocational training. Many of the physical barriers, when viewed objectively, are not as insuperable as they appear to be. Often minor modifications render laboratories and classrooms generally accessible.

The psychological barrier is erected by the handicapped persons themselves, in that they create a barrier of hopelessness based on previous experiences. They have had repeated failures in the past, and they feel that to engage in a new activity, such as vocational training, would only bring them failure again. Every new opportunity for involvement is met with an excuse—until finally the opportunities no longer appear. The psychological barrier is not created overnight but comes about partly as a result of many frustrating, often painful, experiences with another kind of obstacle: the social barrier.

The social barrier is erected by society. Members of society have many misconceptions, biases, and fears regarding the handicapped and as a result impose restrictions on them. Blind people should work in snack bars in government buildings; deaf people should work in printing shops; the mentally retarded should assemble hair curlers, etc. The long list of restrictions is compiled without anyone ever consulting the individuals involved as to what *they* would like to do. Society is quick to place a label on anyone who deviates from the norm. The norm, however, exists only in the minds of particular members of society; since it never remains constant, it cannot be all-encompassing. Indeed, through increased information and training, progress is being made to condition people to accept an individual as competent regardless of a handicapping condition.

Legislation can remove physical barriers, but it cannot remove societal barriers unless a massive educational effort is also undertaken. People fear the unknown, but with knowledge appropriate decisions can be made. Though often not visible, societal barriers pose a real threat to the opportunities for success available to the handicapped and every effort must be made, through increased public awareness, to ensure that they are removed.

Chapter 4 explains in detail how each of the above disabilities is defined and describes the criteria by which students are diagnosed and determined to be eligible for special services.

HISTORICAL PERSPECTIVE

Early settlers came to the United States with the expressed purpose of pursuing their respective occupations, family interests, and religious beliefs without interference from the government. There were two common uniting beliefs that gave these people the strength and determination to survive in this harsh new land: (1) "An individual has much worth and the dignity of that individual must be preserved," and (2) "individuals should be free to earn their livelihoods in whatever way that proves most profitable."[8]

Many of the first settlers had special needs, including the debtors, the misdemeanor criminals, and those who, for some reason, were perceived as being undesirable residents of the mother country. These were the people who were sentenced by the courts to be exported to the colonies as potential settlers instead of being cast into prison. Once they had made the difficult journey from Europe to the colonies, they faced the immediate need to develop skills that would enable them to survive. This they did by transferring the European apprenticeship and indentured servant system to the colonies.

The apprenticeship system had the following objectives:

- to teach a particular trade (the apprentice would learn the skills and mysteries of the chosen trade)
- to give the apprentice a good general education
- to give the apprentice good moral and social training
- to pay off debts incurred by the father in apprenticing the son
- to provide a system of poor relief by apprenticing poor, homeless, or orphaned boys
- to eliminate idleness by forcing the idle into apprenticeship programs

The chief advantages of the apprenticeship system for special needs or disadvantaged youths were that

- it was a good way to bring such youths to the new land
- it allowed an opportunity for them to develop strong and close relationships with adults
- it served to assist some disadvantaged youths to get out of the ranks of poverty
- it involved the entire development of such youths, not just the skill development component.

Some of the problems with the apprenticeship system stemmed from the fact that many of the youths were exploited for purposes other than learning a trade. Also, their masters often failed to provide adequate food, clothing, shelter, and general education. Finally, the long length of the apprenticeship (two to ten years) did much to kill the interest of many of the apprentices.

The other system used to involve special needs individuals in the New World settlements was indenture. Individuals could be indentured to ship captains by the courts. The captains in turn brought their charges to the colonies and sold the papers of indenture to eager employers. Indenture had the following characteristics:

- The master was not required to train the indentured servant in any area of skill or provide a general education.
- The indentured servant had to do any work that was requested.
- The paper of indenture could be sold to another master at any time.
- Children and adults of both sexes could be indentured.
- The indenture paid the cost of transporting the servants to the colonies.
- The period of indenture ranged from one to seven years in length.

The apprenticeship system quickly became confused with the indenture system because of the common characteristic of serving for a period of time. Masters soon wanted only indentured servants because they had only to work them, not train them, and a very large illegal traffic in indentured servants quickly sprang up. The courts of

England sentenced special needs individuals in great numbers to be deported to the colonies. Ship captains would buy the papers of indenture and then sell them at great profit upon arrival in America.

As the apprenticeship system declined into a form of indenture, many young special needs individuals were abused. They were beaten and starved and were not tutored in any skill or provided with a general education. Often such apprentices were forced to flee from their masters in order to survive. Many of these runaways were able to travel west and make a fresh start on the frontier.

For young women, the opportunities for skill training, besides training in the home, were practically nonexistent. Women were not involved in the apprenticeship system, only in the indenture system. They were not taught to read or write. If they did learn to do either, it was by accident rather than by design.

One large group of special needs individuals during this period consisted of the slaves. Much has been written about slavery in the United States, but it bears repeating that it is a tragedy this institution ever existed. Slaves were not perceived as having needs, wants, or desires when it came to planning their lives. Attention to this special needs group would not come until the late 1800s and early 1900s.

The Native American population was viewed by many settlers as an annoying obstacle to development of the West. This annoyance was dealt with in a forthright manner that resulted in many human tragedies. The legacy of human tragedy is still present as Native Americans seek a role in the society of today.

From the earliest days of Jamestown until the 1830s, the conditions described above remained pretty much the same. During the 1830s and 1840s, vocational training was introduced into orphanages and reform schools. This created a twofold set of attitudes that can still be seen today. First, it attached a stigma to vocational education, in that it was perceived as being only for poor children, orphans, and delinquents. Many young persons in need of vocational training would not enroll, because they did not want to be associated with such ''undesirable'' students. Second, poor children, orphans, and delinquents were placed in vocational training programs with no consideration given to the individual student's preferred area of study. A vicious circle was created that did much to limit the opportunities of special needs students. Since vocational training was perceived as being only for special needs students, only special needs students would enroll in vocational education; observers could then say, ''See, I told you that vocational education was only for those kinds of people.'' The advantages of vocational training for students of other kinds were simply not appreciated. Beyond that, many educators feared that vocational education would contaminate general education.

With the coming of the Industrial Revolution in the 1860s, a great demand arose for labor of all types. The apprenticeship system was on its last legs, and the Industrial Revolution sealed its fate. Children, especially homeless or orphaned children, were soon working in factories 14 hours a day, six days a week. The conditions they worked under and the tasks they performed were very dangerous and often injurious to their health.

For the handicapped person, life was even more difficult. It was felt that such people should be removed from society so that normal people would not be contaminated by being exposed to their handicaps. The opportunities for vocational and academic training for such persons were virtually nonexistent.

During the early 1900s, some societal and legislative changes occurred that assisted children in general and special needs students in particular. These changes were due to a growing feeling on the part of the general public that more assistance should be provided to special needs students. For the handicapped, there were isolated pieces of legislation that provided for particular disabilities, such as Public Law 58-171, which promoted the circulation of Braille reading materials among the blind. Some teacher education institutions began to offer classes in special education for their students. States such as New York, Rhode Island, and Ohio began classes for children with various handicaps. But the vocational training of such children at this point was limited to isolated, specific, and repetitive tasks, such as broom making.

For the disadvantaged, there were child labor laws and compulsory school attendance laws that restricted the employment of 8-, 9-, and 10-year-olds. As a result, there was a growing feeling that these students should go into vocational training programs of some kind. There arose a common philosophy that the ''whole boy'' needed to be educated and that vocational training could help in this. It was held that females, in contrast, could acquire their education in the home, for that was where they would spend their adult lives.

The Smith-Hughes Act (Public Law 64-347) was passed in 1917 as an emergency war measure. This act provided the basis for the vocational education movement. For the first time, there was money available for the promotion and development of vocational education in cooperation with the states. The total monies authorized under this piece of legislation amounted to $7 million, with funds set aside at the secondary level in the areas of agriculture, trade and industry, and home economics. Of the $7 million, $1 million was set aside for teacher training.

Under another part of the Smith-Hughes Act, the Federal Board for Vocational Education was established. The primary function of the Board was to supervise the expenditure of federal funds according to the provisions of the act. An often overlooked additional function of the Board was to coordinate vocational rehabilitation programs for handicapped persons. This combination of duties was ideal for the purpose of serving special needs students, primarily the handicapped, in vocational programs. Unfortunately, because of the prevailing philosophy, this duty was not abided by, as demonstrated by this excerpt from Policy Bulletin No. 1, which outlined who was to be served in vocational education:

> The Federal Board desires to emphasize the fact that vocational schools and classes are not fostered under the Smith-Hughes Act for the purpose of giving instruction to the backward, deficient, and incorrigible or otherwise subnormal individuals; but that such schools and classes are to be established and maintained for the clearly avowed purpose of giving thorough vocational instruction to healthy, normal individuals to the end that they might be prepared for profitable and efficient employment. Such education should command the best efforts of normal boys and girls.[9]

As can be seen from this statement, there has been a long dispute about who should receive vocational training. Though vocational training began in institutions of the 1830s to serve the special needs students, the stated policy in 1917 was clearly that vocational education was not meant to serve special populations.

Chapter 2 explains in detail the various pieces of legislation that have been passed pertaining to serving special needs populations. A careful look must be taken at this legislation to gain a clear perspective of the social trends and of the way Congress has reacted to these trends through legislative action. The majority of legislation dealing with special populations has been reactive, that is, laws have been passed after needs have surfaced, rather than as part of plans to serve future needs of high risk citizens.

Since 1917, the United States has survived four major military conflicts (World War I, World War II, Korea, Vietnam), a depression, several recessions, and numerous other tragic and sensitizing events. The decade of the 1960s brought into full force the civil rights movement. Emotions stemming from the Vietnam conflict combined with those stemming from the civil rights movement to bring about a new awareness of the individual differences that exist in society and of how these differences contribute to make the United States function as it does. One theme that emerged during the 1960s was *relevancy*. What was being taught, the work being done, and the programs being offered had to be relevant, and the following kinds of questions began to be asked. How are we serving the handicapped and disadvantaged? What are their rights when it comes to educational planning and program offerings?

The course of the 1970s was determined by the experiences of the 1960s. The time was right for specific pieces of legislation (Public Laws 91-230, 93-112, 93-203, 94-124, 94-482, and 95-93) that would provide the mechanisms through which handicapped and disadvantaged persons could be served and trained. Because of these new social and educational commitments, the 1970s became known as the "total programming decade."

The 1980s has been characterized as the "decade of implementation." The 1970s saw legislation passed, programs developed, and barriers removed, while in this decade there have been the refinement of program offerings, the finalization of barrier removal, and the continuation of societal awareness training. The laws passed in the 1970s dictate that now schools and human service agencies must work together to implement programming for special needs students that is meaningful and realistic.

Deinstitutionalization and *mainstreaming* became two frequently used terms when the concerns of the handicapped were addressed. Deinstitutionalization involves moving handicapped individuals out of institutional settings into community settings where they can live and work successfully. The total benefits resulting from this movement will probably never be fully measured because of the diversity of the individuals involved. However, there are certain benefits that have already been clearly realized. First, deinstitutionalized individuals are being recognized as human beings with full human rights. Second, such individuals are being allowed to work and thus to contribute to their own and society's well-being. Third, these persons are being given the opportunity to develop and mature as citizens in a democratic society. Through this movement, people in our society are, in a sense, looking at themselves and saying, "Yes, all of us are different, but through these differences we can grow, contribute, and love each other for who we are."

As noted earlier, the handicapped were for a long time isolated because they were unique and their uniqueness made them unacceptable in a "normal" society. As the trend of accepting individuals for who they are slowly gained momentum in the 1960s and 1970s, a new word was coined to describe this acceptance: *mainstreaming*. During the middle 1970s especially, this term was used widely to describe programs for the handicapped. Mainstreaming is

> an educational placement procedure and process for exceptional children, based on the conviction that each such child should be educated in the least restrictive environment in which his educational and related needs can be satisfactorily provided. This concept recognizes continuum of educational settings which may, at a given time, be appropriate for an individual child's needs; that to the maximum extent appropriate, exceptional children should be educated with nonexceptional children; and that special classes, separate schooling, or other removal of an exceptional child from education with nonexceptional children should occur only when the intensity of the child's special education and related needs is such that they cannot be satisfied in an environment including nonexceptional children, even with the provision of supplementary aids and services.[10]

The basic premise of the mainstreaming concept is that exceptional and nonexceptional children have common needs. These common needs can serve as a basis for developing various instructional programs. By keeping the two types of students separated, each is being deprived of the opportunity to exchange experiences with and develop an appreciation of the other. It should be noted that mainstreaming does not eliminate special classes or programs for those exceptional students who need them in order to receive an education appropriate to their needs.

When the mainstreaming concept was first promoted, many school officials overreacted, both positively and negatively. The negative reactions resulted from uncertainty and fear. When people embark upon a new adventure, they often are frightened because they do not know what to expect. The same thing occurred when educators were exposed to the mainstreaming concept. The fear came from a lack of previous exposure to handicapped individuals. In their research education programs, only those educators who majored in special education received training in dealing with exceptional students. Also, since the majority of handicapped people were institutionalized or sheltered in homes, the average educator did not acquire any experience with exceptional students. With uncertainty came fear, and with fear came the development of certain negative attitudes. For many teachers, it was easier to say "Those students can't make it in my class" than it was to give them a chance to try. Also, many teachers felt that these students were being unloaded on them, forcing them to act as babysitters for an hour or two. There were instances where teachers were not informed about the students they would be having; they only knew they had to take them. These kinds of situations created, for both teachers and students, real barriers that could have been avoided with adequate information and training.

On the other hand, many school officials were overly confident and took the approach that exceptional students should be mainstreamed into all classes. Exceptional students were placed in advanced math, chemistry, or vocational agriculture classes because they had to be fitted into the entire school program. Many of these random placements resulted in dismal failures. This overly positive approach was unfair to both students and teachers, because there was no team effort made to allow the handicapped students to enter programs where they wanted to be, where they could succeed, and where the teacher could teach effectively. Placement was made only to illustrate the handicapped students could be enrolled in all programs throughout the school, without ensuring that they could succeed.

As educators became better informed and trained, however, the mainstream pendulum began to swing back toward the center. Educators, in cooperation with exceptional students and their parents or advocates, started to establish more effective systems for involving these students in school programs. The earlier mainstreaming concept had carried a connotation of ''returning to'' rather than ''planning for,'' and new terms were now developed to reflect the new ''planning for'' thrust. The new concept was that of the *least restrictive environment*. This concept had been included in the original mainstreaming movement but had not really been explored or defined to the extent it should have been, which was due to the newness of the entire handicap movement.

The concept of the least restrictive environment is that individuals, whatever their exceptional characteristics might be, should have an opportunity to learn and function in an environment that is conducive to their success. Specifically, two things are legally required of public agencies:

> 1. That to the maximum extent appropriate, handicapped children, including children in public or private institutions or other care facilities, are educated with children who are not handicapped; and
> 2. that special classes, separate schooling or other removal of handicapped children from the regular educational environment occurs only when the nature or severity of the handicap is such that education in regular classes with the use of supplementary aids and services cannot be achieved satisfactorily.[11]

The Education for All Handicapped Children Act of 1975 (Public Law 94-142) led to the above guidelines for establishing least restrictive environments and for providing a device through which placement in nonrestrictive environments could be greatly facilitated. This device is the individual educational plan (IEP). The IEP, in its simplest form, is a written statement about a handicapped child that includes the following:

> A statement of the child's present levels of educational performance; a statement of annual goals, including short-term instructional objectives; a

statement of the specific special education and related services to be provided to the child, and the extent to which the child will be able to participate in regular educational programs; the projected dates for initiation of services and the anticipated duration of the services; and appropriate objective criteria and evaluation procedures and schedules for determining, on at least an annual basis, whether the short-term instructional objectives are being achieved.[12]

The IEP is a guide to help facilitate proper programming for handicapped students. Chapter 5 discusses the IEP and its components in greater detail.

A concern for how best to assist handicapped students in moving from secondary school to a productive life within their communities brought about the concept of *transition*. Transition is based on three principles: independence, integration, and productivity. With all of the support models and programs, like restrictive environmental programming and the IEP, in place, handicapped students were completing or aging through secondary schools at a much higher percentage, but without any programs available to facilitate the last big step into the adult world. Transition became the concern in schools, businesses, and human service agencies, which used models and strategies of transition based upon the three principles in order to maximize individual abilities and contributions. Transition will be discussed further in various chapters throughout the book.

Balancing the legislative and societal gains made by the handicapped during the 1970s was the new attention to the barriers facing the disadvantaged. The Civil Rights Act of 1964 and the growing societal acceptance of human differences throughout the seventies greatly aided the involvement of ethnic, cultural, and religious minorities in the educational process. Much, however, still needs to be done in this area in view of the fact that minority youth aged 16–21 constitute nearly one-half of the unemployed even though they constitute only one-fourth of the labor force.

From a historical perspective, the sixties and seventies were an exciting time of social and human development. The eighties seems to be a decade of implementation. Legislation has been passed that enables all sectors of society to participate in school, work, recreation, and community activities. The challenge of the nineties will be to continue to implement activities that will ensure that *all* our citizens will have opportunities to become involved in programs and employment based upon their needs, preferences, and desires, without fear of exclusion or omission. If this can be accomplished, historians will look back at the period between 1960 and 2000 as a time when the obligation to serve all citizens of the United States, with all the attendant challenges, was met.

PROGRAM DESCRIPTIONS

As we have seen, our society has gone through a number of cycles in the delivery of educational services to special needs youth. As a result of some of these cycles, there has been a division of programs that requires a careful inspection of the roles that general, career, special, practical arts, and vocational education play in the total delivery system.

**General
Education**

General education has been defined as education through which one acquires the ability to cope with one's environment.[13] This definition assumes that general education is needed by all students and that specialized education will be offered to enable students to select training that they need to cope successfully with their environment.

Ideally, then, through successful integration of general education and specialized training (such as vocational education), students should be ready to cope with most problems that society or life might present. In order to understand why special needs youth do not fit within this educational framework and do not have the "ideal" skills to cope with life, one must look at the historical development of the objectives of education.

The major objective of public education in America has been to prepare individuals for living, not to prepare individuals to make a living.[14] Americans have long held the view that people who have developed their minds, bodies, and characters through formal exercises in cultural and intellectual disciplines will be better suited to enter occupations than those who have not. Stemming from this view, a hierarchy of education has been created in our schools that allows special needs youth to slip through the cracks of the structure.

At the top of this hierarchical structure is the college preparatory curriculum, obviously designed for those students who will be going on to college. The problem that arises with the components of the hierarchy is that, in many cases, parents who "want something better" for their son or daughter insist that their child follow this curriculum. But students often have no desire to go on to college and would prefer to be in another program. They begin to have scholastic problems, and the situation snowballs until they become discipline problems or drop out of school.

The next layer of the hierarchy is the general curriculum. This curriculum is designed to provide opportunities for students to acquire the basics: reading, writing, and arithmetic. It is an in-between curriculum that prepares the individual neither for college nor for employment after leaving school.

Vocational education is the training of individuals for gainful employment after completion of a specific training program. Vocational education finds itself at the bottom of the hierarchy because of the stigma it has carried as a dumping ground for less capable students.

General education thus finds itself sandwiched between the college preparatory curriculum and vocational education, and, in many cases, there is uncertainty as to what should be done with it. Nevertheless, as a result of this sandwiching, general education finds itself with the challenging responsibility to provide quality educational opportunities to special needs youths so that these individuals can make meaningful and realistic life-directing decisions. Thus, one important part of the general education delivery system should be the provision of career education to these youths.

**Career
Education**

There have been many definitions of career education suggested by different individuals, agencies, and organizations. As a result of these different definitions, career education has been approached from many different presentation modes and concept positions. One widely accepted definition was proposed by Kenneth B. Hoyt, associate commissioner of education (Washington, D.C., 1976). He defines career education as ''the totality of experiences through which one learns about and prepares to engage in work as part of her or his way of living.''[15] In fact, there are a wide variety of ways to develop programs that will provide opportunities for special needs youth to acquire the necessary information base from which they can make a career choice.

Career education is perceived as a flow-through type of education whereby individuals acquire not only information concerning paid employment but information about other aspects of their lives as well. As the hours in a workweek decrease, individuals will have to look for more ways to utilize the rest of their time.

In a sense, people generally have three careers for which they need training: a career in the home, a career in the community, and a career in the workplace. The career in the home is that of a homemaker. The word *homemaker*, as used here, refers to someone who contributes in some manner to the successful operation of the home. Thus, anyone can be a homemaker: a male or female, a boy or girl, a single or married person, a son or daughter. People need to have information and training in order to assume their roles in making a home, regardless of how typical or atypical their situation might be.

The career in the community also takes many forms. Participation in recreational, service, religious, or volunteer activities can be part of a community career. Even if people are not involved in such activities, there is still one community career activity in which they hope to be successful: being a consumer. No one can avoid or ignore this type of community activity: Everyone consumes, in one form or another, the community's services, goods, and activities. And a great deal of preparation is required to enable individuals to assume the critical career role of consumer.

The work world as a source of career education has received much attention, but there is still much developmental work to be done. This is because there are still many unknown variables in the selection, training, and placement of people in a paid employment setting. Vocational education has been the primary deliverer of training for the work world.

The American Vocational Association's *Task Force Report on Career Education* pulls together the various threads of career education and lists them as the ingredients for a comprehensive K–12 career education program. The task force concluded that career education should be designed to help individuals to develop

- favorable attitudes toward the personal, psychological, social, and economic significance of work
- appreciation for the worth of all types and levels of work
- decision-making skills necessary for choosing career options and for changing career directions
- capability of making considered choices of career goals, based on development of self in relation to the range of career options

- capability of charting a course for realization of self-established career goals in keeping with individual desires, needs, and opportunities
- knowledge, skill, and attitudes necessary for entry and success in a career[16]

In order for special needs students to acquire these competencies, individuals who work in the areas that provide career education must understand the components that contribute to the universal concept of career education. These components were identified by Curtis Finch and N. Alan Sheppard in 1974 as the following:

- Career education is an educational philosophy rather than a physical entity or single program.
- Career education begins at grade K and continues through adulthood.
- Career education is concerned with learning about work and involves more than preparation for work.
- Career education provides an orientation toward a work ethic.
- Career education is encompassed in the totality of education.
- Career education consists of all those activities and experiences through which one learns about work.
- Career education provides an awareness, exploration, and preparation function instead of just equipping a person for a specific job.
- Career education seeks to prepare all students for successful and rewarding lives by improving their basis for occupational choice.
- Career education is for all students.
- Career education benefits the entire population.[17]

As can be clearly seen, career education is a broad-umbrella concept that allows for much freedom and creativity in terms of presentation modes and program components. Such freedom and creativity are the major strengths in the delivery of programs for special needs youth.

Special Education

Special education has been defined as "specially designed instruction, at no cost to the parent, to meet the unique needs of a handicapped child."[18] This type of education is intended to serve those individuals who have some type of handicapping condition that requires specialized educational assistance in order for them to develop and mature to the maximum degree possible. These specialized services take a variety of forms, but the basic premise is that they must be offered in the least restrictive environment. Attention to providing the least restrictive environment has been brought about as a result of federal legislation (Public Law 94-142), which has led to a new concern for serving special needs students.

In the not-so-distant past, special needs students (disadvantaged or handicapped) were almost assured of placement in a special education class, which often preceded haphazard placement in a vocational program. Many of these placements occurred because the individuals in charge of placing students in specific programs did not have adequate information about either the students or the appropriate programs. During the past few years, however, there has been a dramatic change in the quality of student placements. Special education is being recognized for the services it can provide rather than viewed merely as a "holding pen" until the student leaves school.

Special education is not by itself a total delivery system but is rather a part of the total educational delivery package. Careful placement must be based upon the individual needs of the student involved. Since special needs encompass both handicapped and disadvantaged students, care must be taken to ensure that an appropriate placement is made based upon a variety of information, not made merely because a student fits into a particular category.

Special education's role is to serve the handicapped student either as a primary deliverer or, if the student is in a regular school program, as a resource service. In addition, there are other special educational services available to classroom teachers. Special education has developed many strategies for working with students who have problems with the formal setting. These strategies need to be utilized to their fullest and shared by all teachers for the benefit of their students.

Vocational teachers, as the result of least restrictive environmental programming, share students with special education teachers. Since these teachers are working toward the development of a quality educational program for the student, it makes good sense for all those involved to care about what is being offered and the methodologies being used and to share their expertise.

As stipulated in Public Law 94-142, arbitrary placement of individuals in special education programs is no longer acceptable without proper justification. Special education should be responsive to individual student needs. But it can only be a part of the total education picture. It cannot, nor should it be asked to, serve all special needs students. Total educational programming is a must.

Practical Arts

Practical arts, as defined by the American Vocational Association (AVA) in 1968, is "a type of functional education predominately manipulative in nature which provides learning experiences in leisure time interests, consumer knowledge, creative expression, family living, manual skills, technological development, and similar outcomes of value to all."[19]

Most practical arts courses are in the areas of general agriculture, home economics, industrial arts, and general business. These courses are generally taught in a daily class period by teachers with degrees. The students enrolled in practical arts courses do not establish specific vocational goals for the training they receive. Rather, they use these training experiences as a basis for making meaningful and realistic career decisions.

As an educational area, practical arts can provide excellent programs for special needs students. The reasons are similar to those noted for vocational education. The students have an opportunity to create, to manipulate, and to possess—three things that are very important for developing students who are having only limited success in school. In addition, special needs students are afforded opportunities to gain new experiences from which they can make career choices that are consistent with their life goals.

Practical arts courses are offered in grades K–12, with the strongest delivery at the junior high level. The reason for this is that it is during the junior high years that students do much of the exploration that will shape the rest of their lives.

Much controversy has occurred on the question whether practical arts should stand by itself or be a prevocational or feeder program for vocational education. This controversy has stopped many students from taking practical arts courses, but it has persuaded others to turn to them. Since each student is unique—because of individual differences and differences in family background, environment, and so on—the dispute should not be allowed to intrude into educational planning for students. Students should be enrolled in practical arts courses—or for that matter, in any other courses offered by the school—based upon their particular needs, interests, and desires, not because they are believed to be moving in this or that direction.

Because of their orientation toward practical application, practical arts courses at the junior high level have in many cases been the difference between a student leaving or remaining in school. The awareness of junior high students of practical arts or vocational programs in a high school can often stimulate their interest in particular areas, bridge the gap between junior high and high school, and keep them from dropping out.

Vocational Education

Vocational education has been defined by the AVA as "education designed to develop skills, abilities, understanding, attitudes, work habits, and appreciations needed by workers to enter and make progress in employment on a useful and productive basis."[20]

Vocational education, so defined, includes the following:

- preparation for jobs requiring less than a baccalaureate degree
- activities and experiences through which one learns to assume a primary work role
- an emphasis on skill development or specific job preparation
- a focus of attention at the upper-middle grades, senior high, and two-year college level
- a physical entity or program rather than an educational philosophy, with the major goal of gainful employment.[21]

The basic goal of vocational education is to take a nonskilled student through a series of training experiences so that at the end of a specified period of time the student will have the skills necessary to enter and succeed in the work world. Vocational education is normally concerned with six major occupational areas: vocational agriculture, home economics, health occupations, trades and industries, business and office education, and distributive education.

Vocational training is generally offered by an instructor with a degree or suitable work experience who meets state certification standards. Students enrolled in vocational programs set specific vocational goals for those programs. The instructional time for vocational classes is normally three hours, which can be divided up in many different ways. The most common is to combine one hour of classroom instruction and two hours of laboratory work.

Vocational education has long suffered from the stigma noted earlier. Working with one's hands has commonly been misperceived as less desirable than working with one's mind. This stigma, which can also be seen in the difference in status between blue and white collar work, is now changing for a variety of reasons, including the following:

- Vocational education offers advantages to vocational graduates over nonvocational graduates.
- Vocational education is training in occupational areas that are in demand and reflective of the needs of today's work setting.
- Vocational education enrolls women in nontraditional occupation areas.
- Vocational education enrolls minority students into programs leading to higher salaried and skilled occupational areas.
- Vocational education is effective in working with existing employed workers to upgrade their competencies, increase their productivity, and enhance promotability.
- Vocational education is effectively enrolling and working with handicapped students.
- Vocational education graduates have a tendency to move into business ownership following their occupational training and work experience.
- Comprehensive vocational education programs have an impact on the economic growth and development in communities.[22]

Vocational education has long been responsive to societal needs. This type of education enables the community to change, expand, or modify programs and training to meet emerging worker and employment demands.

Vocational education is faced with a real challenge and must assume a clearly defined responsibility to serve special needs students. Special needs students who are disillusioned with school do not see the relevance of school to the world around them. Because of the training it offers and the methodology it employs in this training, vocational education is a logical deliverer of educational services to these troubled youths. It involves not only the cognitive aspects of learning but also the psychomotor and affective aspects. Its basis is activity, which troublesome students frequently find lacking in day-to-day school life. Finally, through vocational education, students can see an immediate transference from the school setting to the world around them, whether their area of interest is automotive repair skills or consumer buying knowledge.

Vocational
Special Needs
Programs

Vocational special needs programs are a part of the general vocational education delivery system. Because of our central concern with them, they deserve separate examination and analysis.

A vocational special needs program is a program that is designed to provide the necessary instruction or support service to enable a special needs student to succeed in a vocational or prevocational program.

Vocational special needs programs may take a variety of forms. Such a program may be

- a separate vocational special needs course such as vocational English or vocational mathematics
- a regular vocational class with support materials or modified materials for use by special needs students
- a regular vocational class with a resource teacher in the class to assist the vocational instructor
- a regular vocational class with a special needs resource center for use by special needs students

There can be many modifications and variations of these kinds of programs; hence the above list should not be regarded as all-inclusive.

The key points to be remembered in developing vocational special needs programs are these:

1. The inability to succeed in a regular vocational program should be the basis for identifying students for enrollment in such programs.
2. These programs focus on individuals and their particular needs, not on generalized groups.
3. The inability to succeed is the result, not the cause, of special needs conditions.

Vocational special needs programs or services should neither duplicate nor dilute the offerings of other school programs. To avoid such overlapping, the following objectives of vocational special needs programs should be kept in mind:

- to develop the means for students to complete school
- to enable students to work toward achieving their maximum potential
- to develop the conviction that the individual is a valued person
- to develop the self-confidence necessary to take advantage of employment opportunities
- to develop a desirable attitude toward the world of work
- to allow students to acquire a salable skill

Clearly, vocational special needs programs deal with the skill development component of vocational education. Beyond that, however, much of the instruction focuses on human relations, self-development, and worker attitudes.

To qualify as a special needs program, a vocational special needs program must demonstrate that it

- can prepare the student for employment
- is necessary to prepare individuals for successful completion of a special needs program
- is of significant assistance to individuals in making informed and meaningful choices of occupation

Whether these criteria have been met might be at times difficult to prove. The list does, however, provide some general indicators to help establish program parameters.

DELIVERY OF SERVICES

None of the previously defined program areas can alone provide all the services required by disadvantaged and handicapped students. Each must cooperate with and assist the others to ensure maximum programming opportunities for such students. The process must include longitudinal educational assistance to the students. It is neither fair nor feasible to select a certain area in the process and then say, ''These students are that area's responsibility.'' This is unfair to the programs involved, unfair to the teachers, and, most of all, unfair to the students.

To repeat, public education must develop a longitudinal system of services for special needs students. This would reduce the number of programs that have failed in the past because they were ''too much, too late.'' It would also make it easier to treat the problems rather than just the symptoms.

Upon entrance into the public school system, a student should have a longitudinal plan that provides opportunities for growth and maturity. The opportunities in the plan, their purpose and design, should be clearly outlined.

Kindergarten students enter school with bright-eyed enthusiasm for learning and the world around them. This enthusiasm continues until about the third or fourth grade. Often at this point alienation begins, and then during the rest of the educational journey the child becomes more and more alienated, until a strong pattern of failure emerges.

Through a strong career education program integrated into a strong academic program, general education can greatly encourage students' curiosity and tendency to explore. Students study about careers in the classroom and then have an opportunity to see their newly acquired information applied in their community. They meet and visit with community helpers, view community businesses and industry, and participate in community projects. This career orientation can do much to keep education relevant for special needs students, who are often failure-prone.

As students finish the elementary grades, a concentrated effort must be made by teachers to retain the enthusiasm they brought initially to the school setting and to make the transition from the elementary to junior high school as easy as possible. Disruption and alienation often occur when a student is faced with a new environment. For the student who is unsure and confused about what lies ahead, the potential for failure is greatly enhanced.

During the junior high years, general education should provide additional career education in the form of career exploration. The junior high years are a time of physical and mental growth involving much activity by the student. A comprehensive career education program can offer many opportunities to utilize this activity. Practical arts classes enable special needs students to create, manipulate, and possess. In the academic areas, general education can give the student a tie between career exploration and the three R's. The tie-in comes when, for example, career survival words are learned in an English class and then used in interviewing a worker within the community, or when math skills are used by the student in ordering lumber for a class project.

Another kind of program that can be of great help in involving and retaining the special needs program is known by a number of names, such as experience-based career education (EBCE), hands-on training (HOT), and experience programs in the community (EPIC). Regardless of the name the program goes by, its purpose is to involve the student in both the school and the world of work. Specifically, work experience programs

- help the student gain exploratory occupational experience
- assist in keeping the student in school
- provide in-school class and job support and personal development training
- create a training base for cooperative occupational programs
- provide, at times, programs to enable students to earn badly needed money
- allow students to develop close relationships with school staff members

Since many students leave school between the ages of 14 and 16, the last point regarding close student-teacher relationships needs to be emphasized: The teacher can encourage and assist special needs students in making the transition from junior high to high school. The teacher may take students over to the high school and introduce them to their vocational or work experience teacher for the next year. This kind of visit is much different from the quick orientation tour conducted by high school students each spring for ninth grade junior highers. The transition must be made carefully because, in spite of their carefree and nonchalant attitudes, many students are psychologically fragile and need attentive treatment.

At the high school level, care must be taken in placing the special needs student. As noted earlier, there must be close cooperation between all segments of the student's education program. The general, special, and vocational education teachers must know and share each other's efforts. Each must call upon the others for assistance and strategies in serving special needs students.

CONCLUSION   Special needs students have historically been in need of assistance. In the past, various attempts have been made to serve those individuals who do not fit the expectations of the prevailing society. Many of these attempts have been feeble, to say the least, but at least they provided a base from which improvement could be made. Society has since become more informed, and people have learned to be more tolerant of human differences. This in turn has opened doors for the handicapped and disadvantaged that were previously closed.

As was seen in reviewing the population shifts, both inside and out of school settings, there are dramatic changes occurring within the United States. A common thread runs throughout the data, which is that more and more students are going to be classified as having special needs.

Educators now face a real challenge in defining their role in the educational process for special needs students. Education is no longer the effort of a single person; it is a team effort. This allows everyone—the student, the teacher, the parent, and the school—to benefit from their joint efforts. Special needs students are unique individuals who need special teacher and school support to enable them to complete their schooling successfully.

As a programming concept, vocational special needs education provides opportunities to train, support, and encourage disadvantaged and handicapped students in acquiring vocational skills. The skills and talents of these students are needed. To deprive them of the opportunity to develop these skills and talents or to enter into human relationships is to do a terrible injustice to both the students and society. Educators must renew their commitment to serve *all* the youth who enroll in their programs. They must renew their commitment to take account of the uniqueness of each student. To do less is to cheat everyone involved of a student's opportunity to grow, develop, contribute, and live fully.

Will Rogers suggested this recipe for success: "Mix knowing what you're doing, loving what you're doing, and believing in what you're doing."[23] Teachers of special needs students have a unique opportunity to meet students where they are and to help them go places they never thought possible. This can be done if both students and teachers follow Will Rogers' recipe.

NOTES

1. *Education Week*, May 14, 1986.

2. Ibid.

3. Ibid.

4. U.S., *Federal Register* 42, no. 191, October 3, 1977, 53851.

5. Ibid.

6. Ibid.

7. U.S., *Federal Register* 42, no. 163, August 23, 1977, 42478.

8. Calfrey C. Calhoun and Alton V. Finch, *Vocational and Career Education Concepts and Operations* (Belmont, Calif.: Wadsworth, 1976), 31.

9. Federal Board for Vocational Education, *Statement of Policies, Bulletin No. 1* (Washington, D.C.: GPO, 1917), 17.

10. Council for Exceptional Children, Statement adopted by the 13th Delegate Assembly, Delegate Assembly Final Report, Chicago, April 1976, 6.

11. U.S., *Federal Register* 42, no. 163, August 23, 1977, 42497.

12. U.S., *Federal Register* 42, no. 163, August 23, 1977, 42491.

13. Rupert Evans, *Foundations of Vocational Education* (Columbus, Ohio: Charles Merrill, 1971), 51.

14. Calhoun and Finch, *Vocational and Career Education Concepts and Operations*, 87.

15. K.B. Hoyt, *An Introduction to Career Education: A Policy Paper of the U.S. Office of Education*, DHEW publication no. (OE) 75-00504 (Washington, D.C.: GPO, 1975), 4.

16. American Vocational Association, "Task Force Report on Career Education," *American Vocation Journal* 47, no. 1 (January 1972): 12.

17. Curtis R. Finch and N. Alan Sheppard, "Career Education Is Not Vocational Education," *Journal of Career Education* 2, no. 1 (Summer 1975): 20.

18. U.S., *Federal Register* 42, no. 163, August 23, 1977, 42480.

19. American Vocational Association, *Definitions of Terms in Vocational, Technical, Practical Arts Education* (Washington, D.C.: AVA Committee on Publications, 1968), 16.

20. Ibid., 12.

21. Finch and Sheppard, "Career Education Is Not Vocational Education," 21.

22. American Vocational Association, *Effectiveness of Vocational Education* (Arlington, Va.: AVA Staff, 1979), 2.

23. *The Innovative Educator* (Stillwater, Okla.: Leadership Development Institute, 1979), 3–15.

Chapter 2

The Impact of Federal Legislation on Vocational Special Needs Programming

John D. Bies, Ph.D.

Throughout the history of our country and other democratic countries, there has been a common principle found whenever attempts were made at improving the quality of life and opportunities for the citizenry, namely, that the laws (of democratic nations) have profound effects upon all aspects of life. In the United States, the effects range from the way our government operates to our national defense, from the care of our natural resources to the improvement of our human resources.

Samuel Johnson noted that "the law is the last result of human wisdom acting upon human experience for the benefit of the public."[1] Hence, it is difficult to identify any other actions that have had a more significant and profound impact upon the vocational education of special needs populations than the federal legislation enacted by Congress. As is the case with other areas of legislation, the federal legislative contributions, promotions, regulations, and influences were part of a slow, evolving process. It should be remembered that the Constitution of the United States specifically states that the responsibility of education is to be left to the individual states. Thus, the influence of the federal government in education was at first indirect and abstract. Once a foundation was laid, it was then possible to have a more direct impact upon the educational process.

The term *special vocational needs* was first widely used with the passage of the 1968 amendments to the Vocational Education Act of 1963. (*Vocational special needs* is now the more common term.) In these amendments, Congress clearly identified and defined the special needs population and authorized specific funding formulas for this group. It should not be assumed, however, that vocational education funding for the special needs population first began in 1968. In fact, the unique problems of special needs groups have been addressed by legislative action for well over a century. What must be emphasized here is that it was not until the 1968 amendments that a piece of vocational education legislation clearly and specifically defined and provided funding for the disadvantaged and handicapped.

Prior to presenting information about specific pieces of legislation, it is first necessary to develop a historical framework pertaining to the federal government's evolving role in education. Thus, a brief analysis of this process will be first presented. This will be followed by a closer examination of the specific enactments affecting vocational programming for special needs populations.

FOUNDATIONS FOR FEDERAL LEGISLATION

Under the Constitution of the United States, Congress and the federal government are not responsible for providing an education to all individuals. Instead, the Constitution leaves education as a responsibility of individual states—and at their discretion. Adhering to the strictest interpretation of this delegation of power to the states, Congress was reluctant to usurp the powers of the states by regulating and providing aid to education.

It was not until the Continental Congress enacted the Ordinance of 1785 that a cooperative relationship between the federal government and educational services at the state level was established. Under the ordinance, one section of land was to be set aside for the support of schools within each township. Though the ordinance did not give direct support to schools, it did establish a precedent-setting principle of assisting education at the state level. In 1802, Congress passed the Ohio Enabling Act, which granted land to states for school support and set aside the 16th section of each township for educational purposes. Thus, the foundations for federal contributions to education were laid.

The next major piece of legislation affecting state public education was the Morril or Land Grant Act of 1862. Under the act, assistance was provided through the granting of public lands for the establishment and maintenance of agricultural and mechanical arts colleges and universities. It is interesting to note that this act was passed during the Civil War because of the lack of Southern opposition to the federal governmental interference with states' rights. Once the Civil War ended, land grant institutions were also established for blacks (primarily in Southern states). These were supported by the Supreme Court as being "separate, but equal" (establishing another legal precedent, one that was not overturned for almost 100 years).

With the industrial revolution well under way and the character of the United States changing, the twentieth century brought with it significant changes in the way educational responsibilities were viewed by Congress. The Smith-Hughes Act of 1917 was the first major piece of legislation that provided direct financial support to vocational education. This act was the first to provide direct funding for education at less than the collegiate level in order to train students in agriculture, home economics, and trades and industries. Since then, a number of other acts have been passed to provide funding for public school education and to require federal regulation. As funding and regulations were increased by Congress, so was the extent of the service areas (i.e., distributive education, health occupations, technical education, office education, industrial arts, and special needs). More recent federal legislation will be discussed in greater detail throughout this chapter.

As already noted, the Smith-Hughes Act of 1917 established a regulatory and funding precedent upon which all subsequent job training and upgrading legislation was based.[2] Therefore, it is not surprising that a year later Congress enacted the Smith-Sears Act of 1918 (Public Law 179). The purpose of this act was to provide for the vocational rehabilitation and return to civil employment of those disabled veterans discharged from the armed forces.

Though the Smith-Sears Act was the first enacted law that dealt solely with the rehabilitation of disabled veterans, concern for this population group can be traced back to the founding years of our country. Direct compensation for disabled veterans, however, was not provided until 1865, when returning Civil War disabled veterans were provided with small stipends. Public Law 179, however, was the first federal law and provided direct aid for rehabilitation, and it is therefore considered to be a hallmark enactment in the rehabilitation field.

It should be emphasized here that disabled civilians in need of rehabilitation were not covered by the first rehabilitation act. The rationale offered by members of Congress for their exclusion was that such a show of concern and help for the civilian population would only ''coddle'' them and, in the long run, hurt their chances for returning to the mainstream of full-time employment.

The first comprehensive vocational rehabilitation legislation was signed into law in 1920. The Vocational Rehabilitation Act, also known as the Smith-Fess Act (Public Law 236), provided rehabilitation services for civilians injured and disabled in industrial accidents during civil employment. However, the act provided only for vocational training, with no provision for medical treatment or physical therapy. It was designed to provide services in the areas of training, guidance, and counseling. Furthermore, only limited funding was made available for rehabilitation programs: $796,000 was appropriated during the first year of administration of the program, and only $1,000,000 was appropriated for each of the following three years. Not surprisingly, of the hundreds of thousands of disabled workers needing rehabilitation, only 5,600 were able to take advantage of rehabilitation programs. Though this act was significant (as the first to provide rehabilitation to the civilian population), it is considered to have been a practical failure, because of the myopic funding levels provided by Congress.

Though the Smith-Fess Act failed to meet the needs of a significant portion of disabled workers, it did provide two revolutionary incentives for future legislative action. The first was the use of matching funds on a state-by-state basis. Prior to this time, all funding was based on a population formula or another similar criterion. The Smith-Fess Act legislated the use of a 50-50 matching funds formula, with additional funding determined by a state's population. The second incentive was that the responsibility for the administration of the act and its programs was given to the Federal Board for Vocational Education.

No further rehabilitation legislation was passed by Congress until the early 1940s. This was due to two factors: a change in political philosophy during the 1920s and critical levels of unemployment during the Great Depression. The government reverted to a laissez-faire attitude during the twenties and gave top priority to providing work for the unemployed in the thirties; meanwhile, physically disabled workers were all but forgotten and were forced to fend for themselves.

When the United States became embroiled in World War II, Congress became aware of the critical shortage of industrial manpower caused by the Selective Service draft. To help alleviate this situation, the Bardon-LaFollette Act of 1943 (Public Law 113) was signed into law by President Roosevelt. The intent of this act was to provide the disabled men classified as being unfit for military service with the opportunity to receive vocational training in order to fill manpower needs in critical industries.

Public Law 113 was unique in the annals of rehabilitation legislation in that it was the first such act to include medical services along with vocational training. Fifty percent of all funds were earmarked by the act for rehabilitation services in the areas of medical examinations, corrective surgery, hospitalization, transportation, occupational licenses, occupational tools and equipment, prosthetic devices, and so forth. The act also provided rehabilitation for the mentally impaired, but the effect was limited by the fact that only a small number of mentally impaired individuals were willing or able to take advantage of the services. Rehabilitation services were also extended to the blind, who had previously participated only in programs sponsored by individual state agencies. L.H. Rivers, Jr., has noted that a key provision of the Bardon-LaFolette Act made it possible for states to develop plans that provided rehabilitation services for the blind by transferring operations from state administrations to other agencies serving the blind.[3] Today, there are over 30 states with separate agencies serving the blind.

In 1954, another significant piece of rehabilitation legislation was enacted. This was the Vocational Rehabilitation Act of 1954 (Public Law 565). The intent of this act was to relieve the existing shortages in rehabilitation personnel and facilities. Section 3 of the act provided for the extension and improvement of rehabilitation programs through a 75-25 matching funds appropriation system. Under this formula, the federal government provided 75 percent of the funding for services and projects and the states contributed the remaining 25 percent. This funding system applied only for a three-year period, but is considered to have been quite successful in light of the added services provided for various groups or disabled personnel.

Two additional features of the 1954 Vocational Rehabilitation Act were in the areas of research and training. Funds were provided for research activities that contributed to the improvement and advancement of rehabilitation services, practices, and techniques. High priority was given to those research activities that encouraged the application of findings to practical, field-based rehabilitation services. The act also authorized funds for grants and fellowships for individuals seeking professional preparation in the various areas of vocational rehabilitation. This part of the act continues today to provide professionally trained personnel in rehabilitation services and in medical and paramedical fields.

On October 3, 1967, President Lyndon B. Johnson signed the Vocational Rehabilitation Amendments (Public Law 90-99) into law. The amendments extended federal authorization of funds to provide for a total of $1 billion over fiscal years 1969 and 1970. The major objectives here were to provide grants for research and model projects for the rehabilitation of disabled migrant workers, to establish a national center for the deaf and blind, and to reallot funding for the District of Columbia to achieve a more equitable distribution of rehabilitation monies.

In 1968, Public Law 90-391 was enacted as the Vocational Rehabilitation Amendments of 1968. These amendments further increased the extent and funding of rehabilitation programs and services. The major provisions were

- the creation of additional appropriations for grants for innovative rehabilitation and research and for demonstration and training projects
- the establishment of funding programs for public and nonprofit agencies for the recruitment and training of manpower to provide services to rehabilitation programs
- the authorization of up to 10 percent of the states' allotment for the construction of new rehabilitation facilities
- the expansion of rehabilitation services to include work by optometrists

The Rehabilitation Act of 1973 (Public Law 93-112) was by far the most dramatic and significant piece of rehabilitation legislation ever passed. In effect, this act superseded all previous rehabilitation legislation. The main thrust of Public Law 93-112 was to provide services to individuals with severe handicapping disabilities.

One section of the 1973 act contributed to profound changes in the rehabilitation and hiring of handicapped personnel. This is section 504, which made it illegal to discriminate against qualified individuals on the basis of their handicapping conditions in hiring and in admission into vocational education programs. This section provides that "no otherwise qualified handicapped individual . . . shall, solely by reason of his handicap, be excluded from the participation in, be denied the benefits of, or be subjected to discrimination under any program or activity receiving federal financial assistance."[4] Thus, it makes discrimination on the basis of handicap illegal, with a penalty of losing part or all of federally funded contracts, grants, or services.

Other objectives of the law were

- to promote expanded employment opportunities for the handicapped in all areas of business and industry
- to establish state plans for the purpose of providing vocational rehabilitation services to meet the needs of the handicapped
- to conduct evaluations of the potential rehabilitation of handicapped clients
- to expand services to handicapped clients as well as to those who have not received any rehabilitation services or received inadequate services
- to increase the number and competence of rehabilitation personnel through retraining and upgrading experiences

In 1974, the Rehabilitation Act Amendments (Public Law 93-516) was passed. The intent of these amendments was to provide more equitable services and programming for the blind and those with impaired sight. The major provisions of these amendments established uniform treatment of the blind through agency coordination and cooperation, provided for the administration, in the "spirit of the law," of those provisions that allowed the blind to serve as vendors in public buildings, and authorized a White House Conference on Handicapped Individuals for the promotion and advancement of rehabilitation services and opportunities for handicapped persons.[5]

The last significant piece of rehabilitation legislation was known as the Rehabilitation, Comprehensive Services, and Development Disabilities Amendments of 1978 (Public Law 95-602). These amendments to the Rehabilitation Act of 1973 were designed to coordinate services between the Vocational Rehabilitation Act, Education for the Handicapped Act, and Vocational Education Act. The amendments authorized over $170 million over a three-year period for rehabilitation services, including programs for Indian tribes. In addition, it provided for the establishment of multidisciplinary systems for providing vocational rehabilitation and of reader services for the blind.

Perhaps one of the more important accomplishments of Public Law 95-602 was the establishment of a National Council on the Handicapped. The major functions of this council were

- to establish general policies for, and review of, the operations of the National Institute of Handicapped Research
- to provide advice to the Commissioner of the Rehabilitation Services Administration
- to provide advice on the execution of the act
- to continually review and evaluate all policies, programs, and activities concerning the handicapped

In addition to the establishment of a National Council, the act also provided funding for the implementation of community service pilot programs, as well as for projects with industry. Under Title III of the act, there was a reaffirmation to continue employment opportunities for all handicapped individuals without discrimination. An important addition to the Vocational Rehabilitation Act of 1973 was the inclusion of Title IV: Comprehensive Services for Independent Living, which promoted the individual's need for self-reliance, for support, and for living independently without burden to the family. Under this title, the major provisions were the following:

- establishment of comprehensive services for handicapped individuals
- creation of centers for independent living for the handicapped, including older blind individuals
- counseling, living skills, housing and transportation assistance, health maintenance, and other services that would contribute to and aid in independent living by handicapped individuals

Public Law 98-221, also known as the Rehabilitation Amendments of 1984, was passed. Though not a significant piece of legislation in terms of additional programming, it was important on two counts. First, there was a reaffirmation of existing programs and services for handicapped individuals. Second, there was a structural change in the administration of the act. This administrative change placed all rehabilitation control under the Office of Special Education and Rehabilitation Services.

When people are asked about socialism, socialized government, or social action legislation in the United States, they immediately think of Franklin D. Roosevelt and his New Deal policies and activities. This is only logical, for the legislative enactments and executive policies of the 1930s constituted the first massive governmental thrust toward alleviating the social hardships brought about by a worldwide depression. Programs such as the Civilian Conservation Corps and the Public Works Administration typified the solutions offered to solve the economic and social problems of Americans. **SOCIAL ACTION LEGISLATION**

During the 1960s and first part of the 1970s, a new wave of social action legislation occurred. Unlike their predecessors of the 1930s, the new laws were more than "make work" legislation. The major weakness of the New Deal programs was that they were designed to relieve unemployment only through governmental support projects; they consequently failed to provide any long-term solutions to the complex social and economic problems of the time. The new wave of legislation, in contrast, was aimed directly at eliminating or alleviating economic and social inadequacies.

After World War II, the Employment Act of 1946 (Public Law 304) was enacted to solve the unemployment problem caused by the winding down of war industry activities and the great influx of discharged manpower from the military. The problem was to be solved not only by public funds, but by a declaration of war against unemployment. The act stated,

> The Congress hereby declares that it is the continuing policy and responsibility of the federal government to use all practical means consistent with its needs and obligations and other essential considerations of national policy, with the assistance and cooperation of industry, agriculture, labor and State and local governments, to coordinate and utilize all its plans, functions, and resources for the purpose of creating and maintaining, in a manner calculated to foster and promote free competitive enterprise and the general welfare, conditions under which there will be afforded useful employment opportunities, including self-employment, for those able, willing, and seeking to work, and to promote maximum employment, production, and purchasing power.[6]

Needless to say, Public Law 304 did not end unemployment. It did, however, have two important provisions. The first required the president to prepare and present an annual economic report to the nation; the second established the President's Council of Economic Advisers. Thus, though the act did not eliminate unemployment in the United States, it did provide a means of developing an intellectual base and information source for identifying and developing policies to solve the country's economic problems.

The first act that signaled the oncoming wave of social action legislation of the 1960s was the Area Redevelopment Act of 1961 (Public Law 87-27). The main thrust of this act was to bring business and industry into areas of low economic development and chronic unemployment or underemployment. T.J. Hailstones and F.V. Mastriana note that the main function of the act was to provide financial aid to distressed areas or areas with a surplus of labor.[7] Some of the programs developed under the act were aimed at the training of workers for jobs in newly established industries. These programs were later merged with those of the Manpower Development and Training Act of 1962 (Public Law 87-415).

The latter act, more commonly referred to as MDTA, was perhaps the most significant piece of social action legislation of the 1960s. It was signed into law by President Kennedy to create new programs and techniques to ensure to those who, for any reason, were unemployed or underemployed an "environment guaranteeing employment."[8] Specifically, MDTA set up training, retraining, and job-upgrading programs for individuals with no occupational skills or outdated ones. Title II of the act was specifically designed to retrain unemployed persons who would otherwise be unable to obtain full employment.

Under specifications set by MDTA, four types of job preparation programs were established:

1. institutional training at either public or private institutions
2. on-the-job training at the place of employment
3. demonstration and experimental training programs
4. youth training programs for individuals aged 16–20 who were out of school and out of work

Public Law 88-214, the 1963 amendments to MDTA, expanded job training for unemployed individuals who lacked basic education skills. It authorized training in minimum educational skills through specialized instruction in reading, writing, language skills, and arithmetic. It also designed and expanded programs for the disadvantaged and out-of-school youth aged 16–21. These programs, however, were limited to youth from chronically impoverished environments that were conducive to academic or vocational failure.

Training programs to meet the special needs of workers over age 44 were not available until the passage of the 1966 MDTA amendments (Public Law 89-792). These amendments also provided for physical examinations, minor treatment, and prosthesis for trainees who were not capable of paying for health services. Finally, the act authorized the establishment of experimental and institutional programs to provide job training to inmates of correctional institutions.

Similar to the MDTA, the Economic Opportunity Act of 1964 (Public Law 88-452) was designed to decrease the levels of unemployment among the disadvantaged and unskilled populations of the country. J.W. Rioux has noted that though no general aid to education was provided for in the act, resources were made available for the upgrading of education.[9]

Public Law 88-452 established and funded seven major programs. These were

1. The Job Corps
2. The Neighborhood Youth Corps
3. College Work Study Programs
4. Urban and Rural Community Action Programs
5. Adult Basic Education
6. Education of Migrant Children
7. Adult Work Experience Programs

Of the seven programs, three were specifically designed to reduce immediately the high rates of unemployment for target groups. A brief description of three of the law's more significant programs follows.

The Job Corps was developed for youths aged 16–21 who had continuing records of school failure and displayed an inability to succeed in their communities. The Corps provided residential training centers for young men and women in rural and urban areas and designed programs tailored to meet their occupational training needs. These programs provided for basic education, skill training for the development of occupational competence, and constructive work experience related to the training program.

The Neighborhood Youth Corps was designed for youths who indicated an intention to drop out of school prior to fulfillment of high school diploma requirements or who had left school and wanted to re-enter. The program provided school and work experiences tailored to help students with weak academic interests and to relate their studies to the world of work.

Adult Work Experience Programs were designed to re-educate, train, or retrain parents who were raising children in poverty and who were chronically unemployed and receiving public assistance.

Under the various programs established by Public Law 88-452, a number of special remedial and noncurricular services were provided to program participants. These included rehabilitation and retraining for the physically and mentally handicapped and health, rehabilitation, employment, educational, and related services to those not qualified for military service.

On December 28, 1973, the Comprehensive Employment and Training Act (Public Law 93-203) was signed into law. Commonly referred to as CETA, this act assumed many of the functions of the old MDTA programs. Indeed, with the passage of CETA, MDTA programs under the Manpower Administration were removed and placed under administrative control of the new act. Reflecting the high rates of unemployment in the early 1970s, CETA's primary purpose was to establish programs to provide comprehensive manpower services to the country. The act was aimed at hardcore unemployed youths and adults who had no occupational skills and thus were not contributing to the development of the nation's economy.

Like most social action legislation, CETA was designed as a short-term, stopgap attempt to alleviate the immediate unemployment problem. Job training was aimed at making adults and youths into productive members of society as soon as possible. Thus, training time was usually based on how long it took trainees to secure employment.

Agencies who sponsored CETA programs were from both the public and private sectors, and the training varied from on-the-job training to formal in-class programs. CETA funds assured individual and family support for the trainee and provided monetary incentives to complete the programs. Support services and funds were also available for health and medical care, child care, residential support, transportation, counseling, and remedial instruction. In these ways, and by directing vocational educators to plan their programs in concert with CETA programs, Congress expressed its belief that CETA programming would be an extremely important means for curing the problems of the hardcore unemployed.

Later, the CETA Reauthorization Act of 1978 (Public Law 95-524) was enacted, with two major contributions. The first was the continuation of funding and support for existing CETA functions, such as the various youth programs, the Counter-cyclical Public Service Employment Programs, programs aimed at developing private sector opportunities for the economically disadvantaged, and the Young Adult Conservation Corps. The second contribution, and perhaps the most significant aspect of Public Law 95-524, was the attempt to maximize the coordination of the various plans, programs, and activities aimed at alleviating the unemployment problems of the country. Specifically, the act required that programs involving vocational education, rehabilitation, public assistance, self-employment training, and social services work together to eliminate duplication and counterproductive competition. Thus, the 1978 act refocused the efforts of all relevant agencies on the common goal of turning unproductive individuals into a productive force in the United States economy.

In 1977, the Youth Employment and Demonstration Projects Act (Public Law 95-93), or YEDPA, was signed into law. As an amendment to Public Law 93-103, YEDPA set up two important programs: the Young Adult Conservation Corps and the Youth Employment Demonstration Program. In the Conservation Corps, economically depressed young adults aged 16–23 were provided with employment opportunities of a public nature. For example, the Corps participated in field projects concerned with tree nurseries; wildlife habitat improvement; range management improvement; recreational development, rehabilitation, and maintenance; fish habitat and culture; forest insect and disease prevention and control; road and trail maintenance and improvement; general sanitation, cleanup, and maintenance; erosion control and protection from flood damage; and prevention of drought and other natural damage. Four years later, the Youth Employment Demonstration Amendments of 1981 (Public Law 97-14) was passed, with a continuation of programming and funding.

The most recent piece of social action legislation was the Job Training Partnership Act of 1982 (Public Law 97-300). The purpose of this act was to establish programs to prepare youth and unskilled adults for entry into the labor force and to afford job training to those economically disadvantaged individuals and other individuals facing serious barriers to employment, who are in special need of such training to obtain productive employment.[10]

The importance of Public Law 97-300 was that it established a Private Industry Council to develop job training plans and programming and to provide oversight of these programs. The requirement of training plans places a major emphasis on the accountability of training programs and what they attempt to attain. Here, for the first time, was step-by-step documentation pertaining to the design, administration, and operation of training programs. Specifically, it was required that each job training plan be required to contain the following:

- a complete administrative plan
- a description of services provided
- procedures for identifying and selecting eligible participants
- performance goals
- procedures for selecting service providers
- a budget
- a description of methods for complying with coordination criteria
- coordination of services within a geographic area where more than one job training program center exists
- fiscal controls
- periodic reports pertaining to the progress of the program

The vocational education profession has traditionally been receptive to providing services to students with special needs. In fact, the Smith-Hughes Act of 1917 is said to have established the precedent for funding vocational preparation for the handicapped.[11]

EDUCATIONAL LEGISLATION

The term *special needs* can be traced to the Vocational Education Act of 1963 (Public Law 88-210). This act was the first to define the term to mean individuals with disadvantaging or handicapping conditions that would prevent them from succeeding in a traditional education program. Specifically, the act stated,

It is the purpose of this part to authorize Federal grants to states to assist them to maintain, extend, and improve existing programs of vocational education, to develop new programs of vocational education, and to provide part-time employment to continue their vocational training on a full-time basis, so that persons of all ages in all communities of the state— those in high school . . . and those with special education handicaps—will have ready access to vocational training or retraining which is of high quality, which is realistic in the light of actual or anticipated opportunities for gainful employment, and which is suited to their needs, interests, and ability to benefit from such training.[12]

The act further stated that federal funds could be used for programs providing occupational training to individuals with academic, socioeconomic, and other handicapping conditions. Since it did not mandate or earmark the use of funds for the special needs population, little was done under the act to service this group. As a result, special needs programming was at best randomly funded and haphazardly organized.

Because the special needs population was not being properly serviced by vocational education, Congress, in the Vocational Amendments of 1968 (Public Law 90-576), decided to provide funds specifically for special needs students. These amendments identified two main categories in the special needs population: the disadvantaged and handicapped. The disadvantaged were to receive 15 percent of all vocational education funds and the handicapped were to get 10 percent, for a total of 25 percent.

The 1968 amendments defined the disadvantaged as students with social, economic, academic, or cultural disadvantagements that prevented them from succeeding in the normal school environment. The handicapped were defined as students who were unable to learn successfully because they were mentally impaired; emotionally disturbed; orthopedically handicapped; visually handicapped; had hearing, speech, or other health impairments; or were multihandicapped.

The Educational Amendments of 1972 (Public Law 92-318) further expanded vocational programming and services for disadvantaged and handicapped students. These amendments provided funding and grants to institutions of higher education and to secondary school programs that offered career and occupational education services to students with special needs.

The next major piece of vocational education legislation supporting the special needs population was the Vocational Education Amendments of 1976 (Public Law 94-482). The 1976 amendments, signed into law by President Ford, changed the funding formula for special needs programs and services: They increased the percentage of earmarked vocational education funds from 25 to 30 percent, with 10 percent going to the handicapped and 20 percent to the disadvantaged. The amendments also restricted the definition of the disadvantaged to individuals with social, economic, or academic disadvantagements. Cultural disadvantagement was dropped from the definition, because it was felt that an individual's cultural background and heritage should be viewed not as a hindrance, but as something positive and necessary in the development of a well-rounded individual.

The 1976 amendments had two other major provisions. The first was intended to ensure against sex discrimination in vocational education programs. To this end, the amendments were aimed at promoting vocational education programs for women and men in nontraditional occupations, for example, men in child care and health occupations and women in auto mechanics and machine shop work. The anti–sex discrimination clause was included by Congress not only to eliminate sex discrimination practices in vocational education, but also to help solve the skilled manpower shortage in numerous manufacturing and service businesses and industries.

The second major provision was to establish a cooperative working relationship between vocational education and Department of Labor programs. Specifically, vocational education programs and CETA agencies were required to coordinate their efforts in an attempt to eliminate competitive duplication of programs and services. By requiring this sort of ''cooperative venture,'' Congress hoped to stimulate a more concentrated effort toward eliminating unemployment among those lacking salable skills.

With the backing of President Carter, Congress passed the Department of Education Organization Act of 1979 (Public Law 96-88), which established the Department of Education. The Secretary of Education was elevated to a cabinet level position and divisions were elevated to offices. Thus, special needs programming within the Department of Education fell within two offices: the Office of Vocational and Adult Education and the Office of Special Education and Rehabilitative Services.

Public Law 98-524 was another hallmark in the annals of vocational education legislation. On October 19, 1984, President Reagan signed into law the Carl D. Perkins Vocational and Technical Education Act of 1984. With initial appropriations in excess of $835 million, this act was designed to

> assure that individuals who are inadequately served under vocational education programs are assured access to quality vocational education programs, especially individuals who are disadvantaged, who are handicapped, men and women who are entering nontraditional occupations, adults who are in need of training and retraining, individuals who are single parents or homemakers, individuals with limited English proficiency, and individuals who are incarcerated in correctional institutions.[13]

Not only did this act continue to recognize the needs of both disadvantaged and handicapped populations, but it also recognized the unique problems of the single parent and of individuals who are entering nontraditional occupations. Under Title II of the act, basic state grants were delineated. Monies were set aside for states who met the special needs and enhanced the participation of handicapped individuals, disadvantaged individuals, adults needing training and retraining, single parents or homemakers, individuals participating in programs designed to eliminate sex bias and stereotyping in vocational education, and criminal offenders serving time in correctional institutions.

It has long been the objective of our nation to provide an opportunity for all individuals to receive an education appropriate for securing employment and progressing in an occupation. Given this objective and the rise in economic instability and unemployment in the early 1970s, many individuals outside the field of vocational education turned their attention toward the goal of solving our unemployment problems. Professionals in special education, for example, have always had an interest in the vocational preparation of handicapped students. As a result of such interest and the increased pressure from various special interest groups concerned with the establishment and maintenance of quality educational programs for the handicapped, the Education for All Handicapped Children Act of 1975 (Public Law 94-142) was signed into law on November 29, 1975, by President Ford.

The act states that

> to assure that funds received by the State or any of its political subdivisions under any other Federal program, including Section 121 of the Elementary and Secondary Education Act of 1965 . . . and Section 122(a)(4)(B) of the Vocational Education Act of 1963 . . . under which there is specific authority for the provision of assistance for the education of handicapped children, will be utilized by the State, or any of its political subdivisions, only in a manner consistent with the goal of providing a free appropriate public education for all handicapped children.[14]

Specifically, the Education for All Handicapped Children Act of 1975 requires every state to provide a free and appropriate education, including vocational educational programs, for all handicapped children. However, if a local school district cannot provide such opportunities for their handicapped students, it is responsible for finding these services, regardless of their geographic location and cost, and making them available. It is the clear intent of the law to ''assure that all handicapped children have available to them . . . a free appropriate public education which emphasizes special education and related services designed to meet their unique needs . . . and to assess and assure the effectiveness of efforts to educate handicapped children.''[15]

Thus, the 1975 act is considered to be a piece of civil rights legislation for the handicapped. Since its passage, Public Law 94-142 has had a profound effect upon the total educational environment and in many cases has improved the overall quality of all educational programming. The act, in essence, guaranteed a number of rights to all handicapped children. These rights are specified in its major provisions, which are briefly described here.

- Services provided under the act were for handicapped children aged 3–22 inclusive.
- State allocations were to be made using a percentage formula. Allocations for the first fiscal year, ending September 30, 1978, were determined by multiplying the number of handicapped children in the state by 5 percent. This amount was to be prorated upward to a maximum of 40 percent for the fiscal year ending September 20, 1982.
- States had to identify and establish objectives that would contribute to providing a ''full educational opportunity'' to all handicapped children, a timetable detailing when these objectives were to be attained, and a description of the services, facilities, and personnel needed to attain the objectives.
- An appropriate educational program had to be made freely available to all handicapped children aged 3–18 by September 1, 1978, and to all handicapped children aged 3–21 by September 1, 1980.

- Where applicable, the state had to provide a least restrictive environment (mainstreaming of handicapped students into the regular school programs) for handicapped children aged 3–21.
- Each state had to establish procedures to test and evaluate handicapped students so that they could be properly placed in an educational program. Steps had to be taken to assure that these students would not be discriminated against because of testing procedures.
- The state had to provide procedures for conducting annual evaluations of the effectiveness of various programs meeting the needs of handicapped students.
- Provisions had to be made to fully inform parents of the programs or services which their children were enrolled in or using. Furthermore, the records diagnosing the status of a student's condition had to be made public to the parent or guardian.[16]

Since the passage of the Education for All Handicapped Children Act of 1975, there has been no other major piece of legislation addressing educational and vocational programming for the handicapped population. There have been, however, several amendments extending and tightening services in this area:

- Public Law 95-49, Education of the Handicapped Amendments of 1977, made possible the extension of certain programs and provided for a continuation of authorized appropriations.
- Public Laws 95-561 and 96-341, Education of the Handicapped Amendments of 1978 and 1980, continued federal authorization of program funding, legislated the reorganization of special education into the Department of Education, and continued special education programs in higher education and programs for students from disadvantaged backgrounds.
- Public Law 98-199, Education of the Handicapped Amendments of 1983, extended funding authorizations to centers and services that meet the special needs of the handicapped and to the training of personnel for special needs education.

SUMMARY

Today, the federal government is a major force in providing both financial and programmatic support for the special needs population. This was not always the case, however. Because the Constitution of the United States left the responsibility for public education to the states, Congress and the President were initially reluctant to give any financial or moral assistance to such students. However, the situation changed slowly and Congress now provides help to those with special needs in three broad areas: rehabilitation, social action, and educational programming.

Rehabilitation legislation began with the passage of the Smith-Sears Act of 1918. Between 1918 and 1924, a significant number of rehabilitation programs were initiated for disabled workers. These, however, ceased with the rise of a laissez-faire attitude later in the 1920s and with the unemployment problems of the 1930s. World

War II created a manpower shortage and gave new life to the rehabilitation field. Since the end of World War II, there have been a number of legislative acts concerning rehabilitation. The most significant of these was the Rehabilitation Act of 1973 and its amendments of 1978.

Social action legislation has its roots in the New Deal era of the 1930s. Its revitalization began in the 1960s with the passage of the Area Redevelopment Act of 1961 and the Manpower Development Training Act of 1962. One of the more significant pieces of social action legislation was the Comprehensive Employment and Training Act of 1973. This act provided millions of dollars of federal aid for the training and upgrading of hardcore unemployed and underemployed individuals who were not contributing to the United States economy. The most recent social action legislation of importance was the Job Training Partnership Act of 1982. This law established a Private Industry Council and required a job training plan for all programs.

In addition to rehabilitation and social action legislation, educational legislation has played a significant role in providing program aid for the special needs population. In the Vocational Education Act of 1963 and its amendments of 1968, the special needs group was defined and identified as a population needing more support in our schools. Congress consequently earmarked 25 percent of vocational education monies for special needs students. The passage of the Carl D. Perkins Vocational Education Act of 1984 not only reaffirmed Congress's support for special needs students, but also expanded services and funds provided to them. Probably the most far-reaching and significant piece of educational legislation in this area, however, was the Education for All Handicapped Children Act of 1975. This law, together with its subsequent amendments, is considered to be the civil rights act for handicapped children, in that it guarantees all handicapped the right to a free and appropriate education.

NOTES

1. *Anecdotes of Samuel Johnson* (1786).

2. M.E. Switzer, "Legislative Contributions," in *Vocational Rehabilitation of the Disabled: An Overview*, ed. D. Malikin and H. Rusalen (New York: New York University Press, 1969).

3. L.H. Rivers, Jr., "History of Federal Vocational Rehabilitation As It Affects the Blind," in *Social and Rehabilitation Services for the Blind*, ed. R.E. Hardy and J.G. Cull (Springfield, Ill.: Charles C Thomas, 1972), 69–87.

4. Public Law 93-112 (Rehabilitation Act of 1973), sec. 504.

5. Public Law 92-516 (Rehabilitation Act Amendments of 1974), title II, sec. 206.

6. Public Law 304 (Employment Act of 1946), sec. 2.

7. T.J. Hailstones and F.V. Mastriana, *Contemporary Economic Problems and Issues* (Cincinnati, Ohio: South-Western Publishing Co., 1976).

8. Public Law 87-415 (Manpower Development and Training Act of 1962), sec. 101.

9. J.W. Rioux, "Economic Opportunity Act and Elementary and Secondary Education Act of 1965," *Childhood Education* 42, no. 1 (1965):9–11.

10. Public Law 97-300 (Job Training Partnership Act of 1982), 29 USC 1501.

11. Switzer, "Legislative Contributions."

12. Public Law 88-210 (Vocational Education Act of 1963).

13. Public Law 98-524 (Carl D. Perkins Vocational and Technical Education Act of 1984), 98 Stat. 2437.

14. Public Law 94-142 (Education for All Handicapped Children Act of 1975), sec. 613, (A)(2).

15. Ibid., sec. 3 (C).

16. Ibid., part B.

Balino, A.C. *Manpower in the City*. Cambridge, Mass.: Schenkman Publishing Co., 1969.

Bies, J.D. "Serving Students with Special Needs." *Journal of Epsilon Pi Tau* 3 (1977):39–46.

Blatt, B. "Public Policy and the Education of Children with Special Needs." *Exceptional Children* 38 (1972):537–45.

Brookings, J.B. and B. Bolton. "Vocational Interest Dimensions of Adult Handicapped Persons." *Measurement Evaluation Counseling Development* 18 (1986):168–75.

Burkett, L.A. "Latest Word from Washington." *American Vocational Journal* 52 (1977):9–10.

Conley, R.W. *The Economics of Vocational Rehabilitation*. Baltimore, Md.: Johns Hopkins Press, 1965.

Greene, J. "Applying the Lessons of Research: The Need for Mandated Training in Federal Youth Employment Programs." *Education and Urban Sociology* 14 (1981):55–66.

Hailstones, T.J. and F.V. Mastriana. *Contemporary Economic Problems and Issues*. Cincinnati, Ohio: South-Western Publishing Co., 1976.

Kruger, D.H. "Manpower Planning and the Local Job Economy." *American Vocational Journal* 50 (1975):32–35.

Lewis, J.W. "State Manpower Legislation: An Alternative Strategy." *American Vocational Journal* 50 (1975):65–66.

Lund, D.R., and R.J. Tungman. "Linkages at the Council and Commission Levels." *American Vocational Journal* 52 (1977):33–34.

Marburger, C.L. "The Economic Opportunity Act—and the Schools." *Educational Leadership* 22 (1965):542–48.

Public Law 178 (Vocational Rehabilitation Act of 1918).

Public Law 11 (Vocational Rehabilitation Act of 1919).

Public Law 236 (Vocational Rehabilitation Act of 1920).

Public Law 113 (Vocational Rehabilitation Act of 1943).

Public Law 304 (Employment Act of 1946).

Public Law 565 (Vocational Rehabilitation Act of 1954).

Public Law 937 (Vocational Rehabilitation Amendments of 1956).

Public Law 85-198 (Vocational Rehabilitation Amendments of 1957).

Public Law 85-213 (Vocational Rehabilitation Amendments of 1957).

Public Law 87-27 (Area Redevelopment Act of 1961).

Public Law 87-415 (Manpower Development and Training Act of 1962).

Public Law 88-210 (Vocational Education Act of 1963).

Public Law 88-452 (Economic Opportunity Act of 1965).

Public Law 89-792 (Manpower Development and Training Act Amendments of 1966).

Public Law 90-99 (Vocational Rehabilitation Amendments of 1967).

Public Law 90-391 (Vocational Rehabilitation Amendments of 1968).

Public Law 90-576 (Vocational Education Amendments of 1968).

Public Law 92-318 (Educational Amendments of 1972).

Public Law 93-112 (Rehabilitation Act of 1973).

Public Law 93-156 (Rehabilitation Act Amendments of 1974).

Public Law 93-203 (Comprehensive Employment and Training Act of 1973).

Public Law 94-142 (Education for All Handicapped Children Act of 1975).

Public Law 94-482 (Educational Amendments of 1976).

Public Law 95-40 (Amendments to the Vocational Education Act of 1963).

Public Law 95-49 (Education of the Handicapped Amendments of 1977).

Public Law 95-93 (Youth Employment and Development Projects Act of 1977).

Public Law 95-524 (Comprehensive Employment and Training Reauthorization Act of 1978).

Public Law 95-561 (Educational Amendments of 1978).

Public Law 95-602 (Rehabilitation, Comprehensive Services, and Development Disabilities Amendments of 1978).

Public Law 96-88 (Department of Education Organization Act of 1979).

Public Law 96-341 (Comprehensive Employment and Training Act Amendments of 1980).

Public Law 96-374 (Educational Amendments of 1980).

Public Law 97-14 (Youth Employment Demonstration Amendments of 1981).

Public Law 97-300 (Job Training Partnership Act of 1982).

Public Law 98-199 (Education of the Handicapped Act Amendments of 1983).

Public Law 98-221 (Rehabilitation Amendments of 1984).

Public Law 98-524 (Carl D. Perkins Vocational and Technical Education Act of 1984).

Rioux, J.W. ''The Economic Opportunity Act and Elementary and Secondary Education Act of 1965.'' *Childhood Education* 42 (1965):9–11.

Rivers, L.H., Jr. ''History of Federal Vocational Rehabilitation As It Affects the Blind.'' In *Social and Rehabilitation Services for the Blind*, edited by R.E. Hardy and J.G. Cull. Springfield, Ill.: Charles C Thomas, 1972.

Schwendau, M. and D. Dolman. ''Using JTPA to Prepare Students for Employment.'' *School Shop* 45 (1986):34 + .

Switzer, M.E. ''Legislative Contributions.'' In *Vocational Rehabilitation of the Disabled: An Overview*, edited by D. Malikin. New York: New York University Press, 1969.

Weebink, P. ''Unemployment in the United States, 1930–1940.'' *American Economic Review* (1940).

Chapter 3

Identification and Assessment of Disadvantaged Students

Jerry L. Wircenski, Ph.D.

Who are the disadvantaged? This is perhaps one of the most difficult questions for educators and society in general to answer. When we label someone or some group as disadvantaged, we usually mean that they are disadvantaged in relationship to some criteria—educational level, economic standard, value system, cultural or social standard, or any other criteria individuals use as a yardstick to measure and make comparisons between people. The label disadvantaged is thus often based on personal judgments.

Mario D. Fantini and Gerold Weinstein state that the usual criterion for identifying the disadvantaged is economic—poverty and low social status. But they note further that "the meaning of disadvantaged must be broadened to include all those who are blocked in any way from fulfilling their human potential." They assert that this blocking can take place anywhere: in the inner-city ghetto or in middle- or upper-class suburbs. They state:

> The schools have failed the middle-class child as they have the child from low income families. The affluent child, who comes to the school prepared to succeed in a mediocre, outdated educational process is also being shortchanged, and thus, too, is disadvantaged. Simply because he does his homework, gets passing grades, and eventually graduates, is not necessarily a sign of advantaged.[1]

The early professional literature abounds concerning the characteristics of the disadvantaged. Not surprisingly, there is widespread variation in the literature regarding those characteristics and the causes that produce them. Frank Riessman has described the culturally deprived as

- relatively slow at cognitive tasks, but not stupid
- learning more readily from a concrete approach

47

- pragmatic rather than theoretical, often appearing anti-intellectual
- traditional, superstitious, and somewhat religious
- being from a male-centered culture, except for some major sections of the black subculture
- inflexible and not open to reason about many of their beliefs (i.e., morality and educational practice)
- feeling alienated from the larger social structure, with resultant frustration
- holding others to blame for their misfortune
- valuing masculinity and attendant action, viewing intellectual activities as unmasculine
- viewing knowledge for its practical, vocational ends
- not wishing to adopt a middle-class way of life but desiring a better quality of living, with personal comforts for themselves and their family
- lacking in auditory attention and interpretation skills
- deficient in reading and communication skills generally, and having wide areas of ignorance[2]

Leon Eisenberg has stated that, psychologically, the disadvantaged do not have an individualistic, competitive orientation. Their values tend to be collective group values rather than individualistic, and they perceive advancement as coming from social group forces rather than from individual activity. They consistently require others to prove themselves in any situation and are generally unimpressed by middle-class prestige. They are often lacking in adequate verbal and experiential stimulation, and have not formed the learning sets that are necessary for formal learning.[3]

Ben Seligman has characterized the disadvantaged as lacking the goals and ambitions that characterize the middle class. They have a sense of alienation and isolation leading to fatalistic acceptance of the conditions of poverty.[4] These conclusions are supported by Francesco Cordasco and Eugene Bucchioni, who characterize the disadvantaged as having feelings of fatalism, depending inferiority, and helplessness.[5] The manifested aggressive behavior of the disadvantaged is not channeled into constructive tasks but is directed to those tasks that provide immediate gratification.[6]

Disadvantaged learners are generally described as culturally, socially, educationally, and economically deprived.[7] They are normally below school grade level in achievement. Typically, by the end of the ninth grade, the reading levels of disadvantaged learners are from 2 to 3½ years below grade level, and their abilities in mathematics and other subjects are retarded. Conceptual and reasoning ability are, likewise, below that of nondisadvantaged learners of the same age. Also, typically, disadvantaged learners are apathetic toward school and structured learning situations, in which their experience has been one of low achievement and failure.[8]

Learning Traits   We should caution, however, that disadvantaged learners are not all alike. Cultural and socioeconomic factors, ethnic background, values, abilities, and other factors vary among students. Robert W. Walker has listed learning traits of disadvantaged persons that differentiate them from other learners, but not all of these traits apply to all disadvantaged learners. Walker's list includes the following traits:

- limited ability to use the basic scholastic skills
- limited perception of the value of an education
- lack of motivation to learn
- poor attitude toward the conventional school situation
- weak self-image
- lack of self-confidence
- dependent upon others
- low levels of aspiration
- short interest spans
- argumentative and hostile or passive and apathetic
- resentful of authority
- feeling of 'not belonging'[9]

J.M. Conte and G.H. Grimes have developed a similar list of 13 characteristics. Though similar to Walker's, this list is also presented here because it further delineates the learning characteristics of the disadvantaged. According to Conte and Grimes, the disadvantaged

- seem to be oriented to the physical and visual rather than the aural
- show more interest in content rather than form
- are externally oriented rather than introspective
- exhibit problem-centered, as opposed to abstract-centered, learning characteristics
- use inductive rather than deductive reasoning
- are spatial rather than temporal oriented
- are slow, careful, patient, and persevering (in areas of importance to them) rather than quiet, clever, facile, and flexible
- are inclined to communicate through actions rather than words
- are found to be deficient in auditory attention and interpretation skills
- are very oriented toward concrete applications of learning
- have short attention spans, and experience difficulty in following orders
- are characterized by significant voids in knowledge and learning
- lack the experience of receiving approval for success[10]

Much of the literature that has examined the disadvantaged has concentrated on elements other than personal characteristics. Describing the home life of the disadvantaged, Robert D. Strom noted that there is little opportunity for interaction among

Environmental Characteristics

family members and little opportunity for language exchange.[11] The families of disadvantaged children normally do not have long-range goals. The focus of attention is on day-to-day survival.[12] Leon Eisenberg found that children from disadvantaged families received infrequent attention from their parents and were often left to fend for themselves at a very early age.[13] Disadvantaged children do not receive the parental monitoring of daily activities that middle-class children typically receive. They are free to roam the streets and neighborhoods unsupervised at very early ages, whereas middle-class children of the same age are usually under strict parental supervision.[14]

Leonard M. Ridini and John E. Madden have provided a comprehensive description of the inner-city disadvantaged. They concluded that inner-city youth are generally troubled by the following eight problems:

- possibility of being unemployed and underemployed
- a tremendous amount of loud noise in their environment
- high rates of illiteracy and undereducation
- discrimination
- inadequate health care
- negative self-concepts
- a shortage of competent teachers to teach them effectively[15]

Benjamin Bloom and Robert J. Havighurst describe the parent-child relationship of the disadvantaged family as nonexistent. They state that there is no time allocated for parent-children activities, no shopping trips, no visits to cultural sites, nor even trips to other neighborhoods. There are no joint activities through which the parent and child can communicate and get to know each other.[16]

Herman P. Miller describes the home environment of the disadvantaged child as that of a single parent. Over half of the homes are fatherless, and, in many of the homes where the father is present, he is often absent a good deal of the time. This is especially true in ghetto families.[17] Mario Fantini and Gerold Weinstein describe the family of a disadvantaged child as consisting of many brothers and sisters and many parents and parent substitutes, such as aunts, uncles, cousins, and grandparents, living together. They refer to this situation as an extended family.[18]

Based on the environmental characteristics of the disadvantaged, a number of basic needs become apparent. In review of the needs of disadvantaged youth, Vincent Feck has identified the following:

1. security and stability in their environment
2. successful educational experiences
3. recognition for achievement
4. love and respect
5. legal sources of finance
6. financial management
7. proper housing

8. good health
9. development of basic communication skills
10. salable work skills
11. an appreciation of the meaning and importance of work
12. successfully employed adult or peer work models
13. positive self-concepts
14. job opportunities and qualifications
15. socially acceptable attitudes and behavior[19]

Comparisons of disadvantaged children with those of middle-class children on personal and homelife characteristics show wide discrepancies, as one would expect knowing the plight of the disadvantaged in the United States. Yet some interesting commonalities have been found when studying disadvantaged children and middle-class children in terms of abilities. There is no evidence that disadvantaged children are inherently less intelligent than more privileged children. In discussing the abilities of disadvantaged children, Eisenberg notes that there is often confusion between differences and deficiencies.[20] Disadvantaged children are born into a familial environment that stems from a culture different from that of middle-class children. Disadvantaged children generally are not strong in verbal communication and cognitive skills, because their survival in the subculture of the streets is dependent upon doing rather than talking. They thus assume responsibilities at a far earlier age than do middle-class children. Their skills enable them to survive an active, demanding environment, as opposed to the more formal learning environment of the schools. Martin Deutsch states that disadvantaged children simply enter the schooling situation less prepared and thereby are prone to failure at a very early age.[21] Arthur R. Jensen supports these findings, stating that it is generally conceded that comparing the I.Q. scores of one race, one ethnic group, or one socioeconomic group against those of another reveals little difference in intelligence between or among groups. Children reared in stimulating environments will have a higher intelligence quotient than those reared in less stimulating environments, regardless of group.[22] Research conducted by Thomas F. Pettigrew supports these findings. He states that it has been demonstrated that when any group moves from an unstimulating environment to a comparatively stimulating one, the intelligence quotient will be increased.[23]

Research on the abilities of disadvantaged children seems to indicate that they are not unequal to those of more advantaged children. The disadvantaged have, however, accumulated a wealth of less desirable experiences that inhibit their success in the more formal school environment developed and fostered by the middle-class system of values. There is little doubt that the promise of American education has made little sense to a large segment of the population, including the disadvantaged. Contrary to historical myths, educational sociologists have produced strong evidence that schools serve the socioeconomic structure in which they exist. The schools have generally provided middle- and upper-income youth with the intellectual tools necessary for success in American society. But they have commonly failed to cope effectively with the task of educating the disadvantaged.[24]

In the 1960s, equality of educational opportunity was understood in simple terms. It meant that everyone in society or in education was to be treated equally: one standard, one set of books, one fiscal formula for children everywhere, regardless of race, creed, or color. Success went to the resourceful, the ambitious, the bright, the strong; failure was the responsibility of the individual, certainly not that of the school or society.

In this vein, the answer to the question, Who are the disadvantaged? was best provided by Fantini and Weinstein. They stated:

> The disadvantaged cannot be defined by the race, residence, jobs, or behavior alone. Although we tend to think first of such districts as Harlem, disadvantaged are to be found also in small towns, in the rural slums of back woods Appalachia, in the Spanish borough of El Paso, on American Indian reservations—or on the fashionable streets of Scarsdale. They are black, white, red, and yellow; with or without parents; hungry or overfed; they are the children of the jobless, the immigrant workers, or the unemployed. The only thing they have in common is that all are left out of the process which purports to carry to all human kind, regardless of background: feelings of potency, self-worth, connection with others, and concern for the common good. *Anyone deprived of the means to reach out to these human goals is disadvantaged, for it is the purpose of our democratic social institution to advance the development of these human goals for all people* [emphasis added].
>
> Failure in human goal attainment is therefore a reflection of institutional failure and, until our social institutions in general, and the schools in particular, are equipped to satisfy these goals, full human development is thwarted. Until then we are disadvantaged. Our focus will, of necessity, be on the most obvious institutional casualties, but the implications for all should be recognized.[25]

Summary

There is a wealth of literature regarding the general characteristics of the disadvantaged. There is some disagreement, however, as to the personal characteristics, homelife, and abilities of the disadvantaged. What is evident from the review of the literature is that there is very often a tendency to overgeneralize, to almost stereotype the disadvantaged as being this or that. In fact, it is impossible to paint a composite picture of the "typical" disadvantaged person. When applying definitions or drawing implications from the literature, it is most important to remember that each disadvantaged youth or adult is *an individual*. Each disadvantaged person has certain unique characteristics, which, for purposes of delivering vocational education programs and services, can be drawn together into a composite profile, but only for purposes of implementation.

Reacting to criticism about inequality of educational opportunity, Congress, in the 1960s, passed a series of acts designed to strengthen the public educational system. These acts called attention to students who found it difficult to succeed in traditional classes or courses, many of whom either were far behind in basic educational skills or had already been pushed out or dropped out of school.

The term *disadvantaged* came into widespread use following the passage of the Economic Opportunity Act of 1964. Disadvantaged persons were defined as individuals whose incomes were below minimum levels and who were included in one of the following categories: minority groups, school dropouts, under 22 years of age, 45 years of age or over, and handicapped.[26] At that time, the definition of disadvantaged used in connection with the antipoverty program identified "target groups." The Research and Policy Committee of the Committee for Economic Development stated, "The common meanings of 'disadvantaged' are vague and ambiguous. Frequently the terms 'disadvantaged' and 'poor' are used interchangeably, and the members of some minority ethnic groups are typically assumed to be disadvantaged."[27]

When applied in relation to poverty, the term *disadvantaged* failed to indicate the specific conditions suffered by individual members of the target group that required remedial treatment. The preceding chapter notes favorably the federal legislation regarding special needs learners. Here, it is important to highlight those federal acts that have defined the characteristics and clarified the identification of the disadvantaged. This legislation began with the Vocational Education Act of 1963, signed by President Lyndon B. Johnson on December 18, 1963. In this act, Congress directed vocational education toward the needs of people rather than into rigid categories and target groups. The act called for the vocational education of "persons who have academic, socioeconomic, or other handicaps that prevent them from succeeding in the regular programs of vocational education." The central theme of the act was "programs for people," rather than "people for programs." Although it was a first step in delivering vocational education services to the disadvantaged, the 1963 act "*merely recommended* [italics added] that students who have special needs related to disadvantaged or handicapping conditions be served by vocational education programs."[28]

The Vocational Education Amendments of 1968 went far beyond this "recommendation" by relating appropriations to objectives. The amendments mandated that portions of federal grants to the states be used to provide special programs or services to those who could not succeed in regular vocational education programs without such services. They required that individuals, rather than groups, be identified for special services. They also required that states spend at least 15 percent of their basic state grant funds to pay for services and programs for the academically and socioeconomically disadvantaged. According to Evelyn R. Kay, Barbara H. Kemp, and Frances G. Saunders, "the Vocational Education Amendments of 1968 present an unlimited challenge for states and their school districts to provide special programs and services to ensure vocational education success for the disadvantaged. . . ."[29]

IDENTIFICATION OF DISADVANTAGED LEARNERS IN VOCATIONAL EDUCATION

The 1968 amendments also provided a definition for the term *disadvantaged*. The term was defined as meaning "persons . . . who have academic, socioeconomic, or other handicaps that prevent them from succeeding in the regular vocational education program. . . ."[30]

In 1970, a more inclusive definition appeared in the *Federal Register*. Kay, Kemp, and Saunders, quoting the *Federal Register,* vol. 35, no. 9, May 9, 1970, stated,

> Disadvantaged persons . . . means persons who have academic, socio-economic, cultural, or other handicaps that prevent them from succeeding in vocational education or consumer and homemaking programs designed for persons without such handicaps and who for that reason require specially designed educational programs or related services. The terms include persons whose needs for such programs or services result from poverty, neglect, delinquency, or cultural or linguistic isolation from the community at large, but does not include physically or mentally handicapped persons unless such persons who suffer from the handicap described in this paragraph.[31]

The charge to vocational education was clear; the amendments of 1968 focused on the needs of disadvantaged students, which were to be met through program development, services, and activities.

Title II of the Vocational Education Amendments of 1976 required that 30 percent of basic state grant funds be spent for necessary special services and programs—20 percent for the disadvantaged and 10 percent for the handicapped. The disadvantaged were defined as those persons who have academic or economic handicaps and who require special services and assistance to enable them to succeed in vocational programs. The Division of Vocational and Technical Education of the Department of Health, Education, and Welfare (HEW) provided, in the *Federal Register,* vol. 42, no. 191, section 104-804, a further interpretation by defining *academic disadvantage* to mean a person that "(1) lacks reading and writing skills, (2) lacks mathematical skills, or (3) performs below grade level."[32]

Economically disadvantaged was defined to mean "(1) family income is at or below national poverty level; (2) participant, or parents or guardian of the participant, is unemployed; (3) participant, or parent of participant, is recipient of public assistance; or (4) participant is institutionalized or under state guardianship."[33]

Under title II, eligibility for participation in special programs for the disadvantaged (supported under the title's subpart 4, section 104.801) was limited to the academically or economically disadvantaged who, as a result of their disadvantage, "(1) do not have, at the time of entrance into a vocational education program, the prerequisites for success in the program; or (2) are enrolled in a vocational education program but require supportive services or special programs to enable them to meet the requirements for the program that are established by the state or the local educational agency."[34]

Under the 1976 amendments, in order for persons to have been eligible for special vocational programs, program modifications, and related services under the set-aside and special funds for the disadvantaged, they must have met the following conditions:

1. The individual is excluded from a regular vocational program because of the *effects* of a disadvantagement or
2. The individual shows evidence of being unable to succeed in a regular vocational program because of the *effects* of a disadvantagement, *and*
3. The effect of the disadvantagement is identified by a qualified professional person (teachers, counselors).[35]

The Job Training Partnership Act (JTPA) was passed by Congress in 1982. Although this was not a vocational bill per se, it continues to have a significant impact on the vocational training of youth and adults. As a replacement for the much maligned Comprehensive Employment and Training Act (CETA), this piece of federal legislation represents an ongoing commitment on the part of Congress to provide programs that will assist economically disadvantaged, unemployed, or underemployed youth and adults. Under JTPA, each regional service area receives federal funds through a joint council made up of local business, education, labor, and social service agency personnel; the council is referred to as a private industry council (PIC). JTPA provides for

- basic job training services
- training services for the disadvantaged
- an employment and training program for dislocated workers
- federally administered job training programs (e.g., Job Corps, Native American Program, Veteran's Employment Program)
- other related training and support services[36]

Some of the specific services offered under JTPA might include the following:

- job search assistance, including orientation, counseling, and referral
- on-the-job training, remedial education, upgrading, and retraining
- supportive services such as health care, child care, residential support, and transportation
- payment of needs-based allowances to cover expenses incurred while in training or employment[37]

Eligibility for these services is extended to individuals who are economically disadvantaged, as determined by individual income. There is also a provision in the act for serving the needs of dislocated workers.

None of these early federal directives has had such a far-reaching impact on vocational education for the disadvantaged as the Carl D. Perkins Vocational and Technical Education Act of 1984 (Public Law 98-524). The predominant theme of this legislation can be found in its stated purpose (see also Chapter 2, p. 41) which is to ''assure that individuals who are inadequately served under vocational education programs are assured access to quality vocational education programs.''[38] Five other purposes of the act are closely related to the main purpose. The act is designed to

- promote greater cooperation between public agencies and the private sector in preparing individuals for employment, in promoting the quality of vocational education in the States, and in making the vocational system more responsive to the labor market in the States;
- improve the academic foundations of vocational students and to aid in the application of newer technologies (including the use of computers) in terms of employment or occupational goals;
- provide vocational education services to train, retrain, and upgrade employed and unemployed workers in new skills for which there is a demand in that State or employment market;
- assist the most economically depressed areas of a State to raise employment and occupational competencies of its citizens;
- assist the State to utilize a full range of supportive services, special programs, and guidance counseling and placement to achieve the basic purposes of this Act.[39]

Of the funds available under Title II, part A, of the act, 10 percent is allocated for handicapped individuals, 22 percent for diadvantaged individuals, 12 percent for adults who are in need of training or retraining, 8.5 percent for single parents and homemakers, 3.5 percent for individuals who are participants in programs designed to eliminate sex bias and stereotyping, and 1 percent for criminal offenders.[40]

Until this legislative mandate, federal set-aside funding had been used to pay the costs of supplemental staff, services, or materials in order to provide vocational programming opportunities for all special populations. The provisions of this new legislation refocus the emphasis upon placement in regular vocational programs. The direct cause of this refocusing is the supplemental cost provisions of section 202 (c) (2). Under this section of the act, the federal share of expenditures (50 percent) for the disadvantaged shall be used for supplemental or additional staff, equipment, materials, and services that are not provided to other individuals in vocational education but that are *essential* for disadvantaged individuals to participate in vocational education. If the conditions of disadvantaged individuals require a separate program, federal funds may be used to pay 50 percent of the costs (of the program's services and activities) that exceed the eligible recipient's average per pupil expenditure for regular vocational services and activities.[41]

As in the past, the only basis for identifying students as disadvantaged should be their need for supportive services or special programs designed to meet their unique needs in order to enable them to succeed in vocational education. Furthermore, each student should be identified as an *individual* who cannot succeed, rather than as a member of a particular group of people. With this in mind, some general characteristics are presented as guidance for each of the groups classified as disadvantaged according to the Carl D. Perkins Act. The groups of individuals included under the term *disadvantaged* are academically disadvantaged individuals, economically disadvantaged individuals, individuals with limited English proficiency (LEP), criminal offenders, single parents, and displaced homemakers.

Classification of Disadvantaged Individuals According to the Carl D. Perkins Act

Academically disadvantaged individuals are those who score below the 25th percentile on a standardized achievement or aptitude test, who have secondary school grades below 2.0 on a 4.0 scale (4.0 = A), or who fail to attain minimal academic competencies.[42]

The Academically Disadvantaged

Academically disadvantaged youth typically have a long history of academic failure. Many have already dropped out of school "mentally" if not physically. As a result, their aptitude and achievement test scores are usually much lower than those of their peer group. They also tend to have a record of failure in the important basic skill courses of English, mathematics, and science. Many are already a grade level or two behind their age group in class standing. The academically disadvantaged often come to the educational environment from a different cultural or ethnic background than that of their peers. Furthermore, this background may be one where parents do not provide educational guidance or where a strong emphasis is not placed upon the importance of schooling. An outgrowth of this lack of influence and emphasis is frequent absences from school, tardiness, or behavioral problems.

Academically disadvantaged students often display language or communication problems in school. These problems may include limited English proficiency, poor oral or written communication skills, poor grammar, and poor vocabulary skills.

What happens to these academically disadvantaged youths? Many drop out of school. The attainment of a high school diploma is widely recognized as essential to a successful transition from school to the workplace. Yet 14.4 percent of 1980 high school sophomores left school without a diploma, according to the National Center for Educational Statistics.[43] The reasons most frequently cited for dropping out were dislike for school and poor grades.

Economically disadvantaged individuals are defined as those who come from a family that the state board of a state has identified as low income on the basis of uniform criteria such as the following:

The Economically Disadvantaged

- annual income at or below the official poverty level
- eligibility for free or reduced-price school lunch
- eligibility for AFDC or other public assistance programs

- receipt of a Pell grant or money from other comparable state programs of need-based financial assistance
- eligibility for participation in programs assisted under title II of JTPA[44]

The economically disadvantaged can be found in almost any area of society. But certain areas or regions have a chronically low level of economic activity or a deteriorating economic base, causing such adverse effects as

    A. a rate of unemployment which has exceeded by 50 percent or more the average rate of unemployment in the State, or in the Nation, for each of the three years preceding the year for which such designation is made, or

    B. a large concentration of low-income families, . . .[45]

The plight of the economically disadvantaged is often inseparable from that of the academically disadvantaged—often they are one and the same. Economically disadvantaged youths or adults come from home environments with an extensive record of unemployment or minimal employment. Usually as a consequence of poor academic or vocational training, the economically disadvantaged lack the necessary education to break the cycle of unemployment; poor health, nutrition, and hygiene; welfare; and substandard living conditions or even poverty. Many of the parents are single parents, most often females, who lack essential entry level skills for jobs that require more than manual unskilled labor. Many economically disadvantaged children come from homes where one or more parents have not completed high school or homes where a stable authority figure cannot be found.

The correlation between the noncompletion of high school and poverty is well documented. According to the 1980 census, the number of persons 25 years or older who completed less than 12 years of school number 45 million, or about one-third of the total adult population. In some regions of the country 40–50 percent of the adult population dropped out before high school graduation.

The profound effect of a high school diploma on income becomes clear when one examines the poverty rates of persons with 9–11 years of school and those who have graduated. Persons who had attended high school but did not graduate were twice as likely to fall below the poverty level as those who had received a high school diploma. This difference was found across all age groups for both blacks and whites.

With the increase in the technical nature of many jobs, it appears that a high school diploma is more important than ever before. In 1970, 16 percent of the 22- to 34-year-olds who completed only one to three years of high school were below the national poverty level, according to census figures.[46] In 1981, the rate had already increased to 28 percent.[47]

Many of the economically disadvantaged have resorted to drugs—and to crime to support their drug habits—in an effort to withdraw from the daily environment in which they must live. The economically disadvantaged may be the most difficult segment of the disadvantaged population for vocational personnel to help. The reason for this is the difficulty of breaking a long cycle of economic hardship and the consequences of that hardship. Poor health, poor living conditions, withdrawal from society, drug and alcohol abuse are but a few of the problems.

Those with limited English proficiency (LEP) include individuals not born in the United States or whose native language is a language other than English; individuals from environments where a language other than English is dominant; and American Indian and Alaskan native students who come from environments where a language other than English has had a significant impact on their fluency in English.[48]

The Limited English Proficient

Individuals classified as limited English proficient are in many respects very similar to the academically or economically disadvantaged. Many LEP youths and adults bring to the educational environment a sporadic history of poor performance. This poor performance is reflected in a high rate of absenteeism and tardiness. LEP students often have a high probability of dropping out of school before graduation. As expected, a high percentage of students experience written or oral communication problems when in school. They often simply cannot adjust to cultural and language differences present in the educational environment.

LEP individuals are often also economically disadvantaged. Living conditions are usually less than satisfactory—overcrowded and substandard. Many LEP adults have no employment history or a poor employment history consisting of unskilled, low-paying, service-oriented occupations with very limited advancement opportunities. Yet many have a strong work ethic and a desire to adjust to a society that heretofore has been less than willing to accept them as full members.

A *criminal offender* is defined as any individual who is charged with or convicted of any criminal offense; the category includes youth or juvenile offenders.[49] These individuals are housed in prisons, jails, reformatories, work farms, detention centers, halfway houses, community-based rehabilitation centers, and similar institutions used for confinement or rehabilitation.[50]

Criminal Offenders

The fate of criminal offenders as they serve their sentence is one with which most members of society cannot identify. Criminal offenders share many of the same problems with the economically disadvantaged, problems brought on by financial hardship. This hardship is generally not mitigated, for many employers resist hiring offenders under any circumstances. Even if criminal offenders are successful in securing employment, the supervision requirements (e.g., parole conditions and prohibitions against bonding or licensing) imposed by the criminal justice system often restrict the kinds of job that they may accept.

One of the most important factors affecting criminal offenders is their relationship to the family unit. Criminal offenders are usually members of large extended families. However, the typical social functions of education, guidance, care, food, shelter, and recreation are largely provided by community social institutions instead of by the family unit. Many of these family units are best characterized as intolerable places for children and young adults because of the tensions, disharmony, child abuse, or delinquency which so often prevail.

The criminal offender or the juvenile delinquent more often than not lacks adequate job skills for successfully seeking and holding sustained employment. School can play a major role in the general education and socialization of young adults, and much of the delinquent behavior of young adults can be traced there. Many young adults become increasingly dissatisfied with school, its perceived restrictiveness, its policies, rules, and regulations. As a result, many young adults have a high rate of absenteeism or truancy, experience academic failure, and soon drop out of school. They are consequently ill prepared for the world of work, having no job skills and a low level of literacy. The end result is that they turn to crime in order to survive.

Single Parents

According to the Carl D. Perkins Act, a single parent is an individual who (1) is unmarried or legally separated from a spouse and (2) has a minor child or children for which the parent has either custody or joint custody.[51]

The fate of the single parent can best be discussed from two separate vantage points. These two vantage points are (1) that of the unmarried or legally separated adult and (2) that of the unwed teenage parent. Let us examine each of the single-parent classifications.

The unmarried or legally separated single parent often faces the same type of problems as the academically or economically disadvantaged. Many need extensive counseling assistance in order to enter the educational environment. The focus of this assistance often must be on developing a strong self-concept and an occupational awareness. Like their academically disadvantaged counterparts, many single parents who are unmarried or legally separated need reinforcement in the basic academic skills of English, mathematics, and science in order to partake of additional academic and vocational training. Academic difficulties are not the only problems with which many single parents must cope; economic problems are usually present as well. If this is the case, financial aid and child care services are generally required before the single parent can return to or continue schooling.

The teenage parent (usually female) faces many of the same problems as the single parent, but these are compounded by the difficulties of being children themselves. For teenage parents, extensive interpersonal and family counseling assistance must be provided in order to help them adjust to their new role.

Displaced Homemakers

The term *homemaker* refers to adults who have taken care of a home and family, usually without remuneration; for that reason, they have few marketable skills.[52]

Displaced homemakers generally include the following target groups:

- persons who had been homemakers but who now, because of the dissolution of a marriage, must seek employment
- persons who are single heads of households and who lack adequate job skills
- persons who are currently homemakers and part-time workers but who wish to secure a full-time job
- women who are now in jobs that have been traditionally considered jobs for females

- men who are now in jobs that have been traditionally considered jobs for males and who wish to seek employment in job areas that have not been traditionally considered as job areas for males[53]

Displaced homemakers, like other groups of the disadvantaged, have academic and economic difficulties that block their efforts to gain salable employment skills through vocational education programs. Assistance in the development of basic skills, occupational and personal counseling, financial and child care assistance, and nutrition and health assistance are but a few of the kinds of help needed by displaced homemakers.

For two and a half decades, students, parents, and adults have looked to vocational education to provide some hope for the disadvantaged, to help overcome their alienation from the educational mainstream, to change the cycle of dropping out of school, unemployment, and poverty. But there is still much to be done. A 1976 report of the Senate Committee on Labor and Public Welfare stated that despite the existence of civil rights guarantees and the supposed equality of opportunity, "the vocational education enterprise has made little progress towards ensuring equal opportunities for the disadvantaged."[54] Ever since 1963, vocational education legislation has contained a number of equity provisions designed to address the concerns of all individuals who have a need for, interest in, and ability to benefit from vocational training. Equality of opportunity for disadvantaged youth and adults clearly continues under the Carl D. Perkins Act. The law provides assurances that

Summary

- equal access will be provided in recruitment, enrollment, and placement activities
- equal access will be provided to the full range of vocational programs for all disadvantaged learners, including occupationally specific courses and cooperative education and apprenticeship programs
- information will be provided to students and parents concerning the opportunities available in, and eligibility requirements for, vocational education (at the LEA [local educational agency]) before students enter the ninth grade level[55]

Section 204 of the act states that information be provided to disadvantaged students, and parents of such students, concerning the opportunities available in vocational education at least one year before the students enter the grade level in which vocational education programs are first generally available, but in no event later than the beginning of the ninth grade. Information about the requirements for eligibility for enrollment in vocational education programs must also be included. Furthermore, each student who enrolls in vocational education programs shall receive

(1) an assessment of the interests, abilities, and special needs of such student with respect to completing successfully the vocational education program;

(2) special services, including adaptation of curriculum, instruction, equipment, and facilities, designed to meet the needs described in clause (1);

(3) guidance, counseling, and career development activities conducted by professionally trained counselors who are associated with the provision of such special services; and

(4) counseling services designed to facilitate the transition from school to post-school employment and career opportunities.[56]

Unless and until vocational education addresses the needs of the whole learner, we shall continue to meet only haphazard success. The failure in individual attainment will be a reflection of a failure in our schools in general and in vocational education in particular.[57]

IDENTIFICA-TION AND AS-SESSMENT OF DISADVAN-TAGED LEARNERS

Background

Given the characteristics of disadvantaged learners, one of the major tasks facing vocational and general education personnel is that of identifying individual learners who might be disadvantaged. As noted earlier, it is extremely important to think of each disadvantaged person as an *individual*. Each disadvantaged learner brings to the school environment certain strengths as well as weaknesses, and it is important for the educator to be aware of those unique strengths and weaknesses. Indeed, recognition of such unique learner characteristics is essential in the decisionmaking process concerning matters like instructional staffing, curriculum development, and instructional delivery.

The task of identifying potential disadvantaged learners has been an ongoing problem. A 1976 study by John Walsh and Jan Totten of programs for disadvantaged students in the United States that covered 84 projects in 77 communities in 23 states indicated confusion about the meaning of the term *disadvantaged*. The investigators also found that the identification requirement set by the legislative acts for individuals, rather than for groups, was not met. In fact, they found that there was little understanding of this concept at the state level; individual assessment was defined in terms of whether students met established criteria for enrollment in programs for the disadvantaged. They concluded that ''most states have devoted very little attention to the conceptualization of special vocational education services for the disadvantaged, based on specific criteria for the identification of disadvantaged students and individual assessment of students either eligible or potentially eligible for such services.''[58]

Walsh and Totten found that the states generally used two major criteria, either separately or in combination, for identifying disadvantaged students: ''(1) students who are behind one or more grades in academic achievement, or (2) students who reside in designated target areas (usually high youth unemployment areas, big cities, Title I areas, and areas of rural poverty).''[59] Very often, the criteria actually applied at the local level differed widely between states and between communities within states.[60] Jerry L. Wircenski found the discrepancy in the application of specific identification criteria was also evident in a study of national exemplary cooperative, self-contained, and mainstream programs.[61] One of the most disturbing findings of the Walsh and Totten assessment was that half of the 84 project directors interviewed in conjunction with the project level assessment said that they did not believe the students enrolled in their programs were disadvantaged.[62]

In the literature there is much confusion surrounding the identification process and the application of that process's information. Three basic steps to alleviate the confusion in the learner identification and assessment process are apparent in the literature. They are referral, assessment, and educational planning.

Three Basic Steps to Identification and Assessment of Disadvantaged Learners

Step 1: Learner Referral

The first step, learner referral, is usually made by academic teachers, counselors, administrators, parents, or support staff (i.e., psychologists, nurses, or community agency personnel). The learner referral is generally informal in that attention is called to a student who is having some academic, economic, or social problem. Once the student is identified by referral, most school systems have an established, more formal mechanism whereby the student's special needs can be more readily identified. During the informal referral process, many administrators prefer not to remove the referred student from the regular instructional program until an accurate assessment can be made of the unique problem.

L. Allen Phelps and Ronald J. Lutz have noted that "the referral identification process often removes the student and dangerously labels him or her among the peer group and the instructional staff."[63] The current trend in providing special services for the disadvantaged is to reduce the number of referrals 'out' of regular programs. Furthermore, the excess cost provisions of the Carl D. Perkins Act discourages the establishment of separate programs by funding 50 percent of the cost of the program's services and activities that exceed the average per pupil expenditures. In this way, the stigma of being labeled differently (by placement in programs where disadvantaged learners are segregated from the mainstream of regular classes) is minimized.

Phelps and Lutz make a number of suggestions to assist in-school and out-of school personnel in the collection and reporting of student identification information:

1. Initially, you should review and become familiar with any existing identification criteria, procedures, and/or forms used for the referral of special students in the district. It is important to be familiar with any existing process used in your school district so that the identification utilized here does not result in a duplication of effort. It may also be that some of the identification information has already been compiled on the special needs students in your class.

2. A second activity involves deciding what specific identification information it is important and essential to collect. Most student identification information forms include the following:

    a. Name, age, birthdate, sex, school, and grade placement of student
    b. Name, address, and phone numbers of parents or guardians
    c. Date on which the information is submitted for review
    d. Name of referring teacher, teachers, or, in some instances, parents
    e. Reason for the referral (usually a detailed description of the specific problems the student is encountering)
    f. Special services the student is already receiving
    g. Type of action the referring teacher or professional suggests as being appropriate
    h. Name and title of the individual to whom the identification information is submitted. This is usually the building principal or director of special education.

3. Careful consideration also has to be given to how the student identification information will be collected. Questions of who should compile the information and which information sources are to be used will also influence the identification-referral process. In some instances parents will point out the specific problems to individual teachers or counselors and request that a referral be initiated. In most cases, however, teachers or other school personnel will initiate the referral and utilize their written observation reports as an information base when compiling the necessary information. Parent and student interviews, school records, and numerous other references can and should be also consulted for background information.

4. Once the basic student identification information is collected and summarized, it must be submitted to the appropriate person for action. Whoever this individual is, he or she must have the responsibility and authority for seeing that the referral-identification is acted upon.

5. Depending upon the special services and personnel available and the nature of the student's special need, a variety of actions may then be undertaken by the principal or director of special services. In some cases it may be appropriate to call a meeting of the student's teachers to determine what special considerations or modifications are needed in the student's instructional program. In other cases it may be necessary to have the student's hearing or vision tested or to have some additional educational assessments done to determine more specifically the student's learning or behavioral problem(s).

6. The identification-referral process can easily become bogged down in paperwork and exhaustive procedures. It is best to keep it as simple and as efficient as possible. Collect and report only the basic information needed to establish the student's eligibility to receive the special services he or she will need to succeed in an educational program.[64]

A number of forms have been developed to refer learners who might have some type of disadvantage. A sample referral form currently used for student referral purposes is shown in Exhibit 3-1. A similar learner referral form, developed by Thomas E. Hyde and Jerry L. Wircenski, is shown in Exhibit 3-2.[65]

Both forms are designed to solicit referral information from in-school and out-of-school personnel who suspect that a learner may have some type of disadvantage. Modifications can be made by the school district staff to accommodate local information or criteria. It is essential to keep in mind that merely because a learner is being referred does *not* mean one should conclude that the person is disadvantaged. The function of reaching such a conclusion is the concern of the second stage, the learner assessment process.

General Assessment. Following the initial identification process, the next step is to assess or diagnose the learner's strengths and weaknesses. The purpose of learner

Step 2: Learner Assessment

Exhibit 3-1 Disadvantaged Learner Referral Form A

Directions: Please complete as much information as possible.

Date _____

Student name _____

Grade _____ Subject _____ Sex _____

Referred by _____

Relation to student _____

Referred to _____

Reason for referral _____
_____
_____
_____
_____

How long has this problem existed? _____

Describe action *already* taken
_____
_____
_____
_____

Have parents been contacted? _____ yes _____ no

Parents' names: Father _____

Mother _____

Parents' address _____

Home phone _____ Work phone _____

Parents' reaction _____
_____
_____

Exhibit 3-2 Disadvantaged Learner Referral Form B

Student name _____   Referring person _____
Date _____   Subject area _____
Grade _____   Agency _____
Sex _____   Length of time knowing student _____
Age _____   Referred to _____

The above named student, in my professional judgment, is having difficulties in the following areas:
(Complete as many as apply and provide examples where possible.)

1. Attitude: Overall attitude toward school, adults, peers.
   Comments:

   Poor   Fair   Good   Excellent

2. Social Skills: Ability to get along with peers, adults; participation in soc. act. (clubs, sports).
   Comments:

   Poor   Fair   Good   Excellent

3. Personal Hygiene: Overall general appearance; personal grooming.
   Comments:

   Poor   Fair   Good   Excellent

4. Manual Dexterity: Coordination; ability to work with hands.
   Comments:

   Poor   Fair   Good   Excellent

5. Reading/Writing Skills: Ability to express ideas in writing; ability to read and comprehend.
   Comments:

   Poor   Fair   Good   Excellent

6. Verbal Communication Skills: Orally expresses ideas and opinions.
   Comments:

   Poor   Fair   Good   Excellent

7. Mathematics Skills: Ability to perform basic computations (add., sub., multi., div.).
   Comments:

   Poor   Fair   Good   Excellent

8. Performing at grade level . . . . . yes   no
9. Potential school dropout . . . . . . yes   no   maybe
10. Potential "social" dropout . . . . yes   no   maybe
11. Problems with:

	None	Few	Many
A. Discipline			
B. Acting out behavior . . .			
C. Economic			
D. Law			
E. Drugs/alcohol			
F. Homelife			
G. Others (specify)			

Comments:

assessment is to provide identification information that is useful for staffing, curriculum, and support service planning. The learner diagnosis can be made in any number of learner-assessor experiences. The most common is that of teacher assessment through the teaching-learning process. In this process, observations can be formulated and recorded. A similar diagnosis can be made as a result of a counselor's assessment, through the counseling process, of learner strengths and weaknesses. Likewise, community agency personnel and professionals can utilize the interaction process between student and advisor to diagnose individual problems.

In Exhibit 3-3, L. Allen Phelps presents a learner analysis profile that focuses attention on those criteria that are applicable to adolescents and young adults interested in vocational education.[66] The left side of the learner analysis profile identifies eight broad categories in which observable effects of disadvantages commonly occur. The center column provides a rating scale on which specific "special needs indicators" can be rated from learning difficulty to learning strength. The right side of the Phelps learner analysis profile provides space for documentation. This documentation is especially important to have in order to substantiate accurately the learner's strengths and weaknesses. Classroom teachers, administrators, parents, counselors, and psychologists, as well as community resource agencies and school records, are some of the sources that can be utilized for documentation purposes.

It is important that the documentation process be based on current objective data and facts and not on innuendoes, prejudices, or outdated information. Standardized, norm-referenced achievement and aptitude tests and criterion-referenced tests are possible sources for documentation, although caution must be exercised in evaluating the experiences of students who have not been in the social mainstream of the educational process. School personnel may wish to administer some individual testing to verify referral information or to observe the student directly during test administration.

Program Specific Assessment. As noted, the purpose of the learner assessment step in the identification of disadvantaged learners is to *pinpoint* an individual learner's strengths and weaknesses. Based on the results of the learner assessment process, special services or programs can be identified or designed to accommodate the disadvantaged learner. This may be sufficient in many school systems. It is suggested, however, that one additional task be performed before prescribing a plan of action. That task is to achieve an appropriate perspective.

A system of learner assessment developed by Hyde and Wircenski places a learner's assessment information in perspective with the learner's career choice as well as the career choices of the learner's peers (see Exhibit 3-4).[67] In this system, information is collected on every student who has been referred by school personnel, parents, or community resource agencies—a process similar to that in the Phelps learner analysis profile or other identification-assessment systems. In the Hyde and Wircenski identification system, however, a student's profile is then compared with all other students who have expressed a similar career choice. Such a comparison may show that a student indeed can be identified as having some type of disadvantage, for example, poor reading skills. The student may still be able to succeed in a vocational

Exhibit 3-3 Learner Analysis Profile

Learner: _____	Assessment/Appraisal Team:
School: _____ LEARNER ANALYSIS	_____
Date: _____ PROFILE	_____

Special Need Indicators	Learning Difficulty	Learning Strength	Documentation/Observed Behavior
QUANTITATIVE/ NUMERICAL SKILLS			
Count and Record			
Add/Subtract			
Multiply/Divide			
Measure			
General Number Use			
Money			
Other Quantitative/ Numerical Skills:			
VERBAL SKILLS			
Read			
Spell			
Record Information			
Verbal Communication			
Written Communication			
Other Verbal Skills:			
COGNITIVE SKILLS			
Retention			
Sequence			
Attentiveness			
Planning Ability			
Mechanical Aptitude			
Transfer			
Other Cognitive Skills:			
PERCEPTUAL SKILLS			
Auditory Discrimination			
Form Perception			
Form Discrimination			
Space Perception			
Color Perception			
Touch Discrimination			
Other Perceptual Skills:			
LANGUAGE SKILLS			
Listening			
Nonverbal Expression			
Technical Vocabulary			
Grammatical Expression			
Other Language Skills:			

Exhibit 3-3 continued

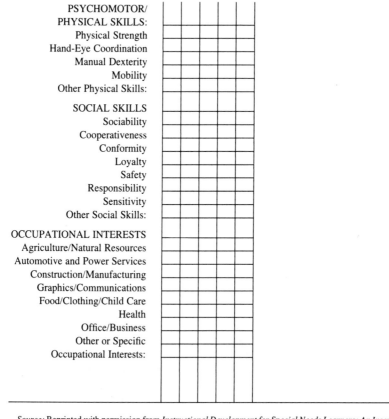

PSYCHOMOTOR/ PHYSICAL SKILLS:						
Physical Strength						
Hand-Eye Coordination						
Manual Dexterity						
Mobility						
Other Physical Skills:						
SOCIAL SKILLS						
Sociability						
Cooperativeness						
Conformity						
Loyalty						
Safety						
Responsibility						
Sensitivity						
Other Social Skills:						
OCCUPATIONAL INTERESTS						
Agriculture/Natural Resources						
Automotive and Power Services						
Construction/Manufacturing						
Graphics/Communications						
Food/Clothing/Child Care						
Health						
Office/Business						
Other or Specific Occupational Interests:						

Source: Reprinted with permission from *Instructional Development for Special Needs Learners: An Inservice Resource Guide* by L.A. Phelps, pp. 47–49, University of Illinois at Urbana-Champaign, © 1976.

program, however, because the skill deficiency may be acceptable when compared to the skill level of successful students already enrolled or satisfactorily placed on the job. Thus, in this instance, the label of disadvantaged is not accurate because the deficiency is *not* detrimental to success in the regular vocational program. In another case, however, the student's reading skills may *not* be adequate for a vocational program without special support services or remedial instruction. In short, educators often are too quick to label learners as disadvantaged without considering the possibility that the learner can succeed in the regular vocational curriculum. The comparison process must of course involve the vocational teacher for each program and must be based on sound data on both successful and unsuccessful program learners.

Exhibit 3-4 Learner Assessment Form

PROGRAM <u>Carpentry</u>

Student name _____

Grade _____

Date _____

Completed by _____

General Directions: Complete the information in Part I for the above named student. Complete Part II for the typical student presently enrolled in this program or successfully completing this program.

CRITERIA	Part I — Rating of the above named student based on referral *and* documentation	Part II — Ratings of students presently enrolled or formally enrolled in program on this criteria				
		Well Below Average	Below Average	Average	Above Average	Well Above Average
Attitude	Poor Fair Good Excellent (Rating)					
Social Skills	Poor Fair Good Excellent (Rating)					
Personal Hygiene	Poor Fair Good Excellent (Rating)					
Manual Dexterity	0 25 50 75 100 (Percentile)					
Reading Ability	0 3 6 9 12 (Grade Reading Level)					

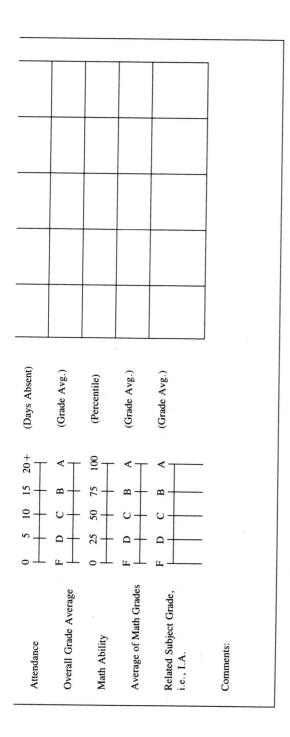

Step 3: Learner Educational Planning

The last step in the learner identification and assessment process is to develop a learner educational plan. This plan focuses on the modifications or support services necessary to assist disadvantaged learners to overcome their disadvantages. The central purpose of the identification and assessment process is to inject some form of change into the teaching-learning process. Its most common impact is the utilization of individualized instruction. The delivery of services for the handicapped—those "individuals who are mentally retarded, hard of hearing, deaf, speech impaired, visually handicapped, seriously emotionally disturbed, orthopedically impaired, or other health impaired persons, or persons with specific learning disabilities, who by reason thereof require special education and related services, and who, because of their handicapping condition, cannot succeed in the regular vocational education program without special education assistance"[68]—through individualized instructions is much more clearly defined as a result of the Education for All Handicapped Children Act of 1975 (Public Law 94-142). This act states that each school system must establish a procedure whereby the educational needs of every single learner, rather than a group or class, are addressed through an individual educational plan (IEP).

Although it is not our intent here to discuss handicapped learners, much can be gained from examining the IEP element for the handicapped stipulated in the 1975 act. The IEP must include

1. a statement of the student's present level of educational achievement in areas such as academic achievement, social adaptation, prevocational and vocational skills, psychomotor skills, and self-help skills
2. a statement of annual goals that describes the educational performance to be achieved by the end of the school year under the child's individualized education program
3. a statement of short-term instructional objectives, which must be measurable intermediate steps between the present level of educational performance and the annual goals
4. a statement of specific educational services needed by the child, including a description of all special education and related services that are needed to meet the unique needs of the child, also including the type of physical education program in which the child will participate
5. the date when those services will be initiated and terminated
6. a description of the extent to which the child will participate in regular education programs
7. objective criteria, evaluation procedures, and schedule for determining, on at least an annual basis, whether the short-term instructional objectives are being achieved.[69]

The 1975 act suggests that an IEP for the handicapped be developed on an annual basis through a planning conference consisting of special education teachers, classroom teachers, administrators, counselors, parents, and community service agency personnel.

There is no similar federal mandate for individualized educational planning for the disadvantaged, yet there has been much discussion about their need. In the absence of such legislative action, vocational educators and school personnel should take the lead in formulating similar learner educational plans for the disadvantaged. The purpose of the identification and assessment process is to bring together individual strengths and weaknesses into a comprehensive and coordinated instructional program. Many forms are available for consolidating information into an individualized learner educational plan. Ann P. Turnbull, Bonnie Strickland, and John C. Brantley offer one of the more comprehensive learner educational plans.[70] Exhibit 3-5 presents their completed IEP for handicapped students, which could be modified for disadvantaged learners. In Exhibit 3-6, L. Allen Phelps offers a much more simplified individualized learner educational plan.[71] Local school districts can adopt one of these two plans or they may design individualized learner education plans more appropriate for their own use.

The initial referral and formal assessment forms discussed earlier contain essential information and documentation that are important for planning purposes. These forms therefore should become part of the learner educational plan.

SUMMARY

This chapter began with an examination of characteristics of disadvantaged learners as described in the literature. Personal and homelife characteristics and ability levels were reviewed. It is apparent from numerous studies that disadvantaged learners have been shut out of the mainstream of American educational, economic, cultural, and social life. The life style of the disadvantaged learner typically has been one of mere existence.

A summary was given of federal legislative acts concerning vocational education that have served to identify and characterize the disadvantaged learner. Noted was the importance of identifying disadvantaged learners in vocational education and of applying the information from the identification process in the learner assessment and learner educational planning stages. Finally, it was shown how certain forms for the identification of disadvantaged learners can be usefully applied in this multiphased process.

It is important to remember that the effort and support of *all* educational personnel are required in the identification and recruitment of disadvantaged and handicapped students and in coordinating the delivery of appropriate services to them. "Cooperation and coordinated planning are essential among all segments of the educational community and the related agencies which serve disadvantaged and handicapped persons."[72]

In the preface of *Resurge '79,* Daniel B. Dunham, then deputy commissioner for occupational and adult education (HEW), stated, "Individuals must not be limited in their career objectives because of age, sex, race, or disability. Vocational education must be provided in an equitable manner to all persons in all communities. That is why it is essential for all educators to know each of their students in terms of their interests and abilities to better meet their learning needs.[73] These words still hold true today. The task of providing job skills for the disadvantaged will not be easy. But if

Exhibit 3-5 Individual Educational Plan

Checklist

Date	Action
9-1-87	Referral by Louise Borden
9-3-87	Parents informed of rights: permission obtained for evaluation
9-15-87	Evaluation compiled
9-16-87	Parents contacted
9-18-87	Legal committee meets and subcommittee assigned
9-28-87	IEP developed by subcommittee
9-30-87	IEP approved by subcommittee

Committee Members

Mrs. Louise Borden
Teacher
Mrs. John Thomas (Sp. Ed.)
Coordinators
Other IEA representative
Mrs. John Doe
Parents
Mrs. Mary Franks
Mrs. Joan Bambara
Mrs. Alice King
Date IEP initially approved
9-20-87

Yearly Class Schedule

Time	Subject	Teacher
8:30-9:20	math	Franks
9:30-10:20	language arts	Bambara (Resource)
10:30-11:20	social studies	Bambara
11:30-12:20	science	Franks
	lunch	
1:10-2:00	art	Shaw
2:10-3:00	P.E.	King

Continuum of Services

	Hours per week
Regular class	20 hours
Resource teacher in regular classroom	
Resource room	6 hours
Reading specialist	4 hours
Speech language therapist	
Counselor	

Identification Information

Name John Doe
School Beecher Sixth Grade Center
Birthdate 5-15-76 Grade 6
Parents'
Name Mr. and Mrs. John Doe
Address 1300 Johnson Street, Raleigh, N.C.
Phone Home none Office 932-8161

Testing Information

Test Name	Date Admin.	Interpretation
PIAI	9-10-87	spell—1.7, math—5.7, read recog—1.7, read comp—N.A., gen. info—6.3
Test of initial consonants (CRT)	9-11-87	knows eight out of twenty-one initial consonant sounds total 20
CRT Reading Checklist	9-12-87	oral comprehension—6th grade reading skills—primary level
Carolina Arith. Inventory (Time)	9-2-87	Level IV
Carolina Arith. Inventory (Number concepts)	9-2-87	Level IV

Special class
Transition class
Others: _____

Health Information
Vision: good
Hearing: excellent
Physical: good
Other: _____

Student's Name   John Doe
Level of Performance   primary reading recognition, 6th grade
comprehension of oral material.

Subject Area   Reading
Teacher   Mrs. Bambara—resource teacher

ANNUAL GOALS: 1) John will successfully complete the primer level of the Bank Street Reading Series.
2) John will recognize and correctly say 90 new sight words.
3) John will master 14 initial consonants.

SEPTEMBER	OCTOBER	NOVEMBER	DECEMBER	JANUARY
Referred	1. Recognize and correctly state the sounds of the initial consonants *b* and *f* 100% of the time.	1. Recognize and correctly state the sounds of the initial consonants *s* and *m* 100% of the time.	1. Correctly recognize and state the sound of the initial consonant *g* 100% of the time.	1. Review and correctly state the sounds of the initial consonants *b*, *f*, *m*, *s*, and *g* 100% of the time.
	2. Recognize and correctly say ten new sight words 100% of the time.	2. Recognize and correctly say ten new sight words 100% of the time.	2. Recognize and correctly say five new sight words 100% of the time.	2. Recognize and correctly state the sound of the initial consonant *h* 100% of the time.
	3. Complete the first three stories of the primer, reading the material with 50% accuracy.	3. Complete the next three stories in the primer, reading the material with 50% accuracy.	3. Complete the next story in the primer, reading the material with 50% accuracy.	3. Review and correctly say 25 previously learned sight words 100% of the time.
				4. Recognize and correctly say five new sight words 100% of the time.

OBJECTIVES

Exhibit 3-5 continued

	SEPTEMBER	OCTOBER	NOVEMBER	DECEMBER	JANUARY
OBJECTIVES					5. Review the previously read stories in the primer, reading the material with 60% accuracy.
MATERIALS		Bank Street Basal Reading Series, Hoffman Phonetic Reading Program, teacher-made materials	Bank Street Basal Reading Series, Hoffman Phonetic Reading Program, teacher-made materials	Bank Street Basal Reading Series, Hoffman Phonetic Reading Program, teacher-made materials	Bank Street Basal Reading Series, Hoffman Phonetic Reading Program, teacher-made materials
AGENT		regular teacher resource teacher	regular teacher resource teacher	regular teacher resource teacher	regular teacher resource teacher
EVALUATION		1. informal assessment 2. Criterion Referenced Test (CRT)	1. informal assessment 2. CRT	1. informal assessment 2. CRT	1. informal assessment 2. CRT

Source: Adapted from *Developing and Implementing Individualized Education Programs*, 2nd ed., by A.P. Turnbull et al., with permission of Charles E. Merrill Publishing Company, © 1982.

Exhibit 3-6 Learner Educational Plan

LEARNING PRESCRIPTION

Learner: _____   Instructional Team: _____

School: _____   _____

Date: _____   _____

A. Appropriate Learning Mode

Directions: Indicate, by numbering, the three most appropriate learning modes for this student. Check others that may also be appropriate.

_____ Audio/visual presentation   _____ Field experience(s)

_____ Observation of goal behavior   _____ Role playing

_____ Interview/conference with   _____ Reading
       knowledgeable person   _____ Audio recording

_____ Experiment/laboratory   _____ Other (specify):
       experience/project

_____ Programmed instruction   _____

_____ Simulation/games   _____

B. Interaction Mode

Directions: Indicate below the situations in which the student will work most productively.

_____ Independently (alone)   _____ Large group

_____ Peer/partner   _____ Individually with teacher or aide

_____ Small group

C. Additional Learning Style Considerations: _____

_____

_____

_____

_____

Source: Reprinted with permission from *Instructional Development for Special Needs Learners: An Inservice Resource Guide* by L.A. Phelps, p. 59, University of Illinois at Urbana-Champaign, © 1976.

---

the disadvantaged do not obtain these skills through vocational education, they may not obtain them at all.

NOTES

1. Mario D. Fantini and Gerold Weinstein, *The Disadvantaged: Challenge to Education* (New York: Harper & Row, 1968), 4–5.

2. Frank Riessman, "The Culturally Deprived Child," in *Learning Activities for Disadvantaged Children,* ed. John B. Bergeson and George S. Miller (New York: Macmillan, 1971), 44–45.

3. Leon Eisenberg, "Strengths of the Inner City Child," in *Education of the Disadvantaged,* ed. M. Goldberg and A.J. Tennenbaum (New York: Holt, Rinehart and Winston, 1967), 78–88.

4. Ben B. Seligman, *Permanent Poverty, An American Syndrome* (Chicago: Quadrangle Books, 1968), 95.

5. Francesco Cordasco and Eugene Bucchioni, *The Puerto Rican Community and Its Children on the Mainland* (Metuchen, N.J.: Scarecrow Press, 1972), 15–465.

6. Seligman, *Poverty*, 95.

7. Charles Oaklief, *Review and Synthesis of Research on Vocational and Technical Education for the Rural Disadvantaged* (Columbus, Ohio: ERIC Clearinghouse on Vocational and Technical Education, August 1971), 3–45; W.F. White, *Tactics for Teaching the Disadvantaged* (New York: McGraw-Hill, 1971); John Walsh and Jan L. Totten, *An Assessment of Vocational Education Programs for the Disadvantaged under Part B and Part A Section 102(b) of the 1968 Amendments to the Vocational Education Act* (Salt Lake City, Utah: Olympus Research Centers, December 1976), 23.

8. Thomas C. Cook, "A Profile of Highly Successful Vocational Teachers of Disadvantaged Students" (Ph.D. diss., Pennsylvania State University, 1978), 108–15; Edgar I. Farmer, "Identifying Pedagogical Competencies Needed to Train Vocational Education Teachers to Teach the Socioeconomically and Educationally Disadvantaged Students in the Inner Cities of Pennsylvania" (Ph.d. diss., Pennsylvania State University, 1978), 52–140.

9. Robert W. Walker, *What Vocational Education Teachers Should Know About Disadvantaged in Rural Areas* (Columbus, Ohio: ERIC Clearinghouse on Vocational and Technical Education, October 1971), 3.

10. J.M. Conte and G.H. Grimes, *Media and the Culturally Different Learner* (Washington, D.C.: National Education Association, 1969).

11. R.D. Strom, "Family Influence on School Failure," in *The Disadvantaged Child: Issues and Innovations*, ed. J.L. Frost and G.R. Hawkes (Boston: Houghton Mifflin, 1966). 379–81.

12. Lawrence L. Le Shan, "Time Orientation and Social Class," *Journal of Abnormal and Social Psychology* 47 (1952): 589–92; William E. Amos, "Disadvantaged Youth: Recognizing the Problem," in *The Disadvantaged and Potential Dropout*, ed. J.C. Gowan and G.D. Demos (Springfield, Ill.: Charles C Thomas, 1966), 9–16.

13. Eisenberg, "Strengths of the Inner City Child," 78–88.

14. David P. Ausubel and Pearl Ausubel, "Ego Development among Segregated Negro Children," in *Education in Depressed Areas*, ed. A.H. Passow (New York: Teachers College, Columbia University, 1963), 109–41.

15. Leonard M. Ridini and John E. Madden, *Physical Education for Inner-City Secondary Schools* (New York: Harper & Row, 1975), 4.

16. Benjamin Bloom, *Stability and Change in Human Characteristics* (New York: John Wiley & Sons, 1964), 77; Robert J. Havighurst, "Metropolitan Developmental and the Educational System," in *Education of the Disadvantaged*, ed. A.H. Passow, M. Goldberg, and A.J. Tannenbaum (New York: Holt, Rinehart and Winston, 1967), 19–31.

17. Herman P. Miller, *Rich Man, Poor Man* (New York: Signet, 1964), 59–80.

18. Fantini and Weinstein, *The Disadvantaged*, 73–74.

19. Vincent Feck, *What Vocational Education Teachers and Counselors Should Know about Urban Disadvantaged Youth* (Columbus, Ohio: ERIC Clearinghouse on Vocational and Technical Education, October 1971), 21.

20. Eisenberg, "Strengths of the Inner City Child," 78–88.

21. Martin Deutsch, "The Disadvantaged Child and the Learning Process," in *Education in Depressed Areas*, ed. A.H. Passow (New York: Teachers College, Columbia University, 1963), 163–79.

22. Arthur R. Jensen, "How Much Can We Boost I.Q. and Scholastic Achievement?" *Harvard Educational Review* 39 (1969): 1–123.

23. Thomas F. Pettigrew, "Negro Intelligence: A New Look At an Old Controversy," in *The Disadvantaged Child: Issues and Innovations,* ed. J.L. Frost and G.R. Hawkes (Boston: Houghton Mifflin Company, 1966), 96–116.

24. Committee for Economic Development, *Education for the Urban Disadvantaged: From Preschool to Employment* (New York: The Research and Policy Committee of the Committee for Economic Development, 1971), 9.

25. Fantini and Weinstein, *The Disadvantaged*, 5.

26. Manpower Administrator, U.S. Department of Labor, *Definition of Term "Disadvantaged Individual,"* Order no. 1-69 (Washington, D.C.: GPO, January 16, 1969).

27. The Committee for Economic Development, *Education for the Urban Disadvantaged.*

28. *Resurge '79: Manual for Identifying, Classifying and Serving the Disadvantaged and Handicapped under the Vocational Education Amendments of 1976 (P.L. 94-482)* (Washington, D.C.: GPO, September 1979), 1.

29. Evelyn R. Kay, Barbara H. Kemp, and Frances G. Saunders, *Guidelines for Identifying, Classifying, and Serving the Disadvantaged and Handicapped under the Vocational Education Amendments of 1968,* DHEW publication no. (OE) 73-11700 (Washington, D.C.: GPO, 1973), 1.

30. Ibid., 2.

31. Ibid.

32. *Resurge '79: Manual,* 5.

33. Ibid.

34. Ibid., 16.

35. Ibid.

36. Michelle D. Sarkees and John L. Scott, *Vocational Special Needs* (Alsip, Ill.: American Technical Publishers, 1985), 10.

37. Ibid.

38. Public Law 98-524 (Carl D. Perkins Vocational and Technical Education Act of 1984), October 2, 1984, 2437.

39. Ibid.

40. Ibid., 2452–53.

41. Ibid., 2450.

42. Sarkees and Scott, *Vocational*, 64.

43. U.S. Department of Education, National Center for Educational Statistics, *Vocational Education Data System* (May 3, 1984), p. 149.

44. Sarkees and Scott, *Vocational*, 12.

45. Ibid., 65.

46. U.S. Department of Commerce, Bureau of the Census, *Characteristics of the Low-Income Population: 1970,* Current Population Reports, series P. 60, no. 81 (Washington, D.C.: GPO, 1972).

47. Ibid.

48. Sarkees and Scott, *Vocational*, 65.

49. Public Law 98-524, Carl D. Perkins Act, 2483–84.

50. Ibid.

51. Ibid., 2486.

52. Ibid., 2484.

53. Sarkees and Scott, *Vocational*, 67.

54. U.S. Congress, Committee on Labor and Public Welfare, *Educational Amendments of 1976; Report to Accompany S.2657,* Senate Report 94-882, 94th Cong. 2d sess. (Washington, D.C.: GPO, 1976), 54.

55. Public Law 98-524, Carl D. Perkins Act, 2545–55.

56. Ibid., 2454

57. Ibid.

58. Walsh and Totten, *An Assessment,* 35.

59. Ibid., 28–29.

60. Ibid.

61. Jerry L. Wircenski, *Meeting the Needs of Teachers of Disadvantaged Programs in Pennsylvania,* Project no. 94-8032 (University Park, Pa.: Pennsylvania State University, Department of Vocational Education, September 1978), 1–274.

62. Walsh and Totten, *An Assessment,* 155.

63. L. Allen Phelps and Ronald J. Lutz, *Career Exploration and Preparation for the Special Needs Learner* (Boston: Allyn & Bacon, 1977), 110, Reprinted with permission.

64. Ibid., 110–13.

65. Thomas E. Hyde and Jerry L. Wircenski, "Developing Career Counseling Instruments," mimeographed (University Park, Pa.: Pennsylvania State University, 1978), 1–15.

66. L. Allen Phelps, *Instructional Development for Special Needs Learners: An Inservice Resource Guide* (Urbana, Ill., University of Illinois at Urbana-Champaign, Department of Vocational and Technical Education, 1976), 47–49.

67. Hyde and Wircenski, "Developing Career Counseling Instruments," 1–15.

68. Public Law 98-524, Carl D. Perkins Act, 2484.

69. S. Torres, ed., *A Primer on Individualized Education Programs for Handicapped Children* (Reston, Va.: Foundation for Exceptional Children, 1977), 52–53.

70. A.P. Turnbull, Bonnie Strickland, and John C. Brantley, *Implementing Individualized Education Programs* (Columbus, Ohio: Merrill, 1978).

71. Phelps, *Instructional Development,* 59.

72. Ann P. Turnbull and Jan B. Schulz, *Mainstreaming Handicapped Students: A Guide for the Classroom Teacher* (Boston: Allyn & Bacon, 1979), 80–97.

73. *Resurge '79: Manual,* i.

REFERENCES

Bergeson, John B., and George S. Miller. *Learning Activities for Disadvantaged Children.* New York: Macmillan, 1971.

Black, M.H. "Characteristics of the Culturally Disadvantaged." In *Learning Activities for Disadvantaged Children,* edited by V.B. Bergeson and G.S. Miller. New York: Macmillan, 1971.

Cobb, R.B., and D.E. Kingsbury. "Special Needs Provisions of the Perkins Act." *VocEd* 60, no. 4 (1985), 27–29.

Cobb, R.B., and E. Mikulin. "Implementing the Special Needs Provisions." In *A Guide to Implementing the Carl Perkins Vocational Education Act.* Alexandria, Va.: American Vocational Association, 1985.

Dunn, R., and K. Dunn. *Educator's Self-Teaching Guide to Individualizing Instructional Programs.* West Nyack, N.Y.: Parker Publishing Co., 1975.

U.S., *Federal Register* 35, no. 91, part II, sec. 102.3 (Definitions), May 9, 1970, 7335.

U.S., *Federal Register,* part XI (Rules and Regulations for Education Amendments of 1976, P.L. 94-482, Vocational Education, State Programs, and Commissioner's Discretionary Programs), October 3, 1977.

Wircenski, J.L. "Are We Really Serving Disadvantaged Youth?" *VocEd* 60, no. 3 (1985), 27–29.

Chapter 4

Identification and Characteristics of Handicapped Students

Stanley F. Vasa, Ed.D.
Allen L. Steckelberg, M.Ed.

Recent legislation and judicial decisions have led to a dramatic change in the provision of educational opportunities for handicapped individuals in the United States. Judicial precedents have established and mandated free access to public educational opportunities for handicapped individuals. Legislative initiatives have come in the wake of judicial rulings. Passage of the Education for All Handicapped Children Act (Public Law 94-142) in 1975 unambiguously made free appropriate public education for handicapped individuals a nationwide declaration. This was further supported and extended by regulations implementing section 504 of the Rehabilitation Act of 1973, which basically requires that institutional recipients of federal financial assistance for education shall provide a "free appropriate public education" to each qualified handicapped person, regardless of the nature or severity of the person's handicap.[1]

Three pieces of legislation provide the definition of a handicapping condition. Public Law 94-142 defines handicapped children as "those children evaluated . . . as being mentally retarded, hard of hearing, deaf, speech impaired, visually handicapped, seriously emotionally disturbed, orthopedically impaired, other health impaired, deaf-blind, multihandicapped, or as having specific learning disabilities, who because of those impairments need special education and related services."[2]

The implementing regulations for section 504 of the 1973 act encompass the definition of Public Law 94-142 by defining a handicapped person as "any person who has a physical or mental impairment which substantially limits one or more major life activities, has a record of such impairment, or is regarded as having such an impairment."[3]

The Vocational Education Amendments of 1976 (Public Law 94-482) provides funding through vocational educational programs to serve handicapped students. The rules and regulations for the amendments set forth a further delineation of the handicapping conditions and programming in vocational education:

''Handicapped'' means: a) a person who is: (1) mentally retarded; (2) hard of hearing; (3) deaf; (4) speech impaired; (5) visually handicapped; (6) seriously emotionally disturbed; (7) orthopedically impaired; or (8) other health impaired person, or persons with specific learning disabilities; and b) who, by reason of the above: (1) requires special education and related services, and (2) cannot succeed in the regular vocational education program without special educational assistance; or (3) requires a modified vocational education program.[4]

In Table 4-1, the definitions of the handicapping conditions from Public Law 94-142 are presented. In later sections of this chapter, we will examine each of the major categories of handicapping conditions most frequently confronted by the vocational education teacher in the public schools. The conditions covered are deaf and hard of hearing, visually handicapped, orthopedically impaired, other health impaired, mentally retarded, seriously emotionally disturbed, specific learning disabilities, and speech impaired.

IDENTIFICA-TION OF THE HANDICAPPED   Under Public Law 94-142, 11 handicapping conditions are officially recognized. The act also provides specific guidelines for the assessment and placement of handicapped students. The evaluation procedures are explicit and require the following:

- tests are provided and administered in the student's native language and validated for the purpose for which they are used;
- tests are administered and selected to best ensure that the skills of a student with a sensory or physical impairment are reflected, rather than the student's sensory or physical limitations;
- no single test shall be used as the sole criterion for placement;
- a multidisciplinary team or group of persons [is formed] including the classroom teacher(s) or other specialist with knowledge of the disability; and
- student [is] to be assessed in all areas related to the suspected disability including, when appropriate, health, vision, hearing, social and emotional status, general intelligence, academic performance, communicative status, and motor abilities.[5]

Considerations in the placement of a handicapped student in a special program are included in the rules and regulations for the implementation of Public Law 94-142. Information from a variety of sources—including standardized tests, teacher observations, social and cultural background, and adaptive behavior—must be analyzed, and the placement decision must be made by a group of persons who are knowledgeable about the student, the meaning of the evaluation data, and the options available to the student.

Table 4-1 Definitions of Handicapping Conditions Under Public Law 94-142

Handicapping Condition	Definition
Deaf	"Deaf" means a hearing impairment which is so severe that the child is impaired in processing linguistic information through hearing, with or without amplification, which adversely affects educational performance.
Deaf-Blind	"Deaf-blind" means concomitant hearing and visual impairments, the combination of which causes such severe communication and other developmental and educational problems that they cannot be accommodated in special education programs solely for deaf or blind children.
Hard of Hearing	"Hard of hearing" means a hearing impairment, whether permanent or fluctuating, which adversely affects a child's educational performance but which is not included under the definition of "deaf" in this section.
Mentally Retarded	"Mentally retarded" means significantly subaverage general intellectual functioning existing concurrently with deficits in adaptive behavior and manifested during the developmental period, which adversely affects a child's educational performance.
Multi-handicapped	"Multihandicapped" means concomitant impairments (such as mentally retarded-blind, mentally retarded-orthopedically impaired, etc.), the combination of which causes such severe educational problems that they cannot be accommodated in special education programs solely for one of the impairments. The term does not include deaf-blind children.
Orthopedically Impaired	"Orthopedically impaired" means a severe orthopedic impairment which adversely affects a child's educational performance. The term includes impairments caused by congenital anomaly (e.g., clubfoot, absence of some member, etc.), impairment from other causes (e.g., cerebral palsy, amputations, and fractures or burns which cause contractures).
Other Health Impaired	"Other health impaired" means limited strength, vitality or alertness, due to chronic or acute health problems such as a heart condition, tuberculosis, rheumatic fever, nephritis, asthma, sickle cell anemia, hemophilia, epilepsy, lead poisoning, leukemia, or diabetes, which adversely affects a child's educational performance.
Seriously Emotionally Disturbed	"Seriously emotionally disturbed" is defined as follows: The term means a condition exhibiting one or more of the following characteristics over a long period of time and to a marked degree, which adversely affects educational performance: (A) An inability to learn which cannot be explained by intellectual, sensory, or health factors; (B) An inability to build or maintain satisfactory interpersonal relationships with peers and teachers; (C) Inappropriate types of behavior or feelings under normal circumstances; (D) A general pervasive mood of unhappiness or depression; or (E) A tendency to develop physical symptoms or fears associated with personal or school problems. The term includes children who are schizophrenic or autistic. The term does not include children who are socially maladjusted, unless it is determined that they are seriously emotionally disturbed.

Table 4-1 continued

Specific Learning Disabilities	"Specific learning disability" means a disorder in one or more of the basic psychological processes involved in understanding or in using language, spoken or written, which may manifest itself in an imperfect ability to listen, think, speak, read, write, spell, or to do mathematical calculations. The term includes such conditions as perceptual handicaps, brain injury, minimal brain disfunction, dyslexia, and developmental aphasia. The term does not include children who have learning problems which are primarily the result of visual, hearing, or motor handicaps, of mental retardation, or of environmental, cultural, or economic disadvantage.
Speech Impaired	"Speech impaired" means a communication disorder, such as stuttering, impaired articulation, a language impairment, or a voice impairment, which adversely affects a child's educational performance.
Visually Handicapped	"Visually handicapped" means a visual impairment which, even with correction, adversely affects a child's educational performance. The term includes both partially seeing and blind children.

Source: Reprinted from *Federal Register,* Vol. 42, No. 163, pp. 42478–42479, United States Government, August 23, 1977.

Vocational educators are a source of input into the placement of students into special programs. Data for the identification of the handicapped students are to be obtained from a variety of sources. Some of these sources are given in Table 4-2.

Decisions about placement should be made on the basis of what program would be most appropriate for the student in the least restrictive environment. The least restrictive environment is defined as

> procedures to assure that, to the maximum extent appropriate, handicapped children, including children in public or private institutions or other care facilities, are educated with children who are not handicapped, and that special classes, separate schooling, or other removal of handicapped children from the regular educational environment occurs only when the nature or severity of the handicap is such that education in regular classes with the use of supplementary aids and services cannot be achieved satisfactorily . . .[6]

The important factor in the placement of handicapped students is that their best interests are taken into consideration. Administrative or instructional convenience in planning the individual education program for the specific student should not be a primary concern. An array of services to serve the handicapped student are available, and they should be used based on the severity of the condition and the necessity for separate programming to meet the student's needs.

Table 4-2 Procedures Utilized in Obtaining Information about Handicapped Students

Source	Use
Standardized Achievement Tests	Comparative data on performance of other students
Individual Intelligence Tests	Indication of student's potential compared to other students
Observation in Classroom	Comparison of student's performance on standardized tests Substantiation of the need for intervention
Adaptive Behavior Scales	Comparative data with the social, emotional, and self-help skills of other students
Interviews	Indication of views of others toward the student and information about how student functions in other environments, e.g., home
Health Records	Information about the student's vision, hearing, and physical health
Parental Interview	Behavior and health history, developmental data, parents' views of student's problems
School Records	Status of student's functioning in academic and vocational classes, attendance, educational history, etc.
Work Samples	Indication of student's functioning in applied school/work placements

INCIDENCE OF HANDICAPPING CONDITIONS

Contrary to common belief, vast numbers of American handicapped children are not enrolled in regular schools. During the 1984–85 school year, 4,363,031 students were served in programs for school-age handicapped children. This number represents 9.29 percent of the total enrollment in the public schools for the 1984–85 school year. Table 4-3 provides a breakdown (by handicapping condition) of the number of handicapped students served and their percentage of the total school enrollment.[7]

Table 4-4 shows where handicapped students were served in the public schools in 1983–84.[8] It is interesting to note that 67.9 percent of the identified handicapped students were served primarily within the regular classroom, with only minimal time spent in special programs. The vast number of students being served in the regular classroom indicates the importance of vocational educators learning to work more effectively with the handicapped learner. A vast majority of the identified handicapped learners are mildly disabled and capable of functioning within the regular school environment with a minimum of outside support services.

In contrast, during the same period (1983–84), 25 percent of the handicapped students were educated exclusively in separate classes. This represents the number of students too severely handicapped to be served in the regular classroom environment. Even smaller percentages of severely handicapped students were served in separate facilities and other educational environments.

Classifying handicapped students into strict categories is more important as an administrative-fiscal tool than as an educational-planning tool. D.P. Hallahan and

Table 4-3 Percentage and Number of School Populations by Handicapping Condition

Handicapping Condition	Percentage of Total School Population	Number Served*
Speech impaired	2.41	1,129,412
Learning disabled	3.91	1,839,292
Mentally retarded	1.52	717,785
Emotionally disturbed	.79	373,207
Other health impaired	.15	69,118
Orthopedically handicapped	.13	58,835
Multihandicapped	.15	71,780
Deaf and hard of hearing	.15	71,230
Visually handicapped	.06	30,375
Deaf/Blind	.004	1,992
Total	9.274	4,366,957

*The figures are for the school year 1984–85.

Source: Progress Toward a Free Appropriate Public Education: A Report to Congress on the Implementation of Public Law 94–142: The Education for All Handicapped Children Act, U.S. Department of Health and Human Services, Office of Education, October, 1985.

Table 4-4 Environments in Which School-Age Handicapped Children Were Served During the School Year 1983–84 by Handicapping Condition

Handicapping Condition	Regular Class	Separate Class	Separate Facilities	Other Educational Environment	Total
Speech Impaired	1,045,187	53,332	15,010	6,483	1,120,012
Learning Disabled	1,383,854	379,869	23,896	3,304	1,790,923
Mentally Retarded	211,739	400,801	97,340	4,705	714,585
Emotionally Disturbed	157,980	130,983	60,859	8,914	358,736
Other Health Impaired	22,780	14,662	5,325	11,147	53,914
Orthopedically Impaired	21,451	22,417	10,114	4,366	58,348
Multiply Handicapped	8,262	27,392	21,629	1,905	59,188
Deaf/Hard of Hearing	27,262	25,344	17,146	720	70,472
Deaf and Blind	259	613	1,097	50	2,019
Visually Handicapped	16,392	5,173	6,864	281	28,710
Noncategorical	15,349	9,718	1,321	1,281	27,669
TOTALS	2,910,515	1,070,304	260,601	43,156	4,284,576
% of Total	67.93	24.98	6.08	1.01	100%

Source: Progress Toward a Free Appropriate Public Education: A Report to Congress on the Implementation of Public Law 94-142: The Education for All Handicapped Children Act, U.S. Department of Health and Human Services, Office of Education, October 1985.

J.M. Kaufman point out the great similarities in learning characteristics, behaviors, and educational needs among the educable mentally retarded, emotionally disturbed, and learning disabled.[9] The labeling of a student as having a specific handicap will not, in itself, provide the classroom vocational teacher with an appropriate teaching strategy. Classroom teachers have to do their own assessment of the specific needs of each identified handicapped student.

The remaining sections of this chapter are devoted to dealing with the handicapping conditions outlined in Public Law 94-142. As there are more similarities than differences among categories of mildly handicapped students, the reader will note in these sections the many similarities that appear in the characteristic and vocational needs of such students.

REVIEW OF HANDI-CAPPING CONDITIONS

The literature yields a number of definitions of *deaf* and *hard of hearing*. There appears to be no generally agreed use of the two terms, partially because the implications of an auditory impairment vary with the person involved and the circumstances. Each professional field involved in the study of hearing impairments classifies according to its particular specialization and purposes. In general, several dimensions of classification have emerged.

Deaf and Hard of Hearing

The degree of hearing impairment has implications for the educator and is, in fact, a major component of the present Public Law 94-142 definition. The degree of hearing impairment is determined by decibel loss as measured by audiometric testing. Table 4-5 shows the estimated relationship of hearing loss to the ability to understand speech. From the table, an educator can infer that consideration of the severity of a hearing impairment is crucial for appropriate educational planning.

Degree of Hearing Impairment

Table 4-5 Estimated Relationship of Hearing Loss to the Ability to Understand Speech

Hearing Loss in Decibels	Ability to Comprehend Speech	Degree of Handicap
0-25	Normal range	Insignificant
25-40	Difficulty with whispers	Slight
41-55	Difficulty with loud and soft normal speech	Mild
56-70	Difficulty with loud speech	Moderate
71-90	Comprehends strongly amplified speech	Severe
91+	Speech not understood under amplification	Profound

Age at Onset of Hearing Impairment

The consequences of a hearing impairment depend, in part, on the point in the individual's development at which the loss occurs. A person born deaf, for example, faces difficulties in speech development usually not experienced by individuals who become deaf in adulthood. Individuals who become deaf later in their development have greater speech and language capacity. In classifying the hearing impaired, those individuals born deaf are often referred to as *congenitally deaf* while those born with normal hearing, but who later lose their hearing, are called *adventitiously deaf*.

Causal Factor

The causal factor (etiology of hearing impairment) has been divided into two types: exogenous and endogenous.[10] Exogenous refers to all causal factors other than heredity, while endogenous includes only heredity.

Location of the Hearing Impairment

The origin of hearing problems can be divided into two types of location used extensively in medical diagnosis and treatment.

Sensory-neural is used to designate hearing loss resulting from inner ear abnormalities. Such hearing loss is sometimes referred to as nerve deafness, because sound does get transmitted to the inner ear but goes no further. The impairment results from the failure of the inner ear to generate the proper signal; the signal is not being transmitted through the auditory nerve pathway to the brain or is not being received by the brain. Causes of this type of damage include meningitis, Rh incompatibility between mother and fetus, pertussis, influenza, measles, trauma, and endogenous factors.

Conductive is used to designate hearing loss resulting from a malfunction of the outer or middle ear that causes sound waves to fail to be transmitted to the inner ear. The outer ear acts as a funnel for sound waves, while the middle ear's three tiny bones (hammer, anvil, and stirrup) transmit these mechanical vibrations from the eardrum to the fluid of the inner ear. Congenital malformations, infections, fluid in the middle ear, and bony overgrowth in the middle ear can block vibrations before they are delivered to the inner ear. Two other common causes of conductive loss are otitis media (middle ear infection) and otosclerosis. In some instances, an individual may suffer a mixed loss of hearing, that is, a combination of conductive and sensory-neural hearing loss.

Incidence

The incidence of predeafness (deafness occurring at or before 19 years of age) in the United States has been estimated, through the National Census of the Deaf Population (NCDP), to be at 2 per 1,000 people.[11] The information in Table 4-3 indicates that approximately 1.5 per 1,000 school-age students are being served in programs for the deaf and hard of hearing. During the 1984–1985 school year, 71,230 students were being served in programs for the deaf and hard of hearing. J.D. Schein and T.D. Marcus report that impairment of hearing is the single most prevalent chronic physical disability in the United States.[12] More persons suffer a hearing defect than have visual impairments, heart disease, or any other chronic disability.

Educational Provisions

The unique educational needs of the deaf and hard-of-hearing student have long been recognized. Simple educational modifications for assisting students with mild hearing losses include assigning the handicapped student to a front row seat, facing the child when speaking, outlining lectures on the blackboard, and making assignments in writing. Hearing-impaired students' most crucial need is for adequate communication between themselves and the teacher, so as to facilitate learning. Since most deaf and hard-of-hearing students experience problems in acquiring expressive language, adequate communication involves both receptive and expressive language components.

The most common measures utilized to improve the deaf student's ability to acquire language skills are the provision of devices that amplify sound and the provision of programs for learning lipreading (also called speechreading) or manual sign language. Amplification is achieved through hearing aids prescribed and fitted by trained professionals. Children are now being fitted with hearing aids at very young ages to allow them to grow up in a ''hearing world'' and to experience the benefits of auditory learning. Education in speechreading and manual sign language is provided in most communities by vocational training centers, colleges, and universities.

The educator must be aware of the degree of hearing that a student possesses in order to make proper adjustments in the curriculum and learning environment. In cases where students have been identified as hearing impaired or deaf and individual educational programs have been developed, professionals who are trained to work with the hard of hearing should be available to provide guidance. Services for hearing-impaired and deaf students extend the full spectrum of services for all special needs individuals presented earlier in this chapter.

Vocational Training and Employment

Based on data from the NCDP, it has been estimated that the proportion of prevocationally deaf people in the labor force is about the same as that for all other people.[13] Approximately 83 percent of the general male population and 44 percent of the general female population are in the labor force, while approximately 83 percent of the NCDP's sample of deaf males and 49 percent of its sample of deaf females are in the labor force.

Schein makes the following statements about the employment of the deaf:

- In terms of personal income, deafness strikes hard. Average earning falls 16 percent below the general average.
- Female deaf persons do less well than male. Deaf women have higher rates of unemployment than women in general.
- In economic terms, deafness is more expensive. Additional expenditures for necessary appliances, extra travel because of inability to use telephone, and the inability to negotiate freely within the marketplace place a burden on the deaf.[14]

Many deaf people, however, may be working at jobs requiring far less education than they have and could be considered underemployed.

The vocational curriculum of the deaf and hard-of-hearing student in the high school need not be different from that designed for the hearing student. Individual differences in talents and intelligence exist among those suffering from hearing impairments, just as they do among those who have normal hearing. In providing for the vocational education of the hearing-impaired student, the instructor needs to make adjustments similar to those for other students, with an emphasis on the teaching strategies previously cited.

Visually Handicapped

The definition of *visually handicapped* focuses on the performance of the student within the educational environment (see Table 4-1 above). Of importance is that the visual impairment limits the student's ability to function in the educational setting. A student who cannot use standard visual materials in the classroom because of a lack of visual acuity would be classified as visually handicapped. The National Society for the Prevention of Blindness defines a legally blind student as one who has a central visual acuity of 20/200 or less in the better eye after correction or who has a field defect in which the widest diameter of the visual field subtends an angle distance no greater than 20 degrees. (The rating of 20/200 relates to the size of symbols on the Snellen Chart. Each rating expresses the standard distance at which a person with normal vision can comfortably read the symbols or letters. For example, a legally blind student can read comfortably no more at 20 feet than a normally sighted child reads at 200 feet.)[15]

The major causes of blindness are the following:

- *Diabetic retinopathy* occurs when tiny blood vessels in the retina hemorrhage due to diabetes. The result is a gradual loss of visual acuity.
- *Cataracts* occur when the lens of the eye becomes cloudy or opaque. They may occur congenitally, as a result of senility or trauma, or as secondary effects of other diseases.
- *Retinitis pigmentosa* is a hereditary disease causing loss of night vision and side vision.
- *Macular degeneration* results when the macula, a small area of the retina, is damaged because of inadequate blood supply, causing loss of central vision.

Blindness may be either congenital or adventitious. Congenital blindness is present at birth. The adventitiously blind person becomes blind due to disease, defective functioning and shape of the eye, or trauma to the eye later in life.

Incidence

Table 4-3 shows that a total of 28,710 visually handicapped students were served in public schools in 1983–84, and that, of this number, over one-half were served in the regular classroom. The percentage of the total school population identified as being visually impaired in 1984–1985 was .06 percent. This figure contrasts with the more generally recognized estimate of incidence of .5 percent for the entire population.

The reason for this discrepancy may be the increase of visual impairment with the onset of aging.

Approximately 75 percent of the legally blind persons in the United States have some usable vision. Of the 1.7 million legally blind persons, 400,000 have no usable vision. In total, about 6.4 million persons in the United States have some degree of visual impairment after correction with eye glasses, contact lenses, etc.[16]

Educational and vocational goals for the blind student are essentially the same as those for a normal student. One goal is to provide blind students with skills that will enable them to take advantage of life's opportunities to the fullest extent possible. Another goal is to provide them with the skills necessary for their functioning at the highest possible level of remunerative employment. When these two goals are achieved, the blind person becomes a self-supporting member of society.

Educational and Vocational Provisions

Barriers to achieving these goals are of two major kinds. First, there are the physical limitations imposed by the student's blindness itself. Available alternatives to sight can enable the blind student to reduce these limitations. Educationally, the adjustments are minimal in most situations; among the available alternatives are talking books, employment of readers, Braille textbooks, and recently developed automatic reading machines that decipher the written word. Teachers can assist by giving good verbal instructions and explaining all written work placed on overhead projectors and the chalkboard.

Second, there are the attitudinal barriers established by sighted persons. These include job discrimination, lowered expectations for blind students, and misguided compassion. These attitudinal barriers restrict the goal of normalization by reducing opportunities and by lowering the self-image of the blind student. Blind persons are capable of a much higher level of functioning than imagined by the general public. Education beyond the normal curriculum involves training the blind student to use available alternatives to sight and to develop coping skills and a positive image.

During the past decade, the number of blind persons in competitive employment has doubled. H.J. Link has estimated that employment or openings in the professional category will, in spite of increased competition, remain high, owing to the development of new occupational areas. The paraprofessional category is seen by Link as containing the greatest number of new opportunities.[17] Section 503 of the 1973 Rehabilitation Act, which requires businesses that provide contract work for the federal government to develop affirmative action plans for the employment of severely disabled persons, should also have an impact on the employment situation for the blind.

Link has noted the following needs in the vocational area:

- more adequate training for job placement personnel
- more adequate evaluation of clients for employment
- reduction of employer resistance to the hiring of the blind
- emphasis on the training of coping and related job skills for the blind client
- use of vocational and technical schools in training blind clients[18]

In summary, blindness has connotations for the general public that cause the potential of blind persons in competitive employment to be underestimated. Attitudinal change is as important to the employment of the blind as is development of adequate skills.

Orthopedically Handicapped and Other Health Impaired

The categories of orthopedically handicapped and other health impaired are treated as distinct in the classification proposed by Public Law 94-142. For our purposes, the two categories can be discussed in the same section, since many of the adaptations of the learning environment require similar considerations on the part of the teacher.

Definitions of orthopedically handicapped and other health impaired are provided in Table 4-1. Some of the major categories included in the classification of orthopedically handicapped and other health impaired are discussed in greater detail in the following sections.

Orthopedic Impairment

Cerebral Palsy. Cerebral palsy (CP) may result from brain damage that has occurred before, during, or after birth or from poor maternal nutrition and health, Rh or A-B-O blood type incompatibility, anoxia, or birth trauma. CP refers to brain damage of the motor areas of the brain, either the cerebrum or the cerebellum, that affect motor control of certain groups of muscles.

CP has been divided into several categories depending on how it affects the child. The American Academy for Cerebral Palsy lists the various types as

- *Spasticity* (increase in muscle tone)
- *Athetosis* (slow writhing movements which conflict with voluntary movement)
- *Rigidity* (extreme stiffness and tenseness of extremities)
- *Ataxia* (poor balance, coordination and difficulty with depth perception)
- *Tremor* (regular and rhythmical involuntary shaking movements)
- *Atonia* (lack of muscle tone, limpness and flaccidity)
- *Mixed* (combination of other forms)[19]

Several other problems are often evidenced in combination with CP, including mental retardation, learning disabilities, emotional problems, seizures, visual impairments, auditory impairments, and speech impairments. Although these problems have a high incidence in combination with CP, the affected child may have none of them.

The associated handicaps can make the CP child a less likely candidate for the regular classroom. However, it is possible that children with less severe CP involvement may be capable of functioning in the classroom. The spastic hemiplegic type (see list above) usually manifests a higher level of intelligence but may have associated sensory impairments. The athetoid child also may have higher intelligence, while children of the rigidity type are usually severely retarded. It is evident that decisions and modifications of the educational program for the CP child must be based on the individual child's needs.

Congenital Anomaly. A congenital anomaly is a birth defect in which the child is without some body appendage or with a deformed appendage, such as a clubfoot or clubhand. The anomaly may also occur in joints or in the spine. The defect may be inherited from one or both parents or be environmentally caused.

Spina Bifida. Spina bifida is a birth defect in which the bones of the spine fail to close. As a result, a sack containing spinal fluid forms in the area of the lower back and is present at birth. The condition is usually treated surgically immediately after birth. The extent to which a disability remains can vary from little or none to paralysis of the legs, impaired autonomic nervous system, functioning difficulties with bowel and bladder control, or lack of any sensation in the lower body. Spina bifida students are usually capable of profiting from regular classroom instruction with only minor adaptation.

Spinal Cord Injuries. Spinal cord injuries may result in paralysis. The area affected is determined by the level at which the spinal cord is injured. If the cord is severed between the fifth and eighth vertebrae, a condition known as a *quadraplegia* results, in which control and sensation in the arms and everything below the point of severance is lost. If the injury occurs below the eighth vertebra, control and sensation is lost in the legs and the injury is referred to as *paraplegia*. In both of these conditions, there is usually loss of bowel and bladder control and often loss of sexual functioning. Other problems, such as physical deterioration of muscles and pressure sores from wheelchairs or braces, arise because of the paralysis and loss of sensation.

Rarely does the injury affect brain functioning. Therefore, victims of a spinal cord injury can be served in a regular classroom as soon as they have sufficient mobility to get there.

Amputation. Amputation is the surgical removal of a limb or a portion of a limb. It is usually performed when tissue has been injured beyond repair as a result of irreversible loss of blood supply to the limb, infections (including bone tuberculosis, cancer, and osteomyelitis), or the removal of congenital anomalies. Amputation is usually followed by the provision of a prosthetic device (artificial limb). When the prosthetic device has been fitted and the amputee has been trained to use it, the individual is capable of functioning well in the regular classroom and in most vocational training settings and job settings.

Contractures. A contracture is a permanent shortening of a muscle due to spasm or paralysis. This term also refers to a condition of high resistance to the passive stretch of a muscle, which may result from abnormal formation of tissue surrounding a joint. A student may suffer a permanent disability or deformity due to the shortening of a muscle caused by the shrinking of damaged tissue. Minor modifications of the regular classroom, if any, are sufficient to accommodate the student with a contracture.

The category of other health impaired includes many medical conditions, both acute and chronic, that afflict students and adversely affect their educational progress. *Other Health Impaired*

This section presents descriptions of several conditions with which the educator may wish to become more familiar. Not all of the health-impairing conditions that the educator may encounter are included, because of the diverse nature of these conditions. However, the following descriptions will provide the educator with information that can be applied to the study and evaluation of other conditions.

Some health-impairing conditions are relatively rare and encountered in the classroom infrequently. Also, not all health-impairing conditions are equally handicapping for the child. Asthma, for example, causes attacks that make breathing difficult, yet for long periods between attacks there may be no obvious, observable symptoms. In contrast, other conditions, such as heart disease, may obviously affect the child at all times. It is important to remember as well that the same impairing condition may vary in severity from student to student. Some students with heart conditions may participate in most classroom activities while others may exhibit marked diminution in their tolerance to the ordinary physical activities of the classroom. Therefore, for a student with a health-impairing condition, educational programs should be planned in light of the student's unique behavioral assets as well as the student's medical classification.

Heart Condition. To assist the educator in understanding medical classifications of heart disease patients, part of the American Heart Association Classification System is reproduced in Table 4-6.[20] The table provides descriptions of the functional capacity of patients with cardiac disease.

As suggested by the classification of Table 4-6, children with heart disease can behave in different ways and can exhibit varying degrees of disability. Children with mild heart conditions may be therapeutically unrestricted but may be so anxious that they behave as if their disability were great. Those students whose tolerance is markedly diminished should be assisted in adjusting to their limits. G. McNutt suggests that individuals with surgically corrected congenital heart disease should be able to function in normal vocational activities.[21] A good rule of thumb appears to be

.

Table 4-6 Functional Classifications of Heart Disease

Functional Classifications

Class I	Patients with cardiac disease but without resulting limitations of physical activity. Ordinary physical activity does not cause undue fatigue, palpitation, dyspnea, or anginal pain.
Class II	Patients with cardiac disease resulting in a slight limitation of physical activity. They are comfortable at rest. Ordinary physical activity results in fatigue, palpitation, dyspnea, or anginal pain.
Class III	Patients with cardiac disease resulting in inability to carry on any physical activity without discomfort. Symptoms of cardiac insufficiency or of the original syndrome are present even at rest. If any physical activity is undertaken, discomfort is increased.

Source: Adapted from American Heart Association Classification System, in *Interviewing Guides for Specific Disabilities: Heart Disease,* U.S. Department of Labor, 1969.

that the student with heart problems should not be pressed to the point of excessive fatigue.

Asthma. Asthma is an episodic, reversible, increased responsiveness of the smooth muscle walls of the lung's airways to various stimuli, resulting in spasms of the bronchial musculature and the production of an excessive amount of mucus, hence the characteristic symptoms: recurrent attacks of labored breathing accompanied by wheezing and coughing.

Asthma is an allergic condition of the lungs. Along with asthma, the afflicted individual is inclined to exhibit other allergic problems, such as eczema, hayfever, hives, and food intolerance.

An asthmatic attack may be a frightening experience for the teacher because of the struggle and gasping for every breath, the color change, and the obvious distress displayed by the child. The attack may be brought on by a specific sensitivity to an allergen, exposure to excessive physical activity, or possibly by an emotional reaction. It is believed that stress lowers the threshold of sensitivity to an attack.

Asthma, like other medical conditions, varies in severity from child to child. In general, asthmatic children should be encouraged to join in ordinary class activities and should be treated as normally as possible. The teacher should be aware of the factors that precipitate an asthmatic attack, have information concerning the proper course of action to follow should an attack occur, and know about any possible side effects or behavioral changes that may be related to the prescribed drugs being used by the student. The requisite information can be obtained from the student's parents and physician, and assistance can be obtained from the school nurse. Generally, afflicted students will regulate themselves, and no artificial restrictions need be placed upon them. However, efforts should be made to avoid exposing such students to the substances to which they are allergic or to cigarette smoke, dust, and other irritants which tend to promote bronchospasm.

Epilepsy. Epilepsy is not a specific disease but is rather a symptom that can be produced by various diseases, tumors, or other injuries to the brain. These injuries result in recurrent, short-lived electrical discharges from the brain, commonly called seizures. These seizures take many forms, depending on what part and how much of the brain is involved. The common types of seizures are the following:

- *Grand mal.* The grand mal is probably the most dramatic type of seizure. All the neurons in the motor cortex discharge simultaneously and the person experiences violent convulsions and complete loss of consciousness. These episodes are often preceded by a warning (aura) which may be visual, auditory, olfactory, or abdominal, or even some other kind of sign that the person recognizes. The attack itself results in (1) an abrupt loss of consciousness; (2) tightening of the muscles with the body rigidly extended (tonic spasm) for usually one to three minutes; (3) jerking movements of the head, arms, and legs (chonic convulsion) lasting two to three minutes; (4) a period of recovery with or without confusion; and (5) a period of sleep. The frequency of attacks may vary from one a year to many a day.

- *Petit mal.* This is the second most common form of epilepsy. The person experiences a sudden fleeting loss of consciousness or a change in posture or muscle tone without warning. No confusion or aberration of consciousness follows the attack. Typically, there is nothing more than a momentary gap in the person's activities with a related gap in memory. Petit mal seizures are most likely to appear before or at puberty and tend to disappear with increasing age, but in some children they give way to grand mal seizures.
- *Jacksonian.* These are localized seizures, beginning in one extremity or side of the face and progressing throughout the arm or leg of the same side, often without loss of consciousness. The convulsion may spread to the other side of the body, in which case the attack becomes generalized, usually with loss of consciousness, as in grand mal seizures.
- *Psychomotor.* In this type of seizure, the person exhibits behavior that is usually purposeful but not relevant to the situation. The attacks may last for a few minutes or may go on for more extended periods. While under the seizure, the person may act as if intoxicated, may be morose and irritable, and may engage in purposeless motor movements. Following the attack, the person has no memory of the incident.

An estimated .5 percent of the population is epileptic, but the condition is not apparent in these people except during seizures.[22] Epilepsy may occur at any age, in any race, and in either sex. Approximately 75 percent of all epileptic seizures begin before the age of 25. Epilepsy occurs in one out of every 50 children.[23]

Special curricular modifications are not necessary for students with epilepsy, but the teacher should be aware of the disruption of concentration and the resultant learning problems that may be created by this disruption. The teacher should also be prepared for the possibility of a grand mal seizure. In this case, the Epilepsy Foundation of America suggests that the steps listed in Exhibit 4-1 be followed.[24]

In general, the epileptic student can participate in nearly all school activities. However, the student's parents and physician should be consulted to determine if any activities should be avoided. Most children with epilepsy are well controlled on medication, have normal intelligence, and can be expected to lead normal lives.

Exhibit 4-1 First Aid for Grand Mal Epilepsy Seizures

Teacher should:

- remain calm
- not try to restrain student
- clear area around student to prevent injury
- not force anything between student's teeth
- when seizure is over let the student rest
- inform the child's parents of the seizure
- turn the seizure into a learning experience for the rest of the class.

Source: Teacher Tips from the Epilepsy Foundation of America, Epilepsy Foundation of America, © 1972.

Diabetes. Diabetes is a metabolic disorder in which the insulin produced in the body by the pancreas is insufficient to properly utilize sugar and starches. In the diabetic, carbohydrate metabolism breaks down, and conversion of sugar and starches into energy or their storage for future use cannot be accomplished as in the nondiabetic. This condition may be due to either the inability of the pancreas to produce enough insulin or the inability of the body to use properly the insulin produced. In either case, an excess of sugar accumulates in the blood (hyperglycemia) and may be excreted in the urine (glycosuria). In severe cases, the body can no longer obtain needed energy from carbohydrates and must draw upon protein and fat as a source of energy. This usually results in a loss of weight and strength. Other symptoms include excessive thirst, appetite, and urination.

Diabetes occurs at all ages and affects approximately 3 million people in the United States. Of these, about 4 percent have onset in childhood.[25]

Treatment of diabetes usually includes insulin injections, dietary regulation, or both. Additionally, the right amounts of exercise and rest are important components of most treatment plans. The most effective control of the disease is obtained when a balance of insulin, diet, and exercise is achieved.

The educator should be aware of symptoms of both high and low blood sugar to assist students with diabetes in the management of their condition and to provide their physicians with information about the students' management plans.

High blood sugar can result in a diabetic coma. This is fairly rare but can be serious if not treated immediately. This condition usually develops slowly and is characterized by dry skin, deep and labored breathing, dry tongue, thirst, excessive urination, a sweet or fruity odor to the breath, and finally coma. Treatment consists of keeping the child warm and resting after immediately notifying the parent, nurse, and physician.

Low blood sugar may result from anything that may increase the child's metabolic rate, such as too much exercise, too much insulin, not enough food, or nervous tension. This is called an insulin reaction. It usually develops rapidly and is characterized by any or all of the following: pale and moist skin, a sudden change in behavior, sweating, extreme hunger, restlessness, headache, and a tired feeling. Treatment of this condition consists of providing the child with a quick energy snack such as pop, a sugar cube, candy, or raisins. If no improvement is seen within five to ten minutes, the parents, nurse and physician should be contacted. If there is doubt about the diagnosis, the situation, according to one authority, should still be managed as if there was a low blood sugar reaction, since the administration of sugars will cause no harm.[26] Each child has individual characteristic signs of low blood sugar; therefore, consultation with the parents and physician may be necessary to know what to look for in that particular child.

The diabetic student can do everything the normal student does, and no restriction of activity is necessary unless specifically prescribed by a physician. Many children may need supplemental snacks, and a quick energy source should be available if a low blood sugar reaction develops.

The attitude toward employing diabetics is becoming increasingly liberal. The trend is to judge each applicant individually rather than to generalize and reject all diabetic applicants. The present policy of the Civil Service Commission indicates that the commission believes that persons with *controlled* diabetes may be good employees and that it is good business practice to hire them.

Educational Provisions

The various orthopedic impairments outlined in this section affect the physical performance of children rather than their intellectual functioning. In most cases—with the possible exception of cerebral palsy, cerebrovascular accidents, and spina bifida—intellectual functioning remains normal. Recently, measures of intelligence that are less dependent upon language have shown that high levels of intellectual functioning exist even in children with cerebral palsy. After an initial period of training in self-help skills, such children are capable of functioning in a normal classroom. Frequently, however, children with severe medical problems may be absent for extended periods of time. Special care should be taken to ensure that students have the basic tool skills necessary to do more complex tasks. The curriculum should include academic as well as career and vocational education.

Modifications may or may not be needed in the physical environment of the classroom, depending upon the particular student. For instance, if a student uses a wheelchair, doors must be wide enough to accommodate it. In some instances, instructional materials should be modified to facilitate handling by the student. In all but the most severe cases, or in cases of orthopedic handicaps accompanied by other handicapping conditions, the regular classroom provides the optimum setting for the orthopedically handicapped or other health-impaired student.

The two major kinds of barriers to the employment of the orthopedically handicapped or other health impaired are attitudinal barriers and architectural barriers. Removal of these two kinds of obstruction can greatly expand employment opportunities. Removal of architectural barriers is particularly important to orthopedically handicapped persons, since they have limited mobility.

With increased technology, less emphasis is being placed on physical abilities and the number of suitable jobs has increased. Hopefully, under new affirmative action programs, attitudinal as well as architectural barriers will diminish.

Mentally Retarded

Mental retardation refers to a general lack of intellectual and social ability in children and adults. The definition given in Table 4-1 is the legal definition for purposes of funding special education programs for the retarded.

The definition of *mentally retarded* encompasses a wide variety of individuals and a vast range of etiologies and manifestations. Among the more than 200 identified causes are

- genetic irregularities, including those inherited and those caused during pregnancy by overexposure to x-rays, infections, and other causes
- illness of the mother during pregnancy, including German measles, malnutrition, and glandular disorders
- trauma during birth, including measles, meningitis, and encephalitis

- glandular imbalance
- malnutrition
- accidents causing damage to brain tissue
- anoxia (lack of oxygen)
- poisons
- understimulation (extreme environmental deprivation resulting in lack of development)

Individuals are considered retarded if their performance on separate measures of intelligence, academic achievement, and adaptive behavior are significantly below the norms of their age-mates. The relationships between these three measures are clearly seen in Table 4-7, which outlines identification criteria for the school-age mildly retarded. To be considered mildly mentally retarded, a child must obtain scores that fall at least two standard deviations below the mean in all three areas. It is recognized that deficiencies in only one or two of these areas is insufficient evidence for a classification of mental retardation. Assessment in all three areas—providing measures of functioning on tests, functioning in school, and in daily functioning within the natural environment—reduces errors in evaluation. Higher functioning in one area indicates abilities not shown in the other areas of measurement and precludes classification of the child as mentally retarded.

Retardation manifests itself differently among different individuals, both in terms of severity and in terms of how individuals function within the same measured range of ability. Several systems have been developed in medical and educational disciplines to classify the severity of retardation. The popular classification systems use standardized intelligence test scores, in part to describe ranges of ability. The systems are used to describe both programs and individuals.

Table 4-8 provides a summary of three popular classification systems: those of the American Association on Mental Deficiency, the American Psychiatric Association,

---

Table 4-7 Identification Criteria for the School-Age Mildly Mentally Retarded

Measurement Area	Measurement Tool	Performance
Intelligence	Individual intelligence tests (e.g., WISC-R).	Full scale intelligence: 70 or less.
Adaptive Behavior	Adaptive behavior scales, observations, observation reports, developmental history, etc.	Significantly below average. Indications of slow or immature development.
Achievement	Standardized achievement scales. Classroom academic performance.	Ratings significantly below age mates (tests 2 standard deviations below mean). Failure or near failure academically.

Table 4-8 Three Classification Systems for Severity of Mental Retardation

Classification System	Level	Intelligence Rating
American Association on Mental Deficiency	Profound	0–24
	Severe	24–39
	Moderate	40–54
	Mild	55–70
American Psychiatric Association	Severe	0–54
	Moderate	55–69
	Mild	70–84
Educational System	Profound	0–24
	Severe	25–39
	Trainable	40–54
	Educable	55–75

and the educational system. It is important to note that the functioning of specific individuals cannot be determined solely on the basis of their inclusion in one of these classifications. The child must be recognized as an individual with a unique set of abilities and preferences. As with normal children, development does not proceed along a linear continuum, and it displays considerable variability as a function of age.

The classification *profoundly retarded* usually implies severe impairment and the need for constant care. Many of the children who fall in this category require institutional care or constant care in the home; they are not capable of self-care. The classification *severely retarded* implies marked impairment in motor, speech, and language development, but the capacity for minimal independence is present. The *moderately retarded* or *trainable* individual is capable of learning self-care skills and of benefiting from training, yet usually requires a sheltered environment. The vast majority of retarded persons fall in the *mildly retarded* or *educable* category. The mildly retarded person can usually be expected to obtain competitve employment and to function in daily community life.

Incidence

During the 1984–85 school year, approximately 717,785 students, or 1.52 percent of the school-age population, were served in programs for the mentally retarded.[27] Table 4-4 shows that approximately 86 percent of the mentally retarded students were served in either regular classrooms or separate classrooms, while only 14 percent were enrolled in separate facilities and other educational environments.

A majority of the mentally retarded fall within the mildly retarded range of ability. This is demonstrated by the fact that, in 1983, approximately 30 percent of the identified mentally retarded were receiving a portion of their educational program in the regular classroom.[28] This supports the contention that vocational educators probably are already serving the mentally retarded in their classrooms.

Since mental retardation includes such a wide variety of etiologies and symptoms, an inclusive definition, by necessity, lacks specific reference to remediation or educational approaches. The standardized tests used to determine classification are used only for comparisons to normed populations and give no information pertaining to the child on a noncomparative basis. Use of classification should be limited to studies of incidence, prevalence, and so forth, and as a means of receiving appropriate special services for the child.

Educational services are typically arrayed in a continuum of levels. These levels range from little or no modification of the regular vocational classroom to basic self-care and occupational therapy in a hospital setting. Table 4-9 represents various alternatives in vocational education programming available to the mentally retarded student. Decisions about placement of students at various levels are based upon information gathered and evaluated for that particular student. The placement decision is based upon the individual needs of the particular student rather than on broad classifications of severity. Within this continuum, the regular classroom represents the least restrictive alternative and is chosen whenever possible.

As can be seen from the incidence figures in the previous section, the vast majority of mentally retarded students (86 percent) are served in a special class or less restrictive alternative. Educational modifications for these students may include additional emphasis on core components, opportunity for additional practice and overlearning, special materials for low reading ability and increased hands-on experience. The prevocational and vocational curriculum for the mildly mentally retarded student may also include greater emphasis on personal and social skills, daily living skills, and career information often acquired incidentally by nonhandicapped students.

Since mildly retarded students generally do not go on to other education, work experience and placement have assumed growing importance within vocational programs in secondary schools. These functions, as well as coordination with other services such as vocational rehabilitation, are designed to ease the transition from the school environment to the work environment.

In considering a mentally retarded person for employment, such factors as education, training, job experience, motivation, attitude, personality, and general health should be considered along with I.Q. scores. The sole use of I.Q. scores in determining placement may underestimate the potential of the student for employment. Many retarded persons are capable of obtaining jobs in the competitive employment market. With proper training, mentally retarded persons have been employed as general office clerks, messengers, office help, mail carriers, stock clerks, sales clerks, domestics, dayworkers, housekeepers, nursemaids, nurse's aides, laborers, construction workers, welders, carpenter's helpers, filling station attendants, metal workers, and upholsterers, as well as in many other responsible positions.[29] A positive approach to vocational education and job placement, which means concentrating on what the retarded person *can* do, greatly improves the chances of achieving competitive employment.

Table 4-9 Alternatives in Vocational Programming for the Mentally Retarded

Least restrictive	Regular vocational program	Regular vocational programs may fit the needs of some mentally retarded students with little or no modification.
	Adapted vocational program	Regular programs are adapted to meet the special needs of students who cannot succeed in regular vocational programs. Adaptations may be in materials, course content, supervision, working style, etc.
	Adapted vocational programs plus remedial services	These programs provide remedial education in basic computational and quantitative skills, communication skills, work attitudes and habits, personal social skills, occupational information, and/or prevocational evaluation as a prerequisite to success in an adapted or regular vocational program.
	Special vocational education	Self-contained vocational programs offer services not possible in a regular vocational classroom and are open only to handicapped students.
	Special vocational schools	Schools may be established solely for the purpose of vocational education of the handicapped. Usually physically removed from the regular school setting. Basic emphasis on prevocational skills and entry level job skills.
	Sheltered workshop	These provide supervised work and training for those individuals not capable of engaging in competitive work experiences. Workshops may or may not be in conjunction with school programs.
Most restrictive	Vocational training in institutional settings	These vocational programs are offered as part of the total educational program in an institutionalized setting.

Seriously Emotionally Disturbed

The seriously emotionally disturbed classification, even as defined by Public Law 94-142 (see Table 4-1), is composed of a complex and multifaceted array of symptoms. The Public Law 94-142 definition reveals certain characteristics of the emotionally disturbed student that are associated with impaired educational performance. In many cases, such children exhibit maladaptive behaviors that interfere with learning. They may be unable to build or maintain satisfactory interpersonal relationships with others. Also, they may be generally depressed, exhibit inappropriate behaviors and feelings, or possess fears, physical symptoms, or schizophrenic symptom patterns.

Behavior that emotionally disturbed children may display includes:

- explosive temper outbursts
- hostile aggression toward others
- extreme withdrawal and lack of involvement with others
- depression and apathy in situations most students enjoy
- unreasonable beliefs about others, such as beliefs about conspiracies
- loss of use of some bodily function (for example, sight or hearing) with no medical explanation
- extreme unrealistic fear of ordinary objects in their environment

The above list is not exhaustive but rather representative of the presenting problems of emotionally disturbed students. Considerable variability in the frequency, intensity, and duration of the problems will be noted.

The identification of the emotionally disturbed child is usually the province of psychiatric and psychological specialists. Recommendations for treatment come from these specialists and from teams of educational specialists. In the screening process, the first step in the identification of emotionally disturbed and behaviorally disturbed children is to determine if their behavior and actions in the classroom interfere with one or more of the following: (1) the learning of other students, (2) their own learning, or (3) the effectiveness of the teacher.

When interference of one of these three occurs, the student has a behavioral problem significant enough to indicate intervention on the part of the teacher. When the problem cannot be alleviated within the regular classroom by the teacher without assistance, a referral is made to the appropriate specialist in the school, often the special education resource specialist. Based upon data gathered from observations in the classroom, test data, and clinical data, the student would be judged either a simple discipline problem, behaviorally disturbed, or emotionally disturbed. A classification of the student as emotionally disturbed would be made if the behavior noted has occurred over a period of time, that it is not a reaction to a specific stressful situation, and it is of sufficient intensity to cause concern on the part of the staff. The decision for placement in a program for the emotionally disturbed would then be based on the duration, frequency, and intensity of the behavior problem.

Incidence

Estimates of the incidence of emotional disturbance in the United States vary considerably because the definition used, the population sampled, and the identification methods employed differ from one investigator to the next. Table 4-3 indicates that .79 percent of the school-age population is currently classified as emotionally disturbed. The number of emotionally disturbed children has been estimated to be 1,100,000.[30] Kirk and Gallagher estimate the number of students with emotional problems which are serious enough to warrant intensive services is in the range of 2 to 3 percent of the school-age population.[31]

Educational
Provisions

In many cases, emotionally disturbed children can function in the regular class with certain behavioral adaptations. They can benefit from regular placement in situations where they are able to observe appropriate behaviors and see that they are regular members of society. They also benefit from being able to function in a milieu that fosters academic pursuits but is still safe and somewhat protected. In other cases, students may receive special services in the school and participate in regular classes on a part-time basis. In still others, students may receive psychiatric or psychological assistance while participating in regular classes. In all cases, however, the educational placement and programming should be consistent with the least restrictive environment provisions of Public Law 94-142 and be appropriate for that child.

There are various approaches in working with emotionally disturbed students in the classroom, but none would be endorsed by most experts as the "correct" method. One approach emphasizes the acceptance of inappropriate symptoms, followed by tolerance (but not acceptance) and finally by limit setting. Another approach involves acceptance of the child's behavior and reflection of the behavior back to the student. Still another stresses provision of understanding, acceptance, recognition, and clarification of feelings. In contrast to these acceptance philosophies is an approach that utilizes systematic procedures to change or modify inappropriate behaviors and to encourage appropriate behaviors. But regardless of the approach, there are many constructive steps that can be taken to provide a realistic, responsible environment for the emotionally disturbed student.

The educator should be cautioned against making generalizations about emotionally disturbed students. The intensity of the presenting problem of individual students varies on a continuum from total withdrawal to extreme hostility. Since the presenting problems vary in symptomatology, intensity, frequency, and duration, the intervention strategies, training programs, and plans for employment must be based on knowledge of the particular student.

Vocational programs and especially vocational programs for the handicapped have traditionally included training in work habits and attitudes, as well as in personal-social skills, since these contribute to training and job success. The Vocational Education Amendments of 1976 includes training in personal-social skills as a component in its definition of vocational instruction. These areas are of primary importance to the emotionally disturbed student, both for vocational training and for future job success.

As in other handicapping conditions, one of the greatest barriers to employment is the attitude of the general public concerning emotional disturbance. Since emotional disturbance is not generally well understood, if often elicits unwarranted apprehension on the part of potential teachers and employers. Vocational educators have the job of preparing both the student and the potential employer to deal with this apprehension.

The learning disabilities field is a combination of three historically separate fields. Until the 1960s, disorders of spoken language, written language, and perceptual and motor processes were viewed as separate areas of interest.[32] During the sixties, these disorders were classified under the label *learning disabilities,* although three theoretical approaches (corresponding to the three former divisions) are still evident in the many definitions and remediation techniques. Because of the vast scope of the field, a behavioral working definition of the learning disabled (LD) student has not evolved.

The current definition in Public Law 94-142 (see Table 4-1) delineates the major earmarks of a learning disability:

Specific Learning Disabilities

- a discrepancy between the student's intellectual level and his/her achievement in specific academic areas
- does not originate from physical disabilities, such as blindness, deafness, or physiological factors
- student's intellectual ability is within the average to above average range of functioning
- poor academic achievement resulting from mental retardation, emotional disturbance, or environmental, cultural or economic disadvantage are excluded[33]

Various authors have attempted to further uncover the characteristics of LD children. One author, Thomas Jeschke, surveyed teachers working with LD students and identified the following ten characteristics that were frequently observed among such children: hyperactivity; perceptual disturbances; language difficulties; specific learning disorders in reading, arithmetic, writing, and spelling; coordination disorders; disorders of attention; impulsivity; memory problems; low frustration tolerance; and poor self-concept.[34]

Other authors have differentiated children by the area of disability[35] and by learning channel defects.[36] The choice of classification system and the extent of its use is dependent upon how the user intends to utilize the classification system in remedying the learning disability.

The procedures followed and the criteria used in the identification of the LD student are presented in Table 4-10. In the identification process, a multidisciplinary team composed of classroom teachers, local education agency personnel, and individuals trained to administer individual tests seeks information about physical, emotional, and environmental factors, intellectual ability, achievement, and classroom behaviors in order to decide whether the student is learning disabled.

Since *learning disabilities* is an umbrella category and could encompass students with mild to severe difficulties, it is possible that a large percentage of the school-age population could be defined as belonging in this category. In general, 2 percent is an appropriate guideline. In fact, in the original legislative actions under Public Law 94-142, a temporary lid of 2 percent was placed on the number of students who

Incidence

Table 4-10 Identification of Learning Disabled Students

Criteria	Learning Disabled	Nonlearning Disabled
Physical, emotional and/or environmental factors	Vision, hearing, physical abilities, emotional stability, cultural/economic conditions not primary factors in school failures	Sensory impairments, physical disability, emotional disturbance, environmental, cultural or economic disadvantage present
Intellectual ability	I.Q. greater than one standard deviation below the mean	I.Q. less than one standard deviation below the mean
Achievement	Elementary: Achievement test scores more than two years below present grade placement in: oral expression, listening comprehension, written expression, basic reading skills, reading comprehension, math calculations, and/or math reasoning Secondary: Scores two years below grade placement and below seventh grade in at least one of the seven areas listed above	Achievement test scores below present grade placement in all areas.
Observations	Observation data indicate lack of self-management skills; behavior which interferes with own or others learning primarily due to frustration in learning	Observation data reveal severe behavior problems and inability to manage self and surroundings
Classroom achievement	Data indicate sporadic or no progress toward goals	Data indicate steady progress toward goals
Meets above criteria	Identification of LD. Move toward placement in LD program	Alternative solution sought

could be labeled learning disabled for funding purposes. This temporary lid was removed after the publication of the identification procedures in November, 1975. In the 1984–85 school year, slightly less than 4 percent of the school-aged population in the United States was being served in programs for the learning disabled. It should be remembered, however, that the incidence figures vary from state to state depending on the rigorousness of the criteria used for identification.

A number of models or methods of delivering services to the learning disabled adolescent are in existence. For the purpose of convenience in describing the various approaches, they have been grouped into five categories: (1) traditional special education, (2) tutorial, (3) survival skills, (4) career education, and (5) composite. The models are presented briefly in Table 4-11, along with comments about the strengths or weaknesses of each. These models, all of which are used in one form or another in school systems in the United States, demonstrate the widely differing purposes, approaches, and philosophies involved in the education of the learning disabled.

Educational and Vocational Provisions

The term *speech impaired* refers to those students who have difficulties with oral language. The educational/legal definition is given in Table 4-1. Most students, especially in kindergarten and primary grades, have difficulties at one time or another with speech, particularly with articulation and syntax. These difficulties are not considered a speech impairment unless they cause substantial deviation from the speech patterns of a student's peers. The speech impaired student presents a picture that is not congruent with the predictable developmental patterns observed in the majority of students.

Speech Impaired

J. Eisenson and M. Ogilvie have pointed out several communication problems that are often confused with speech impairment. These include (1) nonstandard pronunciations and language usage, (2) regional dialects, (3) poor oral reading, (4) immature articulation and fluency patterns, and (5) psychological disturbances that are manifested as speech symptoms.[37]

Speech impairment may be observed separately or in conjunction with other handicapping conditions. Several other conditions—such as deafness, cerebral palsy, and mental retardation—have a high incidence of combination with related speech problems.

In general, speech problems fall into several categories based on the type of difficulty encountered. These include articulatory defects, stuttering, vocal defects, retarded language development, cleft palate speech, language impairment, cerebral palsy speech, and speech defects due to impaired hearing.[38]

Articulatory Defects. The most common types of speech problems are articulation defects. These may include errors of omission ("bo" for "boat"), errors of substitution ("wabbit" for "rabbit"), errors of distortion ("nother" for "mother"), or errors of addition ("puhlease" for "please").

Stuttering. Stuttering is characterized by involuntary stopping, the rapid repetition of certain sounds, or the prolongation of a sound. Stuttering varies in its frequency of occurrence and in its debilitating effects.

Vocal Defects. Vocal defects are defects of pitch, intensity, quality, or flexibility. Pitch becomes an issue when it is inappropriate to the age or sex of the individual. Intensity may be too loud or too soft, in either case interfering with normal commu-

Table 4-11 Models for Delivery of Services to the Learning Disabled Adolescent

TRADITIONAL SPECIAL EDUCATION	*Description*	This model is an extension of the self-contained special classroom. The approach revolves around an emphasis on specific skill acquisition and remediation of academic or process deficits. The program can either be an integral part of the school program or can easily operate as a separate entity with little integration with the regular program.
	Comment	Frequently, the program lacks continuity with the total school curriculum, places insignificant emphasis on career-survival skills, and requires the LD student to be isolated from the mainstream of the school.
TUTORIAL	*Description*	This model is designed to permit the LD student to compete in the regular school program with assistance of support personnel. Alternative instructional procedures to master content are provided to the student. Major emphasis is on one-to-one tutoring or small group instruction with the LD specialist. Regular liaison between the classroom teacher and the LD specialist or tutor is required to accommodate the LD student.
	Comment	Positive attributes include continuity of the educational program for the LD student; opportunity for student to succeed in regular school program; opportunity for regular teaching staff to alter teaching procedures to accommodate the LD student. Weaknesses include that the students are obligated to adjust to the school curriculum, rather than the curriculum being adjusted to the unique needs of the students. The model can also be expensive to operate.
SURVIVAL SKILL	*Description*	This model is frequently used in conjunction with other models. The emphasis is on assisting the LD student to develop coping skills and response patterns to meet the demands of the instructional program, including test-taking skills and teacher-pleasing behaviors. The goals are to teach self-management, assertiveness, and basic student skills. The program can be delivered on a tutorial or small group basis.
	Comment	When carried to an extreme, the model may be providing students short-term skills which have little value in later life. Students who have developed survival skills will be more likely to be successful in the public school.
CAREER EDUCATION	*Description*	The purpose is to permit realistic planning for the "world of work." The model is often organized in three areas: daily living skills, personal-social skills, and occupational and career guidance. The approach provides experiences for the student related to assumption of adult roles. The instructional components are generally delivered throughout the curriculum, with work experiences on either a simulated or actual placement basis as a culmination of the process.
	Comment	A career education component can be excellent as a part of the total program; however, caution is needed to ensure that LD students are not prematurely directed to occupational choices that may not be commensurate with their potential. If emphasis

Table 4-11 continued

		is placed on career preparation, LD students may be encouraged to make occupational decisions based on their weaknesses rather than abilities.
COMPOSITE	*Description*	The model is composed of three parts: self-management instruction, basic academic skill instruction, and career-survival skill instruction. The model differs from the others in the amount of emphasis placed on each component. Basic academic instruction is provided on a tutorial or small group basis only to enable students to make progress. When little or no academic progress is noted, compensation skills are taught. Self-management instruction allows students to become responsible for their behaviors and their environments. Career-survival skills instruction extends through the first three stages of career education: awareness, exploration, and orientation. The emphasis is placed on skills that are important for success in the "world of work."
	Comment	This model has the advantages of each of the previous models and takes into consideration the whole student. The weakness of the model is the pressure placed on the LD specialist to provide the program. The teacher in the model has to have a broad base of training expertise as a teacher and consultant.

nication. Quality problems include breathiness, harshness, and nasality. Flexibility problems are characterized by a monotone.

Retarded Language Development. For most children, language development follows a predictable pattern. Some students who may have had a delay in language onset exhibit language more infantile than that of their peers, including limited vocabulary and simpler sentences, as well as speech omissions and infantile pronunciation of words. The important consideration here is that the lag in language development is outside that normally expected in similar children.

Language Impairment. Language impairment is usually associated with some type of brain damage. This includes students who have difficulties in the acquisition of language and also those who have difficulties from brain damage that has occurred after the acquisition of language. The first type of impairment is often included in the category of retarded language development.

Cleft Palate Speech. Cleft palate speech is caused by an opening in the hard or soft palate that allows air to pass between the nose and the mouth. This results in an impaired ability to reproduce consonants that require a buildup of air and gives speech a nasal quality.

Cerebral Palsy Speech. Defects in articulation and rhythm are caused by impaired motor functioning resulting from brain damage. Detailed information on aspects of cerebral palsy is provided above in the section on orthopedic handicaps and other health impairments.

Speech Defects Due to Impaired Hearing. Speech is largely learned and regulated through hearing and imitation. Impaired hearing is often accompanied by speech problems in articulation, voice, and intensity. Depending on the onset of hearing loss and compensation, the development of language itself may also be impaired.

Incidence

Usual estimates of the incidence of speech impairments range from 2.5 to 5 percent of the school-age population. Table 4-3 indicates that 2.41 percent of the school-age population were served as speech impaired during the 1984–85 school year. Speech impairment as a handicapping condition affects the second largest number of students—26 percent of those served as handicapped. The American Speech and Hearing Association has reported that 75 percent of speech clinicians work at the kindergarten, first, and second grade levels and that only 2 percent work strictly at the high school level, indicating that the prevalence of speech problems is much higher in younger children.[39] Approximately 93 percent of the speech-impaired students were served in regular classrooms and less than 2 percent were served outside the school system during the 1983–84 school year.

Educational Provisions

Remediation of speech impairment is usually the domain of the speech clinician (who is also known in some areas as the speech pathologist or the speech therapist), but the classroom teacher is often valuable as an adjunct provider of services and a referral source. When the child is being seen by a speech clinician, the teacher should consult with the clinician to jointly design a classroom program that complements the clinician's therapy. An additional valuable service provided by the teacher is in the correct modeling of articulation and language usage. Referrals to speech clinicians are a teacher's responsibility; such referrals may become necessary when the child has generally unintelligible speech, severely delayed speech, dramatic voice changes other than those ordinarily present during puberty, debilitating stuttering, or other speech impairments that adversely affect the child's educational performance.

NOTES

1. U.S., *Federal Register,* 42, no. 86, May 4, 1977, 22682.

2. U.S., *Federal Register,* 42, no. 163, August 23, 1977, 42478.

3. U.S., *Federal Register,* 42, no. 86, May 4, 1977, 22678.

4. U.S., *Federal Register,* 42, no. 191, October 3, 1977, 53864.

5. U.S., *Federal Register,* 42, no. 86, May 4, 1977, 22682.

6. U.S.C., title XX, sec. 1412 (5)(6).

7. U.S. Department of Health and Human Services, Office of Education, *Progress toward a Free Appropriate Public Education: A Report to Congress on the Implementation of Public Law 94-142: The Education for All Handicapped Children Act* (Washington, D.C.: GPO, 1985).

8. Ibid.

9. D.P. Hallahan and J.M. Kaufman, "Labels, Categories, Behaviors: ED, LD, and EMR Reconsidered," *Journal of Special Education* 2, no. 2(1977): 139.

10. H.R. Myklebust, *The Psychology of Deafness* (New York: Grune and Stratton, 1964).

11. J.D. Schein and T.D. Marcus, *The Deaf Population in the United States* (Silver Spring, Md.: National Association of the Deaf, 1974).

12. Ibid.

13. J.D. Schein, ''Economic Factors in Deafness,'' in *Yearbook of Special Education* (Chicago: Marquis Academic Media, 1976).

14. Ibid.

15. National Society to Prevent Blindness, *Vocabulary of Terms Relating to the Eye.* Publication no. 172 (New York: Author, 1957).

16. American Foundation for the Blind, Inc., *Facts About Blindness* (New York: Author).

17. H.J. Link, ''Placement and Employment of the Visually Impaired: State of the Art and Identification and Unmet Needs,'' in *Yearbook of Special Education* (Chicago: Marquis Academic Media, 1976).

18. Ibid.

19. W.L. Mineas, ''A Classification of Cerebral Palsy,'' *Pediatrics* 18: 841–852.

20. U.S. Department of Labor, *Interviewing Guides for Specific Disabilities: Heart Disease* (Washington, D.C.: GPO, 1969).

21. G. McNutt, ''Cardiovascular Disorders,'' in *Workshop in Behavior Characteristics of Exceptional Children for Personnel Who Function in Vocational Preparation Programs,* ed. L.R. Kinnison and I.L. Land (Stillwater, Okla.: Oklahoma State University).

22. R.H. Haslam, ''Teacher Awareness of Some Pediatric Neurological Disorders,'' in *Medical Problems in the Classroom,* ed. R.H. Haslam and P.J. Valletutti (Baltimore, Md.: University Park Press, 1975).

23. G.R. Gearhart and M.W. Weishahan, *The Handicapped Child in the Regular Classroom* (St. Louis, Mo.: C.V. Mosby, 1976). See also note 32.

24. Epilepsy Foundation of America, *Teacher Tips from the Epilepsy Foundation of America* (Washington, D.C.: Author, 1972).

25. U.S. Department of Labor, *Interviewing Guides for Specific Disabilities: Diabetes* (Washington, D.C.: GPO, 1973).

26. H.P. Katz, ''Important Endocrine Disorders of Childhood,'' in *Medical Problems in the Classroom,* ed. R.H. Haslam and P.J. Valletutti (Baltimore, Md.: University Park Press, 1975).

27. U.S. Department of Health and Human Services. *Progress Toward a Free Appropriate Public Education.*

28. Ibid.

29. U.S. Department of Labor, Bureau of Employment Security, *Guide to Job Placement of Mentally Retarded Workers* (Washington, D.C.: President's Committee on Employment of the Handicapped in Cooperation with the National Association for Retarded Citizens and the U.S. Employment Service, 1975).

30. Gearhart and Weishahan *The Handicapped Child.*

31. S. Kirk and J. Gallagher, *Educating Exceptional Children* (Boston: Houghton Mifflin, 1985).

32. J.L. Weiderholt, *Historical Perspectives on the Education of the Learning Disabled in the Second Review of Special Education* (Philadelphia: Lester Mann, JSE Press, 1974).

33. U.S., *Federal Register,* 42, no. 86, May 4, 1977.

34. T.A. Jeschke, *An Overview of Learning Disabilities for Classroom Teachers and Parents* (Des Moines, Iowa: Iowa Department of Public Instruction, 1975).

35. H.D. Hammil and P.I. Myers, *Methods for Learning Disorders* (New York: John Wiley & Sons, 1969); R. Valett, *Programming Learning Disabilities* (Belmont, Calif.: Fearon, 1969).

36. J. Stellern, S.F. Vasa, and J. Little, *Introduction to Diagnostic-Prescriptive Teaching and Programming* (Glen Ridge, N.J.: Exceptional Press, 1976).

37. J. Eisenson and M. Ogilvie, *Speech Correction in the Schools* (New York: Macmillan, 1971).

38. Ibid.

39. American Speech and Hearing Association, ''Public School Speech and Hearing Services,'' *Journal of Speech and Hearing Disorders,* Monograph Supplement 8 (July 1961).

Part II

Vocational Special Needs Program Development and Implementation

Chapter 5

Designing Vocational Programs for Special Needs Individuals

Lynda L. West, Ph.D.

This chapter is written as a guide for educators responsible for the task of designing and implementing vocational programs for special needs students. In preparation for this task, it is necessary to identify certain steps in the process that can assist educators to ensure that all issues are considered in the planning stage prior to the implementation stage. The process referred to is called *program development.*

Program development is defined by Fair as vocational education experiences provided for the special needs student, including all the experiences related to vocational instruction of the individual.[1] There are various program components that will be examined. For example, curriculum development is considered a component of program development. However, program development encompasses all other ancillary services that support instruction as well.

There are many contributors to and participants in program development:

- educators (administrators, special education teachers, vocational instructors, and counselors)
- support personnel (resource personnel, facilitators, paraprofessionals, evaluators, and tutors)
- consultants (specialists, teacher educators, and state education agency personnel)
- agency personnel (vocational rehabilitation, mental health, and social services personnel, among others)
- employers
- parents and students

These individuals plan and implement vocational programs for special needs students. Each component of program development is affected by the coordination and cooperation of these participants. The program components will vary by design, but common components can be found in most programs. The components reviewed in this chapter as part of program development are

- program delivery
- professional development
- curriculum development
- transition programs
- program evaluation

Thabet, Jones, and Basile write that educational program development for exceptional learners must be systematic, stimulating, psychologically sound, organized, and well planned and should include high-quality instructional materials to meet the needs and interests of these learners.[2] Educators today are being asked to approach their responsibilities with a degree of professionalism never demanded before in the history of professional education. This chapter identifies the six mandates of the Carl D. Perkins Vocational Education Act (Public Law 98-524) concerning special needs populations and addresses issues that arise in expediting the program development process and ensuring that these mandates are met.

PROGRAM DELIVERY

In 1978, the Center for Vocational Education developed a set of modules in cooperation with the American Association for Vocational Instructional Materials (AAVIM). These modules outlined steps involved in the process of program development. Hamilton et al. write the following:

> Long-range program planning serves as the "road map" for a successful journey through vocational education. Like a road map, a long-range plan must be prepared ahead of time. Planning for the future gives direction to the changes that are necessary. Vocational instructors are usually expected to develop long-range plans for their programs as well as more immediate, annual plans. Long-range plans for vocational education programs need to be developed using an orderly process such as the one that follows:
>
> 1. Talk with knowledgeable people in the field (e.g., state department and university personnel, officers, and leaders in state and local vocational associations) in order to anticipate future developments in vocational education.
> 2. Gather information about the supply and demand for workers in an occupational specialty area. These statistics are critical input for making decisions that will help in the formulation of long-range program plans.
> 3. Become knowledgeable about the long-range plans for vocational education in the community.

4. Develop vocational education program goals (statements of what is to be achieved) based on the knowledge gained from the preceding processes.
5. Estimate resources (e.g., facilities, funds) that will be needed to accomplish the goals which have been set.
6. Develop a systematic plan of activities to get from the present to the future. Include in the plan a means for obtaining feedback to determine progress.[3]

Program planning and the delivery systems have been strongly affected by the Carl D. Perkins Act. According to Sarkees and Scott, there are two broad themes:

- making vocational education programs accessible to all persons, including handicapped and disadvantaged persons, single parents and homemakers, adults in need of retraining and training, persons participating in programs designed to eliminate sex bias and stereotyping in vocational education, and incarcerated persons; and
- improving the quality of vocational education programs in order to give the nation's workforce the marketable skills needed to improve productivity and promote economic growth.[4]

Fifty-seven percent of the funds available from the act are for programs for special needs individuals. These funds are set aside for the following special needs populations: handicapped, disadvantaged, adults, single parents, homemakers, individuals in nontraditional programs, incarcerated individuals, and limited English proficient individuals. Funds from the act can only be used for supplemental or additional staff, equipment, materials and services not provided to other individuals in vocational education and for ensuring that the following services and activities are available to handicapped and disadvantaged students who enroll in any vocational education program:

1. equal access in recruitment, enrollment, and placement;
2. equal access to the full range of vocational education programs available to all students;
3. assessment of individual interests, abilities, and special needs to assist students in the successful completion of vocational education programs;
4. special services, including adaptation of curriculum, instruction, equipment, and facilities designed to meet the special needs individuals;
5. guidance, counseling, and career development activities conducted by professionally trained counselors; and
6. counseling services designed to facilitate the transition from school to employment or other career opportunities.[5]

The law specifically mandates that vocational education programs must be provided in the least restrictive environment in accordance with the Education for All

Handicapped Children Act of 1975 (Public Law 94-142). Consequently, whenever it is appropriate, an individualized education program or any other individual learning plan developed for a special needs individual should include long-term vocational goals and short-term objectives, as well as support services necessary for the individual's participation in vocational education. Separate vocational programs for handicapped students are discouraged by the Carl D. Perkins Act, which funds only excess costs above and beyond the funding level for all students. In addition, if at least 75 percent of the students in a school are categorized as economically disadvantaged, set-aside funds can also be used to pay the costs of services and activities that apply the latest technological advances to instructional programs or to purchase state-of-the-art equipment.

Another legislative mandate that strengthens the Carl D. Perkins Act is Section 503 of the Rehabilitation Act (Public Law 93-112), which requires an employer to make reasonable accommodation for handicapped workers if the employer receives federal assistance over $2500. Section 504 of the same act requires that qualified handicapped individuals not be denied equal access to private or public programs and activities as a result of their disability. The Job Training Partnership Act (Public Law 97-300) specifically targets disadvantaged individuals and includes handicapped individuals if they meet the income eligibility requirements. The purpose of this act is to establish programs to prepare youth and unskilled adults for entry into the labor force and to offer job training to economically disadvantaged individuals and others facing serious barriers to employment. Viewed separately or together, these legislative mandates emphasize the importance of quality vocational programs for special needs individuals.

In order to design and implement effective vocational programs that meet the legislative requirements for special needs students, major consideration must be given to the personnel who will administer and provide direct instruction and support services. The professionals who are or should be directly involved in program development are the following:

- the director, coordinator, or supervisor of vocational education
- the director, coordinator, or supervisor of special education
- vocational instructors
- special education teachers
- counselors
- vocational evaluators
- support service staff

Names of support service staff that meet the various legislative requirements vary from state to state. Such staff are referred to, among other ways, as vocational resource educators, basic skills instructors, supplemental teachers, resource teachers, designated vocational instructors, and vocational facilitators. Regardless of the name, such staff provide instructional support in various forms to special needs students and, in some cases, direct instruction within vocational programs. These services, including instruction, are supported by a combination of federal, state, and local funds. The administration of such services for vocational programs accommodating special needs learners must be accompanied by certain philosophical assumptions if the program is to provide a maximally effective learning environment. These assumptions include the following:

- Mainstreaming in vocational classes for special needs learners is a method of ensuring equal access and offering individual students the opportunity of learning in the least restrictive environment where both educational and social needs can be met.
- Support services and resources are necessary to ensure that individual needs are adequately accommodated.
- All students, including special needs students, should have the opportunity to learn in a positive environment and where their rights and needs are recognized and supported.

Programs based on these assumptions provide the supportive environment that is needed. Administrators and instructors should develop a sensitivity about positive learning environments—environments that benefit not only special needs students, but ultimately all students. Characteristics of a positive learning environment include the following:

- *Instructors serve as good role models.* An instructor who teaches being on time, spending time on tasks, and working well with others provides the kind of example and environment where students learn to start work on time and be prepared and organized. Such an instructor avoids picking class favorites and treats all students with respect, regardless of their level of skill.
- *Instructors are always prepared and organized.* An instructor who spends time in organizing and preparing for classroom and lab instruction is likely to spend more time on tasks and hold student interest—and spend less time on discipline and other things that detract from the learning environment.
- *Instructors develop a fair and equitable grading policy.* An instructor who is well organized and prepared for class knows in advance the assignments, projects, and tests (written and performance-based) that will determine grades. A grading policy should be well thought out in advance and stated in the course syllabus so students understand the grading criteria. This information can also assist the IEP team to determine in advance if any alternative evaluation strategies should be used.
- *Instructors vary their teaching styles.* When teaching new concepts (in order to provide students with different learning styles), every opportunity should be afforded students to master each new skill. A good instructor knows that instructional strategies should be varied and that reinforcement activities are frequently needed.

- *Instructors foster teamwork and the development of employability skills among all students*. In addition to curriculum content, an instructor should design instructional activities that not only provide experiences and opportunities for skill mastery, but also encourage students to work together as a team for the express purpose of developing the critical employability skills stressed by employers.

A positive learning environment is an important element in a successful vocational program for special needs students. There are numerous factors that contribute to a positive learning environment; the above are just a few that illustrate the impact instructors can have on the learning environment. Other factors, such as administrative support, provision of support services, parent involvement, and interdisciplinary cooperation, also contribute to a positive learning environment.

Materials, supplies, and equipment are typically the same for special needs students as for other students, unless certain adaptations are necessary for physical reasons or additional materials are needed to supplement instruction. Specially adapted equipment is usually referred to as *assistive devices* or *rehabilitation technology*. Technology for vocational programs is also allowable for special needs programs that serve the disadvantaged under the Carl D. Perkins Act.

Program and school improvements often result from instituting vocational programs for special needs students. These programs often provide the missing components of a holistic educational program for special needs students. Not only do vocational programs offer skill training, but they also improve basic academic skills and provide better integrated school settings, as well as other direct benefits that accompany instruction in least restrictive environments.

PROFESSIONAL DEVELOPMENT   Among the key factors in successful vocational programs for special needs students are the personnel responsible for administration and instruction. Having enthusiastic and informed personnel delivering instruction and support services makes the difference between successful programming for special needs students and unsuccessful programming. Personnel set the tone for the learning environment. They also determine the curriculum content, identify which support services special needs students receive (by setting priorities for funds), and evaluate the program. Vocational special needs personnel require competencies to accomplish these objectives. Sarkees and Scott identified the following competencies needed by educators working with special needs students:

- ability to serve as role model, possessing appropriate personal-social qualities;
- ability to provide on-going reinforcement of student performance;
- ability to design, develop and utilize individualized instruction;
- ability to stay up-to-date with technology and changes in the field; and
- ability to plan and work cooperatively with other school personnel.[6]

These competencies enable instructors and other educators who are involved in vocational education for special needs students to provide quality programs.

The information and knowledge base from which educators design and develop programs is central to the quality of education. Informed professionals create and implement more effective programs than educators who do not invest the time and energy in professional development. Professional development opportunities for individuals in the field of vocational special needs have increased dramatically in the past decade. Today there are numerous opportunities for exchanging information and resources, including those offered by

- training and retraining
- professional organizations and associations
- journals, textbooks, and resource materials
- inservice programs, conferences, and conventions
- networking with other professionals
- site visitations to other programs
- research and dissemination

Training and retraining refers to courses, programs, etc., that provide a knowledge base to those who work in the field of vocational special needs. Colleges and universities have begun to offer courses that relate to issues, trends, and research in the field of vocational special needs. Courses at the undergraduate and graduate level are sometimes crosslisted between the departments of special education and vocational education. This practice varies by states and institutions of higher education. Undergraduate courses are beginning to provide future teachers with information regarding career and vocational programming for special needs students. The new emphasis on the transition from school to work has certainly aided this effort, as has the Carl D. Perkins Act. Graduate programs are beginning to focus on vocational education for special needs populations and on the transition from school to work. Unfortunately, this trend in the undergraduate and graduate education of personnel involved in the field of vocational special needs only began in the past decade and it still has far to go. Therefore, educators are currently utilizing means for retraining professionals already in the field.

Retraining takes place in a variety of settings and at various institutions, and it utilizes a number of funding sources. The most common means for professionals to receive retraining and updated information include

- conferences, which often highlight information of interest to vocational special needs personnel
- conventions, which can include a variety of programs focusing on current issues, trends, research, and material related to vocational special needs personnel
- workshops, which often feature a short-term, concentrated focus on a specific topic or topics and involve participants in related activities

- inservice programs, which, in one or more sessions, can facilitate an exchange of information for the purpose of program improvement

Usually the various types of retraining cited here are planned and funded by either a professional association, a state educational agency, a consortium of several school districts, a local educational agency (school district), or, in some cases, an individual school that feels a need to fill a void, design a new program, or simply improve current program offerings.

There are a number of individuals involved in facilitating retraining, including

- administrators
- program supervisors
- special education teachers
- vocational instructors
- resource and support staff
- inservice coordinators (if designated)
- teacher educators, consultants, or other specialists
- advisory committee members

These individuals try to structure inservice programs so that they improve educators' skills and increase their knowledge about vocational programming for special needs students.

One benefit of training and retraining activities is networking. Networking is the formal and informal exchange of information among colleagues interested in common issues. Frequently, a professional association provides opportunities for contacts among professionals who design vocational programs for special needs students. Federal legislation, such as the Education for All Handicapped Children Act and the Carl D. Perkins Act, has helped to bring together special educators, vocational educators, and guidance counselors and has mandated the coordination and cooperation of these professionals to provide quality vocational programming for special needs students.

The two most prominent professional associations that provide information to special and vocational educators are the American Vocational Association (AVA) and Council for Exceptional Children (CEC). Within these associations, there are divisions that share similar goals. The Special Needs Division (SND) of AVA and the Division of Career Development (DCD) of CEC are the two divisions that provide the most opportunities for vocational special needs personnel to share valuable information, which aids in the cooperation, coordination, and better communication of professionals. The Guidance Division of AVA is also involved, since the Carl D. Perkins Act mandates guidance and counseling services for the handicapped and disadvantaged.

The SND has one affiliate organization, the National Association of Vocational Education's Special Needs Personnel (NAVESNP), which has separate membership application and dues. However, SND and NAVESNP closely coordinate goals and activities, including conferences and convention programs. Within CEC, the DCD has a liaison committee to improve communication, cooperation, and coordination with various organizations such as the SND, its affiliate organization NAVESNP, and other special interest groups within SND, i.e., vocational evaluators, teacher educators, and state administrators of vocational special needs programs.

While AVA and CEC are the two major organizations which vocational and special educators look to for information and leadership, there are many other related organizations, such as the National Rehabilitation Association (NRA). With the focus on the transition from school to work, there is a growing need for vocational and special educators to work closely with vocational rehabilitation counselors. The Vocational Evaluation and Work Adjustment Association (VEWAA) is a division of NRA; its purpose is to improve and advance the field of vocational evaluation and work adjustment training for persons with disabilities.

Knowledge about professional associations is just the first step in professional development. Active participation, reading journals, attending conferences, seminars, and workshops, and actively working on committees are all part of professional growth and development. Information about these organizations may be obtained from the following addresses:

1. American Vocational Association, including the Special Needs Division and the Guidance Division: 1410 King Street, Alexandria, VA 22314
2. National Association of Vocational Education Special Needs Personnel: Reschini House, Center for Vocational Personnel Preparation, Indiana University of Pennsylvania, Indiana, PA 15705
3. Council for Exceptional Children, including the Division on Career Development: 1920 Association Drive, Reston, VA 22091-1589
4. National Rehabilitation Association: 633 South Washington Street, Alexandria, VA 22314

The professional organizations mentioned above and many other associations provide educators with information, materials, and other resources to assist in designing and implementing vocational programs for special needs students. Professional associations, state education agencies, local education agencies, and teacher educators provide numerous resources, textbooks, and research in the field of vocational education for special needs populations. Professional associations usually sponsor journals for their membership. There are numerous journals that deal with issues within vocational special needs programming and that contribute to the knowledge base for those who design and implement vocational programs for special needs students at both the secondary and postsecondary level. The journals most prominently associated with vocational special needs are the following:

- *Journal for Vocational Education Special Needs Personnel,* published by the National Association of Vocational Education Special Needs Personnel

- *Career Development of Exceptional Individuals,* published by the Division on Career Development of the Council for Exceptional Children
- *Exceptional Children,* published by the Council for Exceptional Children
- *Vocational Education Journal,* published by the American Vocational Association

Professional development is a component of program development in that it emphasizes the importance of professionals keeping current with the growing literature, information, and research required by those who design and implement vocational programs for special needs students. However, administrative support is also required by vocational special needs personnel so that they may comfortably utilize the various opportunities offered by professional development. Some administrators do not emphasize the benefits of such activities or, in some cases, even put barriers in the way, because professional development requires that personnel be away occasionally from the school or workplace. Yet the rewards of such involvement can be enormous, not only to the professionals but also to their individual schools and school districts. Some state education agencies that distribute set-aside funds from the Carl D. Perkins Act have asked local education agencies to sign assurances that they will allow vocational special needs personnel to participate in and attend certain professional development activities, e.g., specific conferences. This alerts administrators early in the school year that vocational special needs personnel will be expected to attend and participate in selected professional development activities. The Education of Handicapped Children Amendments (Public Law 98-199) also sets aside funds to be used for a comprehensive system of professional development, which provides opportunities for special educators to attend inservice programs, conferences, and conventions for the purpose of professional development.

Site visitations to other programs is another professional development activity that offers professionals the opportunity to investigate other program models and resources. Site visitations occur when one or more representatives of a local or state education agency visit another education agency. Site visitations can be used beneficially to

- review administration strategies
- identify effective teaching techniques
- review curriculum content
- review support services, resources, and materials
- observe students involved in programs
- collect information or data for evaluation

Site visitations are useful in designing new programs or planning revisions in current programs.

Chalofsky states that professional development is a process of keeping current, competent, and open to new theories, techniques and values. Professionals must be proactive as their profession develops and grows. Successful professionals internalize the need for professional development so that it becomes a constant process of self-renewal and growth.[7]

A curriculum is only one component in a total program, but it is a central component. A curriculum is the specific instructional content which an instructor guides a student through and which will ultimately result in the student's mastery of a set of skills that will make the student employable.

CURRICULUM DEVELOP- MENT

Wiggs suggests a list of categories to be used during the program planning stages and believes that data should be gathered to assist in the planning. The data categories may include some or all of the following:

- anticipated number of learners
- location of learners
- education, training, or work experience background of learners
- experience in present or related jobs
- job performance requirements versus learners' present skill levels (e.g., learning deficiency ranges)
- language or cultural differences among learners
- motivation of learners
- physical or mental characteristics of learners
- specific interests or biases of learners[8]

By gathering information and analyzing the data, curriculum content is determined and appropriate general learning programs are generated. Also generated are specific learner objectives, support services, instructional methods, materials, and resources.

Curricula have increasingly become competency-based over the past decade. There are various labels which may be applied to competency-based education. Blank identified some of the more common labels: *competency-based instruction, mastery learning, systems approach to education, performance-based instruction, criterion-referenced instruction, individualized instruction, programmed instruction, self-paced learning,* and *instructional system development.*[9] Blank says that even though all of these terms are not entirely synonymous, the kinds of education they refer to are similar and their approach to training has four basic principles:

1. spell out exactly what it is that trainees will learn
2. provide high quality instruction
3. help students learn one thing well before getting on to the next
4. require each trainee to demonstrate each competency.[10]

Competency-based vocational education certainly is characterized by these four principles. In addition, it also provides special needs educators with an avenue for developing appropriate goals and objectives for individual education plans (IEPs) and other individual plans—such as individual vocational education plans (IVEPs) and individual work rehabilitation plans (IWRPs)—that guide a student's instructional experiences and the provision of support services.

Vocational programs that have a well-organized and systematic curriculum have defined their course content. The course content is then stated clearly in the course syllabus. The syllabus is a tool that assists educators in preparing special needs students for entrance into vocational programs and it can aid in developing annual goals and short-term objectives. The course syllabus should include the following:

- *course description:* an outline of course content in narrative form
- *units of study:* a list of major headings taught in the course
- *student competencies:* a list of individual student competencies that will be taught in each unit of study (competencies are also referred to as *tasks* or *skills*)
- *vocabulary:* a short list of basic vocabulary terms considered critical by the instructor for a particular unit of study
- *evaluation:* for each particular unit of study, a list of evaluation methods that will be used to determine mastery (e.g., multiple-choice exams, observation checklists)
- *grading policy:* a statement that outlines the criteria used by the instructor to determine student grades
- *prevocational skills:* a set of skills that will enhance a special needs student's chances for success in a given vocational program (e.g., for a building trades program, a prevocational skill would be the ability to read a ruler to 1/16 of an inch)

Every vocational instructor should have a course syllabus that contains this information in order for the IEP team and various other support service personnel to better utilize all available information for improved IEP planning and for more appropriate program placement of handicapped students and other special needs students requiring special assistance.

Identification of competencies appropriate to current labor market needs is the foundation of a competency-based curriculum. Most often, student competencies are listed as goals and objectives. It is important that the competencies are relevant and that their descriptions are in behavioral terms and as accurate as possible. There are two sources that assist educators in developing and improving vocational student competencies:

1. Occupational Data Analysis System (ODAS) is a computerized system that uses data from three existing data bases to assist business, education, and industry in developing relevant vocational programs.

2. Vocational-Technical Education Consortium of States (V-Tecs) is a consortium of states that develops and shares competency-based vocational technical education information and materials; it is a service of ODAS.

In addition to these resources, state and local vocational advisory committees provide local labor market information that can assist instructors to identify the necessary competencies and develop a list of specific tasks or skills for instruction.

Vocabulary is equally important when examining curriculum and developing vocational programs for special needs students. Technical terms and names of specific tools or equipment are frequently the terms that require additional instruction time. For a special needs teacher or other support service personnel assisting special needs students while they are enrolled in specific vocational training programs, a vocabulary list is beneficial. Such a list can help a student studying for an exam or simply improve the student's understanding of terms used in class. While a vocational instructor develops the course syllabus, identifies student competencies, or constructs examinations, selected vocabulary terms can be identified as potentially difficult, possibly requiring additional instruction time and reinforcement activities.

Resources and materials that may be useful in providing special needs students with supplemental information, instruction, or familiarity with terms are an important part of the curriculum development process. They add an extra dimension to direct instruction. Instructors and support service personnel should constantly be searching for additional resources. Frequently resources or materials can be located through state education agencies, consultants, teacher educators, and regional or state resource centers. Resources and materials can also usually be located through newsletters, guides, journals, or exhibits at local, state, and national conferences and conventions.

There are various monitoring and evaluation techniques that vocational instructors can select to measure student progress and determine mastery of skill competencies. Frequently, there is not just one evaluation technique or method that is the best and it is not uncommon for several evaluation techniques to be used in combination. Sarkees and Scott identify the following evaluation methods as appropriate for use in vocational programs for special needs students:

- student-teacher contracts
- pencil-paper tests
- product checklists
- performance rating sheets
- peer evaluation
- self-evaluation
- safety checklists
- classroom or laboratory behavior checklists[11]

Obviously, each technique is appropriate in different situations and for different outcomes of measuring, evaluating, or monitoring student progress. Each technique or evaluation method has pros and cons, which should be carefully weighed in determining the proper evaluation techniques for each unit of study.

Grading is an integral part of the curriculum development process and must be considered when planning vocational programs for special needs students. Instructors are concerned about the "right" way to grade a special needs student. They are concerned with their own accountability, being fair to all the students, and not "watering down" their standards or curriculum. Sarkees and Scott write, "The grading system for special needs learners should be based upon progress made on specified objectives for a given grading period. It should be fair and reflect the competencies developed by *each* student rather than how well the student performed compared to other students."[12]

Very few preservice training programs train future teachers how to grade special needs students fairly and objectively. Inservice training has been the primary source for developing grading systems used for measuring, evaluating, and grading special needs students who have been mainstreamed into a vocational program. Grading systems for vocational programs should include

- a philosophy of grading
- a list of evaluation techniques that will be used for grading purposes
- a description of the importance of each evaluation method used
- the translation of the point system to a letter grade
- a statement on class participation, attendance, or other variables that will be used in determining final grades

By stating these criteria at the beginning of the semester, all students, the vocational instructor, the special education teacher, and support personnel (if any) will be made aware of the expectations and the teachers can anticipate difficulties and better prepare the students for the evaluation process.

Guliano states that during the process of conducting a class, an effective instructor is one who can teach others (instructional role), keep records of student progress (administrative role), and interact on a personal level with students (interpersonal role).[13] He underscores the importance of instruction and of guiding the learning process. Curriculum and instruction are key elements in program development.

TRANSITION PROGRAMS

Transition from school to work is currently a national mandate from the Office of Special Education and Rehabilitation Services (OSERS) and the Carl D. Perkins Act, which underscores the importance of transition for special needs students. There are a number of key factors involved in transition from school to work. Literature has identified several consistent program components found in most models of transition, including

- *functional curriculum:* instruction that focuses on independent living skills, particularly vocational and employability skills, but on social skills as well

- *integrated school services:* instruction and support services that are provided in the least restrictive environment and that increase interaction with nonhandicapped students
- *community-based instruction:* instruction that is conducted outside the classroom and in or near actual employment settings
- *parental involvement:* utilization of family members for instruction, reinforcement, and assistance with support systems
- *interagency cooperation:* interaction and utilization of various agencies and organizations for the purpose of coordinating services that facilitate the transition process

These program components are fundamental to the transition process and improve instruction, support, and coordination, which are necessary for successful transition from school to work. Frequently they are also the topics of inservice or conference presentations for vocational special needs personnel. These components should be carefully considered when writing an IEP or IWRP and when designing transition programs. It is not surprising that advocacy organizations, parents, and state task forces on transition, as well as educators, are searching for ways to

- design, utilize, and implement functional curricula
- provide better integrated school services
- further implement community-based instruction
- identify ways to utilize or implement interagency cooperation
- create new opportunities and services
- provide all of the above via a logical, systematic approach

Madeleine Will, in a position paper for OSERS, defined transition as the "period that includes high school, the point of graduation, additional post-secondary education or adult services, and the initial years in employment. Transition is a bridge between the security and structure offered by the school and the opportunities and risks of adult life."[14] Will developed a model of transition that has become the framework for many other transition models (see Figure 5-1).

This particular model focuses heavily on high school instruction and includes vocational instruction as well as independent living skills, employability skills, and personal relationships. Will believes that the services and experiences that lead to employment as part of the transition process should become part of the programmatic considerations for the IEP team prior to the student's exiting the educational system. According to her view, transition does not begin in high school; it begins in the early primary grades. There should be a consistent philosophical approach starting in the elementary grades and continuing throughout the student's educational program, not to be completed until the student is employed.

Once students have completed a formal educational program, the transition process is the focus of educators, parents, and adult service providers. The transition process

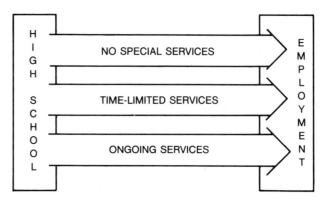
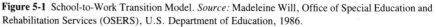

Figure 5-1 School-to-Work Transition Model. *Source:* Madeleine Will, Office of Special Education and Rehabilitation Services (OSERS), U.S. Department of Education, 1986.

may include postsecondary training, assessment, or a variety of other transition services, including

- career or personal counseling
- transportation
- residential assistance
- financial support
- social skills development
- medical care

Designing a transition program is a complex task. It requires individuals who understand the philosophy of transition and can organize and implement a program requiring cooperation from special education, vocational education, vocational rehabilitation, and other adult services providers, as well as from a host of other individuals, such as parents, employers, community representatives, etc.

As a result of the emphasis on transition, some states have begun to develop individual transition plans (ITPs). Many states, however, have chosen to incorporate the ITP into the last two or three years of a student's IEP, either as the focus of the IEP or, in some cases, as an addendum to the IEP. Not all states have uniformly incorporated career, prevocational, vocational, or transition goals into the IEP as yet. However, legislation, court mandates, and state education agencies are setting priorities that are improving the quality of IEPs, instruction, and support services.

Wehman states that training personnel for transition at both the preservice and inservice level is essential. Roles must be defined and training must occur for those who participate in transition programs. He believes that transition from school to work does not occur for most handicapped students because the individuals responsible for transition have not been properly trained. He cites five major categories or clusters of training competencies that will better prepare personnel for transition efforts:

1. community-job assessment skills
2. student assessment
3. job placement and behavior skills
4. onsite job training
5. follow-up and job retention skills[15]

Wehman lists a variety of methods that may be used to train personnel for developing the skills needed for transition programming:

- short-term training

- field work

- summer institutes

- workshops

- ongoing, onsite technical assistance

- interdisciplinary efforts on the part of personnel in vocational education, special education, and vocational rehabilitation and developmental disabilities[16]

Brown, agreeing with Wehman, states that ''too many educators still lack knowledge about career opportunities available to handicapped persons and need to better understand how job-related skills can be viewed creatively when seeking job placement opportunities.''[17] Brown and Wehman both make it clear that to train personnel involved in designing and implementing transition programs is essential.

Brown states that a variety of potentially important issues should be considered by persons responsible for providing preservice and inservice personnel development activities. He writes that instructors should be taught to consider each student's needs in terms of

1. how to best structure/organize instructional contents;
2. how to select appropriate goals and objectives;
3. how to sequence instructional units/activities so that they will be most easily comprehended;
4. the rate at which instructional activities are presented;
5. the frequency of opportunities for students to practice/apply new skills and the proximity of that practice to the instruction;
6. the type of reinforcement that should be provided for positive behavior; and
7. how students can be given feedback about the appropriateness of their behaviors.[18]

Conaway states that transition programs should begin before high school. Consequently, there are some considerations that educators must incorporate in designing transition programs:

- the need for increased emphasis on career education for handicapped students beginning in elementary school
- the importance of including career development objectives in each student's IEP at all educational levels
- the need to continue to improve the quality of supplemental services available to handicapped vocational education students
- the need to increase awareness among special educators of the importance of vocational evaluation.[19]

There are many guidelines for educators who design transition programs for special needs students. Individually they can be considered as steps in a process to assist local educational agencies in planning transition programs. West developed a set of guidelines for local education agencies that were applying for discretionary funds from state education agencies:

1. Select the definition and philosophy of transition which best meets the needs of the local educational agency (LEA);
2. Develop an outline of program options, curriculum options and the support services which are available to students in the LEA;
3. Determine voids in curriculum and program options (as they relate to transition);
4. Develop options to fill the voids;
5. Identify personnel who will be involved in all components of the transition efforts;
6. Organize inservice for appropriate personnel involved in transition efforts;
7. Select and/or develop materials needed for transition efforts;
8. Determine activities for transition efforts;
9. Outline a transition implementation plan for the LEA;
10. Assign specific responsibilities and timelines for each activity identified in the plan;
11. Conduct transition activities;
12. Evaluate transition services;
13. Determine the impact of transition activities and the actual impact on student's transition to employment;
14. Identify and examine transition alternatives/options not previously explored by the LEA; and
15. Plan future transition efforts identified by the evaluations.[20]

Designing, planning, and implementing transition programs is newer to educators than is planning vocational programs. Therefore, training in the area is needed by the personnel involved to familiarize themselves with information regarding the transition process. Professional development for personnel directly ties the components of transition into program development.

Evaluating transition programs is also new to educators. It will be some time before formal data collection can accurately provide information to individuals involved in designing transition programs. Certainly with the priority being given to transition, this will surely come. But until transition programs have progressed, local educational agencies can utilize external review teams of consultants to examine the transition components of a school district. The evaluation team can interview participants involved in the transition program, observe transition activities, review documents, and synthesize their findings into descriptions of strengths and areas of concern and make recommendations. The chair of the transition review team should have an exit interview with the director of vocational education, the director of special education, and any other administrators involved in the transition program in order to go over the initial report and answer any questions the educators might have about the findings. The information gained from the external program review and the final report can be utilized by the local educational agency to assist it in improving its transition program activities, applying for discretionary grants, and developing a more comprehensive transition program.

PROGRAM EVALUATION

In designing a program evaluation for a vocational special needs program, there are various issues that need to be examined to determine the quality and effectiveness of the program. These include issues concerning

- administration of the program
- adequacy of staffing to meet program design
- coordination between vocational education and special education
- identification of the one or more target populations the program intends to serve
- funding sources available to support the program
- purpose of the program
- curriculum content and appropriate course offerings
- resource and support services to supplement individual needs of the target populations
- comprehensiveness of support services
- assurances that the legislative mandates are met

The statement of purpose of a program describes the philosophy and rationale of the program, as well as its goals, objectives, and parameters. The statement of purpose provides direction for administrators in the same way that blueprints provide the framework and parameters for building a house. The administration of a program provides guidance and support as well as facilitating action. Administrators set the guidelines and timelines for activities needed to meet the goals and objectives of a program. It is critical to program design and development that administrators have a clear concept of the program from a broad perspective in order to guide the program and the staff and to identify the necessary steps for program implementation.

Self-evaluation is a process conducted by individuals involved in all phases of the program and its evaluation. Personnel involved in a program evaluation will likely be asked to complete a form that asks a series of questions. The answers to these questions will assist an evaluation team in determining the quality and effectiveness of the program. This type of program evaluation offers the opportunity to collect anecdotal data, which are sometimes lacking yet can offer insight into the quality and effectiveness of a program. Self-evaluation usually is conducted by a committee within the system, but all individuals involved have an opportunity for input. Specifically, each staff member evaluates his or her own performance and contribution to the overall program. At the same time, certain needs will likely emerge, as well as plans for improving the individual's performance and the program's overall effectiveness. These plans and self-directed recommendations will be considered by an external review team.

An evaluation of a special needs program should be designed to examine the philosophy and goals of the program. The goals should be clear, precise, consistent, and measurable. There should be both long-term and short-term goals. The program evaluation typically utilizes several methods of evaluation, including

- self-evaluation (internal review)
- evaluation by an onsite visitation/interview team (external review)
- review of onsite records (external review)

There have been many guides written to describe the evaluation process within vocational education. Program evaluation of vocational education for special needs populations uses the same evaluation procedures; it simply asks a different set of questions to ensure that mandates for special needs populations are being followed. The key questions that are critical to program evaluation of vocational education programs for special needs students are obviously directly tied to the mandates of the Carl D. Perkins Act:

- Is information provided to special needs students and parents that describes opportunities available in vocational education at least one year before the students enter the 9th grade?
- Does each special needs learner that enrolls in a vocational education program receive an assessment of his or her interests, aptitudes, abilities, and special needs?
- Does the information gained from the assessment result in a written plan for each special needs student who enrolls in a vocational education program?
- Does each special needs student who is enrolled in a vocational education program receive special services designed to meet the individual needs identified during a vocational assessment?
- Do special needs students who enroll in vocational education receive guidance, counseling, and other career development experiences from professionally trained counselors?

● Do special needs students enrolled in a vocational education program receive counseling to facilitate transition to postschool employment or other career opportunities?

While these are the primary questions that are mandatory in any program evaluation for vocational programs for special needs individuals, they are certainly not the only questions that should be examined. For example, in planning program evaluation, it is important to know who the evaluation is to be conducted for and what the purpose of the evaluation is. If the purpose of the evaluation is to determine if legislative requirements are being met and to identify the strengths and weaknesses of the program, then it is critical to generate a list of questions that will yield the most useful and accurate information. A sequence of tasks needed to be performed to conduct the evaluation must be established and timelines must be set. Also to be considered is who would be able to conduct the program evaluation fairly and objectively and what resources will be needed to properly conduct the evaluation. Regardless of the nature of the evaluation, it is important to consider what actions or decisions are expected as a result of the evaluation. Hopefully, any program evaluation of vocational programs for special needs students will result in program improvement.

SUMMARY

Nadler defines human resource development as organized learning experiences in a definite time period to increase the possibility of improving job performance and personal growth.[21] His definition closely resembles the account of vocational program development for special needs individuals given in this chapter.

Program delivery is a component of program development because of its examination of the system that provides direct instruction, resources, materials, and support services that together constitute a program especially designed for individual learners who have special needs. The impact of the Carl D. Perkins Act on program delivery specifically concerns the support services and personnel that serve special needs students enrolled in vocational programs and are funded through the act.

Professional development is a component of program development in that it furnishes the necessary information to personnel who provide instruction and support services to special needs students enrolled in vocational education programs. Through various professional development activities and opportunities, professionals in the field of vocational special needs exchange information and increase their knowledge, which results in improved vocational programs.

Curriculum development is the key to the instructional process and is therefore a component of program development. Curriculum content determines the learner's objectives, the selection of instructional strategies, instructional materials, media, tools, equipment, learning facilities, and a host of other things.

The transition process requires information from every other component of program development in order to facilitate the transition of a special needs individual from school to work. It is the final process and it determines if in fact the student is ready to exit the educational system and enter into employment and an independent living situation.

Program evaluation determines if the components, both separately and together, have been effective. It indicates to administrators and teachers whether they have complied with legislative mandates, including abiding by the spirit as well as the letter of the law.

Together these program components constitute the process called program development. Program development should be designed specifically and systematically to create a positive learning environment for special needs students, an environment where learning and personal growth takes place regardless of the conditions that cause a student to be labeled a person with special needs.

NOTES

1. George W. Fair, ''Program Development for Special Vocational Needs Youth,'' in *Handbook of Special Vocational Needs Education,* ed. Gary Meers (Rockville, Md.: Aspen Publishers, 1980), 117.

2. Nancy Thabet, Barbara Jones, and Joseph Basile II, *Research Based Program Development Model for Exceptional Learners* (Morgantown: West Virginia Department of Education, 1985), preface.

3. James B. Hamilton et al., *Evaluate Your Vocational Program* (Athens, Ga.: American Association for Vocational Instructional Materials, 1978), 6.

4. Michelle D. Sarkees and John L. Scott, *Vocational Special Needs* (Alsip, Ill.: American Technical Publishers, 1985), 11.

5. Public Law 98-524, the Carl D. Perkins Vocational Education Act, sec. 204.

6. Sarkees and Scott, *Vocational Special Needs,* 15–16.

7. Neal Chalofsky, ''Professional Growth for HRD Staff,'' in *The Handbook of Human Resource Development,* ed. Leonard Nadler (New York: Wiley and Sons, 1984), 13.3.

8. Garland D. Wiggs, ''Designing Learning Programs,'' in *The Handbook of Human Resource Development,* 7.17.

9. William Blank, *Handbook for Developing Competency-Based Training Programs* (Englewood Cliffs, N.J.: Prentice-Hall, 1982), 7.

10. Ibid., 6.

11. Sarkees and Scott, *Vocational Special Needs,* 338–46.

12. Ibid., 350.

13. Daniel F. Guliano, ''Instructing,'' in *The Handbook of Human Resource Development,* 8.3.

14. Madeleine Will, ''OSERS Programming for the Transition of Youth with Disabilities: Bridges from School to Working Life,'' in *Enhancing Transition from School to the Workplace for Handicapped Youth: Personnel Preparation Implications,* ed. Janis Chadsey-Rusch and Cheryl Hanley-Maxwell (Champaign, Ill.: National Network for Professional Development in Vocational Special Education, 1986), 10.

15. Paul Wehman, ''Transition for Handicapped Youth from School to Work,'' in *Enhancing Transition from School to the Workplace,* 40.

16. Ibid., 40–41.

17. James M. Brown, ''A Model for Enhancing the Transition of Mildly Handicapped Youth into Postsecondary Vocational Education,'' in *Enhancing Transition from School to the Workplace,* 44.

18. Ibid., 57.

19. Charlotte Conaway, ''Vocational Education's Role in the Transition of Handicapped Persons,'' in *Enhancing Transition from School to the Workplace,* 74.

20. Lynda L. West, ''Inservice Training Implications for Teacher Educators in Special Education in the Transition Process,'' in *Enhancing Transition from School to the Workplace,* 139–40.

21. Leonard Nadler, ''Human Resource Development,'' in *The Handbook of Human Resource Development,* 1.3.

Chapter 6

The Modification of Curriculum and Instruction: Catalysts for Equity

Stephen White, M. Ed.

Special needs learners have long been a part of public education, but the modification of curriculum and instruction to meet their needs is a relatively recent phenomenon. A sophisticated awareness of the importance of sound curriculum and instruction for disadvantaged, limited English proficient, and handicapped students is only now beginning to emerge. During the 1970s, programs for the disadvantaged and limited English proficient proliferated. However, these programs focused primarily on affective development, and curriculum modification was viewed as secondary.

Until the transition initiative was articulated at the federal level in 1983, the majority of research efforts in curriculum and instruction for special education occurred at the elementary level.[1] This focus was also evident in regular education and it was not until *A Nation at Risk* was published that the secondary schools were given much attention by educational researchers.[2] Subsequently, instruction in special education at the secondary level was characterized by tutoring of smaller groups of students in the college prep academic courses offered to regular students in the comprehensive high school. Goals were often formulated in terms of developmental growth in reading and mathematics, and specially designed instruction became little more than the modification of content to enable students to pass regular classes. Tragically, programs for special needs learners were too often developed around the master schedule or with a mainstreaming focus without regard to options upon graduation. The focus on maximum access for special needs learners resulted in practices where enrollment was viewed as an end in itself and taken as proof that our schools were providing equal educational opportunity for all.

Today, students with special needs have a right to participate in the full range of educational and extracurricular activities available in the public schools. Special needs educators have played a significant part in this revolution in public education, modifying curricula to enable disadvantaged and disabled students to have access to vocational education programs. Unfortunately, access to the public schools has yet to produce a corresponding access to independent living or employment for special needs learners.

Special needs learners are all too often placed in vocational education because the technology enables them to pass the course, rather than because the training prepares them for employment. As a result, educators applaud when special needs students pass at minimum standards courses in Machine Trades, Electronics, Welding, Office Education, and Typing. Unfortunately, barely passing a Machine Trades course will not provide a special needs student the skills to compete with advanced students for a limited number of apprenticeships. For special needs educators, modification of curriculum and instruction are the nuts and bolts to the special needs student's bridge to independence.

A meaningful discussion of curriculum modification cannot occur until the word "curriculum" is defined. Krajewski and his colleagues found over one hundred definitions of curriculum in the literature.[3]

Joyce and Weil state, "A curriculum is an educational program. It is designed to accomplish certain educational goals and to use specific educational means to accomplish those goals. It consists of the broader environment within which interactive teaching takes place and includes overall content and approaches to it."[4] Curriculum was viewed as a means to an end, and the goal determined the curriculum content used to achieve it. Vocational education by definition is a planned course of study designed to prepare individuals for gainful employment in specific occupations.[5] Employment in a specific occupation is the end that determines the means (the vocational curriculum), and as innovations in the workplace occur, corresponding innovations should be incorporated into the instructional program. Failure to take this into account in the planning process for mainstreaming special needs learners has limited the effectiveness of vocational education for this population and reduced the impact of the access itself. As the twenty-first century approaches, it is imperative that the Nation's commitment to special needs learners encompass more than a commitment to equal access and that it address the substantive issues of access to employment and independent living that arise when considering the modification of curriculum and instruction. Three elements are presented below as a basis for addressing these issues: marketability, curriculum softening, and reciprocal curriculum infusion.

A CONCEPTUAL FRAMEWORK FOR CURRICULUM MODIFICATION

Marketability

The educational team or individual teacher should determine whether placement in a specific program enhances the student's "marketability." Simply because placement in an industrial arts program will give a student skills in woodworking, this does not necessarily mean that the student will gain marketable skills from that experience. A student's age, interest, and aptitude need to be considered in making the determination, as well as the local market conditions, future job outlook, transferability of skills gained from the course, and the skill requirements of the course.

It should be noted that the benefit a special needs student gets from a particular course needs to be weighed against the benefit the student might get from alternative course offerings. Furthermore, the level of competition for available jobs and the degree to which the course directly prepares students for employment need to be considered. This aspect of curriculum selection is implicit in the Carl D. Perkins Act, which requires that all disadvantaged and handicapped students receive an assessment of their interests, abilities, aptitudes, and special needs related to the specific vocational education program.[6] Marketability involves both projecting into the future and carefully examining student abilities and specific program requirements.

The tasks involved in determining marketability require extensive collaboration between the student's advocate and the receiving vocational teacher. In addition, a readily accessible data base with current and accurate information is equally important. The onus for gathering and analyzing this information will typically fall on the committed professional, although a long-range commitment by school administrators can build such a data base through regular review of curriculum content, active advisory councils, comprehensive community-referenced assessments, and concise communication networks.

Curriculum Softening

Curriculum softening is the tendency among educators to provide access for students by reducing the requirements in vocational education programs. This practice may have some merit when applied to traditional academic courses such as American history, but it has little merit when applied to vocational education. Curriculum softening does not include practices that enable students to participate (i.e., taped lectures, transferable physical modifications, use of oral rather than written examinations), but rather it includes the removal of time-and-motion standards and of requirements for accuracy, as well as the wholesale elimination of instructional units.

Several strategies will be discussed later that allow students access to vocational programs in ways that enhance their marketability. Curriculum softening makes a sham of the mainstreaming mandate and the legitimate civil rights the mainstreaming movement embodies. It provides teachers, administrators, parents, and students with a patently false picture of the adult opportunities available following graduation. Equally important, curriculum softening prohibits the selection of an alternative curriculum that might provide the bridge between school and employment, and it furnishes a negative measure for determining the appropriateness of student placements and specific curriculum content.

Reciprocal Curriculum Infusion

Career education was built on the concept of curriculum infusion during the early 1970s.[7] By developing instructional units focused on careers, educators could provide a pervasive career development program throughout the curriculum without diminishing the time-on-task in the core subject areas. This infusion of career-oriented materials is once again gaining support as educators attempt to address the special needs of students throughout the school curriculum. *Reciprocal curriculum infusion* refers to infusion of academic training into the vocational curriculum and a reciprocal infusion of vocational training into the academic curriculum. This reciprocity is particularly necessary for limited English proficient and disabled students, because it reinforces learning concepts across a number of settings; it should be emphasized whenever possible.

A major purpose of the Carl D. Perkins Act was the improvement of the academic foundations of vocational students and the application of newer technologies. Adequate preparation for the twenty-first century will require all students to be as proficient as possible in both academic and technical skills.[8] Reciprocal curriculum infusion provides a focus for addressing both areas of skill simultaneously. Decision-makers will need to weigh each of these elements in selecting the appropriate curriculum in order to ensure that the training enhances marketability, that the academic and technical aspects are reinforced through reciprocal curriculum infusion, and that curriculum softening is avoided.

Vocational teachers need to be willing to say no to enrollment of certain students with special needs and simultaneously be ready to make the modifications that are necessary for others to succeed. The conceptual framework presented here provides a systematic method for making those judgments in a professional manner free of bias or sympathy. Special and other educators will have a tool that will enable them to make decisions based on objective data, rather than on hunches or biases toward vocational education and the workplace. It is unreasonable to expect teachers from nonvocational backgrounds to be as cognizant of skill requirements as vocational educators. Vocational teachers will need to share their expertise, and they have an obligation to be forthright about any given student's marketability following completion of a course.

CONTENT MODIFICATION

The approach to curriculum as a means to an end should guide modifications as well. For example, providing a student with extensive modifications in written materials (size of letters, modified reading levels, pronunciation guides) may allow the student to complete tasks to required levels, but the modifications are probably impractical in the workplace. Because the student is expected to complete the task to the prescribed standard, marketability becomes the relevant factor rather than curriculum softening.

Task analysis has been widely used as a tool to facilitate placement of special needs learners in vocational programs. Gold and Scott define task analysis as "all the activity which results in enough power for the learner to acquire the task. It should represent the most effective use of resources and time (efficiency). Task analysis divides into content, the task and the steps into which the task is divided, and process, the way in which the task is taught."[9] This discussion will be limited to the task analysis of content, leaving the discussion of process to the section on instructional practices.

Vocational educators are usually astute in breaking down curricula into a series of tasks with sequential parts. Competency-based education is an example of task analysis applied to curricula in an effort to enable students to progress at their own pace while maintaining the integrity of the course content. The emphasis by Gold and Scott on efficiency is particularly relevant in education today, as the technology of teaching is such that almost anyone with the physical capacity to perform a task can be taught to do so proficiently.[10] The issue is no longer whether a student can learn the task, but rather how long will it take for the student to become proficient. The use of task analyses to reinforce, explain, and clarify concepts and procedures is a helpful modification for special needs learners in almost any course.

However, the estimated time required for the student to master the task must be considered in the planning process. A simple task "slice" from the vocational curriculum could be used as an assessment tool for all students, and time-and-motion data from the task slice could be legitimately used to make determinations regarding placement in the program. Task analysis provides the instructor with a better understanding of the curriculum and the options for customizing instruction, but it should not be employed to postpone the eventuality of student failure. It provides a means to individualize vocational education and enhances the special needs student's opportunity to participate.

Many researchers advocate an ecological approach, which views behavior as a dynamic part of the interaction between the person and the environment.[11] From an ecological perspective, a special needs student's success in vocational education is dependent as much on the attitudes and behavior of the other students as on the special needs student. Modification of curriculum from this perspective would include awareness training for regular students, presentations by special needs individuals who represent nonstereotypic images, and a set of lessons on interpersonal relations. These modifications will not only promote successful integration into the class, but provide valuable citizenship training in the process. Brief role playing or media presentations at the beginning of a term may help to dispel animosity and promote acceptance by other students and staff.

Donaldson goes one step further and advocates that educational settings be designed so that the special needs learner is given a status at least equal to all other students.[12] Operationally, special needs students would be required to meet the same standards for behavior and suffer the same consequences for violations. The ecological aspect is particularly important in the transition from school to employment. The ability to ask supervisors for assistance, follow directions, respond to criticism, listen without interrupting, and offer help to coworkers have all been found to be important variables in the workplace, and terminations are frequently related to the absence of these basic skills.[13]

Curriculum softening should not be used to deny students access to programs that can enhance their marketability. Many special needs learners will have serious difficulty completing a full apprenticeship program. Fitzpatrick developed a program that required all students to follow three circular tours, each more difficult than the previous tour and each corresponding to a career level for industrial entry.[14] In this way, some students with special needs were able to complete the first or second tour and still enter the workforce at a career level. Use of this cyclical approach necessitates competency-based instruction to manage each student's path through the program. Vocational education, perhaps more than traditional curriculum offerings, lends itself to competency-based instruction, where students progress at their own pace within certain parameters. The curriculum is not compromised as it would be if the instructor were to soften the curriculum, and the student's training definitely enhances marketability.

It is estimated that the information half-life (the time period during which half of the information in a field becomes outdated) of certain fields is as short as six years.[15] The changes created in the workplace by this phenomenon are difficult to anticipate and virtually impossible to predict regarding specific occupations or trades.

A cost-effective method for reducing the negative impact of such change is the cluster method of curriculum organization, implemented in Oregon as early as 1971.[16] Each cluster is based on job tasks, duties, and content common to related occupations, and the common tasks become the high school level curriculum for clusters such as trade, technical careers, and business careers. In Oregon, the cluster approach was set within a comprehensive career education framework where career specialization occurred at the postsecondary level. For special needs students, this approach offered a thorough background in career education and a foundation in particular clusters, but it had an undetermined impact on employment levels for the majority of handicapped and disadvantaged students who did not continue their education after high school. As a result, special vocational programs were developed primarily to meet specific job-training requirements.

The cluster method of developing common skills was a forerunner of the ''prep-tech'' and ''prep-human services'' courses developed during the 1980s.[17] Clusters form a basis for learning technical principles and concepts germane to specific career clusters while retaining the flexibility and adaptability needed to respond to changes in the workplace. Four steps are included in the process of developing a career cluster.

First, a meaningful task analysis must be completed that identifies requisite benchmark skills for each related course.

Second, the task analyses for each related curriculum must be compared to determine which skills overlap and which benchmark skills are shared. Curriculum mapping was developed by Fenwick English as a means of determining exactly what is taught in a curriculum and the amount of time spent teaching it.[18] This approach to curriculum analysis has been widely used in two principal ways: (1) to determine discrepancies between the official curriculum and the curriculum followed in the classroom and (2) to determine discrepancies among the staff who implement the curriculum. By placing the official curriculum on a grid and asking staff to indicate which components are taught and how much time is spent on those components, such discrepancies can be identified with little difficulty. Curriculum mapping can be applied to vocational departments to determine benchmark skills in the same way it has been applied to American history to determine the discrepancies noted above.

The third step in developing a clustered curriculum is to rearrange common curriculum elements in the emerging cluster curriculum and to determine whether the cluster is a practical investment of time and energy. For example, do equipment needs militate against clustering for the occupations in question? Does the specific course more appropriately stand alone as a separate but essential course? Will the cluster result in ''watered down'' curricula for fundamental areas that require lengthy and detailed training? All these questions need to be resolved.

Finally, the curriculum should be developed from the contributing courses, then field-tested, revised, and implemented.

A combination of the circular (or cyclical) method of curriculum design and the cluster approach is depicted in Figure 6-1. This model provides a means for modifying curricula to enable students to develop marketability in a wide array of career entry points without softening the curricula. Special needs students, as well as advanced students, gain a foundation in the principles of career clusters and acquire skills specific to existing or emerging jobs.

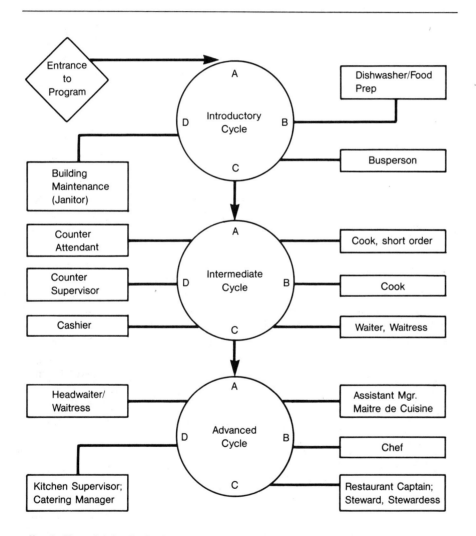

Key: A = Human Relations B = Food Preparation C = Customer Service D = Management

Figure 6-1 A Maximum-Employment Curriculum Model: Food Services

In a restaurant occupations cluster, foundation principles could be taught with specific entry level spinoffs available after completing each cycle. For students desiring to enter the workforce in the shortest time, occupation-specific entry level training would take place following the initial cycle of cluster skills training. For students desiring to maximize their educational training, entry into occupation-specific training would occur after the third or final cycle, or at the postsecondary level.

For vocational educators, this model has both advantages and serious disadvantages. It enables educators to modify a curriculum so that students with a much wider range of abilities can be served. Each cycle enables certain ability groups to spinoff into specific occupational training with a realistic chance of employment. Students with lower abilities and those with higher aptitudes are able to find their functioning level in the vocational program. Stigmas are removed and special needs students receive the same basic instruction as advanced students. Competency-based instruction has been widely used in vocational education, and it provides an effective method for vocational educators to accommodate a curriculum for a range of individual differences.[19] By applying the same strategies to the model in Figure 6-2, an even wider range of students can be served. Moreover, each cycle has a specific kind of occupational training as an outcome, and the framework builds upon benchmark skills that have application horizontally across the cluster as well as vertically within the course content. In this way, the model can respond in a limited way to unforeseen changes in the marketplace.

The primary disadvantage of a cyclical cluster approach is related to the investment of time and effort. It is a tedious, time-consuming process to conduct a quality task analysis for one course, let alone to develop cycles from benchmark skills across several courses and instructors. Where circular tours and career clusters have been developed separately, the process has been accomplished over several years, with considerable administrative and staff support. The practice of building competence in several units and then repeating the cycle at higher skill levels is gaining support in regular education curriculum development. Researchers have found that students acquire certain skills most successfully when the concept is introduced in the primary grades and expanded in successive years through the use of cyclical instruction with increasingly difficult operations.[20]

There is considerable research that suggests that for many special needs students, training should occur in the setting where the skill will ultimately be used.[21] A major change that broadened the concept of gainful employment and signaled a significant shift in services for disabled persons was the development of the concept of supported employment.

Supported employment is a reaction to the assumptions of the developmental model that once characterized sheltered workshops and, to a lesser degree, vocational rehabilitation services. Employment options were developed along a continuum from activity centers to competitive employment.[22] Workers were expected to acquire the necessary skills prior to advancement to the next, less restrictive level. This dichotomous arrangement, where an individual was either ''gainfully employable'' or ''not gainfully employable,'' served to perpetuate a system of segregated services and to inhibit access to educational opportunities and employment. Supported employment provided a method for developing an open-ended array of jobs that did

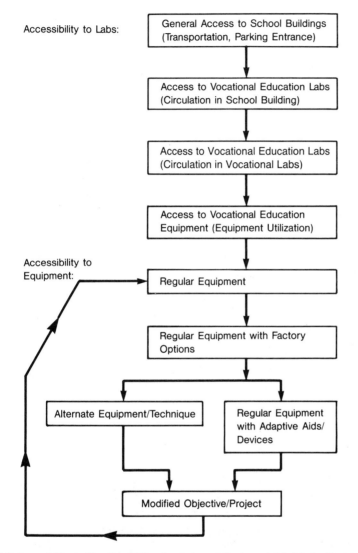

Figure 6-2 Accessibility to Vocational Education Labs and Equipment: Models for Decisionmaking. *Source:* Adapted from *Accessibility to Employment Training for the Physically Handicapped* by T.L. Erekson and A.F. Rotatori, p. 11, with permission of Charles C Thomas Publisher, © 1986.

not require a competitive performance level. It also provided the support services needed for workers to compete where they had been unable to do so previously. (Transportation, job coaches, training for co-workers, job analyses, and matching workers to jobs are just a few examples of support services.) As a result, a new job market has developed for special needs workers who were previously denied entry to paid, integrated employment.

Vocational educators will need to modify curricula to reflect the changes brought about by the introduction of supported employment. Jobs such as a copperplate engraver can be modified in the workplace to allow a special needs worker to perform as a copperplate engraver's helper, engraving prescribed numbers or types of plate but leaving the calibration of settings to someone else. A student may lack the decisionmaking skills to work independently as a janitor, buy may be able to empty the trash as part of a team effort. On a more sophisticated performance level, a special needs worker may be able to operate the tire changer in a large tire shop, but be unable to perform all the duties of the fully apprenticed worker, who does automotive diagnoses, wheel alignment, and invoice management. Virtually any job can be divided into components that can be performed efficiently by special needs learners, regardless of whether the special need is a language barrier, physical disability, or mental handicap. Furthermore, curriculum modifications that result in career entry units short of full apprenticeship or certification will be needed in the years ahead to meet the retraining needs of the nation. For special needs workers, these changes will provide a vehicle to enter the workforce and retain employment once they enter. Since being gainfully employable is no longer clearly defined, the job market and vocational education can no longer offer students single comprehensive performance options.

Advocacy training has been suggested as a content intervention that is achievable through curriculum infusion. It is based on the philosophy that the more aware students are of their own needs and the systems that exist to accommodate them, the greater their capacity to take action to satisfy those needs.[23] Suggested primarily for disabled workers, advocacy training can be helpful to other special needs populations, as well as to regular students.

The use of special instructional materials, review loops, additional practice, and allowance for reading or oral deficits during testing and student evaluation are sound practices when they do not result in curriculum softening and when marketability is enhanced. Many of these practices will be discussed in the sections on equipment modification and instructional practices.

The emphasis of this section has been on the modification of the vocational curriculum to provide units with potential career entry for each student. The use of circular tours and career clusters can facilitate this process if implemented carefully and with the end product of employment clearly in mind. Students with special needs do not need a separate curriculum, but the common curriculum must be flexible enough to reflect the demands of the marketplace. Vocational educators will need to have a thorough knowledge of the task analyses that constitute their curriculum and, most important, a willingness to compare job analysis data with the characteristics of a potential student with special needs. Finally, instructors should have an understanding of curriculum modification that allows them to make sound decisions regarding marketability and curriculum infusion while recognizing the dangers of curriculum softening.

MODIFICATION OF TOOLS AND EQUIPMENT

In vocational education, the adaptation of tools and equipment is integral to the instructional program. Bruelhide identifies six factors for planning, constructing, and testing equipment modifications: (1) safety of use, (2) simplicity, (3) availability of materials, (4) expense, (5) ease of construction, and (6) resultant restriction of tools and equipment for other students.[24] It is the author's contention that this list should be considered within the conceptual framework presented earlier in this chapter, with particular focus on the likelihood that the training will enhance each student's marketability. Bruelhide stresses this aspect when he notes, "Use of regular equipment where possible is very important because it is *regular* equipment that will be available in business and industry where the disabled student will be employed."[25] Figure 6-2 presents a model for decisionmaking that examines the physical ecology of facilities as well as equipment.

Kingsbury views the modification of tools and equipment as a process that allows the special needs learner accessibility and promotes the dignity of the student, while maintaining the integrity of the vocational program.[26] Despite the explosive growth in rehabilitation technology, the numerous ecological dimensions of the vocational laboratory and the workplace make the identification of all possible modifications a laborious task. Kingsbury developed a list of possible solutions to common problems that can also be applied to unexpected problems. The list is presented in Table 6-1. Many of the modifications suggested can be applied to curriculum content and instruction as well as to modification of tools and equipment.

A considerable volume of professional literature has focused on the unique learning needs of the disadvantaged worker, the displaced homemaker, the mature worker in need of retraining, the disabled worker, the limited English proficient (LEP) worker, and the dropout and potential dropout.[27] Much of it examines factors (e.g., student motivation, decisionmaking, counseling, and support services) that have been shown to impact learners favorably (particularly the potential dropout, displaced homemaker, and disadvantaged learner) but that fail to address the instructional process.

THE SPECIAL NEEDS OF TARGETED GROUPS

The field of limited English proficiency has been plagued by a longstanding debate between advocates of English as a second language (ESL) and advocates of bilingual education. The former approach borrows the resource model from special education, providing the support necessary for limited English proficient students to succeed in regular English-speaking classes. The latter approach attempts to help students learn English by teaching students partly in English and partly in the language spoken in their homes. Vocational education is confronted with an additional issue that arises regarding educational programs for limited English proficient students: limited time periods. For the adult who lacks functional skills in English, neither approach is satisfactory. The ESL approach implies the need to follow the developmental sequence in English instruction, while the bilingual approach requires dual instruction in basic subjects.

Lansing Community College developed a comprehensive "Intensive Technical English Language" program that allowed limited English proficient students to acquire the technical English needed in vocational programs in the shortest time.[28] Rather than adhere to a developmental language instruction program that prohibited entrance into vocational programs until after a prescribed level of English language was mastered, the college provided instruction in both areas simultaneously. The

Table 6-1 Example Problem-Solving Questions with Rehabilitation Technology Solutions

Questions	Possible Solutions
Is there a problem with:	
Access	Remove barriers, change doorknobs to levers.
Movement	Rearrange materials for freedom of movement, flexible table with lifts.
Safety	Eliminate danger, use jigs or fixtures to hold hot material in welding.
Mobility	Reposition job site, provide ramps to classroom lab or move class setting.
Difficult Procedure	Simplify approach, use a digital volt-ohm meter to measure electrical forces.
Judgment	Reduce the need, present measuring cups in lab activities.
Counting	Change procedures, use check sheets for tasks or visible samples in labs.
Measurement	Provide a standard, use colored lines on a precut board.
Reading Materials	Provide tape recording of materials, use devices such as voice emulators.
Strength	Provide a tool or assist, use of a hoist or holder.
Touch or Feeling	Texture surface, use sandpaper textures glued to switches and colored guides.
Vision	Improve lighting or develop orientation guides, use VCR equipment to magnify reading material.
Hearing	Develop alternative teaching methods, use visual models or examples to illustrate material.

Source: Reprinted from *Vocational Special Needs,* 2nd ed., by M.D. Sarkees and J.L. Scott (Eds.), p. 237, with permission of American Technical Publishers, © 1985.

"intensive" aspect of the language instruction was that only the language of the workplace was taught, using oral drill practice and putting an emphasis on reading comprehension. With this population, as with other special needs groups, research has not been done on whether particular instructional strategies are more appropriate than others for homogeneous groups.

Fortunately, a significant body of applied research in learning theory with disabled students has been conducted. Mentally retarded individuals learn in essentially the same manner as normal individuals. Gold and Scott report that "learning consists of an initial period of responding at chance followed by a sudden onset of learning, or a point where the child makes an insightful solution to the problem."[29] The retarded individual takes longer to attend to the relevant dimension than the normal individual, but once the individual attends to the relevant dimension, learning occurs at essentially the same rate as for a normal person. The implication for instruction is clear: For retarded students, instructional delivery must be structured to enable them to attend to the relevant dimension as quickly as possible. Additional trials will be necessary, as retarded students take longer to identify the solution.

Developing a set of learning needs for learning disabled students is a much more difficult task. Neurological dysfunction, an uneven growth pattern, a discrepancy between achievement and potential, sensory-motor impairment, perceptual-motor impairment, problems in short-term memory, and the absence of other handicapping conditions as the primary disability contribute to labeling someone as having a specific learning disability. To complicate things further, many students have difficulty in mathematics only, or in reading and function normally in all other subjects. MacMillan, Keogh, and Jones, in an exhaustive analysis of research on mildly handicapped learners, note the following:

> Taken as a whole, then, there is consistent evidence that both mildly retarded and LD children have deficient organizational skills (which may be interpreted as attention problems), but that they can be helped to use strategies to advantage. However, without external prompting they appear to employ inefficient organizational strategies, to rely on rote memory, or apparently to use no strategy at all.[30]

Students with disabilities need to increase their capacity for attending to the relevant dimensions of instruction. Prompts, additional practice, and clearly defined procedures enhance their ability to learn. The authors caution, however, that the bulk of special education research has not been concerned with teaching, but with the differences between handicapped and nonhandicapped learners.

An area that has received considerable attention across special needs groups is assessment and prescription for learning styles. Learning style is often associated with the overlap of individual differences in intellectual abilities and personality characteristics. While assessment of learning style or "learning preferences" can be a useful tool for modifying ecological aspects of a curriculum, its study has yet to yield definitive recommendations for delivery of instruction.

Research on dropouts and potential dropouts provides some data regarding the instructional process. Batsche surveyed 44 directors of exemplary programs representing over 25,000 students and found that clearly communicated performance standards and clearly defined learning outcomes were ranked as two of the most important program factors in dropout prevention.[31] The same study, however, re-emphasized the value placed on the affective domain by leaders in the field.

How can vocational educators prepare instructional formats to maximize their effectiveness with the array of special needs learners without sacrificing services to the majority of their students who do not qualify as members of a targeted group? What guidelines should determine the format for delivering instruction to special needs and regular students? The next section will address that issue by suggesting a three-pronged conceptual framework and by describing a specific special education approach to illustrate that framework.

A CONCEPTUAL FRAMEWORK FOR INSTRUCTIONAL PRACTICES

While modification of content, equipment, tools, and materials evolved considerably through the collective efforts of vocational educators, modification of instruction lagged behind.

If the expertise of vocational educators is the main ingredient affecting quality curriculum, then special educators hold the key to the development of quality instructional methods. This follows from the fact that disabled students face the entire spectrum of barriers to learning; hence the need for special instruction. Special education is in fact defined as specially designed instruction to meet the unique needs of a handicapped child.[32] However, MacMillan, Keogh, and Jones state that most special education research has been more concerned with cognitive and developmental psychology than with teaching. They note, ''The challenge before us is to study the instructional process directly, rather than to continue to be preoccupied with variables such as administrative arrangements and labels, influences that account for little variance in achievement differences.''[33] Vocational educators can no longer afford the luxury of unsystematic instruction that is driven by climate and curriculum alone. Programs that require reliance on additional personnel or individualized one-on-one instruction are impractical in the long run. The following suggests a framework for addressing these issues and an approach typifying the specially designed instruction that all students can benefit from.

Teaching with Examples

Special needs learners in vocational education have a limited amount of time to acquire a marketable skill or the prerequisites for postsecondary training. For this reason, an instructional format should be efficient and cost-effective in terms of time invested and skills acquired. Teaching with examples, as opposed to teaching by example, involves viewing the learning process as essentially a matter of attending to the relevant dimensions that distinguish one item or concept from another. This focus on discrimination between correct and incorrect items is most efficiently taught with several examples. Correct examples should be from as wide a range as possible, thus ruling out misinterpretations of what the relevant dimensions are. Incorrect examples are even more effective teaching tools, because when an item that is similar to the correct item is presented as incorrect, all the similarities are also ruled out as relevant dimensions. In this way concepts, definitions, rules, and sequences can be taught efficiently.

Vocational education lends itself to this approach, because so many curriculum areas have qualitative discriminations that must be mastered before the student can be considered competent. For example, a home economics or foods course will teach students how to bake and decorate a cake. Concepts such as consistency, smoothness, texture must be applied with considerable accuracy. The same is true for mechanics courses, which stress the need to be able to determine the right degree of tension or torque when applied to automotive parts. Machinists are concerned with tolerance levels, typists with proofreading. These critical skills cannot be taught efficiently by requiring students to define *smooth* or describe tolerances of one-hundredth of an inch. Students learn to identify these concepts when they have the opportunity to experience them through examples. Identification of one or two carefully chosen correct examples and one or two carefully chosen incorrect examples can rapidly teach students the accepted range. For instance, in a home economics lesson on fabrics and color, what better way to teach the differences among the myriad shades of blue than to use examples?

Consistency of instruction is the developing of specific instructional strategies that are applied uniformly with all students. It does not entail that presentations should be rote and uninteresting, but that they should be introduced in a consistent manner to indicate to students when to attend, what to attend to, and how to respond. If the instructional strategy is sound, special needs students will be able to learn and advance through the program with regular students.

Consistency of Instruction

Competency-based instruction, which allows students to proceed at their own pace, will make it impossible to introduce material that is new to all students simultaneously. However, review for one group can be the introduction of new material for another. Consistency of instruction also means the effective teacher will instruct in an interactive mode during each class period. The instructor needs a cost-effective method that allows for instruction with the largest group possible. Zahorik suggests for regular educators that "a limited but realistic repertoire of teaching methods will result in better teaching than a multitude of inappropriate ones."[34]

Consistency of instruction is necessary because vocational education involves laboratory work requiring the assistance, observation, and tutoring of individual students. To expect vocational or academic instructors to maintain program integrity while providing individually designed programs to a growing and diverse special needs population is absurd unless that instruction can be provided simultaneously to special needs, regular, and advanced students. A concise teaching strategy applied uniformly will allow students at various points in the curriculum to benefit from periodic instruction in large groups. This does not mean forsaking the special needs learner. What it does mean is that instruction should be presented so the special needs learner understands the concepts and skills clearly as he or she proceeds through the course of study. If the student with special needs can grasp the material presented, the vast majority of regular students will be able to as well.

The instructional format needs to provide multiple opportunities for students to respond including by verbally and physically performing tasks that can be immediately critiqued by the instructor. It does not require an extensive written data system. Rather, the instructional format should guarantee the instructor that there will be multiple responses from the students. One response per student per minute is not unreasonable. This interaction provides students with a constant flow of qualitative information that enables them to make ongoing evaluation of their skills as they are developed, while providing feedback to the instructor regarding the effectiveness of the delivery. Quality instruction does not require additional staff, because the power of a systematic interactive teaching method like direct instruction provides a mechanism for vocational instructors to teach more in less time.

Interactive Teaching

This conceptual framework should remind the educational community that instructors need to develop strategies that meet the needs of all their students and they should not surrender responsibility for the instructional process to paraprofessionals or to the peers of the vocational students. Vocational instructors should solicit assistance regarding instructional technique from special services personnel rather than tutoring services for individual students.

The framework presented here for modification of instruction is similar to that advocated by regular and special educators and supported by research on effective schools.[35] The specialized instructional techniques are as necessary for disadvantaged, limited English proficient, incarcerated, and gifted students as they are for disabled and regular students, and a wide range of strategies that meet these criteria have been successfully implemented across handicapped and nonhandicapped populations since the passage of Public Law 94-142.[36] The following section will focus on one empirically validated and widespread instructional program that holds considerable promise for vocational educators: direct instruction.

DIRECT INSTRUCTION

Direct instruction is a generic term, but it also refers to a discrete educational program developed in the 1960s by Siegfried Engelmann.[37] In the latter sense, *direct instruction* refers to a complex systematic approach to instruction that can have a considerable impact on curriculum content (design) and on instruction (delivery) as it has been defined here. Direct instruction has been chosen for this discussion because the underlying structure is built on the following rule: "Teach more in less time."[38] This focus on utility is salient to any discussion about the need for vocational educators to modify their instruction.

Engelmann lays the foundation for his theory with the statement, "A theory of instruction begins with the assumption that the environment is the primary variable in accounting for what the learner learns."[39] To enable teachers to teach more in less time, direct instruction provides a set of delivery skills built upon the following assumptions:

- All learners possess the capacity to learn any quality from examples within the limitations of sensory receiving mechanisms.
- All learners generalize learning on the basis of the sameness of the quality learned from examples.
- It is possible to design the delivery of instruction to communicate faultlessly one interpretation.

By manipulating the presentation of concepts and items, direct instruction assumes that anything can be taught to anyone. The only limitations reside in the acuity of the learner's sensory input systems (hearing, vision, taste, smell, and touch). While this discussion will draw heavily on the theoretical basis of direct instruction, the following U.S. Department of Education statement about direct instruction should also be kept in mind: "When teachers explain exactly what students are expected to learn, and demonstrate the steps needed to accomplish a particular academic task, students learn more.''[40]

A model for modifying curricula was presented earlier in this chapter. The following two sections identify nine principles of direct instruction and articulate them within a framework of three response paradigms.

The following principles are suggested here as critical to a successful instructional program for all students, including those with special needs:

Principles of Direct Instruction

- Teach one thing at a time.
- Provide students with multiple opportunities to respond to each lesson.
- Reinforce students for correct responses throughout the lesson.
- Correct errors immediately by reteaching through one of the three response paradigms (see next section).
- Review each lesson at the beginning, middle, and end.
- Keep the pace of interaction quick and ''rhythmic.''
- Signal clearly (let students know when lessons begin and when they are expected to respond).
- Give students opportunities to respond verbally and physically.
- Keep the process interactive.

It should be noted that these nine principles apply to the actual teaching or presentation of new material and previous material for review or mastery. They are not considered essential for practice or independent skill development (e.g., working on a lathe following instruction). However, direct instruction should occur several times each class meeting, and practice without it is hard to distinguish from tutoring. Teachers are certified to distinguish them from tutors, and they have an obligation as professionals to provide ''teaching'' frequently.

Teaching one thing at a time is recommended as the best practice for ensuring that there are no misinterpretations of the teacher's delivery. It does not require that the presentation should be so simple as to lose the advanced students. Rather, it requires focusing the instruction on what the teacher wants to convey and delivering instruction through examples that convey the concept or skill.

For a teacher to provide multiple response opportunities, the lesson will have to include several junctures where feedback is encouraged and solicited. Direct instruction materials recommend as many as 10–15 responses per minute.

Reinforcement of correct responses should provide more than ''warm fuzzies.'' When a teacher indicates the correctness of a response, all students benefit by recognizing what a correct response looks like. The correct response provides one more example of correctness and provides feedback to all students on what is not correct as well.

Corrections need to be timed as close to the occurrence of the errors as possible. If too much time lapses, the learner will consider an error a correct response or unimportant. This may lead to distortions in any subsequent instruction. The direct instruction model assumes that errors result from two causes: inattentiveness and lack of knowledge. To distinguish the two, the teacher should observe where the student is looking and what the student is doing prior to the cue presentation. Looking away or interfering behavior prior to the cue shows obvious inattentiveness. The teacher should respond by praising an attentive student. If the inattentive student at some point returns to the task, the teacher should provide praise at that time. If errors are caused by a lack of knowledge, the teacher should examine the pace and signal used in the delivery and consider using the teaching paradigms discussed in the next section. What might have given the wrong interpretation to the teaching sequence? A good rule of thumb is to expect Murphy's Law to operate at all times (Whatever can go wrong, will go wrong!) and to plan the delivery with concise directions and examples that communicate one and only one interpretation to the learners.

Reviewing continually allows the teacher an opportunity to "firm" the skills previously presented and at the same time enables the student to demonstrate the strength of the skill when it is separated from the immediate teaching interaction. This procedure will build not only skills taught previously, but the current lesson's skills as well.

Pacing should be tailored to the age and maturity level of the students. Obviously, teaching adults with a rhythmic presentation and canned signals and praise will be fruitless. At the same time, teaching adults with a monotone, disinterested approach will be equally disastrous. Pacing also includes the organization of materials and the instructor's preparation. These time-consuming elements of quality instruction communicate to students a teacher's interest in them, the value the teacher places on each student's time and energy, and the value the teacher places on the content and the course.

Signals are cues given by the teacher that tell students when to respond, including when to listen and when to make a verbal or physical response in unison. Without clear signals, only the verbal and higher-performing students will respond. As a result, the instructor will be unable to judge how effective the instruction has been and whether the delivery communicated a correct or an incorrect interpretation. Lower performers learn to copy the responses or stop responding altogether. By having to respond in unison, all students respond and "more is taught in less time."

Each signal should have three parts. First, the teacher gives directions. Second, the teacher provides a thinking pause. Last, the teacher cues the reponse, effectively indicating "Respond now." The cue is usually a physical one, but can be accompanied by certain words. Physical cues include the use of a hand clap, finger snap, or drop of the hand, as well as pointing at or touching a specified item. Verbal cues include introductory statements such as "Your turn," "Watch me," "Say it!" "Listen," or "Tell me." It is critical for any cue that all students understand when to respond, and an effort needs to be made to tailor the cues to the age and maturity level of the students. Adult learners, for example, may not appreciate the cue "Say it!" but by explaining the value of periodic responses in unison, the vocational educator should be able to develop discrete cues that are appropriate for all levels of instruction.

Vocational education lends itself to a wide variety of educational experiences, not the least of which is hands-on performance of practical skills related to the "real world." Direct instruction has been associated primarily with academic instruction, but each of the nine principles can be applied to hands-on curricula across the vocational education spectrum (both in the laboratory and in the classroom).

The teaching process must be interactive in order to count as direct instruction. Interactiveness is the cornerstone of the modification of instruction for special needs learners. Failure to recognize and remediate deficits when they occur leads to distorted understanding of course content. Frequent ongoing interaction provides the teacher with feedback, keeps the learners on task, and provides a dynamic to teaching that is essential if students are to reach their potential.

Instructional Response Paradigms

This section suggests that instructors divide skills into three types—rules, comparisons, and sequences—and design their instructional format around the type of skill that needs to be learned. Table 6-2 presents the three response paradigms.

The rule paradigm is used whenever the skill requires that the learner memorize it. This may mean being able to conceptualize the effects of analog noise on linear digital systems in an electronics curriculum or simply to learn the correct procedure for dusting in a building maintenance program. In both cases, processes need to be mastered and committed to memory; hence the response paradigm for "rules."

Typically, the teaching cycle incorporated in the rule paradigm or any other should take no more than two minutes, including reteaching and correcting errors. Obviously, direct instruction lends itself to considerable independent practice, which is consistent with the logistics of vocational education curricula. Using the example of learning to dust, Table 6-3 illustrates the teaching interaction following the rule paradigm.

The advantage of direct instruction in vocational education is that it provides many opportunities to enhance an interaction, such as pauses, hands-on practice, and verbal presentation of the interaction by the teacher while demonstrating it physically. Direct instruction also lends itself to considerable creativity in building the student's response level. In this case, the instructor can mix and match verbal and performance questioning, leading by demonstrating the initial dusting step and refining the student's ability to discriminate between correct and incorrect dusting by dusting, for example, below knee height (or by violating other rules for dusting to review previous lessons). This provides the student the opportunity to provide feedback to indicate the current skill level and at the same time avoids rote learning. Notice that only one skill is taught at a time.

The second paradigm (comparison) presented in Table 6-2 is for those tasks that require either a definition or comparison. For the most part, items that require comparison to define a quality should be taught with this paradigm, such as tolerance levels, measurement gradations, and tool identification. However, rather than clutter

Table 6-2 A Set of Direct Instruction Response Paradigms

		Paradigm		
Presentation		*Rule*	*Comparison*	*Sequence*
Type	*Description*			
Model:	Instructor demonstrates (models) the task or states the concept.	X	X	X
Lead:	Instructor and learners perform task together while repeating concept.	X		
Test:	Instructor asks students to perform task independently.	X		
Alternating Test:	Instructor juxtaposes examples in such a way as to require students to attend to relevant features of item. Instructor presents vastly different examples of correct possibilities and incorrect items that are minimally different from correct item. This rules out features that may lead to misinterpretation of meaning.		X	
Delayed Test:	A test of the item presented later in the lesson, providing opportunity to separate skill from cycle and require students to perform skill out of context.		X	
Guided Practice:	Students participate in performing sequence while instructor provides minimal verbal and/or physical support required for students to perform skill in fluid timely fashion.			X
Solo Practice:	Students perform sequence unassisted, while instructor provides immediate feedback following task.			X

the student's thinking with lengthy definitions, the paradigm allows the instructor to teach this kind of task in the most efficient and effective manner, presenting only the clues the learner can use.

The comparison paradigm requires that the students be tested on a wide range of correct items and with minimally different incorrect items. The more similar the incorrect items, the stronger the instruction will be. Students need to attend to the single dimension that possesses the quality of "correctness." The instructor should

Table 6-3 An Example of a Teaching Interaction for a Rules Instruction Paradigm

	Teacher Statement	Student Response
Model:	"Watch closely. Dust and clean all flat surfaces between knee height and your overhead reach every day."	Student observes.
Lead:	"Say it with me this time. Dust and . . . . clean all. . . . . flat surfaces between . . . . knee height and . . . . overhead reach every. . . . . day!"	
Test:	"Your turn. Show me what should be dusted everyday."	Student demonstrates.

present this mix of correct and incorrect items until the student identifies accurately the relevant dimension, whether it is the degree of torque required in diesel mechanics, the accepted tolerance range for a machinist, or which consent form is required by a medical records clerk. A minimum of ten examples should teach the meaning in less than one minute. Later in the lesson, the teacher should complete the comparison paradigm with a delayed test, providing an additional indicator of the strength of the learning that has occurred.

The third paradigm (sequence) presented in Table 6-2 is for those tasks that cannot be taught in isolation. This is very similar to the rules paradigm, where first the skill is modeled and then the teacher leads the student and finally tests the student unassisted. A rule is a discrete concept that stands by itself, while a sequence is a related set of skills, procedures, or concepts that have little meaning or instructional value in isolation. For that reason, a sequence is taught from beginning to end, with guided practice during the sequence to be introduced only when needed. Again, vocational education laboratory settings lend themselves to this third paradigm.

These detailed instructional techniques require considerable inservice time and extensive skill in data collection and analysis for implementation. Also, the implementation of any interactive instructional format will require substantive administrative support.

PROGRAM GUIDELINES

The first guideline for program development pertains to input into the decisionmaking process. It is unacceptable for a single professional to make decisions regarding entrance into or exclusion from vocational education for special needs learners. Because placement is a collaborative issue that affects the sending instructor, counselors, vocational instructor, and administration, some sort of screening process should be instituted that provides for input from all concerned. One danger of institutionalizing such an approach for special needs learners while proceeding with "business as usual" for students without identified special needs is the possibility of denying access merely by instituting additional barriers to placement. Administrative issues surface here and the critical role school administrators play in facilitating quality services for all students is clear. A solution to this problem of screening could be found by simply instituting in the counseling office a screening process for *all* students. A team approach is essential for quality programming. Special needs learners need an individualized program plan much more than individualized, one-to-one instruction.

The second guideline for educators involved in the development of programs for special needs learners is to design them with a long-range vocational goal in mind (at least five years in the future). For special education students, the individual education plan (IEP) is required to provide services in the least restrictive environment. A more appropriate instrument for maximizing a student's access to the larger society might be the ''least restrictive employment.''[41] This concept has been defined to mean paid, integrated employment with maximum opportunity for job security, career advancement, and personal satisfaction. Modification of the IEP team process to examine long-range adult outcomes prior to designing a program is relatively simple, and such examination can be applied with all special needs students through the team process advocated earlier.

The third guideline is inherent in the Carl D. Perkins Act, which requires a comprehensive assessment of the interests, aptitudes, abilities, and special needs of handicapped and disadvantaged students who enroll in vocational education. Vocational assessment must address those skills that are going to be necessary in the workplace of the future rather than rely on norm-referenced work samples that reflect the workplace of today's industrial society, which even now is becoming more information oriented. Assessments must address the long-range prospects for students, provide optimum communication among decisionmakers, and still identify strengths and skill deficits for each student.

The fourth guideline is that a range of vocational programs need to be developed that can provide a dynamic to the course offerings and allow each student to develop specific marketable skills. This applies to work experiences obtained through cooperative education and to the classroom and laboratory experiences typically associated with vocational education. Least restrictive employment can guide the selection and monitoring of these options.

The final guideline for program development combines aspects of the conceptual frameworks delineated earlier in this chapter. Vocational programs for special needs learners need to prepare students for gainful employment as defined in the Carl D. Perkins Act and concurrently to provide the specially designed instruction as defined by the Education for All Handicapped Children Act. In short, the definitions of vocational and special education should be used as barometers of program adequacy for any placements in vocational programs.

These five guidelines fit neatly with the concepts of marketability, reciprocal curriculum infusion, and curriculum softening. In addition, they are congruent with teaching with examples, interactive teaching, and consistency of instruction.

IMPLICATIONS FOR ADMINIS-TRATORS

Throughout this chapter, references have been made to the role of the school administrator in modifying curriculum and instruction for special needs learners. It should be clear to the reader that for the educational community to move beyond cosmetic "equity" to substantive skill development, a serious shift in delivery systems will be required. Unfortunately, the legal mandates of the Education for All Handicapped Children Act were not replicated in subsequent federal reauthorizations of vocational rehabilitation, special education, or vocational education. At best, local administrators must choose between accepting money for program innovation and suffering the consequences of refusing it.

Vocational special needs education requires greater administrative input than traditional areas of education, because access requires collaboration. Curriculum modification requires input from multiple sources and necessitates administrative approval. In addition, many of the decisions affecting special needs students are procedural in nature, again requiring administrative direction. Each of the five guidelines described in the previous section addresses administrative concerns that cannot always be delegated to others.

Modification of instructional practices at the building level can also be influenced greatly by the school administrator responsible for teacher evaluation. Emphasis on improved instruction as opposed to accountability can facilitate positive change quickly. For these reasons, the school administrator plays a pivotal role in any special needs program.

What reasons are there for local school administrators to invest time and energy in significant curriculum modification and the implementation of highly specific instructional programs? Perhaps the most convincing reason is that such investment is in the best interest of the school system, the teachers, the community, and, certainly, the entire student body. A vocational program that provides students with occupational competencies that result in employment—employment that corresponds to the widest range of student abilities and interests—fulfills a very important public education mission.

A second reason for proceeding with significant curriculum modification and putting a renewed emphasis on instructional improvement is that the long-term benefits include enabling local education agencies to accomplish their mission in a cost-effective manner. A shop teacher who uses a competency-based curriculum with several occupational entry points and uses as well a concise interactive teaching method can accommodate many more students than a shop teacher who teaches using an inefficient curriculum and requires additional staff to accommodate special needs students who would otherwise fail. Failure to utilize a conceptual framework for determining entrance into vocational programs may result in the presence of special needs students in programs they do not belong in. The traditional approaches that have characterized our schools require students to complete a full term, even if the instructional units that realistically are of benefit may be completed in four to five weeks. An effective program will enable students to exit prior to the term's end, allowing a second special needs student to enter.

Dollars and cents inevitably play a role in efforts to improve instruction or modify the curriculum. Despite budgetary restraints at all levels, the federal commitment to education continues in the form of "seed" money for innovation, program improvement, and model programs. Several federal sources, most notably the Carl D. Perkins Act, focus the bulk of their resources on meeting the special needs of our citizens through employment and training.[42] Administrative commitment to the concept of educational equity and excellence in our schools is demonstrated in a willingness to secure the resources necessary to improve instruction for all students.

Curriculum development will need to go beyond submitting district level mastery-learning charts to school boards. Administrators will need to take the lead in developing incentives that encourage vocational, alternative, and special educators to examine their curricula, combine their relative expertise, and develop quality, employment-related curricula. It is not enough to be satisfied with increased enrollments or even happy students. The effective administrator will look for results in terms of adult outcomes.

SUMMARY

This chapter examined the historical tendency in the educational community to focus more on providing access than on providing growth in functional skills for special needs students. A conceptual framework was then developed for selecting vocational programs on the basis of three components: marketability, curriculum softening, and reciprocal curriculum infusion. Marketability concerns both the future job market for a particular set of skills and a student's aptitude for competing for those future jobs. Curriculum softening was described as the tendency among educators to provide access for special needs students by reducing program requirements, a useful concept for pinpointing what should be avoided. Reciprocal curriculum infusion concerns an often overlooked need: the need to modify the sending environment as well as the receiving environment in order to enhance each student's potential for succeeding.

The next section discussed the importance of task analysis, ecological curricula, cycles of training, clusters, and maintenance of specific occupational training as the foundation for vocational education. Instructors who develop expertise in any of these areas will be better equipped to serve special needs learners. Modification of equipment and tools was then discussed, and examples of decisionmaking processes for modifying equipment, facilities, and the environment to meet specific special needs were provided. The failure of researchers to identify differences in actual learning for specific special needs groups was mentioned, and a framework for modifying instruction was described.

Teaching with examples, consistency of instruction, and interactive teaching were presented as critical factors for effective instructional delivery. Teachers who incorporate these principles into their instructional program will be apt to serve a wider range of students than teachers who do not. Direct instruction was then described in terms of nine instructional principles and three presentation paradigms designed for varying task structures. Teamwork, long-range planning, meaningful vocational assessment, a range of vocational program options, and the integration of vocational education and special education were described as guidelines for program development. If applied systematically, these guidelines will help address the systemic elements within the public schools that need to be modified if special needs education is to be both realistic and effective. The discussion then shifted to implications for school administrators. The administrator was viewed as the key individual for affecting changes in either curricula or instruction. This is because the administrator has the capacity to set the tone, establish the process, and guide staff in making meaningful decisions regarding vocational special needs education.

When the transition initiative was launched, Assistant Secretary of Education Madeleine Will noted, "Approximately 8 percent of the gross national product is spent each year in disability programs, with most of this amount going to programs that support dependence."[43] Dropout rates for disadvantaged youth are still much higher than for other socioeconomic groups, and a shrinking labor pool will need to be supplemented by workers currently segregated from society in order to fill an increasing demand for entry level employment into the twenty-first century.[44] It is indeed in the best interests of all public schools and all school administrators to address these issues head on and to support the transition from the cosmetic equity of school access to the substantive equity of access to real employment and postsecondary training opportunities.

For the vocational special educator, the challenge of modifying curricula and instruction is enormous, and it will not be accomplished overnight with any quick fix methods, or even with single instructional formats such as the direct instruction model described here. It should be an ongoing process and will require collaboration that examines, sometimes painfully, those areas of education that have been loosely coupled together in our public schools. The principles of teacher autonomy within the classroom and the absolute discretion in how a curriculum is presented will need to be modified in favor of improved instruction to students. We should not pat outselves on the back for mainstreaming special education students or maintaining potential dropouts in secondary school if the end result is chronic unemployment and disappointment. Equity for special needs students will be realized when curricula are modified to allow the widest number of students entrance into skill-building curriculum units linked with the workplace and when instruction is provided systematically by all teachers.

NOTES

1. G. Thomas Bellamy and Barbara Wilcox, "Secondary Education for Severely Handicapped Students: Guidelines for Quality Services," in *Critical Issues in the Education of Autistic Children and Youth*, ed. B. Wilcox and A. Thompson (Washington, D.C.: Department of Education, Office of Special Education, 1981, Mimeographed), 1.

2. National Commission on Excellence, *A Nation at Risk: The Imperative for Educational Reform* (Washington, D.C.: Author, 1983),4; William A. Firestone and Robert E. Herriott, "Effective Schools: Do Elementary Prescriptions Fit Secondary Schools?" (Philadelphia, Pa.: Research for Better Schools, June 1982), 4; Marvin Cetron, *Schools of the Future* (New York: McGraw-Hill, 1985), 156.

3. Robert J. Krajewski, John S. Martin, and John C. Walden, *The Elementary School Principalship: Leadership for the 1980s* (New York: Holt, Rinehart, and Winston, 1983), 105–6.

4. Bruce Joyce and Marsha Weil, *Models of Teaching* (Englewood Cliffs, N.J.: Prentice-Hall, 1972), 319.

5. Public Law 98-524 (Carl D. Perkins Vocational Education Act of 1984), sec. 521, (31).

6. Ibid., sec. 204 (c)(1).

7. David C. Gardner and Sue Allen Warren, *Careers and Disabilities: A Career Education Approach* (Stamford, Conn.: Greylock Publishers, 1978) 115; Rupert N. Evans, Kenneth B. Hoyt, and Garth L. Mangum, *Career Education in the Middle/Junior High School* (Salt Lake City, Utah: Olympus Publishing Company, 1973), 16–17; Washington State Commission for Vocational Education, *Options for Equivalent*

Credit in the High School Curriculum: A Guide for Local Decision Making (Olympia, Wash.: Author, 1986), 19.

8. Carl D. Perkins Act, sec. 2; John Naisbitt, *Megatrends* (New York: Warner Books, 1982), 6; Marvin Cetron, *Schools of the Future*, 19; Arthur L. Costa, "The Need to Teach Students to Think," in *Developing Minds: A Resource Book of Teaching Thinking,* ed. Arthur L. Costa (Alexandria, Va.: Association for Supervision and Curriculum Development, 1985), 1.

9. Marc W. Gold and Keith G. Scott, "Discrimination Learning," in *Training the Developmentally Young*, ed. Beth Stephens. (New York: The John Day Co., 1971), 425.

10. Siegfried Engelmann and Douglas Carnine, *Theory of Instruction: Principles and Applications* (New York: Irvington Publishers, 1982), 4; G. Thomas Bellamy et al., *Community Programs for Severely Handicapped Adults: An Analysis of Vocational Opportunities* (Eugene, Ore.: University of Oregon, 1980), 2; Norris G. Haring and Richard L. Schiefelbusch, *Teaching Special Children* (New York: McGraw-Hill, 1976), 382.

11. Janis Chadsey-Rusch, "The Ecology of the Workplace," in *School-to-Work Transition Issues and Models* (Champaign, Ill.: Transition Institute, 1986), 61–68; Terry G. Cronis, Charles Forgnone, and Garnett J. Smith, "Mild Mental Retardation: Implications for an Ecological Curriculum," *Journal of Research and Development in Education* 10, no. 3 (Spring 1986): 72–75.

12. Joy Donaldson, "Changing Attitudes Toward Handicapped Persons: A Review and Analysis of Research," *Exceptional Children* 46, no. 7 (April 1980): 507.

13. Charles L. Salzberg et al., "Social Competence and Employment of Retarded Persons" (Logan, Utah: Utah State University, 1986, Mimeographed), 2, 6, 9, 38; Benjamin Lignugaris/Kraft et al., "Social Interpersonal Skills of Handicapped and Nonhandicapped Adults at Work," *Journal of Employment Counseling* 23, no. 1 (March 1986): 20–30; Cheryl Hanley-Maxwell et al., "Reported Factors Contributing to Job Terminations of Individuals with Severe Disabilities," *Journal of the Association for Persons with Severe Handicaps* 11, no. 1 (1986): 45–52.

14. Mike Fitzpatrick, "Machine Trades Curriculum" (Everett, Wash.: Sno-Isle Vocational Skills Center, 1986, Mimeographed), 1.

15. Jay McTighe and Jan Schollenberger, "Why Teach Thinking: A Statement of Rationale," in *Developing Minds: A Resource Book of Teaching Thinking*, 3.

16. Monty Multanen, "Vocational Education for a Productive Society: The New Oregon Model" (Salem, Ore.: Oregon Department of Education, 1986, Working Draft), III-1.

17. Ibid, III-2; *Principles of Technology* (Bloomington, Ind.: The Agency for Instructional Technology, 1986, Brochure).

18. Fenwick English, "Curriculum Mapping," *Educational Leadership* 37 (April 1980): 558–59.

19. State Board of Vocational Education, *Competency-Based Vocational Education in North Dakota* (Grand Forks, N. Dak.: Author, 1983), 4–7.

20. Thomas A. Romberg and Thomas P. Carpenter, "Research on Teaching and Learning Mathematics: Two Disciplines of Scientific Inquiry," in *Handbook of Research on Teaching*, 3rd ed., ed. Merlin C. Wittrock (New York: Macmillan, 1986), 85; Robert Calfee and Priscilla Drum, "Research on Teaching Reading," in *Handbook of Research on Teaching*, 829; E. Fennema, "The Relative Effectiveness of a Symbolic and a Concrete Model in Learning a Selected Mathematical Principle," *Journal for Research in Mathematics Education* 3 (1972): 236–37.

21. G. Thomas Bellamy et al., *Community Programs for Severely Handicapped Adults: An Analysis of Vocational Opportunities* (Eugene, Ore.: Center on Human Development, 1980), 2, 11, 17–19; Sherril Moon et al., *The Supported Work Model of Competitive Employment for Citizens with Severe Handicaps: A Guide for Job Trainers* (Richmond, Va.: Virginia Commonwealth University, 1986), iv.

22. G. Thomas Bellamy et al., *Mental Retardation Services in Sheltered Workshops and Day Activity Programs: Consumer Outcomes and Policy Alternatives* (Eugene, Ore.: Center on Human Development, 1982), 11–12.

23. Jane Razheigi and E. Jewell Ginyard, *Total Career Development and Independent Living Skills for Handicapped Students* (Washington, D.C.: American Coalition of Citizens with Disabilities, 1984), 1–2.

24. Kenneth L. Bruelhide, *Special-Needs Education Material for Vocational and Industrial Education: A Bibliography* (Bozeman, Mont.: Montana State University, 1986), 1–61.

25. Kenneth Bruelhide, *Special Needs Education Material for Vocational and Industrial Education: A Planning Guide for Vocational Area Teachers* (Bozeman, Mont.: Montana State University, 1986), III-6.

26. David Kingsbury, "The Use of Rehabilitation Technology for the Redesign of Tools and Equipment," in *Vocational Special Needs: Preparing T & I Teachers*, ed. M.D. Sarkees and John L. Scott (Alsip, Ill.: American Technical Publishers, 1985), 237.

27. James M. Weber, "Vocational Education and Its Role in Dropout Reduction," *Facts and Findings* 4, no. 2 (Spring 1986): 4–6; Lily Wong Filmore and Concepcion Valadez, "Teaching Bilingual Learners," in *Handbook of Research on Teaching*, 675; E. Paul Torrance, "Teaching Creative and Gifted Learners," in *Handbook of Research on Teaching*, 633.

28. Center for Student Support, "The Tempo Project" (Lansing, Mich.: Lansing Community College, 1983, Mimeographed).

29. Marc Gold and Keith Scott, "Discrimination Learning," in *Training the Developmentally Young*, 425.

30. Donald L. MacMillan, Barbara K. Keogh, and Reginald L. Jones, "Special Education Research on Mildly Handicapped Learners," in *Handbook of Research on Teaching*, 698.

31. Katherine Batsche, "Indicators of Effective Programming: Examining the School to Work Transition for Dropouts," *Journal for Vocational Special Needs Education* 7, no. 3 (Spring 1985): 27–30.

32. Public Law 94–142 (The Education for All Handicapped Children Act).

33. MacMillan, Keogh, and Jones "Special Education Research on Mildly Handicapped Learners," 717.

34. John A. Zahorik, "Let's Be Realistic about Flexibility in Teaching," *Educational Leadership* 44, no. 2 (October 1986): 50–51.

35. Engelmann and Carnine, *Theory of Instruction, 17;* Cetron, *Schools of the Future*, 17; William G. Huitt and John K. Segars, *Characteristics of Effective Classrooms* (Philadelphia, Pa.: Research for Better Schools, 1980), 19–22.

36. Madeline Hunter, *Reinforcement Theory for Teachers* (El Segundo, Calif.: TIP Publications, 1967), 1–2; Francis P. Hunkins, *Questioning Strategies and Techniques* (Boston: Allyn & Bacon, 1972), 11–20; Robert M. Smith, "Designing an Instructional Environment: Strategies for Teaching," in *Clinical Teaching: Methods of Instruction for the Retarded*, 2d ed., ed. Robert M. Smith (New York: McGraw-Hill, 1974), 93–102; M. Eaton et al. "Precision Teaching: Extending the Boundaries," *Journal of Precision Teaching* 4, no. 3 (1983): 53–67.

37. Wesley Becker, "Direct Instruction: A Twenty Year Review" (Paper presented at the XVI Annual Banff International Conference on Behavioral Science, March, 1983), 1; Engelmann and Carnine, *Theory of Instruction*, 4; Huitt and Segars, *Characteristics of Effective Classrooms*, 15–16.

38. Becker, "Direct Instruction: A Twenty Year Review," 1.

39. Engelmann and Carnine, *Theory of Instruction*, 4.

40. United States Department of Education, *What Works: Research about Teaching and Learning* (Washington, D.C.: Author, 1986), 35.

41. Stephen White, "Least Restrictive Employment: The Challenge to Special Education." *Career Development for Exceptional Individuals* 10, no. 1 (Spring 1987).

42. The Carl D. Perkins Act; The Job Training Partnership Act of 1981; The Amendments to the Education for All Handicapped Children Act (Public Law 98-199); The Vocational Rehabilitation Reauthorization Act of 1986; The Social Security Act of 1980, sec. 1619A, 1619B.

43. Madeleine Will, *OSERS Programming for the Transition of Youth with Disabilities: Bridges from School to Working Life* (Washington, D.C.: Office of Special Education and Rehabilitation Services, 1984), 1.

44. Tom Mirga, "At-Risk Youth Seen Posing Costly Threat to Nation," *Education Week* 5, no. 10 (November 6, 1985): 5; Lynn Olson, "'Shocking' Waste of Youths Cited in Study of Hispanics' Schooling," *Education Week* 4, no. 15 (December 12, 1984): 17; National Commission on Excellence, *A*

Nation at Risk, 8–9; Tom Mirga, "Reform Has Ignored 'At-Risk' Students, Inquiry by Advocacy Group Concludes," *Education Week* 4, no. 19 (January 30, 1985): 10; Cetron, *Schools of the Future,* 6–7, 13–14, 17, 89.

REFERENCES

Carlson, Richard O, Art Gallaher, Jr., Matthew B. Miles, Roland J. Pellegrin, and Everett M. Rogers. *Change Processes in the Public Schools.* Eugene, Ore.: Center for the Advanced Study of Educational Administration, 1965. pp. 11–34.

Creighton, Cynthia. "A Common Sense Guide to Reasonable Accommodation." *VocEd Journal of the American Vocational Association* 56, no. 3 (April 1981):55–58.

Gill, Douglas H, David E. Cupp, and Duane E. Lindquist. "A Consortium of Vocational Education and Special Education." *The Journal for Vocational Special Needs Education* 8, no. 2 (Winter 1986): 25–27.

Gold, Marc W. *Try Another Way Training Manual.* Champaign, Ill.: Research Press, 1980.

Hill, Janet W., et al. "Demographic Analyses Related to Successful Job Retention for Competitively Employed Persons Who Are Mentally Retarded." Richmond, Va.: Virginia Commonwealth University, 1985. Mimeographed.

The National Commission on Secondary Vocational Education. "The Unfinished Agenda: The Role of Vocational Education in the High School." Columbus, Ohio: Author, 1984. pp. 23–26.

Parent, Wendy S., and Jane M. Everson. "Competencies of Disabled Workers in Industry: A Review of Business Literature." Richmond, Va.: Virginia Commonwealth University, 1985. Mimeographed.

Rusch, Frank R., Jeff McNair, and Lizanne Stefano. *School-to-Work Research Needs.* Champaign, Ill.: Transition Institute at Illinois, 1986. pp. 1–22.

White, Stephen, Hugh Smith, Gary Meers, and Joseph Callahan. "The Key to Transition: Merging Vocational and Special Education." *The Journal for Vocational Special Needs Education* 8, no. 1 (Fall 1985):15–18.

BIBLIOGRAPHY

Beckwith, John A. *Special Needs Students in Vocational Education: A Procedures Manual to Help Disadvantaged and Handicapped Students.* Boise, Idaho: Idaho State Division of Vocational Education, 1984.

Cetron, Marvin, and Thomas O'Toole. *Encounters with the Future: A Forecast of Life into the 21st Century.* New York: McGraw-Hill, 1982.

Gugerty, John J., and Lloyd W. Tindall. *Tools, Equipment and Machinery Adapted for the Vocational Education and Employment of Handicapped People—Supplement.* Madison, Wis.: Vocational Studies Center, 1983.

Hoy, Wayne K., and Cecil G Miskel. *Educational Administration: Theory, Research, and Practice.* 2d ed. New York: Random House, 1982.

Levin, Henry M., and Russell W. Rumberger. *Educational Requirements for New Technologies: Visions, Possibilities, and Current Realities.* Palo Alto, Calif.: Stanford Education Policy Institute, 1986.

"On Integrated Work: An Interview with Lou Brown." In *Competitive Employment: Service Delivery Models, Methods, and Issues.* Edited by F.R. Rusch. Baltimore, Md.: Paul H. Brookes Publishing Co., 1986.

Sher, Jonathan P. "School-based Community Development Corporations: A New Strategy for Education and Development in Rural America. In *Education in Rural America: A Reassessment of Conventional Wisdom.* Edited by Jonathan P. Sher. Boulder, Colo.: Westview Press, 1974.

Walker, Hill, Scott McConnell, Deborah Holmes, Bonnie Todis, Jackie Walker, and Nancy Aolden. *The Walker Social Skills Curriculum: The Accepts Program.* Austin, Texas: Pro-Ed, 1983.

Chapter 7

Cooperative Work Experience Programs for Students with Vocational Special Needs

David Kingsbury, Ed.D.

Cooperative work experience programs are vocational education programs that combine classroom studies with occupational experience in the community. In order to use cooperative vocational education to educate youth with special needs, there are several points to be considered: (1) the needs, abilities, and interests of the student, (2) the different types of programs, (3) the match of the student to the proper type of program, (4) the placement of the student in the community, (5) the choice between classroom education and the community-based setting for various parts of the learning, and (6) the transition of the student with special needs into the community after the student graduates or articulates from the program.

TYPES OF COOPERATIVE EDUCATION PLACEMENT PROGRAMS

The use of cooperative education methodology has produced a large number of program types for the educator to choose from. Some common types of work programs are examined in this section.

Regular Vocational Education Cooperative Programs

Regular vocational education has three commonly expressed goals for graduates from secondary school. The goals are (1) preparation for direct employment, (2) preparation for postsecondary education placement, and (3) career exploration. Cooperative vocational education programs have allowed traditional vocational programs to place students in the community in paid positions related to their career goals. The students are then able to practice their skills and develop their job placement networks. The entrance of students into such a program has been predicated upon the completion of certain requirements in technical skill areas that would be used on the job. For example, a student would normally have a certain skill level in keyboarding on a computer before being placed in a secretarial position at a local bank through an office education program.

Such cooperative applications in vocational education are found in such traditional secondary vocational education clusters as the following.

Distributive and Marketing Education (DME). DME is a vocational program that prepares students in the skills of management, direct sales, economics, and marketing systems. Many service and information jobs fall under this category.

Trade and Industrial Education (T & I). T & I programs concentrate on materials and the fabricating processes involved in the workplace. Many students learn the manufacturing process involved in the development, manufacture, and repair of such things as cars, small engines, printed circuit boards, wood products, and other items that are produced in mass amounts. This area is often associated with high technology, e.g., computer applications, robotics, laser beam technology, and fiber optics. Construction, welding, and small engine repair also fall within this area.

Business and Office Education (OE). OE is a program that develops the skills of students in office management, data base engineering, and information processing for jobs in today's business and governmental organizations. Obtainment of office jobs, e.g., as secretary or office administrator, in a variety of organizations is many times the outcome of this type of program.

Home Economics Education (HE). Home economics is the study of the process and skills that support a family unit in the management of a household. Training in such areas as family and daily living, clothing and textiles, nutrition, and child development fall under this category. Obtainment of a job such as day care professional or home economist or a job in food preparation, cooking, and preparation for the realities of family life is often the outcome of this type of training.

Agriculture Education (Ag Ed). Ag Ed is concerned with the production of food in all its aspects. Students in this type of program learn a variety of skills, depending on the focus of the program. For example, the study of livestock, crop production, soil conservation, forestry, or greenhouse management fall under the scope of selected agricultural programs. Students who would articulate from this type of training might also find related employment in other areas of agriculture, such as finance, sales, or machinery repair.

Regular Cooperative Vocational Education Programs with Modification

Many students who have a special need would benefit from these regular vocational programs with the provision of support services or modification of program prerequisites. The development of alternative job placements, appropriate support services in the classroom, and on-the-job training allow for the inclusion of these students in these regular programs. For example, a student might well succeed—in a greenhouse program for growing flowers—specifically in the planting and weeding of plants, but might not have the academic capacity to study and understand genetics in the prerequisite portions of a cooperative vocational education program in agriculture. In this case, a review of program entrance policy, program modifications, and possible support services would be in order to allow the student to be successfully placed in this type of program. Such placement and assessment processes are based on the assumption that the regular cooperative vocational educational program staff have the capacity to adapt the curriculum and provide the support services in an appropriate manner.

There are situations where either the individual or the program precludes placement of the individual in a regular or modified cooperative vocational education program. In this case, a cooperative vocational education program designed for students with special needs is an option. Some common types of special vocational education cooperative programs are the following.

Special Vocational Education Cooperative Programs

Work Experience and Career Exploration Programs (WECEPs).   A WECEP is a program for students who are 14 to 15 years old and who are not finding success in a regular school program. A WECEP allows students to participate in work stations in the community and also to explore different available job opportunities. It is a program that affords the students opportunities for earning wages and experiencing success in a school-related program. Often, students enrolled in a WECEP would be likely to drop out of school if it were not for the program. The students who make up the population of WECEPs are a mixture of delinquent, disadvantaged, limited English proficient, single parent, and handicapped youth. Such programs are useful options for students who seemingly see little transfer from the classroom setting to real life.

Work Experience Disadvantaged Programs (WED).   WED programs are senior high adaptations of traditional cooperative vocational education programs. A WED program does not attempt to have students learn the technical skills needed in school and then apply them to a work setting in the community. Rather, the strategy is to place students in job settings that require few technical skills and then have them work on personal human relations skills, develop job-seeking and job-keeping skills, and come to see that learning is the key to advancement. The students involved in this type of special vocational education program often come from backgrounds that leave the students with severe economic or academic handicaps. Typically students in such a program have the natural ability to succeed in traditional vocational education programs, but because of the difficult conditions from which they come, they lack the ability, economic well-being, or motivation to do so.

Work Experience Handicapped Programs (WEH).   A WEH program is a program designed for students whose handicapping conditions are of such magnitude that they could not succeed in a traditional cooperative vocational education program, even with support services and curriculum modifications. In a WEH program, students are taught the basic survival skills necessary to seek employment, work adjustment skills needed to get along in work settings, and career exploration skills that assist students in making transition plans for postsecondary placement. Students in this type of program have common learning deficits in terms of vocational development. The program therefore has standard and individual curriculum options available to educate the students in the classroom setting and at community on-the-job training sites.

Individually Designed Vocational Education Programs (IDVEPs). An IDVEP is for an individual with a handicapping condition for whom none of a school's vocational options are appropriate. In such a situation, a variety of strategies and techniques are used that often include a cooperative work experience. Students involved in an IDVEP often have developmental or learning difficulties that prevent them from meaningful learning transfer from the classroom to community. Wehman and Warrington[1] each have identified sheltered or supported community work options as major components of a functional training program of this type.

CHARACTERISTICS OF COOPERATIVE VOCATIONAL EDUCATION

In using any of the above programs with special needs students, certain components are usually contained within the structure of the program. In a quality program, the following factors should be considered:

- Cooperative vocational education brings the resources of the school and community together in an individually integrated program for students.
- Cooperative vocational education selects or combines learning on the job and learning in the classroom through the use of an individual training plan.
- The educator in charge of the program is called a teacher-coordinator and has a reduced classroom teaching load and an increased administrative and managerial–public relations role. Teacher-coordinators act as absentee supervisors and advocates for the students to ensure that all agreements and labor laws are being adhered to and that the educational requirements of the students are being met.
- The students involved in vocational cooperative programs have schedules that are integrated by the teacher-coordinators, which ensures alternating periods of school and work so as to maximize the benefits of both.
- The students receive instruction in the school or at the community site in areas such as academics and certain technical skills in order to meet the students' individual educational needs.
- The students' experiences are planned so that such experiences will enhance their employability and career goals.
- The program coordinator is familiar with vocational education, training in community sites, and has an organized advisory committee.
- The program has a complex and ongoing relationship with other organizations to facilitate the transition of the student to postsecondary training or directly to employment.

COMPONENT FUNCTIONS OF COOPERATIVE PROGRAMS

To understand better the situation in which the teacher-coordinator operates, it is essential to view the various parts of a cooperative vocational education program and see how they fit into place. An analysis of a work program is presented in Figure 7-1.

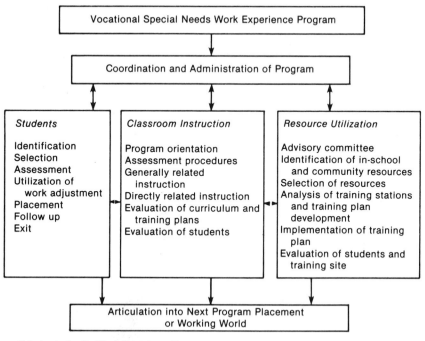

Figure 7-1 Analysis of a Work Experience Program.

In this diagram, it is possible to view the major components involved and to visualize the interaction between them.

The professional who makes a cooperative program come together is the teacher-coordinator. In 1986, the Minnesota Department of Education issued the following list of coordinator responsibilities:[2]

THE ROLE OF THE TEACHER-COORDINATOR

1. Develop community or training work stations that are appropriate to the students' vocational abilities, interests, and aptitudes.

2. Obtain an employability training agreement between a student and an employer concerning roles and responsibilities. (The agreement is to be signed by the parents, student, employer, and teacher-coordinator.)

3. Ensure that proper general safety instructions are provided by a coordinator or employer to a student prior to job or community placement.

4. Maintain a regular visitation schedule to observe students at work and to assist employers to fulfill their responsibility to the students.

5. Develop a transportation system utilizing all available district and community resources. (This frees the coordinator from that responsibility and liability.)

6. Act as a child study team member, where possible, in designing plans for individual students; utilize rehabilitation counselors, psychologists, social work-

ers, counselors, instructional staff, parents, and others as individual cases warrant.

7. Develop and maintain a realistic training plan designed to meet the individual vocational needs of a handicapped student involved in a vocational training program. This plan must be attached to the student's IEP.

8. Develop procedures for periodically evaluating each student's progress toward maximum employability. There should be no less than four evaluations per year.

9. Coordinate (with the child study team) the in-school educational program, which may include assisting students who enroll in additional mainstream courses.

10. Conduct an employability skills seminar for a minimum of 50 minutes per day or 200 minutes per week for all assigned students. Alternative teaching methods are essential to ensure adequate understanding of the subject matter.

11. Maintain and be in compliance with records required by the state department of education and the state and federal departments of labor.

12. Maintain accurate records of parent contacts and an observation log of work site visitations, as well as communications with division of rehabilitation services, members of Joint Training Partnership Act (JTPA) organizations, and other personnel.

13. Work with administration, counselors, other specified staff, parents, ancillary resource personnel, and service agencies to secure services available during high school and develop concrete transition plans.

14. Utilize all available community resources for the students while they are in the program. These resources may include the probation officer, psychologists, the public health service, social services, a job service, etc.

15. Maintain and improve professional growth through involvement in continuing education professional organizations and state and national conferences.

16. Establish and utilize an advisory committee.

17. Assist in the proper due process procedure designated by the child study team or the individual school district.

18. Promote advancement in an occupational area or exploration in varied occupations.

19. Be informed about the insurance policies of the school district and the employer.

20. Maintain open communication with general educators, the principal, vocational director, and special education director to assure support.

21. Encourage students to become involved in student organizations in order to gain leadership skills.

Aside from the responsibilities of a coordinator, there are some other things often overlooked in the development of programs. Professionals who become involved in cooperative education programs for the purpose of occupational outcomes for youth with special needs should consider the following points.

Professionals involved in cooperative education involving occupational outcomes should have a background in, or at least a working knowledge of, the curricula and services available in the present public school. For example, if a school possesses a typing program for students with equipment, curricula, and instruction, it makes no sense for a special education teacher to segregate the instruction of typing and perform the same task in a resource room.

Vocational education professionals and special education professionals must learn about each other's services and work collaboratively to develop and produce a cooperative program for the student with handicapping conditions. This is not inter-agency cooperation; professionals of both kinds are members of a larger organization called a school.

Professionals involved in the development of a cooperative model for the occupa-tional development of special needs students must have an understanding of the resources and capacities of the community around the school. It is not sufficient to talk about cooperation with people in business; one must overtly seek out the opinions and needs of the business community and make an effort to satisfy both the needs of the students and of the community. This is often done with the use of an advisory committee made up of members of the business community.

Skills in matching a student to the curriculum and job must be mastered by professionals in cooperative programs. Many times the only real transition link for handicapped youths is a community-based cooperative program. This alternative to classroom education is often advocated for those youths who, for whatever reason, do not transfer learning from the classroom to the community.

Teacher-coordinators should both have and model genuine concern for students and be able to care for them even if the students' behavior is sometimes unacceptable. The ability to separate feelings and behavior is important—to be able to say, "I like you, but I don't like your behavior."

Teacher-coordinators should have the ability to give and receive feedback. They will often have access to information that can be difficult to deal with or to confront others with. Specific training techniques, such as active listening and honest con-fronting, should be learned well enough so that the coordinators are able to under-stand the total message being sent to them.

Teacher-coordinators should have the ability and willingness to use their resources and other's resources in a cooperative manner. It is far easier to cooperate with other agencies if they trust that what the coordinator is doing is for the good of the student and not just using up their budget.

Teacher-coordinators should have the ability to develop, organize, and indi-vidualize instruction for paraprofessionals and business people to carry out. In this capacity, teacher-coordinators should have the actual skills of task analysis, curricu-lum development, lesson design, and stand-up training; they must be able to "train the trainer" who will be working with the student at a community work site.

Teacher-coordinators should have the ability to accentuate the positive and elimi-nate the negative. They must be positive people who believe in what they are doing and show positive feelings about the students, the school, and the program to employers, community agencies, and others. They should not be afraid of showing enthusiasm, which is one mark of an effective program.

Professionals involved in a cooperative vocational education program for youths with special needs are the key figures in making the program function.

TRAINING SITE LOCATION AND DEVELOPMENT

There are a variety of techniques that can be used to locate and select training sites. While the following list is by no means exhaustive, it presents a useful array of strategies for training site location and development, which are essential parts of a cooperative work experience program. The geographic area surrounding the school of a potential cooperative program must be carefully investigated and training sites identified. In this process, the following considerations should be kept in mind.

1. *Geography*. What is the geographic relationship of the school to community business and industrial sites? Where are the industrial parks, shopping malls, and downtown areas that need to be considered?
2. *Initial Identification of Training Sites*. Once the teacher-coordinator has identified the basic geographic area, the next step is to identify places of employment by a review of Chamber of Commerce listings for the community, yellow page directories, directories of businesses at shopping malls, and city directories of registered businesses and industries.
3. *Identification Analysis*. After the development of a list of possible training sites, refinement of the list by looking at critical factors will help in the selection of probable training sites. Some factors that might be considered in the refinement process are

   - the size of the business
   - the proximity to students' places of residence
   - the access to public or private transportation
   - the physical accessibility of the site
   - the type of business activity that occurs at the site
   - environmental and safety considerations
   - the number of employees
   - future applications of training for students

4. *Identification Analysis Process*. After an initial identification of probable training sites, additional data need to be gathered. Some strategies that can be used in the gathering of this information are the following:

   - Call the business in question and simply ask for a brochure or other literature that might be available. Information thus obtained helps the teacher-coordinator understand the business environment better.
   - Visit the business area to find out firsthand the kind of physical space and plant functions within the business or within similar businesses.

- Identify the chain of command within the business. In developing policy for allocating jobs, it is a mistake to assume the personnel director is the person with whom to start. It is the general manager or the president of the company who tells the personnel director whom to hire. Once support of the top management has been gained, then it is possible to go to the personnel manager with a legitimized plan for the development of the training site.
- Review all of the data gathered and organize the information so as to give quick and accurate access to it.

5. *Initial Training Site Contact*. After a teacher-coordinator has narrowed down the list of training sites, it is time to make initial site contact. At this point, a phone call is essential. The call should be made to the highest identified contact (or contacts) within the business. During this call, the teacher-coordinator should identify himself or herself as a representative of the school agency, establish the purpose of the call, and try to set up an appointment with the business contact. The first appointment with the business contact should last no more than 30 minutes.

6. *Training Site Appointment*. One of the purposes of a training site appointment is to begin building a relationship of trust with the top management in order to facilitate the development of the training site. Trust is usually built on three factors: time, disclosure, and performance. Because of the importance of these three factors, the teacher-coordinator should be sure to arrive on time for the appointment. The teacher-coordinator should also approach the initial meeting as an opportunity to develop a winning outcome for the employer and for the school and students. In the initial contact, it is important to sell the school as a provider of services and to understand the vested interests of the business. In addition, the different viewpoints of the school and the business should be understood and taken into account (see Table 7-1).

7. *Initial Interview Outcomes*. As a result of the initial interview, a number of important outcomes should occur. The outcomes of a successful initial interview are the following:

- The teacher-coordinator should understand what the business does and what the vested interests of the business are.
- The employer should understand what business the school is in. In addition, the employer should know that there are a number of types of training that the school is interested in helping to provide, ranging from direct employment to nonpaid job shadowing.
- The employer should understand the different types of employment and training incentives that can be arranged through the school.
- The teacher-coordinator should have the commitment of the employer to legitimize further contacts with the organization and to move on to the next step in the site development process.

8. *Training Site Analysis*. The next step of the training site development process is to arrange an onsite visit for the purpose of gathering additional data on the

Table 7-1 Communications with Industry

When people in business and education meet together, they need to be aware of differences in the meaning of key terms. For example, the terms below mean the following to persons in the different areas.

TERM	University	Schools	Industry
long-term	20 years	5 years	this afternoon
results	looks good on report	looks good in FTEs	contract in hand
we learned a lot	we learned a lot	we learned a lot	we lost money on this
instruction	classroom lecture; internship	classroom; lab; on-the-job training	classroom; on-the-job training; one-on-one; film what works
flexibility	changing in next five years	changing next year	changing this afternoon
information	I think that	I'm sure that	the facts say
costs	free is good	cheap is good	nothing good is free!
qualifications	distinguish between BA and BS	certification degrees	can you get *results*?

jobs that are performed at the specific location. At this meeting, efforts should be made to visit with a number of individuals involved in the business. Among the people to visit are the personnel manager, the production or service managers, and some actual production or service workers doing the type of work that has training site potential. There is no easy procedure for doing a training site analysis. Each site requires its own mixture of sensing, observation, interviewing, and review. The outcome of this first step of analysis should be the identification of some distinct jobs presently existing that could be used by the cooperative program or the identification of some parts of jobs that could be put together to form a new job that could be used by the program.

9. *Prototype Curriculum Development.* After the initial analysis of specific jobs, the teacher-coordinator should put together a prototype functional curriculum of the actual tasks and processes that would result in a particular job being done within the parameters of acceptable performance to the business organization (for example, the tasks involved in changing bed sheets and blankets in a specific hotel). The prototype curriculum should encompass at least part of some job defined at the business establishment.

10. *Curriculum Validation.* After the development of the prototype curriculum, the results should be shared with the actual workers and managers involved with that aspect of the job to see if there needs to be any modification of the curriculum.

11. *Training Site Contracting.* At this stage, the capacity of the business to participate as a cooperative training station should be established, and it should be determined what type of training station it should be to be most useful. The teacher-coordinator should enter into written training agreements with the the business and be ready to match the training station with a particular cooperative education application and with student trainees.

There are a number of ways that an identified training station can be used to provide education to a student. The way that is most effective for a given station depends on the capacity of the station and the needs of the student. The most common types of placement fall into two major categories: (1) paid training and (2) nonpaid training.

USES OF VOCATIONAL COOPERATIVE EDUCATION TRAINING SITES

In the use of a paid training station, a variety of options can be employed. The variation of the application depends on the amount of supervision and support given the student during the employment training period. The two options are described below.

Paid Training Placements

In this option, the student is placed at the training site and the supervision and training of the student is handled primarily by employees of the business at the training site. Instruction is designed by the teacher-coordinator, but carried out by the employees. The student is an actual employee of the business and is responsible for performing certain functions at the place of business.

Periodic Supervision and Support by School Personnel

In this option, the school assumes the full responsibility for the business functions being performed and has a full- or part-time staff person at the job site. The support person's function is to teach the students the specific tasks involved in performing the job. The students will be supervised during all phases of work and be taught general job skills that can be taken to the job market. The support staff person is an employee of the school or in some cases, a part-time paid employee of the business (although still attending classroom functions at the school). Since the primary functions of the job are the responsibility of the school support staff person, who is answerable for the job production and who teaches the job skills curriculum to the students, it makes good sense to place a number of students at the same training site, using a staggered schedule. For example, a part-time, 20-hour-a-week job can provide 20 hours of direct instruction to a number of students. Programs with one or two support staff persons can therefore provide a large amount of direct supervised training for students in a safe, well-managed, yet realistic work site.

Ongoing Supervision and Support by School Personnel

There are a number of financial reasons for businesses to develop an ongoing relationship with a cooperative vocational program. It is imperative that the teacher-coordinator understand the federal, state, and private initiatives to motivate businesses to hire students who have special needs. Some of the financial incentives to hire these students are the following.

Financial Incentives for Businesses to Accept Student Trainees

Special Subminimum Wage Allowances. The Wage and Hour Division of the U.S. Department of Labor will allow special wage certificates to be written in order to prevent curtailment of opportunities for employment of individuals who are impaired by age, physical or mental deficiency, or injury at wages lower than the minimum wage but not less than 50 percent of such wage. The wages must be commensurate with those of paid nonhandicapped workers in industry in the vicinity for essentially the same type, quality, and quantity of work.[3]

On-the-Job Training Funds. The National Association for Retarded Citizens (NARC) encourages businesses to hire students who meet the following criteria. The student must be (1) at least 16 years old, (2) unemployed for at least seven consecutive days, officially enrolled in school, or working part-time but seeking full-time employment, and (3) mentally retarded, with a full-scale IQ of 80 or below (as measured by a standardized intelligence test).[4]

Interagency Incentives. Hendricks-McCracken found it is possible to access other funds available through JTPA and the Division of Rehabilitation Services.[5] Coordinators should check for additional state or federal tax incentive plans that might currently exist.

Nonpaid Training Placements

There are situations where paid training stations are not available. Times of economic hardship or a lack of preparation on the part of a student might make a nonpaid training placement the most appropriate setting for the student. Again, the type of nonpaid training placement depends on the type of supervision that is available at the training site.

Periodic Supervision and Support by School Personnel

Where a student needs to explore career options and has not made a decision on what direction to take in occupational training, a nonpaid job shadowing activity is often a good choice. The student is assigned to follow and interview an actual worker at the training station site and gain knowledge by observation of and interaction with the worker. The student is not an employee of the business but is on an individual field trip designed by the teacher-coordinator (although under the supervision of an employee of the firm).

Ongoing Supervision and Support by School Personnel

There may be situations where the school is able to provide full-time support staff at a site in order to supervise the career exploration and training activities of students who are still not at the level of employability. In this case, a student would learn the tasks of the job in the community setting, but the student would have to qualify as a school trainee and not as an employee.

Legal Implications of Nonpaid Training and the Fair Labor Standards Act

There is great concern that students could be abused and taken advantage of in a nonpaid training situation. The criteria used to determine which activities are nonpaid training and which are paid work must meet labor law standards. For training to be nonpaid rather than work, the following criteria should be met:

- The training, even though it involves the actual operation of a business, is similar to that given in a vocational school.
- The training is for the benefit of the student.
- Students do not displace regular employees but work under their close observation.
- The employer providing the training derives no immediate advantage from the activity, and on occasion his or her work may actually be impeded.
- Students are not necessarily entitled to a job at the conclusion of the training period.
- The employer and the students understand that the students are not entitled to wages for the time spent in training.[6]

A work experience coordinator should take great care to understand the state's interpretation of laws concerning the use of business sites and the application of state and federal laws concerning students. The effort will likely be repaid, for a nonpaid training site can add a great deal to a vocational training program for students who, for whatever reason, cannot receive an appropriate vocational education in the school setting.

THE PLACEMENT PROCESS: MATCHING THE STUDENT TO THE TRAINING SITE

In examining the many crucial aspects of a student–training site match, it should be remembered that the match is partly determined by the size and complexity of the training site, by the mix of paid and nonpaid opportunities, and by the fit of these opportunities with the student's abilities, needs, and interests. In the matching process, the coordinator should go through a vocational assessment procedure to ensure the student has the maximum opportunity to explore options, is challenged educationally, and receives the support services needed to develop to his or her full occupational potential.

In order to match students and training sites in a systematic way, the coordinator should develop a series of tools and procedures that will facilitate the matching process. A matching process should contain the following steps.

1. The first step should be initial explanation to the student, the parents, and the child study team (if appropriate) of the vocational paid and nonpaid training sites that are available through the cooperative vocational education program. These options should be presented in an orderly fashion, with written or pictorial information that the student can understand. Options that are not presently available to the student should also be discussed if the available training does not interest the student.
2. The next step should be to determine which vocational option in the cooperative program would be appropriate for the student. This could be accomplished by a review of the cumulative records of the student, followed by a one-on-one interview to explain the options, the career growth patterns of those options, and the skill requirements at the various training sites.

3. After the initial interview with the student, the coordinator should develop a placement assessment plan to test the student and discover the student's interests, as well as possible supervision and support needs. Such a plan should point out the critical questions that need to be answered, the methods for answering the questions, and the tentative decisions that might be reached by the assessment process (see Exhibit 7-1). The assessment plan should be shared with the student's parents and with the child study team if the student has a handicapping condition.

4. Implement the assessment plan by having the student participate in the activities contained in the assessment plan. In this process, the teacher-coordinator (and other staff as needed) should use various methods, such as job shadowing, interest testing, and actual training tryout activities (where the student participates in a training activity at several different identified training sites). In training tryouts, the initial prototype curricula developed at each of the sites during the identification and contracting process should be used. The tasks identified in a prototype curriculum should be organized in such a fashion that the student can be observed during the training tryout process. The tasks can be listed and scored by a simple process and then analyzed for areas of productive placement and for possible support and service needs (see Exhibit-7-2).

5. After the student has completed the activities outlined in the assessment plan, the results should be analyzed. The procedures to be used are as follows:

- Each of the critical factors from the training tryout activity should be scored. The results of the assessment should facilitate decisionmaking as to the readiness of the student to participate at the selected training site.

- For each area of need (performance problem), a decision should be made in conjunction with the student and the support service team to either identify resources to modify the need, modify the task at the training site, provide appropriate support and supervision, or combine some or all of these strategies; the choice decided upon should provide the best training station option for the student.

- If the student is handicapped, the vocational assessment should be part of the IEP process.

- If the student is disadvantaged or otherwise has a special need, the teacher-coordinator should identify the required support services and add the information to the student's record.

6. Development of the student training plan and actual placement of the student at a training station should take place at this time. Based on the assessment activities, the teacher-coordinator should know the stage of readiness of the student for different training sites. If it appears that a business has openings that match a particular student's abilities, needs, and interests, then the coordinator is in a position to implement the vocational training process. Some cautions are in order here, however. Difficulties can arise in various ways, including by

Exhibit 7-1 Sample Assessment Planning Form

STUDENT NAME _____

1. PRELIMINARY CUMULATIVE FILE ANALYSIS AND INTAKE INTERVIEW INDI-
   CATES:

   _____
   _____
   _____
   _____
   _____

2. TENTATIVE ASSESSMENT PLAN

QUESTIONS	CRITICAL FACTORS	PROCEDURES
CLASS SKILLS		
LEARNING STYLE		
BASIC SKILLS		
COMMUNICATION SKILLS		
SOCIALIZATION SKILLS		
VOCATIONAL INTERESTS		
ENVIRONMENTAL CONCERNS		

CONCLUSIONS AND TENTATIVE SUPPORT SERVICES NEEDED

ASSESSMENT TEAM MEMBER SIGNATURE

_____

STUDENT SIGNATURE

_____

PARENT SIGNATURE

Source: Reprinted with permission from *Vocational Assessment: A Guide to Improving Vocational Programming for Special Needs Youth* by D. Kingsbury, pp. 23–25, Bemidji State University, © 1986.

Exhibit 7-2 Sample Performance Observation Record Sheet

STUDENT _____   PERFORMANCE
DATE _____   OBSERVATION SHEET
PERFORMANCE SAMPLE _____
INSTRUCTOR _____

TASK LISTING	CAN DO	CAN'T DO	DIFFICULT TO DO
1.			
2.			
3.			
4.			
5.			
6.			
7.			
8.			
9.			
10.			

NOTES: (OBSERVATIONS)

PERFORMANCE

BEHAVIOR: STUDENT'S REACTION TO
PERFORMANCE SAMPLE

CONCLUSIONS FROM OBSERVATIONS

Source: Reprinted with permission from *Vocational Assessment: A Guide to Improving Vocational Programming for Special Needs Youth* by D. Kingsbury, p. 29, Bemidji State University, © 1986.

- trying to force students to be at training sites where the employers are not ready to work with the program
- trying to force students to accept jobs or training sites that they do not want
- failing to communicate fully with parents about the training site opportunities and the transportation and time commitments involved
- assuming that one can always make a perfect match of a student to a job
- using only traditional hiring procedures for the students (some students will never be hired through traditional competitive hiring practices, but they can gain great occupational proficiency by use of power training methodologies and should be trained at fully supervised paid or nonpaid training stations)
- being unaware of the labor law restrictions that apply to the program
- failing to give each student the safety training appropriate to the training station

TRAINING PROCESS ADMINISTRATION

In conjunction with the appropriate placement of the student, a coordinator must make everyone understand what is involved in the program and ensure documentation and feedback about what is happening at the community site. To do this, a series of documents and forms should be used in the actual training process. Some sample forms from the Minnesota State Department of Education that can be used are provided below. They include the following:

- A work experience employability agreement (see Exhibit 7-3) clarifies the roles of the participants in the cooperative work experience program, ensuring their understanding and documenting it with signatures.
- A training plan (Exhibits 7-4, 7-5, and 7-6) is used to schedule the work and school experiences of the student learners and to ensure vocational quality for the students. Exhibit 7-5 illustrates a training plan that is very unstructured to a specific job but that could be developed to meet individual student and employer needs. Exhibit 7-6 presents a form used by the St. Paul public schools; the form includes an area for academic skills training as an in-school responsibility. (Training plans will be dealt with in greater detail in the section on classroom instruction.)
- Proper identification and due process forms are required if students are handicapped. (Also, the vocational assessment forms in the student-job match should be attached to the IEP.)
- Age verification forms are required if the student is not 18 and wishes to participate in a WECEP or other cooperative program.

A variety of other forms should be considered that would document certain functions and thus aid in coordinating the cooperative work experience program. These include the following:

Exhibit 7-3 Work Experience Training Agreement

Student _____   Employer's Name _____

Social Security # _____   Employer's Address _____

Job Title _____   Job Supervisor _____

Work Schedule: Monday ____ to ____   Work Starting Date _____
                  Tuesday ____ to ____
                  Wednesday ____ to ____   School Year _____
                  Thursday ____ to ____
                  Friday ____ to ____   Wages Per Hour _____

ALL PARTIES CONCERNED AGREE TO THE FOLLOWING RESPONSIBILITIES:

Employer's Responsibilities

1. Employer will provide a minimum of 15 hours of work experience and career exploration per week and will provide work of instructional value as outlined in the training plan.
2. Employer will provide supervision and evaluation by an experienced and qualified person and will keep coordinator informed of student's progress.
3. Employer will give the same consideration to student employees as is given to similar employees in regard to safety, health, social security, general work conditions, and other regulations of the firm.

Coordinator's Responsibilities

1. Coordinator is to select appropriate work stations with responsible job supervisor and safe working conditions.
2. Coordinator will visit each student periodically at the work station and will consult regularly with the job supervisor.
3. Coordinator shall endeavor to adjust complaints with the cooperation of all parties concerned, and shall have the authority to transfer or withdraw a student from the program.
4. Coordinator will communicate with each student's parent or guardian when necessary.

Parent's or Guardian's Responsibilities

Parent (or guardian) agrees to let the student participate in the community-based employment program and to cooperate with the school in meeting requirements of the program.

Student's Responsibilities

1. Student will cooperate with school and employer in meeting rules of the program.
2. Student will not report to work on days when absent from school except with special permission of the coordinator.
3. When absent from school, student will notify the coordinator by 8 a.m. and will also notify the employer that he/she will be absent.
4. Student will consult with coordinator before changing hours or days of work, or before quitting job.
5. Student will inform parent or guardian about any change in work/school schedule.

Student _____   Employer _____

Parent (or guardian) _____   Coordinator _____

Source: Reprinted from *Vocational Education Work Experience Programs for Handicapped Youth*, p. 56, Minnesota Curriculum Services Center, Minnesota Department of Education, 1986.

Exhibit 7-4 Training Plan for a Gasoline Service Attendant

I. Title of Job: Service station attendant

II. Job Description: Cleans and maintains station and driveway, handles customer relations on the driveway, sells accessories, cleans and polishes cars, lubricates cars, and makes minor repairs. Learns some fundamental principles of management.

III. Career Objective: Service station manager

IV. Areas of experience and training:
    A. Station care—housekeeping and maintenance
    B. Driveway service
    C. Carwash, clean-up, and polish
    D. Lubrication
    E. Tire, battery, and accessory sales
    F. Minor repairs
    G. Buying and ordering procedures
    H. Principles of station management

V. Details of areas of experience and training:

	Planned Learning	
	In Class	At the Training Station
A. Instruction in station care		
1. Driveway housekeeping and maintenance	X	X
2. Restroom cleaning		X
3. Lubrication department		X
4. Stockroom		X
B. Instruction in driveway service		
1. Six-step driveway service	X	X
2. Windshield, battery, tires	X	X
3. Underhood inspection and sales	X	X
4. Cash register operation and checkout	X	X
5. Making additional sales	X	X
a. radiator hose		
b. fan belt		
c. oil additive		
d. oil filter		
e. lubrication		
f. battery		
g. lights		
C. Instruction on carwash, clean-up, and polish		X
D. Lubrication		
1. Study and use of lubrication manual	X	X
2. Servicing of major parts	X	X
3. Wheel lubrication		X
E. Instruction in tire, battery and accessory sales		
1. Tire brands, sizes and selling points	X	X
2. Battery sizes and selling points	X	X
3. Other accessories	X	X
F. Instruction on minor repairs		
1. Tire change and repair		X

Exhibit 7-4 continued

	Planned Learning	
	In Class	At the Training Station
2. Muffler and tail pipe change		X
3. Brake adjustment and repair		X
4. Car tune-up procedure	X	X
5. Cleaning or steaming motor		X
G. Buying and ordering procedures		
1. Taking inventory	X	X
2. Determination of minimum number of items to keep on hand		X
3. Ordering, so as not to order more than necessary	X	X
4. Display for maximum sales	X	X
H. Principles of station management		
1. Acquaintance with required records	X	X
2. Lease or rental arrangement with major oil company		X
3. Staffing and hiring personnel		X
4. Financing	X	X
5. Requirements		X
6. Importance of station location		X
7. Payroll		X

Source: Reprinted from *Guide for Work Education in Manitoba's Public Schools*, p. 63, Ministry of Education, Winnepeg Manitoba, Canada, 1976.

- a personal data sheet, which provides vocational diagnostic information
- a student agreement form (see Exhibit 7-7), which documents specific obligations of the student not covered under the training agreement
- a parent-school agreement form (see Exhibit 7-8), which records the responsibilities of the school and the parents and highlights activities not covered under the training agreement
- a rating sheet for student evaluation (see Exhibit 7-9), which can be used as a periodic device to help keep track of the student's progress on the job
- various forms to provide a transportation and coordination log to help the coordinator keep track of student visits, mileage, and dates of important upcoming events

CLASSROOM INSTRUCTION IN A COOPERATIVE WORK EXPERIENCE PROGRAM

A common question asked by new coordinators is, "What do I teach?" Part of the answer can be given by considering two types of instruction: (1) general related instruction, including the curriculum applicable to a student who is entering or maintaining a job, and (2) direct instruction that pertains to the specific job that a

Exhibit 7-5 Sample Training Plan for Work-Study

3 Copies:
  1-Training Sponsor
  1-Student
  1-Teacher-Coordinator   Work-Study Program Training Plan

Student-Learner _____ Birth Date _____
Social Security No. _____ Job Title _____ O.E. No. _____
  Training Station _____
  Address _____
  Supervisor(s) _____
Job Definition: _____

Description of Training Station Duties:
  1. _____
  2. _____
  3. _____
  4. _____
  5. _____
  6. _____
  7. _____
  8. _____
Career Objective(s): _____
_____
_____
_____
_____
_____

Training Experiences or Objectives	School Instruction Group or Individual	References and Evaluation	Time Schedule

Source: Reprinted from *The Work Experience Handbook: Vocational Education Work Experience Program for Handicapped Students*, pp. 64–65, Vocational Technical Division, Minnesota Department of Education, 1977.

Exhibit 7-6 Sample Training Needs Assessment Form

TRAINING PLAN*

Name of Student _____   Employing Organization _____

Job Title _____   Job Supervisor _____

CHECK OR LIST ALL AREAS OF INSTRUCTION

ON THE JOB	IN SCHOOL

Interpersonal Skills

ON THE JOB	IN SCHOOL
___ Coordinate Tasks with Co-Workers	___ Job Application Skills
___ Develop Responsibility to Job	___ Job Maintenance Skills
___ React Appropriately to Criticism	a. Interest and Aptitudes
	b. Responsibilities
___ Deal with Public/Customers	___ Daily Living Skills
___ Use Proper Procedures to Report Absences	a. Personal Appearance
	b. Social Contact
___ Supervise Other Employees	___ Job Safety Instruction

List of Training Station Tasks	Academic Skills
_____	___ Reading
_____	___ Writing
_____	___ Spelling
_____	___ Grammar
	___ Alphabetizing
Equipment Skills	___ Number Identification
_____	___ Basic Math Skills
	___ Metric System
_____	___ Problem Solving
	___ Sequencing Tasks
_____	___ Emergency Procedures
	___ Preventative Safety/First Aid
Job Safety Instruction	___ Specific Safety Skills
	a. Machine Use
_____	b. Tool Use

These are examples of tasks from different jobs which may be indicated on the Training Plan under "List of Training Station Tasks."

*Dishwasher
  Collect dirty dishes, pots, and utensils
  Empty bus pans

*Office Worker
  Filing
  Writing letters

Exhibit 7-6 continued

*Dishwasher
  Scrape food off pans, plates, etc.
  Arrange items in washer racks
  Sort silverware
  Read and adjust gauges on washer
  Stack clean items, arrange on shelves
  Wipe tables, mop floor

*Cashier
  Make change
  Write sales slips
  Credit card processing

*Dining Room Attendant
  Take food and drink orders
  Place orders with cooks
  Set tables
  Serve food and beverages
  Clear tables

*Bus Person
  Clear and wipe tables
  Carry bus pans to kitchen

*Housekeeper
  Change bed linens
  Clean tables, ashtrays, wastebaskets
  Clean bathroom, replace towels, etc.
  Vacuum floor

*Office Worker
  Addressing letters
  Use telephone book
  Keep records

*Laundry Attendant
  Place laundry in washer and dryer
  Sort, fold and stack clean laundry
  Read labels and laundering directions

*Gas Station Attendant
  Pump gas
  Change, mount, and repair tires
  Clean windshields
  Check and add oil, transmission fluid
  Give directions
  Make change
  Credit card processing
  Take inventory
  Stock shelves

*Sales Clerk
  Make change
  Write sales slips
  Credit card processing
  Weighing/measuring
  Read labels
  Take inventory
  Fill orders
  Record keeping
  Clean and stock shelves

Directions: List appropriate items on Training Plan under "Equipment Skills."

EQUIPMENT LIST

Adding Machine	Elevator	Pipe Polisher
Cash Register	Film Splicer	Scales
Clothes Washer/Dryer	Garbage Disposal	Soft Drink
Coffeemaker	Gas Pump	Telephone
Deep Fryer	Grill/Oven	Typewriter
Dishwasher	Hydraulic Lift	Tire Changer
Electric Mixer/Blender	Iron	Vacuum Cleaner
Electric Slicer	Microwave	Welder

*To be attached to training agreement

Source: Reprinted from *Teacher Coordinator Handbook: Secondary Vocational Community Based Employment Programs*, Pub. 7879008, pp. 117–118, St. Paul Public Schools, 1978.

Exhibit 7-7 Sample Agreement for Enrolling in a Work-Study Program

---

STUDENT AGREEMENT

The Work-Study Program has been discussed with me by the teacher-coordinator and I understand that through enrolling in this program:

1. I am not guaranteed a job. My teacher-coordinator and I will work together to find a job which seems suitable for me and then it is up to the employer-coordinator and me to discuss the requirements and responsibilities of the job, and to decide if I am to be hired.
2. I am to be paid for my community work experience.
3. I am to have a combined school-work week which does not exceed 48 hours.
4. I understand that I will be required to take the Vocational Skills Class as a part of the Work-Study Program.
5. I understand that I will be present and on time each day, both in school and at work. I will report for my classes each school day that I work unless cleared through my teacher-coordinator.
6. I will notify my employer and teacher-coordinator as far in advance as possible if I am unable to report for work.
7. I will tell my teacher-coordinator about any problems that are giving me trouble in school or on the job.
8. I understand my school supervisor or employer will rate my work regularly and discuss my progress with my teacher-coordinator. The grade for my job training and class will be based on these ratings and interviews.
9. I understand the responsibilities connected with my job and am accepting this training of my own free will.
10. I will obey the rules and policies of my employer and the school.
11. I may be dropped from the program if I leave my job without the consent of the teacher-coordinator or if I do not live up to the terms of this agreement.
12. I will be given the first chance to be in the next year's Work-Study Program if I successfully live up to the terms of this Agreement.

Date _____   Student _____

Coordinator _____

Source: Reprinted from *The Work Experience Handbook: Vocational Education Work Experience Program for Handicapped Students*, p. 59, Vocational Technical Division, Minnesota Department of Education, 1977.

---

student is exploring at a training station. In this section, we look at both components of the classroom curriculum.

General Related Instruction

General related instruction is based on the assumption that there are common survival skills necessary for all persons who enter the world of work. It is important that this general curriculum fits into the career development and education of a given individual. One way of viewing this instruction is in the context of a career development continuum, as shown in Figure 7-2. The Division of Vocational Education in the Ohio State Department of Education has listed the steps of career development in

Exhibit 7-8 Parent or Guardian Information and Consent Form for Work-Study Enrollment

---

PARENT-SCHOOL AGREEMENT FORM
WORK-STUDY PROGRAM

The major objectives of this program are: (1) to help develop the student's basic educational skills, (2) to improve his/her knowledge and attitudes about the world of work, and (3) to develop social skills that will help the student to achieve "full employment" when he/she completes schooling.

Your son or daughter will receive high school credits through participation in the Work-Study Program. Because the Work-Study Program differs in many ways from most general high school programs, the following statements are made to aid your understanding of some of the important parts of the program.

1. This is a three-year program and each student is admitted to the first year on a trial basis.
2. Parents are responsible for the medical needs of the student when the student is not on school property.
3. Regular school and job attendance is a responsibility of parents or guardians.
4. Parents should not contact the employer without first consulting the teacher-coordinator.
5. The teacher-coordinator will attempt to place the student in a work-training experience that tries to develop his/her abilities to the highest possible level.
6. The student must maintain an average or better performance at school and on the job.
7. The student may be shifted from one job to another from time to time or he/she may be removed from a training experience as the teacher-coordinator and/or employer decides.
8. The student will remain with the original training station throughout the school year. Necessary changes must be cleared through the coordinator.
9. Classes, while in school, will be used to develop the student's abilities.

We/I request and authorize Independent School District #_____ to release my son/daughter _____ from school during the hours scheduled on his/her class schedule for individual on-the-job experience.

Date _____　_____
　　　　　　　　　　　　　　　　　　　　　Parent or Guardian Signature
Date _____　_____
　　　　　　　　　　　　　　　　　　　　　Teacher-Coordinator Signature

Source: Reprinted from *The Work Experience Handbook: Vocational Education Work Experience Program for Handicapped Students*, p. 61, Vocational Technical Division, Minnesota Department of Education, 1977.

---

a series of stages that approximate the stages of development that occur in the K–12th grade experience. The five steps are given below:

1. *Career Motivation:* The stage from kindergarten through sixth grade, during which students form ideas about work and gain some sense of what work involves.
2. *Career Orientation:* The stage in which there is development of concepts involved in various kinds of work and in the lifestyles and environmental factors that are related to them.

Exhibit 7-9 Sample Work Experience Rating Sheet

RATING SHEET FOR STUDENT-TRAINEE'S WORK EXPERIENCE

Marking Period _____ Date _____

Name of Student-Trainee _____

Name of Employer _____

Instructions: Under each of the headings below, you will find numbered responses. Read carefully
and then choose the response which most closely describes the student-trainee as the heading
relates to him. Place the number of the response in the blank located at the left of each heading.
Below the responses is a space titled "comments," which may be used if additional information seems necessary. The first heading, "school level," is rated as an example:

___ School level
1. Nursery
2. Elementary
3. Junior High
4. Senior High
5. College
Comments _____

___ Punctuality—Does the student report to work on time and continue to work until quitting time?
1. Frequently arrives late and quits early.
2. Has seldom been late and rarely quits work early.
3. Always prompt and always works until quitting time.
Comments _____

___ Personal Appearance—Do the student's clothing and grooming "fit" the job?
1. Has poor dress habits and needs to improve his grooming.
2. Has acceptable appearance; could make some improvement.
3. Usually is very careful of his appearance.
4. Always presents an appropriate well-groomed appearance.
Comments _____

___ Cooperation—Does the student-trainee cooperate with his boss and co-workers?
1. Does not get along with his boss or co-workers.
2. Is indifferent or often ignores co-workers.
3. Is polite and friendly when working with others.
4. Is always friendly and courteous to others.
Comments _____

___ Reliability—Can the student be depended upon to do a good job?
1. Cannot be depended on; requires constant supervision.
2. Often must be reminded of duties; generally has to be carefully supervised.
3. Generally performs all assigned duties; requires average supervision.
4. Is a good dependable worker; requires little supervision.
Comments _____

___ Care of Equipment—Does the student take proper care of his/her tools and equipment?
1. Seldom uses or takes care of his/her tools and equipment properly.
2. Sometimes uses his/her tools and equipment improperly and/or without the proper care.
3. Usually uses his/her tools and equipment properly and gives them proper care.
4. Always uses his/her tools and equipment properly and gives them proper care.
Comments _____

Exhibit 7-9 continued

___ Poise—Does the student do his/her work with confidence and self-assurance?
1. Needs more confidence, tries to avoid or get out of difficult situations.
2. Usually confident, handles most situations satisfactorily.
3. Confident, usually handles difficult situations satisfactorily.
   Comments _____

___ Attitude Toward Work—Does the student seem to like his/her work and show interest in learning more about his/her job?
1. Seems to dislike the work; has no desire to learn.
2. Is willing to work, but shows no interest or enthusiasm in job.
3. Seems to enjoy work, but is willing to "stand still" and not advance.
4. Shows interest in work and has a desire to learn.
   Comments _____

___ Job Skills—Does the student have the necessary skills and knowledge to be successful on his/her job?
1. Has a definite lack of skills and knowledge.
2. Has limited knowledge; is lacking in some essentials.
3. Has an average grasp of the essential skills and knowledge.
4. Possesses all of the essential skills and knowledge.
   Comments _____

___ Work Habits—Does the student have the necessary work habits to do a good job?
1. Has poor work habits and doesn't know how to organize his/her work.
2. Has fair work habits but sometimes doesn't see things that should be done.
3. Has good work habits and looks for extra work to do.
   Comments _____

___ Improvement and Progress—Does the student's quality of work show satisfactory progress or improvement?
1. Shows little or no improvement.
2. Is learning slowly and has shown only slight improvement.
3. Learns fairly quickly and remembers instructions; is making normal progress.
4. Learns fast; seldom forgets; is making good progress.
   Comments _____

THANK YOU FOR YOUR EXCELLENT COOPERATION.

Source: Reprinted from *The Work Experience Handbook: Vocational Education Work Experience Program for Handicapped Students*, pp. 68–69, Vocational Technical Division, Minnesota Department of Education, 1977.

3. *Career Exploration:* The stage in which students experiment with or investigate a variety of jobs to see if the job requirements match their needs, abilities, and interests.
4. *Vocational Education:* The stage in which students begin learning, either through a classroom or cooperative approach, the specific job skills that will make them employable.
5. *Preprofessional Education:* The stage in which a student makes some tentative choices calling for college instruction and hence begins a college preparatory course of study.

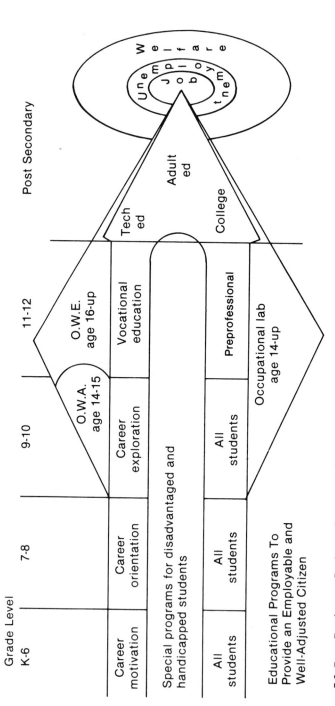

Figure 7-2 Career Development Continuum. *Source:* Reprinted from *Ohio's Career Development Continuum*, Career Development Service, Division of Vocational Education, Ohio Department of Education.

Some common units of instruction that teacher-coordinators have found useful are listed in the monograph *Work Experience Curriculum Outline and Bibliography,* issued by the Minnesota Curriculum Services Center.[7] These common units, to be taught by topical outline, are shown in Exhibit 7-10. The Exhibit 7-10 outline could be modified to include more topics or to sequence topics according to the individual student's needs. In planning the instruction, the coordinator must use a curriculum plan. Such a plan includes the days of presentation, the method of delivery, the depth of competency mastered, and the evaluation methods appropriate to the student.

Direct Instruction

The second major kind of instruction is direct instruction for a specific training station. This instruction is usually implemented by means of a training plan. A training plan is an outline of the major parts of instruction that are to be learned by the student for a specific job. The responsibility to learn these tasks is placed on the student, and the responsibilities of implementation are delegated to the training station site or to the classroom instruction site. Some training plans list only the tasks to be performed, with a checklist for evaluating whether they will be learned in school or on the job. Other plans go into greater detail concerning the schedule of experiences that will be provided and also include the time of completion.

Some coordinators discover that the full implementation of a training plan is a time-consuming and difficult task. Yet it is the training plan that determines the quality of a cooperative vocational education program. Although coordinators may differ about the procedures for designing and implementing a training plan, Harless and Swanson and Gradous each endorse a systematic process for industrial training situations.[8] Guidelines include the following:

- Secure or develop a job description for the training station where students are to be placed. From this job description and from the training station analysis procedures, develop and validate a prototype curriculum.
- With the prototype curriculum in hand, develop competency or performance measures that indicate acceptable productivity for the tasks performed. From this listing, develop a profile of successful behaviors for the training station.
- With safety considerations in mind, field-test the initial units of the prototype curriculum at the training station with the appropriate amount of supervision. Depending on the learning transfer ability of the student, supplement with direct instruction in the classroom setting.
- Adjust the training for the student's individual learning style and productivity performance levels, and set target learning goals.
- Implement the curriculum for the student at the training station.
- Follow up and ensure that the student is progressing at the training station in terms of technical and social skills. In addition, ensure that the situation is still appropriate for the training being conducted. For example, new equipment installed at the training site may dictate that a special unit of curriculum be taught and a previously developed training unit be disposed of.

Exhibit 7-10 Common Units of Instruction

I. Program Orientation

    A. Intake Procedures
        1. Referrals
        2. Staffing
        3. Home visits and conferences (parent involvement)
        4. Forms (training plans, agreements)

    B. Assessment Procedures
        1. Goals and contract development
        2. Vocational inventories

    C. School Program Coordination
        1. Scheduling (classes, transportation)
        2. Support staff
        3. School and work policies
        4. Appropriate vocational courses (skills)
        5. Training site selection

    D. Advantages of Staying in School

II. Safety on the Job

    A. Survey of Student Training Site
        1. Emergency information and procedures
        2. Job safety needs

    B. General Safety Procedures
        1. Materials handling
        2. Protective clothing and equipment
        3. First aid
        4. Home safety
        5. Self-protection (robbery, assault, rape)
        6. Related safety topics (attitudes, safe driving)

III. Employment: Obtaining, Maintaining, and Terminating a Job

    A. Job Preparation
        1. Self-evaluation (skills, interests, personal hygiene)
        2. Personal information (data card, letters of application)

    B. Job Analysis

    C. Job Sources

    D. Job Seeking Techniques
        1. Using the telephone
        2. Reading maps
        3. Reading want ads
        4. Using the telephone directory and yellow pages

    E. Job Application

    F. Job Interview
        1. Interview preparation (manners, dress)
        2. Follow-up

    G. Basic Job Performance
        1. Work habits
        2. Work attitudes

    H. Job Termination

IV. Decision Making

    A. Learning the Decision-Making Process

    B. Applying the Decision-Making Process
        1. Peer problems and community problems

        2. Family problems
        3. Job problems
        4. School problems

    C. Clarification of Values

    D. Planning Careers

V. Basic Employment Skills

    A. Communication (listening, writing, spelling)

    B. Arithmetic (sales, commissions, weights, measures)

    C. Business Machines (adding, cash register)

    D. Transportation (bus scheduling, car pooling)

    E. Timekeeping

VI. Significance of Work

    A. Different Skill Levels

    B. Dynamic Nature of Work

    C. Purpose of Work (lifestyles)

    D. Social Problem Solving

    E. Equal Opportunities and Work

VII. Development of Self-Awareness

    A. Personality

    B. Values and Goals

    C. Interests

    D. Skills and Abilities

    E. Physical Health and Grooming

    F. Character and Social Traits

    G. Personality and Job Success

    H. Development of Self-Concept
        1. Assertiveness
        2. Self-acceptance

VIII. Interpersonal Skills

    A. Employer-Employee
        1. Mutual expectations
        2. Need for rules
        3. Need for authority
        4. Fringe benefits
        5. Worker satisfaction

    B. Co-Worker

    C. Customer

    D. Family

    E. Group Dynamics (peer relationship)

IX. Career Exploration and Development

    A. Job Clusters

Exhibit 7-10 continued

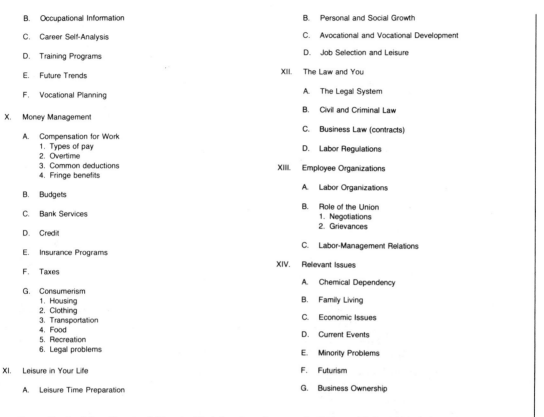

B. Occupational Information

C. Career Self-Analysis

D. Training Programs

E. Future Trends

F. Vocational Planning

X. Money Management

  A. Compensation for Work
      1. Types of pay
      2. Overtime
      3. Common deductions
      4. Fringe benefits

  B. Budgets

  C. Bank Services

  D. Credit

  E. Insurance Programs

  F. Taxes

  G. Consumerism
      1. Housing
      2. Clothing
      3. Transportation
      4. Food
      5. Recreation
      6. Legal problems

XI. Leisure in Your Life

  A. Leisure Time Preparation

B. Personal and Social Growth

C. Avocational and Vocational Development

D. Job Selection and Leisure

XII. The Law and You

  A. The Legal System

  B. Civil and Criminal Law

  C. Business Law (contracts)

  D. Labor Regulations

XIII. Employee Organizations

  A. Labor Organizations

  B. Role of the Union
      1. Negotiations
      2. Grievances

  C. Labor-Management Relations

XIV. Relevant Issues

  A. Chemical Dependency

  B. Family Living

  C. Economic Issues

  D. Current Events

  E. Minority Problems

  F. Futurism

  G. Business Ownership

Source: Reprinted from *Vocational Education Work Experience Programs for Students with Special Needs Curriculum Outline and Bibliography*, pp. 1–5, Vocational Technical Division, Minnesota Department of Education, 1977.

Following are some additional tips about the design of training plans for business and industry:

- The training plan should be individualized for each student's needs and relate to the functional skills demanded at the training site.
- The training plan should take into account the student's career development needs.
- The training plan should be developed through a cooperative effort by the teacher-coordinator, the student, the employer, and the person with direct supervision and training responsibility.
- The training plan should be simple, realistic, and flexible enough to meet both student and employer needs.
- The training plan should be an ongoing curriculum development process, not a document developed at the beginning of the year and filed away.

- Copies of the training plan should be open to review and be distributed to the student, the employer, and the coordinator.

**COORDINA-
TION OF
INSTRUCTION
IN THE COOP-
ERATIVE
VOCATIONAL
PROGRAM**

In the successful cooperative work experience program, the coordinator is able to blend the general related instruction and the direct instruction with the identified support services needed to have the student succeed in occupational development. To understand more clearly how to manage this blend of activity and education, assume that the person in charge of the cooperative vocational program is the teacher-coordinator. In this situation, the student learners begin their occupational development by participating in an initial vocational assessment process. Through this process, the students begin to learn about their skill, needs, and interests. Support services and appropriate training stations are matched and the students begin to learn functional occupational skills.

For example, a week of instruction might occur at the start of the year with a schedule like the one presented in Table 7-2. The teacher-coordinator, assuming the major responsibility for instruction at the start of the year, begins individual instruction on Tuesday. On Thursday, some individual instruction occurs cooperatively in small groups.

However, as the year progresses and the students become familiar with the program, the pattern of instruction gradually changes. Through participation in small group instructional cooperative learning and in individualized direct instruction, the students' skills increase. The instruction plan then begins to resemble the schedule shown in Table 7-3.

Using this schedule of instructional management, the teacher-coordinator instructs the students how to take responsibility and how to set up their own instructional methodology.

The advantages of such a system of instruction are as follows:

- The students learn how to take responsibility for their own learning.
- The curriculum of the program is allowed to progress and evolve based on the students' progress and on training station changes.

Table 7-2 Week of Instruction: Beginning of Year

Monday	Tuesday	Wednesday	Thursday	Friday
Teacher directed lock-step lecture on safety on the job	Teacher directed individual activity for students on specific units	Teacher directed large group film on safety on the highway	Teacher directed small group instruction on safety rules in school and home	Teacher directed class meeting. Guest speaker on safety

Table 7-3 Week of Instruction: Later in the Year

Monday	Tuesday	Wednesday	Thursday	Friday
Teacher directed instruction on decision making for career choices	Small group student directed instruction on exploring career choices, still somewhat structured through teacher coordinator	Student directed individualized instruction on specific remediation or job skill training	Student and teacher directed lab experiments on small job sample experiences	Teacher directed large group film selected by student committee

- Once the structure is established, it allows students to transfer in and out of the program with a minimum of time loss. The teacher-coordinator can supplement lost instructional time with a particular student without necessarily hindering the progress of other students.
- The system allows for many individual differences among students.
- Once the system is developed and field-tested, it allows for development and expansion in a variety of occupational areas, but it still provides the general learning that all students should have.

The disadvantages of such a system are as follows:

- Some teachers continually feel the need to instruct and direct the students' activities and thus fail to let the system work.
- The system takes a lot of initial effort to organize, implement, and monitor.
- This type of instructional program does not resemble the traditional secure classroom approach that many educators are most familiar with.

An important part of the natural responsibility of a cooperative vocational program is the movement of a student into direct employment or into a postsecondary training program. There are a number of tactics and strategies that a teacher-coordinator should use through coordination with appropriate school personnel. The steps involved in the articulation of a student with special needs into the community are as follows:

THE FOLLOW-UP AND TRANSITION OF THE SPECIAL NEEDS STUDENT

1. Identify the adult service agencies in the local area and implement a working relationship with the contact representatives.

2. Develop a transition team for future programming after graduation or for present programming if efforts in securing appropriate training stations do not meet the needs of students.

3. Develop formalized interagency agreements with the adult service providers and the school district to facilitate meeting case management responsibilities, providing consistent services, maintaining client eligibility standards, and making vocational placements.

4. Ensure the provision of appropriate data gathering on students so that the student outputs match the service and placement requirements of the job market and the adult service providers.

5. Collect follow-up data from employers, postsecondary schools, and adult service providers to find out what is happening to program graduates. Be sure to modify program activities as needed.

SUMMARY

Applications of cooperative vocational education, as adapted for youth with special needs, have been explored in this chapter. With the use of energy, creativity, cooperative relationships, and sound methodology, it is possible to educate students with special needs to their fullest potential. Educators who are challenged by the ideas and procedures discussed in this chapter should pursue their particular interest by talking to others in the field and by doing additional reading in cooperative vocational education. The results of such follow-up can be very rewarding.

NOTES

1. G. Warrington, *Vocational Education Non-paid Community-based Career Exploration and Supported Work Options* (White Bear Lake, Minn.: Minnesota Curriculum Services Center, 1986); P. Wehman and P. McLaughlin, *Vocational Curriculum for Developmentally Disabled Persons* (Baltimore, Md.: University Park Press, 1980).

2. C. Delaney, R. Dittmer, L. Hagestuen, B. Haskins, B. Jaehne, P. Johnson, R. Koebnick, J. Lauritsen, K. Munsch, and J. Zollar, *Vocational Education Work Experience Program for Handicapped Students: Teacher-Coordinator Handbook*. White Bear Lake, Minn.: Minnesota Curriculum Services Center, 1986, p. 6.

3. U.S. Department of Labor, *Regulations, Part 524: Special Minimum Wages for Handicapped Workers in Competitive Employment*, WH publ. no. 1316 (Washington, D.C.: GPO, 1985), sec 524.1(C)(1).

4. Warrington, *Vocational Education Non-paid Community-based Career Exploration*, p. 37.

5. K. Hendricks-McCracken, *A Community Based Employment Training Pilot Program: An Interagency Agreement That Works* (Bemidji, Minn.: Bemidji State University, 1986).

6. Warrington, *Vocational Education Non-paid Community-based Career Exploration*, pp. 49–50.

7. C. Engel et al., *Work Experience Curriculum Outline and Bibliography* (St. Paul, Minn.: Minnesota Department of Education, 1977).

8. J. Harless, *An Ounce of Analysis (Is Worth a Pound of Objectives)* (Newnan, Ga.: Harless Performance Guild, 1975); R. Swanson and D. Gradous, *Performance at Work: A Systematic Program for Analyzing Work Behavior* (New York: John Wiley & Sons, 1986).

REFERENCES

Asumma, C., D. Blomster, M. Gavin, W. Gulbrandson, J. Henricks, J. Joosten, D. Kingsbury, D. Revsbeck, B. Richter, R. Rubato, J. Schneck, G. Schwang, and T. Skaja. *Vocational Assessment: A Guide to Improving Vocational Programming for Special Needs Youth*. Bemidji, Minn.: Bemidji State University, 1986.

Bichner, J., L. Brizinski, N. Crewdson, G. Cronquist, V. Hoff, D. Jenson, E. Osland, and D. Shawbold. *Teacher-Coordinator Handbook: Secondary Vocational Community Based Employment Programs.* White Bear Lake, Minn.: Minnesota Curriculum Services Center, 1978.

Delaney, C., R. Dittmer, L. Hagestuen, B. Haskins, B. Jaehne, P. Johnson, R. Koebnick, J. Lauritsen, K. Munsch, and J. Zollar. *Vocational Education Work Experience Program for Handicapped Students: Teacher-Coordinator Handbook.* White Bear Lake, Minn.: Minnesota Curriculum Services Center, 1986.

Engel, C., B. Fields, M. Noesen, K. Gorsky, C. Haskins, M. Henderlite, and C. Kasma. *Work Experience Curriculum Outline and Bibliography.* St. Paul, Minn.: Minnesota Department of Education, 1977.

Harless, J. *An Ounce of Analysis (Is Worth a Pound of Objectives).* Newnan, Ga.: Harless Performance Guild, 1975.

Hendricks-McCracken, K. *A Community Based Employment Training Pilot Program: An Interagency Agreement That Works.* Bemidji, Minn.: Bemidji State University, 1986.

Ohio Department of Education. *Ohio's Career Development Continuum.* Columbus, Ohio: author, no date.

Swanson, R., and D. Gradous. *Performance at Work: A Systematic Program for Analyzing Work Behavior.* New York: John Wiley & Sons, 1986.

U.S. Department of Labor. *Regulations, Part 524: Special Minimum Wages for Handicapped Workers in Competitive Employment.* WH publ. no. 1316. Washington, D.C., GPO, 1985.

Warrington, G. *Vocational Education Non-paid Community-based Career Exploration and Supported Work Options.* White Bear Lake, Minn.: Minnesota Curriculum Services Center, 1986.

Wehman, P., and P. McLaughlin. *Vocational Curriculum for Developmentally Disabled Persons.* Baltimore, Md.: University Park Press, 1980.

Chapter 8

Identification and Utilization of Support Services in Serving Vocational Special Needs Students

Susan B. Asselin, Ph.D.

The goal of vocational special needs education is to develop the occupational competence of individuals and provide them with basic academic and social skills to make career choices and become productive citizens of our society. Providing vocational training and employment services to special populations is mandated in legislative initiatives concerning education as well as rehabilitation and labor.

This goal cannot be attained without involvement of professionals from all levels of education from elementary through postsecondary, personnel from rehabilitation, social services, and other human services agencies, and parents and employers. The development of a sequential, appropriate career-vocational preparation program is crucial to the success of special needs populations.

The career-vocational preparation process begins in the elementary years with basic academic skills, social skills, and independent living skills. Although these skills are introduced in the elementary years, they are continually reinforced throughout the educational process. Special needs students also develop at the elementary level an awareness of careers and the requirements for those careers. At the secondary level, students actually explore a variety of careers through prevocational programs such as industrial arts, business, or home economics. Prior to enrollment in a specific occupational program, special needs students undergo a vocational assessment of interests, aptitudes, and abilities. If a student experiences difficulties in obtaining or maintaining occupational competencies, then a program of work adjustment may be provided.

The ultimate goal for special needs students is job placement at either the secondary or postsecondary level. For some students, continued postsecondary education may be appropriate; for others, placement in a job. If students are placed in a job, there is usually a need to provide continued follow-up services and reinforcement of occupational and job-keeping skills. Subsequent to job placement, special needs individuals require opportunities to develop independent, community living, social, leisure, and family living skills. With an appropriate sequence of steps in career-vocational preparation (as outlined), environmental and attitudinal barriers against special populations can be eliminated and full integration into the community facilitated.

DIVERSITY OF VOCATIONAL SPECIAL NEEDS

The career-vocational preparation process is comprehensive and must involve coordination of professionals from a variety of disciplines, settings, and programs in order to serve the diverse population of special needs students.

Student Population

In the early 1970s, about 1 percent of the enrollment of vocational education was composed of handicapped students. The latest figures reveal that 2.7 percent of the vocational education enrollment is composed of handicapped students, about 15.4 percent is composed of disadvantaged students, and .9 percent is composed of limited English proficient students.[1] Not only have enrollments increased, but so has the diversity of students within these categories (i.e., the disadvantaged and handicapped). Currently, disadvantaged populations include migrants, offenders, those with limited English proficiency, and those who are dropouts or potential dropouts from secondary programs. Programs for more severely handicapped and gifted students in vocational education serve to further expand the range of potential students.

Postsecondary programs in community colleges, vocational-technical centers, and trade schools; human service agencies such as vocational rehabilitation, sheltered workshops, day activity centers; and supported employment programs all provide special needs individuals with vocational training and employment opportunities. Beyond the academic and occupational skills provided at the postsecondary level, additional support services address the personal, social, and family needs of adult learners. Vocational training, employment, and myriad support services required at the postsecondary level result in an even more diverse group of professionals involved in helping special needs students make the transition from secondary education to postsecondary education and eventually to the world of work and independent living.

Professionals

The most effective delivery of career-vocational preparation involves professionals outside vocational and special education. Even the definition of a vocational special needs professional appears to be changing. Individuals from the fields of rehabilitation, vocational counseling and evaluation, social and community services, human services, and labor are becoming interested and active in developing pre-employment and employment skills of special populations. This diversity of philosophies, background education, and experiences must be coordinated to provide the best possible vocational program for special needs populations.

Vocational special needs programming spans the entire lifetime of an individual and is no longer restricted to secondary education. Career education, academic skills, and independent living skills at the elementary level provide the foundation for secondary vocational preparation. At the junior high level, careers are explored; and at the senior high level, students enroll in career preparation courses. At the postsecondary level, pre-employment and occupational skills are further developed, with a greater emphasis on independence and self-sufficiency.

The setting for skill development is dependent on the severity of a student's special need, the availability of resources or programs, and the ability of service providers to work together. In secondary and postsecondary education, vocational training programs provide a continuum of services that promote placement in the least restrictive environment. The instructional setting may be (1) a self-contained program in a special or regular school, (2) a regular vocational (mainstream) program, with support services from special education, remedial education, vocational resources, or support personnel, or (3) a regular vocational program with no support services. Placement decisions are made based on the severity of the handicap or learning problems, local manpower resources, program availability, and the willingness of teachers to serve special needs students.

Setting

Other vocational training options besides occupationally specific vocational programs are available to special needs students. These include cooperative work experiences, which are part of many vocational programs and even some apprenticeship programs. On-the-job training in competitive employment can provide even the more severely learning handicapped person with positive work experiences. Research has shown that when classroom instruction is reinforced by placement in an actual job setting, a special needs student's chance of success is greatly increased.[2] A variety of on-the-job training options can be utilized and matched to the needs of the population served. Programs that feature sheltered enclaves, mobile work crews, and supported work with job coaches or trainers report a high success rate for severely handicapped individuals.[3]

Disadvantaged and handicapped students may receive training through a specialized job training program or in a postsecondary vocational program at a vocational technical center, trade school, or community college. Vocational rehabilitation, sheltered workshops, industry job training programs, and colleges provide postsecondary training as well. Various levels of support services may be provided to special needs students in community colleges or universities through a student services coordinator. Special assistance may include instructional aids or materials, tutors, notetakers, adapted equipment at work stations, or career and personal counseling to ensure the students' success at the postsecondary level.

While prevocational and specific vocational skills were the early focus in vocational special needs programs, the emphasis has been expanded to include life skills, independent living skills, consumer skills, home and family living skills, self-help and health skills, mobility skills, and job seeking and keeping skills. This is in line with a study by the National Commission on Secondary Vocational Education on the

**Vocational
Special Needs
Program Focus**

role and function of vocational education: *The Unfinished Agenda*.[4] In this report, the commission recognized the importance of teaching personal, communications, employability, and specific occupational skills as well as the foundations for career planning and lifelong learning. It has long been recognized that occupational competence and acceptable personal and social skills contribute to success in the workplace and home. These skill areas must be addressed in the educational program of special needs students as early as kindergarten and then reinforced for success in ongoing vocational programs.

SUPPORT SERVICES

The Carl D. Perkins Act defines handicapped and disadvantaged individuals as those who require special or related services and assistance in order to be successful in vocational education programs. This section will explore support services at the secondary and postsecondary level.

Secondary Level Services

At the secondary level, a variety of support services are available. Special education or remedial education can provide individualized instruction to develop basic academic, social, and independent living skills needed for success in vocational programs. Vocational teachers can reinforce basic skills learned in special education.

Special and vocational educators have a tool to develop programs that reinforce these skills: the individualized education program (IEP). The IEP is designed for handicapped students. When an IEP is developed by the special education teacher in conjunction with the vocational education teacher, deficiencies in basic skills can be targeted and skill strengths reinforced. The IEP is composed of information on a student's present level of functioning, educational goals and objectives, and criteria for evaluation. If a handicapped student is to be placed in a vocational program, then a vocational goal and vocational objectives must be included in the IEP. This provides vocational and special education teachers with an opportunity to review the data in the IEP, discuss the student's strengths and weaknesses, and prescribe an instructional program for success in prevocational or vocational training. This should be done prior to placement in a specific vocational program.

Another support service that should be provided prior to placing a handicapped or disadvantaged student in a prevocational or vocational program is vocational assessment. Vocational assessment is a process for screening students and determining their interests and abilities in relation to specific occupational programs. Assessments are administered by a trained vocational evaluator in a school-based or rehabilitation setting. The evaluator discusses the results with special and vocational educators and the student is placed in the most appropriate program, with specific guidelines for instruction that meets the student's individual needs.

The results of the vocational assessment may suggest that the special needs student will benefit from physical or occupational therapy. Physical therapy may be needed to develop the student's mobility, dexterity, or gross or fine motor coordination. More specifically, the physical therapist may prescribe exercises to strengthen muscles, coordinate body movements, or increase mobility of joints. An occupational therapist focuses on functional daily living skills such as dressing, writing, eating, and grooming. Assistive devices may be designed and modifications in the home environment suggested to maximize independence.[5]

Some school districts provide courses for special needs students to develop career or occupational readiness. These courses are typically offered before enrollment in occupationally specific vocational programs. Students work on developing a self-concept and career awareness and orientation, as well as work habits, and job seeking and keeping skills. As a follow-up, students may be placed in a supervised work experience program. Work experience programs are designed to reinforce classroom instruction by providing students with realistic, concrete learning experiences. A similar program may be offered as a work adjustment program.

Special needs students may be placed in vocational programs only to discover that specific work habits and attitudes are inadequate to maintain employment. A work adjustment program developed by a work adjustment instructor in cooperation with the vocational and special education instructors pinpoints problem areas and prescribes an instructional plan. The types of skills needed might include following directions, punctuality, adequate speed and accuracy of work, cooperation with co-workers, and responding well to criticism. Careful planning ensures that the student's deficiencies are remediated so that the student can return to the vocational program.

Another support service needed by special needs students is counseling. Special needs students may come from economically or socially unstable family situations or be under the care of foster families or probation officers. These conditions can negatively affect a special needs student's interactions and performance at school. The negative effect may be exaggerated by low self-esteem and lack of self-confidence. These types of problems often manifest themselves in the classroom as problems in attitude, attendance, motivation, performance, and behavior. A school guidance counselor is the best individual available to assist students in developing skills to overcome these problems. Individual counseling sessions may be prescribed to help a student work out feelings of anger, hostility, or fear. Then a vocational program that reinforces appropriate behaviors and satisfactory performance can be developed by the guidance counselor and the vocational and special education teachers.

In addition to guidance counselors, school districts may employ a vocational school psychologist. The role of a vocational school psychologist is varied. It includes administering vocational-related assessment and diagnostic procedures, conducting personal-social counseling for independent living and employment, providing referrals to school and community services, and conducting inservice training of teachers in areas such as learning style or behavior management.[6] Although vocational school psychologists are relatively new to vocational special needs, their expertise in assessment, counseling, and consultation related to vocational education is an excellent resource for vocational special needs students.

School-based support services may be provided by vocational special needs or resource (support) personnel. These individuals may be trained in both special and vocational education. Their primary role is to provide indirect or direct service to special needs students in vocational programs.[7] Indirect service involves assisting teachers in adapting instructional materials, teaching techniques, or equipment. If they cannot provide the service themselves, resource personnel may refer the teachers to others. For example, a resource person might ask the maintenance department to construct or adapt laboratory facilities. Schools using resource personnel rely on them to coordinate linkages between vocational and special education teachers and adult service agencies such as rehabilitation services. Direct service to students involves working with individuals or small groups of students in the vocational classroom or laboratory. Vocational resource personnel can assist the vocational teacher by teaching prerequisite skills, reinforcing specific skills, or making modifications to meet learning styles of special needs students.

If vocational resource personnel are unavailable, paraprofessionals may be employed to assist vocational teachers and special needs students. While paraprofessionals are unable to plan and prescribe instruction, they may implement a vocational teacher's lesson plan. Paraprofessionals may also be used to tutor individuals or small groups of students, freeing the teacher to work with special needs students. An extra pair of eyes and hands during laboratory extends the influence of the teacher during instruction. Besides direct teaching assistance, paraprofessionals may help prepare equipment, consumable supplies, and audio-visual materials for instruction and maintain records and observe student behaviors.[8]

Peer tutors function in the classroom similarly to paraprofessionals. Peer tutors for special needs students are most effective if they are trained in directing instruction, developing rapport, reinforcement strategies, and observation, among other things.[9] Not only do the tutors help special needs students, but their own learning is enhanced by the experience. Peer tutors are readily available to vocational teachers.

Outside agencies may be utilized as support services for students at the secondary level. The transition-from-school-to-work movement and recent legislative initiatives have increased the involvement of adult service agencies at the secondary level. As an example, vocational rehabilitation services may assign handicapped students to a caseworker as early as the ninth grade. Several states are using a case management approach in which vocational rehabilitation counselors are based in public schools to work with special and vocational educators. An individualized work rehabilitation plan (IWRP) is developed cooperatively between vocational education, special education, and rehabilitation personnel before the student graduates from secondary school. This collaboration involves sharing assessment information gathered by personnel from special education, vocational evaluation, and vocational education. The result is a well-designed, appropriate rehabilitation plan.

Support services from community agencies and organizations take on greater significance at the postsecondary level. In vocational special needs, the concern should be with the whole person, not with the person just as a vocational student. Studies have shown that students who are unsuccessful on the job possess deficiencies in personal and social skills, but not in occupational competence. If special needs students do not know how to cope with daily living problems or whom to contact for assistance, then all the job skill preparation will have been wasted. Students need to be informed at the secondary level what agencies are available. Support services include legal, social, health, employment, counseling, and financial services; these are among the potential resources available to students.

Postsecondary Level Services

The special needs student's postsecondary plans will determine what specific support services should be provided. For instance, if the individual attends a community college or university, an equal opportunity or student services professional may assist the student in instruction, counseling, or mobility. If employment is chosen, the appropriate adult service agency may provide support services in securing and maintaining employment.

Vocational rehabilitation is the typical adult service agency for handicapped adults. Eligibility for services depends on there being a mental or physical handicap that is a substantial obstacle to employment and there being a reasonable expectation that the individual can benefit from vocational training. In some states, the visually impaired and mentally retarded may be served under other state agencies, but the services are similar. Available services include medical treatment, artificial appliances, vocational training, family and personal counseling, job placement and follow-up, independent living, and physical and occupational therapy. The goal of vocational rehabilitation is to restore the individual to physical, social, mental, and economic usefulness.

Vocational rehabilitation may broker services from other agencies or refer its clients to these agencies. One such type of agency is the independent living center (ILC). Peer counseling, job search assistance, wheelchair repair, health care referral, physical accommodation, transportation, and attendant care are among the services provided by ILCs. The focus of these centers is on developing the whole person— cognitively, physically, emotionally, and socially. An important aspect of ILCs is that they are operated by disabled individuals.

Related to the concept of independent living are the services offered by rehabilitation homemakers or independent living specialists. The focus of such services is the development of self-care and self-dependence in the home. Counseling and training in areas such as consumer skills, family finances, meal planning and preparation, child care, family living, nutrition, and housing are provided by a home economist trained in rehabilitation techniques. Vocational rehabilitation, cooperative extension, social services, and hospitals employ rehabilitation homemakers or independent living specialists.[10]

Social and health services are also utilized by special needs adults. Social services provide support to families to help solve personal and financial problems by administering benefit and service programs. Benefit programs include Aid to Dependent Children (ADC), food stamps, fuel assistance, medical assistance, and emergency relief services. Service programs include employment, foster care, child protection, family planning, volunteers, and counseling for abused spouses. The health department offers programs such as clinics for well babies, maternity care, immunization, and family physician programs. While these programs concern the special needs individual and the family, employment services focus on providing opportunities for the special needs individuals to become economically independent, productive citizens.

Employment training for special needs individuals is available from a variety of sources. The Job Training Partnership Act provides job training for disadvantaged youths and adults. Special needs individuals who are economically disadvantaged or handicapped qualify for this training. Services under the act include job search assistance, career counseling, basic academic skill training, occupational awareness and exploration, and work experience programs, as well as literacy and bilingual programs.

Supported work programs are becoming readily available both to handicapped youths and adults. These programs provide employment opportunities carefully monitored by a job coach. The job coach is actively involved with the special needs individual on the job site during training. Off-the-job-site time is spent dealing with transportation, independent living skills, program development, and advocacy.[11]

Supported employment may also involve job placement with groups of handicapped individuals, as in a mobile work crew or enclave. A mobile work crew moves from one job site to another with a supervisor. An example might be in grounds maintenance, where a mobile work crew could be part of a mobile lawn care business. An enclave is a small group of handicapped workers employed with nonhandicapped workers. The onsite supervisor provides assistance to the handicapped individuals, as do the co-workers and employer. An enclave of handicapped workers may occur as an assembly line component in a factory.

Transition support services for handicapped individuals are more than employment related. Vocational competence is the goal of vocational programming, but personal, social, leisure, and family skills are also important.[12] These latter require that there be even greater collaborative efforts between agencies and organizations that serve special populations than would otherwise be necessary.

COOPERATION AND COORDINATION

As vocational special needs personnel attempt to work with individuals from education, rehabilitation, and human services and with parents and employers, some difficulties may be encountered. While most of these individuals represent agencies that have a similar goal for handicapped or disadvantaged clients, they often operate without a basic knowledge of one another. This lack of knowledge may result in duplication of services or even gaps in services. Barriers to cooperation and coordination of efforts must be identified and dealt with before professionals develop a working relationship.

Recognizing Barriers

One way of identifying barriers is proposed by Wiant, Warmbrod, and Pratzner.[13] They describe four dimensions of an interorganizational framework for interactions between human service organizations. In this model, interactions are categorized into situational, structural, process, and outcome dimensions. Descriptions of the four dimensions follow:

1. The *situational dimension* deals with conditions that should be present for interagency relationships. These include recognition of a need to share common resources, an awareness of one another's agency, and a commitment to a common goal.
2. The *structural dimension* involves specific aspects that regulate or govern each organization, the perceived power of each organization, and the interrelatedness and involvement of the organizations.
3. The *process dimension* is an extension of the structural dimension to encompass the working relationship between the organizations. This relationship includes the flow of information and resource between the organizations, as well as the conflicts that may occur.
4. The *outcome dimension* represents the definition of a common goal between organizations, and an analysis of its effectiveness for the impact on all organizations.

Common barriers to effective interactions between education, rehabilitation, and human service agencies include the following:

1. Situational Dimension Barriers:

   - lack of knowledge about other agencies or organizations that provide services to special needs youth
   - lack of coordination among the school-based IEP and human service agency program plans (such as the individualized work rehabilitation plan)
   - feelings of possessiveness concerning the well-being of special needs individuals
   - lack of commitment to work cooperatively with other agencies at all levels of an organization

2. Structural Dimension Barriers:

   - administrative structure and the regulations under which agencies and organizations operate
   - failure to include the special needs individual, the family, the school, the human service agency, and the employer in the decisionmaking process
   - failure to base decisions on adequate vocational assessment data

3. Process Dimension Barriers:

   - lack of continuity of services from school to adult agencies, with no agency responsible for articulation into adult agencies
   - lack of a system for sharing vocational information and assessment data among schools and human service agencies[14]

Eliminating Barriers

Given that knowledge about other organizations is the key to developing cooperation among service providers, steps need to be taken to collect information about all potential agencies that meet the needs of handicapped and disadvantaged youths and adults. Sarkees and Scott[15] describe a process that facilitates acquiring an understanding of other agencies. This process includes (1) sharing agency information, (2) identifying necessary services, and (3) determining common services. Sharing agency information is comparable to the structural dimension. It is important to get to know an agency's or an organization's goals and philosophy, administrative structure, operating procedures, funding sources, organizational flow charts, and clientele.

The next step in the process is to identify what services handicapped or disadvantaged individuals need from each agency. This is comparable to the situational dimension. Such services may include vocational training, vocational assessment, job seeking and keeping skills, job placement and monitoring, and training in social, leisure, and independent living skills. At the same time, needed services that are beyond the scope of each agency are also identified.

When the final step in the process, identifying common services, is reached, existing services and needs are then matched to those available through other agencies. This is comparable to the structural dimension. The existence of a gap or a duplication of services can be determined collaboratively. While this process involves an initial series of steps, there are also some more specific techniques for developing coordination of services.

Techniques for Collaboration

The IEP is the primary tool for promoting collaboration between vocational education and special education at the secondary level. The development of the vocational goals and objectives for each handicapped student in a vocational program is the responsibility of both vocational and special education teachers. The occupational competence of the student is a common goal for both teachers, and the assessment information on the IEP provides substantial data for making placement and instructional decisions. While the IEP is developed for handicapped students, some vocational teachers develop training plans for all students who are employed in work experience programs. With the recent emphasis on transition, school districts are developing individualized transition plans (ITPs). These transition plans involve not only school personnel, but also adult service agency personnel from rehabilitation or mental retardation, for example. The development of any individualized plan is time consuming, and most schools find that more personnel are needed in order for planning to be successful.

Vocational resource (support) personnel across the nation are becoming the main link between special and vocational education in developing IEPs and ITPs. These resource personnel provide assistance in the assessment, placement, and monitoring of special needs students in vocational programs.[7] They are also responsible for developing cooperation between education and adult service agencies to ensure special needs students make the transition from secondary education to postsecondary education or employment and receive the necessary services.

With the emphasis on transition from school to work, some states are assigning handicapped students to a case manager early in the high school years. The case manager is from the agency or organization that will serve the student in adulthood. Efforts are made to ensure that the student receives an appropriate education, assessment, and placement. This requires communication between the agency, the special needs individual, the parents or guardians, and school personnel.

Comprehensive programming must involve professionals working cooperatively to develop vocational, social, academic, and emotional competence among vocational special needs individuals. Articulation between educators and rehabilitation personnel must begin early and continue until the special needs individual is self-sufficient. Support services provided in elementary, secondary, and postsecondary education and by adult service agencies must be coordinated. Currently, no one agency is charged with the responsibility for this coordination. Therefore, it is up to vocational special needs professionals who are experienced in working in inter-disciplinary programs to provide the leadership.

SUMMARY

NOTES

1. National Center for Educational Statistics, *Vocational Education Data Systems* (Washington, D.C.: Department of Education, 1982).

2. S. Hasazi, B. Gordon, and C.A. Roe, "Factors Associated with the Employment Status of Handicapped Youth Exiting High School from 1979 to 1983," *Exceptional Children* 51, no. 6 (1985): 455–69.

3. T.T. Bellamy, R. Horner, and D. Inman, *Vocational Training of Severely Retarded Adults* (Baltimore, Md.: University Park Press, 1979); M. Hill and P. Wehman, "Cost Benefit Analysis of Placing Moderately and Severely Handicapped Individuals into Competitive Employment," *Journal of the Association for Persons with Severe Handicaps* 8 (1983): 30–38.

4. National Commission on Secondary Vocational Education, *The Unfinished Agenda: The Role of Vocational Education in the High School* (Columbus, Ohio: Ohio State University, National Center for Research in Vocational Education, n.d.).

5. R.M. Goldenson, *Disability and Rehabilitation Handbook* (New York: McGraw-Hill, 1978).

6. T.H. Hohenshil, J.W. Shepard, and C.F. Capps, "Vocational School Psychology: Serving Special Needs Students," *Journal for Vocational Special Needs Education* 4, no. 1 (1982): 5–8.

7. S.B. Asselin, "DACUM Approach to Vocational Resource Teacher Education" (Paper presented at the National Conference on Secondary, Transitional, and Postsecondary Education for Exceptional Youth, Boston, Mass., March 1985).

8. S.F. Vasa, A.L. Steckelberg, and L.U. Ronning, *Guide for Effective Utilization of Paraprofessionals in Special Education* (Lincoln, Nebr.: University of Nebraska-Lincoln, Department of Special Education, 1983).

9. S.B. Asselin and A.G. Anderson, "Peer Tutors: An Idea That Works," *Journal of Vocational Special Needs Education* 8, no. 2 (1986): 21–24.

10. L.O. Schwab, "Vocational Homemaking and Independent Living in Rehabilitation Facilities," in *Rehabilitation Facility Approaches to Severe Disabilities*, ed. J.G. Cull and R.E. Hardy (Springfield, Ill.: Charles C Thomas, 1975).

11. P. Wehman and J. Kregel, "A Supported Work Approach to Competitive Employment of Individuals with Moderate and Severe Handicaps," *Journal of the Association for Persons with Severe Handicaps* 10, no. 2 (1985): 4–7.

12. A.S. Halpern, "Transition: A Look at the Foundations," *Exceptional Children* 51, no. 6 (1985): 479–86.

13. A. Wiant, C.P. Warmbrod, and F.C. Pratzner, "Interagency Linkages: A Field Study," *Facts and Findings* 2, no. 16 (1984): 1–7.

14. H.W. Johnson, J.A. McLaughlin, and M. Christensen, "Interagency Collaboration Driving and Restraining Forces," *Exceptional Children* 48 (February 1982): 395–99; L.W. Tindall and J.J. Gugerty, *Improving Vocational Education and Employment for Handicapped People: A Process for Facilitating Interagency Linkages in Wisconsin* (Madison, Wis.: University of Wisconsin-Madison, Vocational Studies Center, 1982).

15. M.D. Sarkees and J. Scott, *Vocational Special Needs* (Alsip, Ill.: American Technical Publishers, 1985).

Chapter 9

Vocational Assessment: The Evolving Role

Carole A. Veir, Ed.D.

Peterson and Hill define vocational assessment as ''a holistic approach which considers an individual's total career development . . . [whose purpose] is to collect and provide objective career information for parents, educators, the student, and others to use in planning appropriate educational experiences to enhance the student's employability.''[1] Dahl, Appleby, and Lipe provide further definition: Vocational assessment is ''a comprehensive process conducted over a period of time, involving a multi-disciplinary team . . . with the purpose of identifying individual characteristics, education, training, and placement needs, which provide educators the basis for planning an individual's program . . .''[2] Vocational assessment is a continuous process of collecting information that can assist in making decisions regarding students' educational needs; such information can provide the opportunity for a more holistic approach to planning program placements and activities. It is clear from these definitions that vocational assessment activities should be part of an ongoing process of collecting, analyzing, integrating, and evaluating information about an individual student's vocational progress.

For a number of years, the terms *vocational assessment* and *vocational evaluation* have been used synonomously to refer to the activities yielding information about the employability skills and needs of handicapped persons, including recent high school students. While there are fundamental differences between vocational assessment and vocational evaluation, both have an appropriate place in the vocational progress of handicapped students. (Disadvantaged students, unless they are also handicapped, do not undergo vocational evaluation.) Although the differences and similarities have been argued about for years, it was not until the passage of the Carl D. Perkins Vocational Education Act of 1984 (Public Law 98-524) that the need to define both fields more clearly became evident.

Roberts says that ''the goal of work [vocational] evaluation is to answer these four questions: (1) Is the client ready to decide on a job training area? (2) If so, what?

DEFINING VOCATIONAL ASSESSMENT

(3) If not, why not? and (4) What is the treatment plan to bring about client and/or environmental changes so that the client can make the decision?"[3] Others have defined vocational evaluation as "identifying an individual's physical, mental and emotional abilities, limitations, and tolerances in order to predict his/her current and future employment potential and adjustment."[4] Numerous others, such as Pruitt, McCray, Neff, Hoffman, Levinson, and Sankovsky, have given similar definitions. Each definition is based on the premise that the evaluation is being conducted to determine individual competencies, needs, and adjustments for placement in a work environment.

However, it is clear that with the consistent use of the phrases "completing successfully the vocational education program" and "special services . . . designed to meet the needs identified" in the Carl D. Perkins Act, the act's assessment assurances require school-based, classroom-based assessment information to be gathered prior to an individual student's entry into a vocational program in order to determine his or her ability to complete successfully the school-based vocational program. Given the wording of these phrases, work-oriented evaluation would appear to be inappropriate. However, that should not eliminate vocational evaluation services for those handicapped students who may need further assistance in determining possible jobs and the development of appropriate employability skills specific to a job (i.e., work adjustment). Additionally, evaluation is usually a one-time, summative process that may last from six days to six weeks, and the short timeframe does not allow for the continuous formative feedback needed in a school setting. There is a place for both types of information for some handicapped students, but vocational assessment information is clearly meant to be school-oriented.

As the roles of vocational assessment and vocational evaluation continue to evolve, there will be many debates regarding the place and use of both types of information. The changes that have resulted from new legislation with a school-based, curricular focus have brought shifts in the nature of delivery, placement, services, personnel, and ultimately of the programs themselves.[5]

Impact of Federal Legislation

Handicapped and disadvantaged students throughout the years have been consistently overrepresented in the ranks of the unemployed and underemployed.[6] Several federal legislative mandates of the last decade have sought to alleviate some of the problems associated with the unemployment and underemployment of these students by creating more appropriate placements and by providing assistance for special needs students in career and vocational education programs. Among the federally mandated programs are the Education for All Handicapped Children Act of 1975 (Public Law 94-142), sections 503 and 504 of the Vocational Rehabilitation Act of 1973 (Public Law 91-112), section 123 of the Job Training Partnership Act (Public Law 97-300), and most recently the Carl D. Perkins Act.

Although the Education for All Handicapped Children Act required testing and placement of special education students (including students in vocational education), little attention has been given to providing any assessment related to vocational programming prior to placement of handicapped students. Disadvantaged students are not included under this act. It was not untl the Carl D. Perkins Act that vocational assessment appeared specifically in a legislative mandate. Now, as a result of both of these acts, handicapped and disadvantaged students are assured appropriate placement in regular vocational education programs as part of the vocational preparation process. General information to assist in developing assessment profiles for disadvantaged students can be gathered from tests required by chapter I, migrant education, and state mandated bilingual education programs.

In addition to requiring vocational assessment of handicapped and disadvantaged students enrolled in programs receiving federal dollars, the Carl D. Perkins Act requires other assurances related to the educational programs for these students. These assurances make certain that school districts and local schools are making programs accessible to handicapped and disadvantaged students and are taking steps to improve the quality of the vocational programs these students are enrolled in. Specifically, the act requires districts to sign assurances that "vocational education programs and activities for handicapped individuals will be provided in the least restrictive environment" (reinforcing section 612(5)(B) of the Education for All Handicapped Children Act) and "whenever appropriate be included as a component of the individualized education plan" (as required by section 612(4) and section 614(a)(5) of the Education for All Handicapped Children Act).[7] The Carl D. Perkins Act further stipulates that "vocational education planning for handicapped individuals will be coordinated between appropriate representatives of vocational education and special education."[8] This leaves no doubt that the parties are required to collaborate to determine the individual student's program. The Carl D. Perkins Act goes on to state that

> each local education agency shall, with respect to that portion of the allotment distributed in accordance with section 203(a) for vocational education services and activities for handicapped individuals and disadvantaged individuals, provide information to handicapped and disadvantaged students and parents of such students concerning the opportunities available in vocational education at least one year before the students enter the grade level in which vocational education programs are first generally available in the State, but in no event later than the ninth grade, together with the requirements for eligibility for enrollment in such vocational education programs.[9]

It also states that

> each student who enrolls in vocational education programs and to whom subsection (b) [see preceding quotation] applies shall receive assessment of the interests, abilities, and special needs of each student with respect to completing successfully the vocational education program; special services, including adaptation of curriculum, instruction, equipment, and facilities designed to meet the needs described [above].[10]

These mandates require state assurances (passed on to the local districts) that vocational assessment is to be provided in order to better identify the needs of each individual student to facilitate successful vocational program completion. These needs may require special services, curricula, instruction, equipment, facilities, or personnel; they are to be considered and provided (if necessary) to assure successful completion of the vocational education program.

There are several things that are noteworthy in the legislation: (1) No mention is made of work-related evaluation for job placement or adaptation, and (2) parents of handicapped and disadvantaged students and the students themselves are to be notified no later than the ninth grade of the opportunities available in vocational education and the requirements for eligibility. These can be interpreted to mean that vocational assessment should be completed no later than the beginning of the ninth grade so that the parents and students know which of the opportunities available may be most appropriate and where the student stands in relation to the requirements for eligibility. This vocational assessment information is needed no later than the ninth grade so that the parents and students can begin taking a realistic look at the appropriate available options. However, neither the summary of major provisions nor the summary of comments and responses in the final rules and regulations of the act mention the assessment requirement, nor how to implement the mandates. Therefore, state and local agencies should read and interpret the language with caution, though it would appear sound educational practice to present assessment information prior to discussing placement options that may be based on eligibility requirements.

Caution should be taken in using the vocational assessment information to narrow or screen out possible placements. It is important to note that the references to vocational assessment pertain to high school settings. The act requires "local educational agencies," not "eligible recipients," to make vocational assessments. Therefore, postsecondary settings are not required to provide vocational assessments, although it is strongly recommended. Vocational rehabilitation work evaluations would be appropriate for handicapped adults at that level.

Although not specifically mentioned in the act, it is advisable when collecting data for the vocational assessments of disadvantaged students that chapter I, migrant education, bilingual education, Indian education, or other service providers for disadvantaged students be consulted and considered in formulating decisions. Personnel working with economically and academically disadvantaged students have valuable data (as well as valuable insights) that can assist in developing an assessment profile for the students.

The law requires local education agencies to establish identification procedures to systematically locate disadvantaged students—those who are academically or economically disadvantaged and those having limited English-speaking skills—but it allows considerable discretion in interpreting the criteria and developing local policy guidelines. (Criteria to assist agencies in identifying disadvantaged students can be found in the Federal Register, August 18, 1985, p. 33233.) Again, utilizing the resources and data already available through programs such as chapter I, migrant education, Indian education and bilingual education and other programs serving students categorized under the Carl D. Perkins Act as disadvantaged could save a local school considerable time and effort. This is particularly true when expertise is needed with regard to cultural and linguistic variables affecting the educational progress of the student. The process of identification is not as difficult with regard to special education students, who will usually be identified through routine and annual special education procedures.

A major focus of the Carl D. Perkins Act is to provide expanded quality programs, services, and equal access to handicapped and disadvantaged students.[11] In order to develop relevant and appropriate goals and objectives to fulfill this mandate and provide these needed services, a more complete picture—indeed a holistic vocational profile—must be developed for each individual student. There has gradually been involvement of an increased number of persons in vocational programs, and a systematic planning process has been developed.[12] The Vocational Rehabilitation Act, particularly sections 503 and 504, and the Education for All Handicapped Children Act and its amendments (Public Law 98-199), as well as the Carl D. Perkins Act, assure that handicapped and now (through the Carl D. Perkins Act) disadvantaged students have the same right as other students to participate in vocational programs.

Numerous federal acts now provide incentives through federal funds to assist handicapped and disadvantaged students to better prepare for work through successful completion of vocational programs and courses at the secondary level. The Carl D. Perkins Act requires, invites, and makes possible the coordination of vocational education, special education, community-based organizations, Job Training Partnership Act (JTPA) activities, vocational rehabilitation, and public and private trainers in order to serve the handicapped and disadvantaged populations.

The legal requirements for vocational assessment provide a framework for the goals and benefits of vocational assessment. They rely upon the collaboration of various personnel to provide the information and support for comprehensive vocational assessment and services. Vocational assessment provides the basic outline for planning vocational programs for special needs students, with the outcomes or benefits being the successful completion of the vocational program, better job preparation, and eventually gainful employment.

Purpose of Vocational Assessment

Vocational assessment clearly has as its goal the gathering and providing of information to assist in making necessary modifications in the course or program curriculum, materials, instruction, and equipment to assure successful completion of the vocational program; to tailor the necessary modifications to an individual student's actual needs in the course or program; and to allow ongoing assessment throughout the duration of the student's program.

The process of gathering, analyzing, and evaluating the various data should provide, at a minimum, personnel, parents, and the student some insight into the student's specific

- abilities and needs
- learning styles

- requirements regarding teaching techniques and support services
- prerequisite or entry-level skill needs for a particular cluster, program, or class
- requirements for adaptations in materials, curriculum, facilities, and equipment
- areas of vocational interest
- psychomotor skills and dexterity
- realistic and obtainable goals and skills

In addition, schools or programs may use vocational assessment as a means of finding out information related to

- work habits
- work attitudes
- previous work experiences
- job readiness skills (grades 11 and 12)
- possible training and employment potential
- future needs for assessment, education, and training

The usefulness and necessity of the profile information in these six areas will have to be determined by the philosophy of the school district or by local program options, as well as by the nature and severity of the handicap or disadvantagement. The more severe the problem, the more specific and in-depth the information must be to determine and plan appropriate placement and programs. In some instances, a comprehensive assessment profile for a handicapped student may include formal vocational evaluation information to determine the student's job work potential and counseling needs and to predetermine actual job training situations.

Benefits of Vocational Assessments

For all special needs students the assessment should lead to a profile of ''instructionally relevant'' information through which appropriate placements in the regular vocational program can be developed, regardless of the ''appropriateness'' of one individual's program needs in relation to another.[13] Peterson summarizes the goals of vocational assessment as being to ''(a) determine whether students have adequate prerequisite skills for various types of vocational education programs; (b) suggest effective teaching techniques and institutional modifications for special students; (c) suggest needed support services; (d) provide the vocational teacher with improved information about the student; and (e) bridge the gap between special educators and vocational educators.''[14]

Among the benefits that result from achieving these goals should be

- a larger number of special needs students leaving school with more salable skills
- fewer students experiencing frustration and failure
- better preparation for postsecondary education or employment[15]

- more students being placed in programs in which they are more interested and for which they are more prepared and suited
- better preparation of students for entering the next phase of training
- more students having a realistic view of limitations and strengths
- more appropriate counseling
- obtainable program goals and objectives
- ongoing evaluation information leading to better feedback
- appropriate modifications in curriculum, facilities, equipment, delivery techniques, and student evaluation
- greater motivation to learn about the world of work and explore alternatives[16]
- greater motivation to learn and apply academic knowledge to concrete experiences
- a profile of information upon which to build a bridge for transition into the world of work or postsecondary training

These benefits do not exhaust the list. They do, however, represent the kind of benefits that parents, students, and school personnel can expect. In a 1981 position paper, the National Association of Vocational Education Special Needs Personnel (NAVESNP), a Special Needs Division affiliate of the American Vocational Association, stated that ''comprehensive vocational assessment services are considered to be an invaluable tool for use in career education planning for all students. However, students with special needs, especially handicapped or disadvantaged, should have priority in receiving comprehensive vocational assessment [evaluation] services.''

The goals are clear and many of the benefits are known. However, it will undoubtedly be some time before all of the benefits are apparent to parents, educators, students, or other personnel involved with serving special needs students.

TYPES OF ASSESSMENT

It is important that schools look at a variety of sources to determine and gather the data needed to make appropriate placements and program decisions. The Carl D. Perkins Act provides a framework for the areas needing to be tested at a minimum (interest, abilities, and special needs) and it makes clear that the assessment is to be targeted at school-based program placement. This has accelerated interest in vocational assessment and has prompted personnel to re-evaluate the assessments they conduct. In doing this, schools are beginning to develop models that relate the assessment activities to instructionally relevant purposes rather than to continue with the process and instrumentation emphases that have previously dominated the field.[17] This philosophy is not new, however. Trying to understand the performance of students in their current ecology has been advocated by Ysseldyke for many years.[18]

Traditional approaches to assessment, notably vocational evaluation, have been based upon the assumption that measures of existing aptitudes, interests, and traits can be used to predict subsequent learning, performance, and adjustment. Contemporary assessment, on the other hand, includes those practices that clearly link the purposes and outcomes of assessment with the goals and techniques of instruction and other forms of service and intervention.[19] Contemporary assessment requires the outcomes to have direct implications for program planning.[20] Desired information relates to school-based curricular needs and not, as with most traditional vocational processes, to employment suitability. The need now is to focus on information related to school-based curricular needs, with vocational evaluation for employment suitability intervening at a later stage in the educational program (i.e., 11th or 12th grade) to enable postsecondary decisions and vocational rehabilitation services to be designed.

The focus of vocational assessment in the school-based arena has changed in nature and purpose because of the Carl D. Perkins Act. This does not mean, however, that many of the types of assessment schools have been conducting are no longer appropriate. Students who have mild handicapping conditions (e.g., learning disabilities) will still have fewer formal assessments than the more severely handicapped. The more severely handicapped student will need more comprehensive and extensive assessment and may require a more formal, work-oriented evaluation format, such as the traditional vocational rehabilitation evaluation, if the student is unable to function in a regular classroom situation. An actual evaluation of work ability may be the best and most direct method to ensure appropriate placement.

There are at least two types of assessment that will provide part of the necessary information for developing a student assessment profile from which appropriate placement and program decisions can be made. The types of assessment used are determined by the information desired and needed for the student profile. The two basic types shall be referred to as *informal assessment* and *formal assessment*.

Informal Assessment

Informal assessment, often referred to in conjunction with criterion-based assessment, differs from formal assessment in four major areas: objectives, setting, personnel conducting the assessment, and materials used. The objectives of informal assessment include

- identifying students with learning problems
- identifying students who may be potential failures
- diagnosing students' strengths and academic needs
- providing information to assist in modifying the curriculum and lessons
- assisting in the identification of appropriate classroom materials based on classroom skills
- utilizing classroom teachers or other personnel familiar with the curriculum[21]

Optimally, these objectives are carried out in the local school setting (whether at a regional vocational technical center or school, a feeder school, or other similar local site), utilizing vocational programs developed specifically around local employment opportunities. The personnel conducting the assessment are most likely to be the vocational special needs specialist or the vocational teacher. Special education or

other personnel familiar with the vocational course content and programs are frequently asked to help with or conduct parts of the assessments. The materials used for
informal assessment vary, but usually include criterion-referenced instruments and
other similar informal materials.

Informal information that may be readily gathered by vocational personnel
includes course observational data and anecdotal records of student behavior and
performance. The information usually concerns such topics as

- functional educational levels
- prevocational skills and readiness
- educational records
- general coordination, motor skills, and stamina
- prior work experiences
- ability to follow directions
- relationships with peers
- responsiveness to authority
- ability to manipulate equipment
- classroom management strategies
- work attitudes
- punctuality and reliability
- learning styles
- reading levels
- specific skill needs
- informal work samples
- vocational and career interests
- vocational program tryouts
- health and medical records
- work and social habits
- family history

Records and data used should be reviewed to ensure they are current, relevant,
valid, factual, specific, and dated. Exhibit 9-1 presents a suggested format for setting
down vocational assessment profile information. Vocational personnel or vocational
special needs personnel can develop an assessment profile with this information.
Interviews may be particularly useful, as they can yield information about self-
perceptions, home environment, goals, social relationships in and outside of school,
learning strategies, fears, etc. Exhibit 9-2 is an example of a student interview form.
It is not always realistic to expect all vocational personnel to have the time to conduct
all the interviews or gather all the data needed by a multidisciplinary team. In districts
or schools where there are vocational special needs coordinators or teachers, or where
special personnel have been trained, they too can contribute to the information-

Exhibit 9-1 Vocational Assessment Information Form

VOCATIONAL ASSESSMENT—INFORMATION DEVELOPMENT
Disadvantaged/Handicapped Secondary Students

Component: _____

	What occurs presently	When it occurs	Who is responsible	What is done with the information
E X I S T S				

	What should occur	When it should occur	Who should be responsible	What should be done with the information
N E E D E D				

Source: Courtesy of Brian Cobb, University of Vermont. Form was developed for Vocational Assessment Institute, Juneau, Alaska, Summer 1986.

Exhibit 9-2 Student Interview Form

Student Interview

Name: _____ Date _____ # _____

Age: _____ DOB: _____ M_____ F_____

Parent's Name _____ Living with? Y   N

School: _____ Grade: _____

What classes do you like the most? _____

  Why? _____

What classes do you like the least? _____

  Why? _____

Jobs or responsibilities around home? Y   N   Describe: _____

_____

Paid work: Y   N   Describe: _____

_____

Parent's occupation: _____

Hobbies or favorite activities: _____

_____

What classes would you like to take? _____

_____

After high school do you want . . .

  A job Y   N   Describe: _____

  More education Y   N   Describe: _____

_____

Describe any handicaps you might have: _____

_____

Source: Courtesy of CAVEC Project, Southeast Regional Resource Center, Juneau, Alaska.

gathering process. However, a teacher familiar with the student may be able to contribute significant data without it becoming a time-consuming task.

Criterion-referenced instruments are another means of gathering significant data for the multidisciplinary team. These tests compare the performance of the student to a specific and predetermined level of desired task performance. Criterion-referenced instruments can accurately measure the area or content they are developed to test. Student test performance is accepted as typical and reliable. This type of testing compares a student's current performance to a specific level of desired task performance in the course or program.[22] Criterion-referenced instruments are particularly useful in the case of safety procedures, where 100 percent accuracy is desired. The level of performance selected as the criterion is the most appropriate level for the skill or set of skills to be learned.

Checklists, interviews, paper-pencil performance, and rating scales are examples of criterion-referenced tests. In developing checklists and rating scales, the teacher should list only behaviors critical or necessary for adequate performance of a given task. The vocational teacher must directly and systematically be able to observe the

Examples of Criterion-Referenced Instruments

performance traits and behaviors of the learner. Checklists are most often used to determine proficiency in cases where the student must perform a specific task to be successful. Rating scales evaluate the quality of the product or service performed by the learner. A Likert scale of 1–5 is frequently used in such ratings.

Paper-pencil performance is another criterion-referenced instrument developed to assist teachers in making decisions. These are usually developed by the vocational teacher to assess knowledge in a specific occupational area. They can be used for screening, pre- or posttesting, or as part of the formative evaluation process. The standards used are often those expected in business and industry. The instrument can contain questions with true-or-false, multiple-choice, or fill-in-the-blank answers or question-responses. However, caution should be used when developing this type of test instrument for special needs learners. This may not be the most appropriate way to test children who have a variety of learning needs, because of vocabulary, readability, and format variance. Consideration of the instrument's usefulness should center on the question, "Would they be asked to respond like this on the job?" Alternative methods that are more appropriate may be used, e.g., demonstration or audio feedback.[23]

Work samples are another type of criterion-referenced instrument. These samples are used to measure a student's ability to perform a specific task that represents or is a sample of the tasks within the vocational area the student is interested in. This instrument usually requires students to perform the most common tasks in the vocational area in order of frequency and to identify tasks that are representative of the occupation as a whole.

When developing work samples, teachers should choose five tasks from the chosen area and then select one to develop as a work sample based on answers to these six questions:

- Which tasks are most representative of the occupational area?
- Which tasks require a progression from simpler to more complex?
- Which tasks require gross and fine motor skills?
- Which tasks do not require too much reading?
- Which tasks can be completed in a short period of time?
- Which tasks are complex enough to allow frustration and persistence to surface?[24]

Learning style inventories can also be of great value to the placement and program planning process. These can be constructed at a local level, or existing instruments can be used. Locally, efforts to identify learning styles should rely on dominance screening, open-ended questions, and questionnaires. The C.I.T.E. Learning Styles Instrument has been widely used in the area of vocational special needs (see Exhibit 9-3).

Guidance for
Vocational
Teachers

As vocational teachers become increasingly involved in administering teacher-constructed instruments for screening and placing special needs learners and for

Exhibit 9-3 C.I.T.E. Learning Styles Instrument

	Most Like Me		Least Like Me	
1. When I make things for my studies, I remember what I have learned better.	4	3	2	1
2. Written assignments are easy for me to do.	4	3	2	1
3. I learn better if someone reads a book to me than if I read silently to myself.	4	3	2	1
4. I learn best when I study alone.	4	3	2	1
5. Having assignment directions written on the board makes them easier to understand.	4	3	2	1
6. It's harder for me to do a written assignment than an oral one.	4	3	2	1
7. When I do math problems in my head, I say the numbers to myself.	4	3	2	1
8. If I need help in the subject, I will ask a classmate for help.	4	3	2	1
9. I understand a math problem that is written down better than one I hear.	4	3	2	1
10. I don't mind doing written assignments.	4	3	2	1
11. Written assignments are easy for me to do.	4	3	2	1
12. I remember more of what I learn if I learn it when I am alone.	4	3	2	1
13. I would rather read a story than listen to it read.	4	3	2	1
14. I feel like I talk smarter than I write.	4	3	2	1
15. If someone tells me three numbers to add I can usually get the right answer without writing them down.	4	3	2	1
16. I like to work in a group because I learn from the others in my group.	4	3	2	1
17. Written math problems are easier for me to do than oral ones.	4	3	2	1
18. Writing a spelling word several times helps me remember it better.	4	3	2	1
19. I find it easier to remember what I have heard than what I have read.	4	3	2	1
20. It is more fun to learn with classmates at first, but it is hard to study with them.	4	3	2	1
21. I like written directions better than spoken ones.	4	3	2	1
22. If homework were oral, I would do it all.	4	3	2	1
23. When I hear a phone number, I can remember it without writing it down.	4	3	2	1
24. I get more work done when I work with someone.	4	3	2	1
25. Seeing a number makes more sense to me than hearing a number.	4	3	2	1
26. I like to do things like simple repairs or crafts with my hands.	4	3	2	1
27. The things I write on paper sound better than when I say them.	4	3	2	1
28. I study best when no one is around to talk or listen to.	4	3	2	1

Exhibit 9-3 continued

	Most Like Me			Least Like Me
29. I would rather read things in a book than have the teacher tell me about them.	4	3	2	1
30. Speaking is a better way than writing if you want someone to understand what you really mean.	4	3	2	1
31. When I have a written math problem to do, I say it to myself to understand it better.	4	3	2	1
32. I can learn more about a subject if I am with a small group of students.	4	3	2	1
33. Seeing the price of something written down is easier for me to understand than having someone tell me the price.	4	3	2	1
34. I like to make things with my hands.	4	3	2	1
35. I like tests that call for sentence completion or written answers.	4	3	2	1
36. I understand more from a class discussion than from reading about a subject.	4	3	2	1
37. I remember the spelling of a word better if I see it written down than if someone spells it out loud.	4	3	2	1
38. Spelling and grammar rules make it hard for me to say what I want to in writing.	4	3	2	1
39. It makes it easier when I say the numbers of a problem to myself as I work it out.	4	3	2	1
40. I like to study with other people.	4	3	2	1
41. When teachers say a number I really don't understand it until I see it written down.	4	3	2	1
42. I understand what I have learned better when I am involved in making something for the subject.	4	3	2	1
43. Sometimes I say dumb things, but writing gives me time to correct myself.	4	3	2	1
44. I do well on tests if they are about things I hear in class.	4	3	2	1
45. I can't think as well when I work with someone else as when I work alone.	4	3	2	1

Source: Courtesy of A.M. Babich et al., Center for Innovative Teaching Experiences, Murdock Teaching Center, Wichita Public Schools.

programming and evaluating programs, they must also become more proficient in developing instruments.

Guidelines for constructing, administering, and interpreting these criterion-referenced instruments include the following:

- Keep the format simple and concise.
- Items should reflect specific program objectives necessary to obtain competencies or reach the standards of the trade or vocation.
- Items should be organized sequentially from least difficult to most difficult.
- Instructions should be short, simple, and easy to understand or they should follow the sequence of the items.
- The readability level should be carefully checked.
- Items that are not required by the industry or trade should not be required.
- A variety of items and techniques (visual, demonstration, written) should be used to allow for individual differences. These should be proportionate to their actual use in the industry or trade setting.
- Time standards for completion should be realistic, adapted for individual needs, yet otherwise as close to those of the trade or industry as possible.
- Test retakes and allowances should be considered for mastery level standards.[25]

Informal testing instruments have several advantages over norm-referenced tests. Informal tests are

Advantages of Informal Instruments

- developed for a specific program area
- able to adjust criteria
- adaptable to meet different learning needs of students
- developed locally
- able to fit with a school's information needs
- usable for a variety of purposes
- usable in the identification, planning, and evaluation of programs

Informal instruments present difficulties for many districts because they

Disadvantages of Informal Instruments

- require significant time to develop
- usually require some training on the part of vocational education personnel
- may require more money to be invested for staff time than a district or school can invest
- may require assistance be provided, at least initially, in developing appropriate instrumentation
- may overburden teachers

Informal testing, in particular, with criterion-referenced testing instruments, can offer a great deal of information about an individual student not available from a standardized or norm-referenced testing instrument. Additionally, the information is related to the specific school or district curriculum so that predictions regarding student success can be made on a more individualized basis.

**Formal
Assessment**

Formal assessment involves the use of commercially produced instruments. The major objectives of formal assessment include

- classifying students for placement or services
- attempting to identify internal strengths and weaknesses of students
- finding the source of the difficulties a student is experiencing
- providing more specific information for the more severely handicapped student regarding modifications in the design, implementation, and evaluation of programs

Formal assessment, due to the nature of the tests, often does not provide specific enough information to plan or modify classroom materials and activities to meet the needs of a student. It also often does not involve classroom teachers who know or will be responsible for serving the child. These are two good reasons for including extensive informal assessment along with formal assessment.[26]

Formal assessment instruments include

- achievement tests
- intelligence tests
- standardized interest inventories
- personality inventories
- social maturity tests
- aptitude and dexterity tests

Assessments using these instruments may be conducted by staff in the school or district (e.g., psychometrists, psychologists, counselors, and vocational special needs personnel). Vocational teachers must look carefully at the academic skills required for successful completion of each course. Many courses have academic skill requirements in math and reading based on the course text rather than on the actual requirements needed for an occupational area. Academic skill requirements should be viewed in light of students' ''achievement'' scores as well.[27]

For students with more severe handicapping conditions—and depending on the nature of the local school program—more formalized evaluation work-oriented tests may be given. This is generally done in a testing center outside of the local building by trained evaluators. Also, such tests generally are of a more summative nature and are conducted only once prior to placement. They include

- computerized vocational aptitude tests
- commercial work samples
- commercial work evaluation systems

The addition of information from such tests to the information from informal assessments provides comprehensive data for the multidisciplinary team to review in their determination of the appropriate placement and services for the student. One note of caution: Testers should avoid "overtesting" the student. In addition, testers should not administer to students, especially disadvantaged students, tests incapable of yielding reliable information on which decisions can be made (e.g., giving intelligence tests to limited English proficient students). Tests, particularly the more formal instruments, should be given with a specific purpose in mind, for a specific need that merits attention, or for other viable reasons—not simply for the sake of collecting more data. Unreliable data can hinder, rather than help, the placement and programming of a student.

Utilizing formal instruments to gather some of the information for an assessment profile has several advantages. These include, but are not limited to the following:

Advantages of Formal Instruments

- Student performance is measured in reference to a large number of other individuals or to similar individuals (depending on the test), providing for program assessment as well.
- Formal instruments generally yield more reliable information than criterion-referenced tests (depending on what information is being sought and what it will be used for).

Formal instruments can present difficulties or be inappropriate for many schools or districts. Among other disadvantages, these tests

Disadvantages of Formal Instruments

- may be time-consuming
- may be expensive to purchase and costly, in staff time, to administer
- often require a special setting in which to be administered
- require specially trained personnel to administer them

These formal instruments also present the following problems:

- The students being tested may not be representative of the normative groups with respect to which the tests were standardized.
- A student's performance is compared to other students and not to the student's previous performance or to school criteria.
- The testing environment may appear threatening.
- The test may not be pertinent to the local or district program objectives.
- Diagnostic information from the test may not be useful in helping a teacher determine modification needs (e.g., it may result in scores rather than useful task analysis data).

Formal assessment can provide significant data that may be useful in determining appropriate placements, programs, and services. For many handicapped students, formal assessment may already be completed and the data available. For disadvantaged students, the multidisciplinary team should determine what, how much, and why formal assessment is needed. Again, assessment instruments should be administered with sensitivity to the reliability of the data gathered, taking into consideration the linguistic and cultural backgrounds of both the norm group and the student. The more severely handicapped student may need additional formal testing and perhaps even formal work-related evaluation.

Three Fundamental Domains

In determining what type and how much assessment is to be done, the three areas required by the Carl D. Perkins Act—interests, abilities, and special needs—must be considered. Cobb takes these three areas to be the "three fundamental domains" of vocational assessment and refers to them by the terms *vocational interest, vocational achievement,* and *vocational aptitude*. Information and data gathered from these three domains yields a significant amount of the total information needed to develop an assessment profile for an appropriate school-based placement.

Vocational Interest

Vocational interest testing attempts to identify occupational areas of enduring interest to the student.[28] This is often difficult to determine for handicapped and disadvantaged students, because of their lack of knowledge about the world of work in general. Such students may also lack the necessary verbal abilities or vocabulary to express their interests. An interest inventory should be administered frequently. Annual or biannual testing may be necessary, depending on the individual student, to ensure the program continues to be appropriate.

There are two basic types of interest inventories: verbal and picture. The verbal inventory generally consists of a written list of jobs or activities; students then indicate degrees of preference for each job or activity (or area). Picture inventories consist of a series of pictures, often slides, which students respond to and use for indicating their preference of jobs. The picture inventory is often more appropriate for special needs learners; it has an adjustable response rate and mode and may be shown to more than one student at a time. Vocational interest data can also be collected, among other ways, through

- student and parent interviews
- student visits to local vocational programs
- student visits to local job sites
- informal work samples and career exploration programs[29]

Vocational interest testing is similar to aptitude testing in that it attempts to assess inherent and unobservable traits and thereby to predict future performance (especially in the classroom) regardless of the immediate experiences of the student.

Vocational Aptitude

Vocational aptitude tests are for discovering inherent or natural talents that can help a student learn and adequately perform a task within an occupational area. Aptitude testing is important to vocational teachers in the school setting because it provides additional information regarding the level of difficulty a student may have in learning and also provides insights into the student's present level of functioning. It is important when choosing a test that it measure the aptitude required for the occupations for which vocational training options are available in the school, district, or vocational center. This is important, as it may prevent inappropriate and time-consuming placements that may ultimately end up in failure or an occupational mismatch for the student. Care should be taken when using the aptitude information to predict job performance for handicapped and disadvantaged students who have had no work experience.

Vocational aptitude tests are available in basically three formats: paper-pencil tests, performance-based tests, and work samples. Paper-pencil tests can serve as broad screening devices for mildly handicapped students (severe students may need more screening). Caution should be used with handicapped and disadvantaged students, however, as the reading skills required often yield invalid results. Performance-based tests primarily test students' ability to work with their hands (finger dexterity and small and large motor skills, depending on the test). Work samples evaluate a group of aptitudes associated with a particular job area or type of work. When choosing an aptitude test, one should choose the test that is most appropriate for the individual student's needs, as well as one that focuses on vocational programs available in the school or area center.[30]

Vocational Achievement

The third fundamental domain is vocational achievement. Instruments in this area test present levels of functioning, but do not attempt to make any predictions regarding the future success of the student. Such tests can be thought of as essentially entry level performance tests.[31] They assist the vocational teacher and multidisciplinary team in knowing how well the student is currently functioning so that placements, modifications, and services needed to begin the vocational program may be determined. Every school or district conducts achievement tests. Again, caution should be used: One should not take the achievement tests to provide totally valid or reliable information. The results must be interpreted in light of the nature and severity of the student's handicapping condition, the testing environment and situation, and the cultural and linguistic factors that may affect the results.

It is important to consider classifying the assessment data into the three fundamental domains so that the multidisciplinary team can better interpret the data they possess and determine the areas in which more or different testing may be needed to develop a well-rounded assessment profile. The information gained from these three assessment areas must be used by the multidisciplinary team to relate classification or placement decisions to training or program decisions by integrating the information to develop appropriate training objectives.[32]

The types of assessment discussed in this section should fulfill the requirements of the Carl D. Perkins Act that there be "assessment of interests, abilities, and special needs of . . . students with respect to completing successfully the vocational education programs . . ."[33] Figure 9-1 shows types of assessment and lists methods for gathering information for each type.

Learning Style
Special Ed. Teacher Test
Vocational Teacher Test
Classroom Observation
Work Sample
Parent Questionnaire
Vocational Tryout
Student Interview

Vocational Achievement
Standardized Tests
Special Education Tests
Regular Teacher Assessment
Parent Interview
Vocational Tests
Curriculum-Referenced Tests

Physical Skills
Dexterity/Coordination Tests
Medical Exam
Physical Education Teacher
Observation
General Work Samples

Vocational Interests
Picture/Verbal Interest Tests
Student Interview
Parent Interview
Student Questionnaire
Tour of Job Sites
Tour of Vocational Programs

Vocational Aptitudes
Vocational Interest Tests
Work Samples
Vocational Class Tryouts
Job Tryouts

Figure 9-1 Types of Assessment and Methods for Gathering Information. *Source:* Adapted from *Guidelines for Vocational Assessment of Handicapped Students,* Texas Education Agency, Austin, Texas, 1986.

MULTIDISCI-PLINARY TEAMS

Prior to the Carl D. Perkins Act, vocational assessment was conducted mainly by vocational rehabilitation evaluators, a few psychologists, and a few special education diagnosticians. The tests often yielded inappropriate or incomplete results. Many of the results attained by vocational rehabilitation personnel unfamiliar with public school vocational programs were work-related evaluations rather than school- and curriculum-related evaluations. The tests were not able to provide information to determine program, curriculum, and service modifications that would tend to increase successful vocational program completions in the school or vocational center. The results of the tests, in isolation from other information, were of limited use. Psychologists and special education personnel emphasized academic skill training, yet often used the information from testing to screen students out of programs and placements rather than to assist in determining appropriate programs, services, or modifications. Additionally, psychologists, while knowing about diagnosis, handicaps, and educational programs, lacked knowledge about vocational assessment and programming. Not all vocational assessment is, or should be, based on psychological tests.

On the other hand, vocational teachers, while knowledgeable about vocational programs, often lacked the skills and training to deal with special needs students. Counselors, too, have not traditionally been trained to work with special needs students and often lack knowledge regarding procedures to assist in appropriate program planning. Little, if any, effort was made to assess the needs of the disadvantaged student or to involve any personnel in working with the disadvantaged student or aiding in placement decisions. The result has been isolated areas of information on which to base decisions and very few (less than 10 percent) IEPs for handicapped students with vocational education on them.[34] The Carl D. Perkins Act, together with a slow change in philosophy, has brought about the realization that there is a need for a group of experts to be involved with the student's total education program and to work together to determine an appropriate vocational program. This holistic viewpoint has made it necessary for groups of experts from a variety of disciplines, who may never have worked together before, to share information and decisionmaking. The combined efforts of these experts can provide new and expanded opportunities to all special needs students.

Personnel Involvement

Coordinating the efforts of the array of personnel serving special needs students is an administrative task unlike those that schools have had to deal with in the past. Although each of the persons involved has worked with special needs students previously, there has been no coordinated effort to provide a holistic viewpoint for decisionmaking, especially as it relates to vocational education. Coordination of this effort raises some of the following questions:

- Who should be involved?
- What types of data will each person be responsible for?
- What school or vocational sites will each person work at?
- Will each person be on each multidisciplinary team, and if not, by whom and how will the choices be made?
- Who will administer what testing instruments?
- Who will determine the timelines for testing and data collection?
- Who will be responsible for student schedules?
- Who will be responsible for arranging, coordinating, and monitoring needed special services?
- How and by whom will the testing instruments be chosen?
- What unit will be responsible for the cost of the instruments?
- Who will be responsible for testing schedules?
- What unit will be responsible for the cost of outside personnel when they are needed?

- What unit will pay for and furnish transportation when it is needed?
- How and by whom will the program or student be monitored and evaluated?
- Who will be responsible for writing the necessary reports?
- Who will be responsible for home contacts, permission-for-testing letters, and other related items?
- What unit will provide and pay for special services and determine what services will be available?
- What unit will provide and pay for paraprofessional assistance?
- Who will relieve vocational teachers and other teachers from their class responsibilities so they may participate in multidisciplinary team meetings when necessary?
- Who will provide and pay for necessary inservice training?

Finding solutions to these and similar questions requires a coordinated effort. As a first step, a team leader, a vocational resource (special needs) specialist, and an administrator (or other person in charge) must find out from each of the potential team members what their objectives, priorities, and needs are. This will ensure that all aspects of assessment and planning are covered throughout the process of development. Several states (e.g., Missouri and Georgia) have trained vocational special needs personnel who can assist or provide the administrative services necessary to meet these coordination needs. Other states are beginning to develop a vocational special needs position for this purpose, while some states are relying on the good faith efforts of local school personnel and building administrators.

With respect to specific areas, such as determining timelines, problems can be handled through the existing channels set out in the rules and regulations of the Education for All Handicapped Children Act that cover handicapped students. Forms, testing notifications, referrals, etc., can also use the current formats developed for handicapped students, with slight modifications for vocational purposes. The handicapped formats can also be used, with modifications, for disadvantaged students, thereby saving time and money. However, care must be taken to ensure that the modifications make it clear that the student is not being referred to, tested for, or placed into a program for handicapped children.

The number and kind of personnel involved in the assessment process depend on a number of factors:

- the nature of the special need
- the type of personnel available
- the time available for assessment
- the nature of the information needed
- the type of information already available

Table 9-1 lists suggested roles and responsibilities of team members.

Table 9-1 Suggested Multidisciplinary Team Roles and Responsibilities

What	Who	When	How	Considerations
A) Identification and referral	Special education, vocational education, guidance counselors, vocational special needs	When staff determine that employment training is appropriate	Interview assessment instructor Parent interview Student interview Demonstrated interest (industrial arts, part-time employment, etc.) Aptitude testing, if available	Is school best training environment? Are necessary special services available?
B) Program planning	Special education, vocational education, vocational special needs, parents, students, counselors, others as needed	After program placement is decided After curriculum is chosen Prior to placement At end of the school year	Achievement tests Informal observation Teacher-made performance samples that are curriculum-referenced Close procedures from text Curriculum-referenced math tests	Determine present levels of performance along the continuum of competencies in the curriculum chosen Determine student placement in chosen curriculum Necessary support special services/needs Information to assist in determining annual and short-term goals/objectives
C) Placement	Special education, vocational education, guidance counselors, vocational special needs, parents	After a determination of appropriate placement has been made and after determination has been made that a particular vocational education or training program appears appropriate	Interests tests Aptitude tests Matching reading/math skills Visit vocational classrooms Job shadowing	Does student have necessary basic skills to survive chosen curriculum (reading, math, language, or other)?

Table 9-1 continued

What	Who	When	How	Considerations
		It is determined that necessary support services are available		
D) Monitoring	Special education, vocational education, vocational special needs, parents	Ongoing	Teacher-made tests Observation Informal interviews with student and instructor Evaluation of course programs, products	Is a monitoring device appropriate? Is it frequent enough? Too frequent? Are appropriate adjustments made?
E) Program evaluation	Special education, vocational education, vocational special needs, parents, students	Annual review of IEP	May need to review or re-administer aptitude, interest, or other tests if curriculum changes are necessary	Did curriculum meet interests/ abilities? Was training environment appropriate? Other training needs? New curriculum areas? Follow-up, on the job needs to complete transition to work

The focus of the new mandates for vocational assessment requires that personnel be knowledgeable about the vocational programs available in the school, district, or vocational center. This may require inservice training for personnel not previously involved with vocational programs. In addition, inservice training may be required for personnel to understand the terms and definitions involved with special needs students. These personnel cannot maximize the successfulness of the vocational assessment process if they are not apprised of the nature of the assessment, the program, or the students for whom the program is intended.

Figure 9-2 lists the personnel suggested to be involved with the vocational assessment process for each of the special needs groups.

Vocational assessment achieves its purpose best if there is a multidisciplinary team effort. In the case of the disadvantaged student, there may be several personnel who have not been involved with such processes before, but who are included to ensure that a holistic coordinated program is developed for the student. Vocational and special education personnel must assume the largest portion of the responsibility for assessment information. Vocational teacher involvement within the total process, especially for students not entering vocational education for the first time, should be emphasized and used resourcefully, as the vocational teacher often knows the student better than do other school personnel. The vocational teacher can provide practical applications of the recommendations and can help the student to see a correlation between the academic skill areas and future success.[35] Using vocational and other personnel who are directly involved with the school or district vocational programs and who are knowledgeable about the student's needs in the school ensures that there is a focus on the local school district's curriculum.

The New Focus

Each school or district must develop its own definition of the roles and responsibilities of the personnel involved in the assessment and multidisciplinary team process. The following guidelines are to assist the school in beginning that development.

Roles and Responsibilities

Handicapped	Disadvantaged (Economically & Academically)	Limited English Proficient
Parent/Guardian	Parent	Parent
Vocational Teacher	Student, when appropriate	Student, when appropriate
Regular Teacher	Vocational Teacher	Vocational Teacher
Special Education Teacher	Migrant Teacher	Indian Ed. Teacher
School Psychologist	Indian Ed. Teacher	Bilingual Teacher
Administrator/Principal	Chapter I Teacher	Principal/Administrator
Various Support Personnel as needed	Chapter II Teacher	Local Employer, when needed
Student, when appropriate	Principal/Administrator	Guidance Counselor
Vocational Needs Personnel	Social Worker	Others as needed
Local Employees, when needed	Local Employer, when needed	
Others as needed	Guidance Counselor	
	Others as needed	

Figure 9-2 Suggested Personnel for a Multidisciplinary Vocational Assessment Team

- *Counselor:* Helps facilitate parental involvement; talks to students about decisionmaking; may do some testing; assists in scheduling courses.
- *Parent:* Provides background information on developmental growth, behavior patterns, learning style, medical status, and possible areas of occupational interest; provides information on other services from the community that are being provided but that the school may not be aware of; provides confidence and support for the student throughout the educational process.
- *Special education teacher:* Informs team members of nature of handicapping conditions and possible effects on successful completion of programs; provides records and background information; assists in the development of criterion-referenced tests; suggests modifications; may do some testing; assists in development of goals and objectives; suggests support services; carries out his or her portion of the IEP and monitors student progress with the vocational teacher.
- *Building administrator:* Assures process is in place and appropriate procedures are followed; makes sure support services are available; supports parent and student efforts; supports team recommendations and monitors follow-through; oversees vocational assessment activities.
- *Vocational instructor:* Assists in the development of work samples, situational assessments, or other criterion-referenced testing instruments for his or her particular vocational (occupational) area; collects assessment data via traditional instructional evaluation procedures as well as those collaboratively established with other assessment personnel; conducts specific training assessments;[36] shares information and develops communication with other personnel involved in the student's program; modifies curriculum; provides ongoing formative evaluation information as needed or requested; ensures student's goals and objectives are being followed and met; may conduct some of the assessment testing.
- *Bilingual or ESL (English as a second language) teacher:* Provides background information on the student regarding cultural and linguistic influences that may affect performance in the vocational program; assists in modification of curriculum; maintains communication with parents; provides language assistance, services, or tutor as needed; may conduct assessments.

This is not, of course, a comprehensive list of either the personnel involved or their roles and responsibilities. It is meant to provide an example of the types of roles and responsibilities that may be considered for key personnel in the process. Roles will vary from district to district and perhaps even from school to school. However, a basic framework of reference should be developed to ensure a clear understanding of each person's part in planning and conducting the vocational assessment process.

THE ASSESSMENT PROCESS

The Committee on Vocational Assessment of NAVESNP, formed in 1981, made the following statement regarding the vocational assessment process: ''Formal vocational assessment should occur approximately one year prior to placement in vocational education. . . . This will usually occur around the ninth or tenth grade.'' (A similar statement could be made about informal assessment.) Although the Carl D. Perkins Act does not specifically state when the vocational assessment process is to occur, it provides some guidance. The intent of the act was to assure vocational assessment was done prior to students' enrolling in vocational programs. How else could parents receive accurate information or schools make appropriate placement decisions or even write the programs? It is also clear that the assessments should take place no later than the beginning of the ninth grade. Because the act requires districts to develop an individual planning component for all students (handicapped and disadvantaged) included in the vocational assessment process, a decisionmaking model for vocational assessment must be developed.

Privacy of Records

There are federal regulations regarding access to records for handicapped students. School districts may have additional policies for handicapped students, as well as policies covering access to educational records for disadvantaged students. Teachers and other personnel involved in the vocational assessment process should inquire into the district's and school's policies regarding the access to and use of student records. Districts may also have policies concerning interviews. Again, the teacher and other personnel should check the district or school policy manual. Social workers or other personnel may be required to accompany the teacher on interviews or family visits.

A Decision-making Model

Establishing a process for vocational assessment involves a series of steps. Once multidisciplinary team members have become familiar with roles and responsibilities and with the types of assessments from which information can be drawn, they must establish a process or cycle for assessment. Before initiating this process or cycle, several questions must be answered, including the following:

- What will the process (cycle) timelines be?
- How often should testing be done?
- What will the assessment delivery model be?
- How will the data be used?
- What forms and permission letters need to be developed?
- What and where are the placement options?
- What existing items can be used?

The answers to these questions may be determined by state regulations, district policy, or local guidelines. It is advisable to check all of these. At any rate, answering the above questions (and those already suggested for developing multidisciplinary teams) should provide the necessary information for establishing an assessment process. Figure 9-3 presents a suggested decisionmaking model for the referral, assessment, planning for, and placement of handicapped and disadvantaged students in vocational education programs.

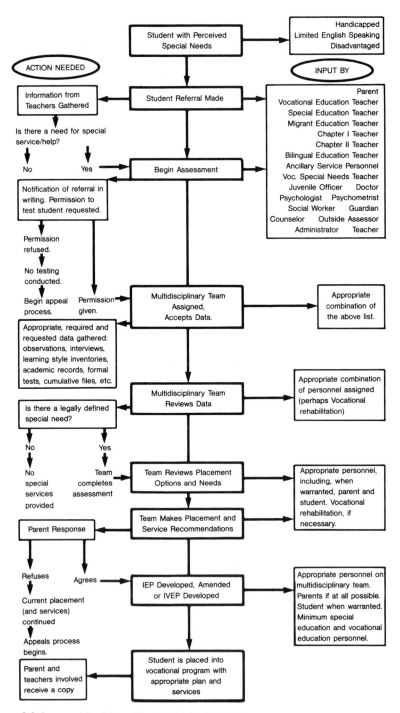

Figure 9-3 Suggested Decisionmaking Model for Establishing an Assessment Process in Vocational Education

To identify students eligible for special vocational services, it is important to remember that the handicapped or disadvantaged student must demonstrate a condition that prevents him or her from ''completing successfully'' their vocational program without special assistance or services. The term ''completing successfully'' is not defined in either law or regulation, and interpretation is left to the local education agency.[37] Exhibit 9-4 presents a sample referral form.

Identification and Referral

Handicapped students, for the most part, will already be in some type of program for assistance in academic areas by the time the student reaches ninth grade or is ready to enter the vocational program. Identification and referral of disadvantaged students may have occurred, but the referrals will be mostly for academic assistance. The class of disadvantaged students comprises the economically and academically disadvantaged, the limited English proficient, migrants, dropouts, and potential dropouts. This class may include students receiving services through ESL programs, chapter I, migrant education, chapter II, Indian education, and other programs designed to serve disadvantaged students. Frequently, disadvantaged students demonstrate aca-

Exhibit 9-4 Sample Vocational Assessment Referral Form

Vocational Assessment
Referral Form

Student name: _____ M   F   Age: _____
School: _____ Grade _____

Why is this person being referred for vocational assessment? (What type of information would you like to get from the assessment?)
_____
_____

Specific questions you desire answers to:
1. _____
2. _____
3. _____
4. _____

School and community information:
Student's present program placement: _____
Past or current vocationally related programs or classes:
_____
_____
_____

Classroom strengths: _____

Classroom weaknesses: _____

Attendance: Good   Average   Poor

Source: Courtesy of CAVEC Project, Southeast Regional Resource Center, Juneau, Alaska.

demic, social, motor, and communication skill needs similar to those of handicapped students.[38]

Care must be taken, however, to ensure these disadvantaged students are not classified as handicapped unless they clearly have a handicapping condition. Particular care should be taken with regard to referrals to speech and learning disability programs. A small number of students may be both handicapped and disadvantaged. Generally, disadvantaged students do not have program profiles or records in a centralized location or document. Every effort should be made to gather all current and available files into one location before beginning further assessment for developing the assessment profile. This will avoid costly and unnecessary duplication of efforts. Prior to the Carl D. Perkins Act, there were no assurances of assessment required for disadvantaged students. Therefore, it is important that as much information as possible be drawn from existing sources so that a holistic view of the needs of the students can be used to plan further assessment. It will also allow for maximum assurance of an appropriate placement and a successful completion of the vocational program.

Team Begins Assessment

It is important that parents are informed about and aware of the actions and services impacting on their child. Parents of handicapped students are required to provide permission prior to the individual testing of their child. Parents of disadvantaged children, too, should be informed of actions the school is about to take regarding their child. Exhibits 9-5 and 9-6 are examples of letters requesting from parents permission to test students for possible vocational placement with special services. Some populations may need these permission letters (and other materials) in a language besides English or they may need other means of communication. If the parent of a special education child refuses permission, the due process procedure may begin. It would be advisable for schools to develop similar due process procedures for disadvantaged students.

Team Assigned

Once permission to test has been given, the multidisciplinary team may take a more in-depth look at the data available, conduct various vocational tests, request further testing, or seek more data. At this point, personnel needed as part of the programming process are assigned to the team.

Team Reviews Data

At this stage, the members of the team decide whether the student has sufficient special needs to necessitate special services to aid in completing the vocational education program. If the student is not found to have special needs requiring special services, then no plan is developed and no services are provided under the Carl D. Perkins Act. This does not preclude services from another source. If the student is found to have sufficient needs, the team gathers information to begin reviewing placement options.

Exhibit 9-5 Sample Permission Form for Student Assessment

Student Number _____

Date _____

PARENT/GUARDIAN PERMISSION FOR STUDENT ASSESSMENT

_____ School would like to provide an assessment
for _____ to assist in planning and providing vocational education
    (Student's Name)
services and/or programs appropriate to his/her needs. We believe this assessment should be
conducted for the following reasons: _____
_____.

In general, this assessment would include: _____
_____
_____.

The assessment would be conducted by: _____
_____.
                    Title(s) of person(s) involved in the assessment

It is important that you be aware and understand that you have the following rights: (1) To review
all records related to the referral for this assessment; (2) To review the procedures used in the
assessment; (3) To refuse permission for the assessment; (4) To be informed of the results of the
assessment.

So that we may know your decision, please CHECK ONE of the boxes below, sign this form and
return it to the school as soon as possible. Thank you for your cooperation.

Sincerely,

_____

Principal

. . . .

_____ Permission is given to conduct the assessment as described.
_____ I do not give permission to conduct the assessment.

_____

Student's Name

_____   _____
Parent/Guardian Signature   Date

Source: Courtesy of CAVEC Project, Southeast Regional Resource Center, Juneau, Alaska.

At this point the team must decide whether they have sufficient data or need more
data. This includes data on the nature of the vocational programs and classes being
considered and the matching of those to the needs and abilities of the students. Exhibits 9-7 and 9-8 provide examples of checklists that can be used to determine the
best match. The team must consider not only the student's abilities, needs, etc., but

**Review of
Placement
Options**

Exhibit 9-6 Sample Referral Notification Letter

PARENT NOTICE

(Name and address of parent)

Dear _____:

Your (son/daughter) is being referred for a comprehensive vocational assessment to determine vocational interests, abilities, and aptitudes. A plan for helping your child develop vocational skills will be based on this assessment and other information.

During vocational assessment, students are tested in small groups with a variety of techniques, including interest surveys, "hands-on" job samples, education assessments, etc. Some students prove skillful in complex tasks such as assembling apparatus; others find success in work requiring a high degree of creativity, while still others find repetitive tasks to be a challenge.

Career information gained from the testing is shared with the student. A format report is also given to the school to assist in planning future school programs.

The vocational assessment will occur on the following dates: _____, at the following location: _____.

We appreciate your cooperation in this process. A permission form has been enclosed. Please contact me or your school if you have any questions.

Sincerely,

Vocational Assessment Specialist
School District

Source: Adapted from form developed by Project KEYE, Klein ISD, Spring, Texas.

also the entry and exit levels of the courses, the adaptability of the curricula, materials, etc., and the types of special services needed in the courses (or programs). All options for placement should be considered to ensure that the student will be placed in the least restrictive and most appropriate environment.

Placement Decision and Service Recommendations

After consideration is given to all of the data, information, and other available inputs, the team (including the parents if possible) decides on a vocational placement and the services and adaptations recommended for successful completion of the chosen program. If the parents do not agree with the placement recommendation, the handicapped student may stay in his or her present placement while due process proceedings are begun. In the case of a disadvantaged learner, the district may choose to place the student anyway. If the parents agree, the team develops, modifies, or amends the current IEP for the handicapped student and the individual vocational

Exhibit 9-7 Student Inventory Form

STUDENT INVENTORY

Student Name: _____ Teacher: _____

+ Student Strength   ○ Student Weakness

INFORMATION INPUT
Sources:
_____ Textbook
_____ Worksheets
_____ Lecture
_____ Discussion
_____ A-V Material
_____ Audio Tape
_____ Concrete Experience
_____ Observation

Structure:
_____ Directed
_____ Independent
_____ Peer Tutor
_____ 1-1 Adult
_____ Small Group Learning
_____ Large Group Learning

INFORMATION OUTPUT
Test Format:
_____ Short Answer
_____ Essay
_____ Multiple Choice
_____ True-False
_____ Matching
_____ Computation
_____ Word Problems

Assignments:
_____ Worksheets
_____ Short Papers
_____ Term Papers
_____ Lab Projects
_____ Media Projects
_____ Oral Reports
_____ Group Discussion
_____ Computation
_____ Word Problems
_____ Charts/Graphs

OTHER CLASS REQUIREMENTS:
_____ Notetaking
_____ Outlining
_____ Use of Reference Manuals
_____ Independent Research
_____ Measuring (to _____ inch)
_____ Skimming/Scanning

_____ Memorization
_____ Correct Spelling
_____ Punctuality
_____ Coming to Class Prepared
_____ Participation in Class Discussion

STUDENT LIKES: _____

STUDENT DISLIKES: _____

IS HOME AMENABLE TO HELPING WITH STUDENT'S PROGRAM? _____Yes _____No
SUGGESTED IVEP ANNUAL GOAL AREAS: _____
_____
_____
_____
_____

Source: Courtesy of Brian Cobb, University of Vermont. Form was developed for Vocational Assessment
Institute, Juneau, Alaska, Summer 1986.

Exhibit 9-8 Course Description Form

COURSE DESCRIPTION

Course Title: _____   Teacher: _____

+ Used Frequently   − Used Somewhat   ○ Used Seldom

INFORMATION INPUT
  Sources:
    _____ Textbook
    _____ Worksheets
    _____ Lecture
    _____ Discussion
    _____ A-V Material
    _____ Audio Tape
    _____ Concrete Experience
    _____ Observation

  Structure:
    _____ Directed
    _____ Independent
    _____ Peer Tutor
    _____ 1-1 Adult
    _____ Small Group Learning
    _____ Large Group Learning

INFORMATION OUTPUT
  Test Format:
    _____ Short Answer
    _____ Essay
    _____ Multiple Choice
    _____ True-False
    _____ Matching
    _____ Computation
    _____ Word Problems

  Assignments:
    _____ Worksheets
    _____ Short Papers
    _____ Term Papers
    _____ Lab Projects
    _____ Media Projects
    _____ Oral Reports
    _____ Group Discussion
    _____ Computation
    _____ Word Problems
    _____ Charts/Graphs

OTHER CLASS REQUIREMENTS:
    _____ Notetaking
    _____ Outlining
    _____ Use of Reference Manuals
    _____ Independent Research
    _____ Measuring (to _____ inch)
    _____ Skimming/Scanning

    _____ Memorization
    _____ Correct Spelling
    _____ Punctuality
    _____ Coming to Class Prepared
    _____ Participation in Class Discussion

GRADING CRITERIA: _____

EXTRA CREDIT POLICY: _____

ATTENDANCE POLICY: _____

HOMEWORK POLICY: _____

MAKE-UP WORK POLICY: _____

Source: Courtesy of Brian Cobb, University of Vermont. Form was developed for Vocational Assessment Institute, Juneau, Alaska, Summer 1986.

education program (IVEP) for the disadvantaged student. A sample IVEP is presented in Exhibit 9-9.

Student Placement

After the IEP/IVEP is developed and after all persons involved have copies of the program plans and know their responsibilities and roles, the student is placed in the appropriate vocational program with special services as outlined in the IEP/IVEP. This is the culmination of the program planning and placement activities.

Monitoring and Evaluation

Placing the special needs child into the appropriate program with supportive services is the first half of the process. When developing the program and IEP/IVEP, attention must also be given to monitoring and evaluating the program, as well as the progress of the student and his or her re-assessment needs. Figure 9-4 outlines a process for monitoring and evaluating the special needs program and student progress.

The IEP/IVEP in Motion

Once the student is placed in the appropriate program, it becomes the responsibility of the vocational teacher(s), special education teacher(s), vocational special needs personnel, and other persons given responsibility through the IEP/IVEP to ensure that the goals and objectives are being met. Meeting the goals may involve special services (e.g., occupational therapy), special personnel (e.g., an individual reader or paraprofessional), special or modified equipment, materials, or techniques and methods of delivery, adapted curriculum, and modified facilities. It will involve guidance, counseling, and career development activities.

Program and Student Progress

Collecting data throughout the school year—instead of once a semester or once a year—is more likely to yield reliable data on which further decisions can be made. This formative documentation results in flexibility and allows changes in the program or student plan (IEP/IVEP) to occur as the need arises, thus ensuring the student is on the most successful path to completing the program objectives. It also enables problems to be dealt with as they arise and yields more accurate information about the nature of the changes needed for the student. To collect such data, teachers need to know how to conduct frequent and informal measurements of student progress. Having ongoing information also allows the vocational teacher to determine the student's readiness for further training or need for further assessment.

Programs and Progress

Utilizing the formative data, a more reliable evaluation can be made of the vocational program appropriateness as well as student progress in the program. This evaluation should be done annually. The course profile, the IEP/IVEP, the goals and objectives accomplished, and other pertinent summative data should be used to determine the appropriateness of the specific program, how successful the student has

Exhibit 9-9 Sample Individual Vocational Education Program Form

Individual Vocational Education Program (IVEP)

Student's Name _____   Vocational Program _____

Annual Goal(s): _____   Special Needs: Academic ☐
_____   Economic ☐
_____   Limited English Speaking ☐
_____

OBJECTIVES	EVALUATION METHOD	ACTIVITIES/MODIFICATIONS	DATE TO BE COMPLETED	PERSON RESPONSIBLE	MONITORING

NOTES:

Student's Strengths:

Limitations:

Teacher _____

Administration _____

Program Coordinator _____

Date _____

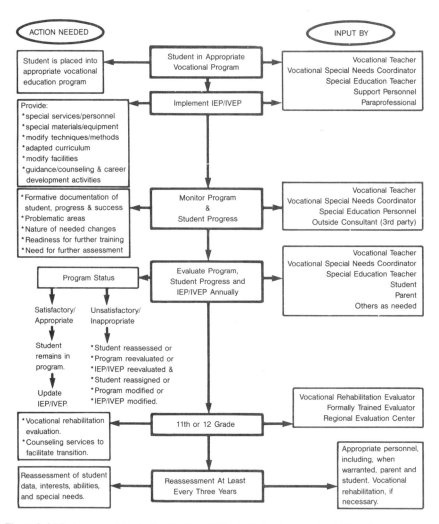

Figure 9-4 Monitoring and Evaluating the Special Needs Student in Vocational Education

been in the program, and whether changes should be made to better meet the student's needs. If the personnel or team responsible find the student is making satisfactory progress and the placement appears appropriate, then the student remains in the program. The IEP/IVEP is updated to reflect continuing goals and objectives for the coming semester or year. If it is decided that the student's progress is unsatisfactory and the goals and objectives on the IEP/IVEP or the program are inappropriate, then three things may take place: (1) the program placement may be re-evaluated, (2) the goals and objectives on the IEP/IVEP may be re-evaluated or rewritten, or (3) the student may be re-assessed in certain areas. The result may be that (1) the student is assigned to another program, (2) the current program is modified, or (3) the IEP/IVEP is adjusted to better meet the student's needs. Students may need one kind of skill to enter the program and yet another kind to exit it and enter into another program or employment. This, too, should be considered to ensure accuracy as well as to enable determination of eligibility for vocational rehabilitation services.

By the 11th or 12th grade, the multidisciplinary team, together with others working with the student, should be able to use the data gathered to formulate ideas about the student's abilities as they relate to postsecondary options. The vocational teacher is a key person in this formulation. He or she has worked closely with the student and will be able to provide specific information regarding the student's abilities, skills, and vocational knowledge. At this point, it is appropriate to request the services of the vocational rehabilitation personnel. Some students will have had full or partial vocational evaluations when initially preparing for placement in a vocational program. However, the majority of students will not have had these evaluations. **Vocational Rehabilitation**

Vocational evaluations are of particular importance at the 11th or 12th grade level, as they assist school and nonschool personnel in using the data to facilitate the transition from high school to a postsecondary or job placement or to provide further assistance through vocational rehabilitation or other agencies. It is appropriate at this level to have more work-oriented information rather than school-based curriculum information. It is critical that vocational rehabilitation and school personnel work together to determine programs and placement for the student as he or she finishes this phase of life and moves into the next (postschool) phase. A cooperative effort can greatly facilitate this transition by providing the necessary services to meet the student's school and postschool needs.

Utilizing a three-year assessment model, based on the special education requirements, has several advantages, including that **Three-Year Assessments**

- students who are also special education students do not have to have two different cycles of testing
- personnel involved can plan their assessment needs
- use of vocational rehabilitation services, given that a data and service base has been established, is facilitated

Figure 9-5 shows a flowchart with suggested assessment timelines. Regardless of the assessment model used, the results should be suitable for the development of an IEP/IVEP and useful to the classroom teacher implementing the plan.

The assessment process is designed to allow the testing to take place in a variety of settings. Districts may wish to consider the following settings or develop their own: **Assessment Delivery Models**

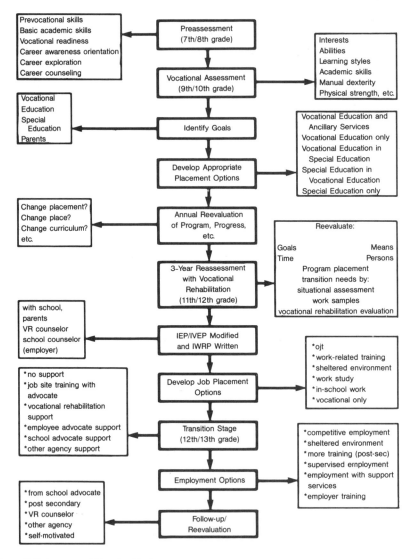

Figure 9-5 Assessment Planning Cycle

- school-based assessment center
- special education classroom
- vocational education classroom
- community-based assessment center
- cooperative assessment center (servicing several districts)
- regional assessment center
- occupational exploration setting

- district assessment center
- mobile assessment center[39]
- vocational assessment consultant/itinerant
- contracted assessment services
- regional or district services cooperatively hired or contracted

Future Directions

To ensure continued services and program success for vocational special needs students, cooperative support must be developed. Some of the options to be explored in the future are the following:

- cooperatively funding assessment and program development
- creating vocational training programs, including courses on special needs students and assessments
- creating special education training programs with a focus on vocational education and vocational assessment
- developing policies and procedures for vocational special needs and vocational assessment at state and local levels that outline procedures, responsibilities, personnel, funding, etc., for vocational special needs education
- making state and federal level funding more readily available for developing vocational special needs personnel training programs
- ensuring better coordination with vocational rehabilitation
- ensuring more coordination with other school personnel involved in the vocational assessment process (e.g., bilingual education, migrant education, etc.)
- understanding and utilizing better the funding sources for providing services and personnel for vocational special needs students (e.g., JTPA, special education, vocational rehabilitation, chapter I, migrant education, etc.)

SUMMARY

This chapter began with an overview of the differences between vocational assessment and vocational evaluation as delineated under the Carl D. Perkins Act. It is apparent from the literature, however, that there is a need for further understanding of these complex areas. The Carl D. Perkins Act offers some guidance.

The impact of the new mandates on a variety of disciplines in the school setting is just beginning to be felt. The assurances of vocational assessment for disadvantaged and handicapped students will require school (and some nonschool) personnel to cooperatively seek appropriate placement, programs, and services if the intent of the law is to be met.

The types of assessment and personnel involved in the assessment process were identified to assist districts in developing assessment teams and to help clarify the roles and responsibilities of each person involved in a holistic approach to assessment and program planning.

Finally, a suggested model for planning the assessment process, conducting the assessment, and evaluating the results of the decisions (for the program and students) was discussed. This model will hopefully provide personnel with guidance in developing their own programs and assessment process.

It is clear that the Carl D. Perkins Act presents challenges for schools and personnel involved with special students. In the aftermath of all the legal processes needed to fulfill assurances, the training and new responsibilities of personnel, the newly coordinated efforts of school personnel to learn about and deal with new areas, let us not forget we are here to serve the students. Special students need special people to fulfill the intent of the vocational assessment process. This chapter provides only a framework which schools can use in beginning to work with the evolving vocational assessment process.

NOTES

1. Mike Peterson and P. Hill, *Vocational Assessment of Students with Special Needs: An Implementation Manual* (Commerce, Tex.: East Texas State University, Occupational Curriculum Laboratory, 1982), 1.

2. T. Dahl, J. Appleby, and D. Lipe, *Mainstreaming Guidebook for Vocational Educators Teaching the Handicapped* (Salt Lake City, Utah: Olympus Publishing Co., 1978), 103.

3. C.L. Roberts, "Definitions, Objectives, and Goals in Work Evaluation," *Journal of Rehabilitation* 36 (1970):13–15.

4. Proceedings of a Training Institute in Work Evaluation (Richmond, Va.: Virginia Commonwealth University, 1966).

5. R.B. Cobb and Dave Larkin, "Assessment and Placement of Handicapped Pupils into Secondary Vocational Education Programs," *Exceptional Children* 17, no. 7 (March 1985):1–14.

6. C. Bell and L. Burgdorf, *Accommodating the Spectrum of Individual Abilities* (Washington, D.C.: Clearinghouse Publications, U.S. Commission on Civil Rights, 1983).

7. Public Law 98-524 (Carl D. Perkins Vocational Education Act of 1984), title II, part A, sec. 204(a)(3)(a).

8. Ibid., sec. 204(a)(3)(B).

9. Ibid., sec. 204(b).

10. Ibid., sec. 204(c)(1)(2).

11. Edward Levinson, "Vocational/Career Assessment in School Psychological Evaluations: Rationale, Definitions, and Purpose," *Psychology in the Schools* 21(1984):112–17.

12. Patricia Sitlington, "Vocational Assessment and Training of the Handicapped," *Focus on Exceptional Children* 12, no. 4 (1979):1–11.

13. Cobb and Larkin, "Assessment and Placement," 7.

14. M. Peterson, "Vocational Special Needs and Vocational Evaluation: A Marriage of Two Fields," *The Journal of Vocational Special Needs* (Spring 1981):15–18.

15. M. Sarkees and J.C. Scott, *Vocational Special Needs* (Alsip, Ill.: American Technical Publishers, 1985), 4–6.

16. R.B. Cobb, "A Curriculum-Based Approach to Vocational Assessment," *Teaching Exceptional Children* (Summer 1983):316–20.

17. Cobb and Larkin, "Assessment and Placement," 1–14.

18. J.C. Ysseldyke and P.E. Mirkin, "The Use of Assessment Information to Plan Instructional Interventions: A Review of Research," in *The Handbook of School Psychology*, ed. C.R. Reynolds and T.B. Gatkin (New York: John Wiley & Sons, 1982), 4.

19. A.S. Halpern et al., *Contemporary Assessment for Mentally Retarded Adolescents and Adults* (Baltimore, Md.: University Park Press, 1982), 1.

20. Ibid., 4.

21. *Puzzled about Educating Special Needs Students?* (Madison, Wis.: University of Wisconsin-Madison, Wisconsin Vocational Studies Center, 1980), 383.

22. *Handbook for Vocational Support Service Teams in Maryland* (Baltimore: Maryland State Department of Education, Division of Vocational-Technical Education, 1984), 1–235.

23. Roberts, "Definitions, Objectives, and Goals," 13–15.

24. *Puzzled,* 399.

25. *Handbook for Vocational Support*, 1–235.

26. *Puzzled*, 417.

27. Greg Weisenstein, *Vocational Special Education Curriculum Guide* (Seattle, Wash.: University of Washington, n.d.), 29–85.

28. Cobb, "Curriculum-Based Approach," 217.

29. Peterson and Hill, *Vocational Assessment*, 41.

30. Ibid., 40.

31. Cobb, "Curriculum-Based Approach," 217.

32. *Puzzled*, 417.

33. Carl D. Perkins Act, part A, sec. 204(c)(1).

34. Levinson, "Vocational/Career Assessment," 114.

35. Paul McCray, *Vocational Evaluation and Assessment in School Settings* (Menomonie, Wis.: University of Wisconsin-Stout, Research and Training Center, 1982), 20.

36. Pam LeConte, "The Impact of the Carl D. Perkins Act on Vocational Assessment: How We Can Meet the Mandate" (The Issues Paper, Second National Forum on Issues in Vocational Assessment, Dallas, Texas, March 13–15, 1986), 117–22.

37. Cobb and Larkin, "Assessment and Placement," 1–14.

38. *Assessment: A Key to Appropriate Program Placement* (Columbia, Mo.: Missouri LINC, Department of Special Education and Department of Practical Arts and Vocational-Technical Education, College of Education, 1986), 45.

39. McCray, *Vocational Evaluation*, 10.

Part III

Vocational Special Needs
Support Services

Chapter 10

Career Education for Special Needs Youth

Ronald J. Anderson, Ph.D.
Marlene I. Strathe, Ph.D.

The concepts of career and vocational education and their interrelationships are sometimes misunderstood by educators, partly because these two educational components are delivered in the schools as separate curricula. To better understand the relationship between career and vocational education, it is important to define career education, examine its relationship to human development, examine existing career development models, and review the methods used to include career education in the school curriculum.

DEFINITION

Different definitions of career education have evolved over the years, and even to date there appears to be little agreement regarding the adoption of a single all-inclusive definition. For example, Hoyt offered this early definition of career education:

> the total effort of public education and the community to help all individuals become familiar with the values of a work oriented society, to integrate those values into their personal value structure, and to implement those values in their lives in ways that make work possible, meaningful, and satisfying to each individual.[1]

In contrast, the recent definition provided by Kokaska and Brolin shifted the focus from that of earlier definitions:

> Career education is the process of systematically coordinating all school, family, and community components together to facilitate each individual's potential to economic, social, and personal fulfillment.[2]

It is clear that the above two definitions of career education have somewhat different emphases. Hoyt's definition is oriented toward work and the values placed on work by the individual.[3] Such work values are to be taught through the public education system. The Kokaska-Brolin definition emphasizes the coordination of instruction within career education for the purpose of developing the individual's personal fulfillment in different aspects of his or her life.[4] Two major differences that emerge from these two definitions involve the focus on work and the coordination functions of the schools. While definitions historically have had varying emphases, the more contemporary definitions appear to de-emphasize the concept of work and focus on fulfillment opportunities. The personal fulfillment focus of career education is especially important in regard to persons with handicaps, for such fulfillment has been a major construct of the career development theoretical framework.

CAREER DEVELOP-MENT THEORY

While definitions of career education provide educators with a basis from which to implement a career development curriculum in the schools, the theoretical foundations of such a curriculum are equally important. Needless to say, there are a number of career development theories that facilitate a better understanding of how individuals are drawn to or select different occupations. Some theories are perhaps more useful than others. In particular, developmental theories seem highly useful, because school curricula are typically organized around developmental learning models. Other career development theories offer a different perspective and may have varying degrees of value depending on the needs of the individual.

Isaacson organized career development theories into five major categories: (1) trait and factor, (2) social learning, (3) situational, (4) personality, and (5) developmental.[5] Broadly, the trait-factor theory has its basis in the matching of individual traits with factors required for successfully performing a particular job. This theory can be understood by thinking of a person who fits a specific stereotype, e.g., someone who is personally aggressive and outgoing becoming a salesman.

The social learning theory is founded on the behaviorist theory and holds career choice to be a function of four factors. These factors are (1) genetics, (2) environment, (3) experiences, and (4) task approach skills. All of the factors interact to shape and regulate an individual's career choice.

The situational theory is harder to describe, because the factors controlling career choice are seen as existing outside of the individual. Perhaps the clearest example of the situational theory is the concept of supply and demand. Many individuals are often drawn to jobs or occupations that are in low supply but for which there is a high demand. Another external factor that often determines work situations for an individual is the economic rewards of a job.

Although theories in each of the above three categories have made contributions to a greater understanding of career development, the personality and developmental theories have been the most influential. One of the personality theories cited by Isaacson is Roe's Circular Model,[6] which attempts to explain the choice of career that an adult makes by the childhood relationship with his or her parents and by the emotional and social atmosphere of the home. Roe theorizes that a child raised in a home that was warm, loving, and accepting would develop a nondefensive adult personality orientation. Such an individual would be more likely to engage in careers involving service, business contact, organization, general culture, and arts and entertainment. Isaacson points out, however, that Roe's theory has lacked major research to support it.[7]

Another personality-based theory is Holland's Vocational Choice Theory.[8] Holland believes that an individual expresses his or her personality through vocational choices and that the occupation the individual chooses also reinforces specific occupational personality traits. Holland asserts that satisfaction with a particular job is one outcome of the interaction between an individual's personality and the work environment.

Holland has used his personality theory to classify specific personality characteristics into six broad categories: (1) realistic, (2) investigative, (3) artistic, (4) social, (5) enterprising, and (6) conventional.[9] Under each of these category types, Holland has listed several descriptors that delineate personality characteristics that often influence individuals to enter certain occupations. Persons with highly social personalities, for example, utilize their skills in working with other individuals. Such individuals prefer occupations in the areas of education, social service, government, music, and dramatics. Usually persons with social personalities perceive themselves as leaders, good communicators, popular, and aggressive. They also possess positive self-concepts and tend to have good verbal abilities and poor quantitative skills. It is important to note that Holland's personality categories are not independent of each other; that is, some characteristics are common to more than one category. Similarly, rarely does one person possess personality traits that exclusively represent only one personality category; rather, most individuals' personalities are a collection of dominant and subordinate traits.

The impact of Holland's personality theory on career choice has been considerable. The application of personality theory on career choice, however, is usually seen at the later stages of career development. Even though personality theory has provided a better retrospective understanding of how and why career choices are made, developmental theory also appears to have significant relevance for educators, since the American school system is developmental in its approach to educating children.

Isaacson identified Donald Super as one of the most influential theorists on the topic of career development.[10] Super's contribution to the understanding of career development involves his trying to explain occupational selection through a mixture of individual personality, life experiences, self-concept, interests, abilities, and tolerances. The relationships or interactions among personal traits can and do qualify an individual for a number of occupations. However, Super proposes that occupational choices and adjustments are also the result of continuous change. Such change is brought about by a set of experiences that a person accumulates over a period of time through work situations, vocational preferences and competencies, and self-concept development. Thus, career development and choice are seen as a dynamic processs.

Super's contribution to career education is perhaps more clearly evident through his career development theory.[11] Super has identified five major stages of career development: (1) growth, (2) exploration, (3) establishment, (4) maintenance, and (5) decline. The growth, exploratory, and establishment stages are the most important. Regarding career education, Super asserts that during the growth stage the individual is forming attitudes and behaviors that play a significant part in assuming a career role. The exploratory stage is probably the most dynamic of all, since it is characterized by three phases of development, namely, fantasy, tentative, and realistic. During the first period, children fantasize about possible career choices. In most cases children indicate, when asked, that they want to be a cowboy, nurse, policeman, firefighter, or doctor. Although children express these choices, they frequently soon forget them and move on to another choice.

Through the tentative phase, children begin to narrow their career choices; however, they are often unsure whether or not the choices are appropriate given the availability of jobs. In addition, some children attempt to evaluate the nature of a particular occupation and the time that would be needed to acquire the necessary training for it.

The realistic phase provides the individual the opportunity to make concrete decisions about career options. At this point, a person will usually determine what, if any, training will be needed, how much it will cost, how much time will be needed to obtain the required training, and how available are jobs.

The organization of career development stages has been viewed somewhat differently by Tiedman and O'Hara.[12] Although they take account of an individual's personality in the making of career choices, Tiedman and O'Hara believe that personality interacts with society to organize and identify with work. The role of personality is a way of differentiating an individual's own uniqueness while the individual attempts to integrate with or adjust to others. Like Super, Tiedman and O'Hara view career development as spanning a lifetime.

Tiedman and O'Hara also believe that an individual passes through two major periods of career development: anticipation and implementation/adjustment.[13] The period of anticipation includes four substages: (1) exploration, (2) crystallization, (3) choice, and (4) specification. The period of implementation/adjustment includes three substages: (1) induction, (2) transition, and (3) maintenance.

During the period of anticipation the individual begins at the exploration substage by evaluating a wide range of possible career options in relation to him- or herself. After considering a wide range of possibilities, the individual narrows the options and attempts to acquire a better understanding of the choices made. Crystallization occurs by narrowing career choices based on the individual's goals, personality, and values. The next substage involves choice, specifically, the choosing of careers that are congruent with the individual's goals. The final stage is specification, which allows the individual the opportunity to more clearly view him- or herself in a chosen career role.

Regardless of the career development theory that might be utilized to guide career development curricula in the schools, it is obvious that appropriate career education can have a significant impact and lead students to make informed career selections. Career selection for special needs students is even more important than for non–

special needs students, since many do not have the opportunity to be exposed to as many options.

In general, the organization of most career development models is based on career development theory. These models have incorporated the general stages identified in developmental theory for application and use in the schools. Kokaska and Brolin have identified four major stages of career development: (1) awareness, (2) exploration, (3) preparation, and (4) placement, follow-up, and continuing education.[14] This model offers young children, those in the primary grades, an opportunity to become aware that adults perform different jobs in different situations. Through exploration, school-age children learn about different occupations and what training or additional education would be needed to become qualified for a specific occupation. In the preparation stage, the student makes at least a preliminary decision concerning what occupation he or she would like to prepare for and engage in during the initial stages of education or training. After completing the preparation stage, the student then enters the placement stage and the work force.

CAREER DEVELOP-MENT MODELS

The Iowa Career Development Model has stages similar to those identified by Kokaska and Brolin, but differs slightly in two areas.[15] The Iowa model begins with the awareness stage and follows with the accommodation, exploration, and preparation/exploration stages. This model has included the accommodation stage, which allows the student the opportunity to identify with a worker or as a worker. Additionally, the Iowa model has adopted a combination stage (preparation/exploration) as its final stage.

Ending with the combination preparation/exploration stage reflects the fact that, in some cases, secondary-aged students have not yet completed the exploration of career options. At the same time, other students may have completed their exploration and are prepared to enter the preparation stage of career development.

The school-based career education model developed by Dr. Gary Clark provides yet another perspective on career education.[16] His model is congruent with the Kokaska-Brolin and Iowa models, but possesses a vertical as well as a horizontal point of view. Clark's model focuses on four basic educational content elements during the elementary school years: (1) values, attitudes, and habits, (2) human relations, (3) occupational information, and (4) acquisition of job and daily living skills.[17] Throughout the secondary school years, students have different training options from which to draw, depending on their career goals or needs. These options include (1) college preparation courses, (2) vocational, technical, or fine arts courses, (3) cooperative or work study programs, and (4) work evaluation or work adjustment.[18]

Clark recognizes that career education does not cease after the secondary school years and he displays further educational options during the postsecondary period. One of the unique features of the Clark model is that it provides the flexibility of exiting educational programs at the completion of each horizontal level. Perhaps the most unusual aspect of his model is that Dr. Clark accounts for a number of special needs students who have the ability to pursue and complete high levels of education.

All three career development models, however, recognize that each stage of development does not occur in distinctly segmented stages of life. For example, someone could become aware of a new career sometime during adulthood, and indeed significant career changes in adulthood are becoming more and more frequent.

Although it is generally recognized that career choices change from time to time and that career development is a lifelong process, these models do provide at least a basic structure around which a career education curriculum can be developed. Undoubtedly, career education models provide educators with guidance concerning curriculum content and the schedule according to which such content should be delivered. To illustrate this point, career awareness content and activities should be initiated during the primary grades, whereas preparation content and activities should be delivered at the end of the secondary years or during the postsecondary period.

CAREER EDUCATION CURRICULUM

As previously discussed, career development is a lifelong process that involves the interaction of personality, values, societal needs, experiences, education, and life styles. Since career development encompasses so many aspects of an individual's life career, education curricula must be broad-based and should pervade the individual's total educational experience. Career development should not be left to chance or accident. It should be systematic and comprehensive.

To be systematic, comprehensive, and appropriate for special needs students, career education curricula must include several modifications. These modifications involve logically sequencing content to provide adequate learning opportunities. Of course, sequencing curriculum content to provide needed experiences will require greater coordination among educators.

Another modification involves a shift in focus from a content base to a process base. Educators will need to think about how a given student will best learn needed skills. In most circumstances, students with special learning needs will require concrete learning experiences.

Educators must also keep in mind that career education is a lifelong learning process. In view of this, special needs students may require more time than other students to master skills necessary to reach their maximum career development potential. Extension of time for the acquisition of skills does not mean, however, that educators should sacrifice the appropriate sequencing of curriculum content.

In 1978, the Council for Exceptional Children developed a position paper that outlined a number of career education objectives for exceptional children. These career education objectives seem appropriate for all special needs learners, including the disadvantaged. The list of career education objectives is provided below.[19]

1. To help exceptional students develop realistic self-concepts, with esteem for themselves and others, as a basis for career decisions.

2. To provide exceptional students with appropriate career guidance, counseling and placement services utilizing counselors, teachers, parents and community resource personnel.
3. To provide the physical, psychological and financial accommodations necessary to serve the career education needs of exceptional children.
4. To infuse career education concepts throughout all subject matter in the curricula of exceptional children in all educational settings from early childhood through postsecondary.
5. To provide the student with opportunity to leave the school program with an entry level saleable skill.
6. To provide career awareness experiences which aim to acquaint the individual with a broad view of the nature of the world of work, including both unpaid and paid work.
7. To provide career exploration experiences which help individuals to consider occupations which coincide with their interests and aptitudes.
8. To provide exceptional individuals programs with occupational choices covering the widest possible range of opportunities.
9. To help insure successful career adjustment for exceptional students through collaborative efforts of school and community.

In its position paper, the Council for Exceptional Children attempted to incorporate the best that career education could offer to exceptional children. If career education is to become a reality for handicapped and disadvantaged learners, how to deliver career content and skills becomes a concern and must be addressed.

There are two methods of delivering career education content and skill training. The first method involves the infusion of career content through existing course structures. This method allows educators to apply math, reading, or social studies concepts to career education. By teaching career concepts through a math class, for example, the student is afforded the opportunity to use math principles in relation to a career skill. More specifically, special needs students could apply math skills by completing time cards, making change, or conducting personal banking business.

The concept of infusing career education in the regular curriculum may be somewhat confusing, since educators may argue that all skills taught are related to career education. It is important to keep in mind that many special needs students may not understand the relevance of basic skills for achieving career benefits unless it is specifically pointed out or taught in the context of a specific utility.

Life-Centered Career Education

Brolin has developed 22 competencies in three curriculum areas that address daily living skills, personal social skills, and occupational guidance and preparation.[20] This career education curriculum has its foundations in the basic skills needed to function effectively as a person within the context of a larger community. It should be noted that Brolin's competency-based career curriculum model is designed to be infused into existing courses offered in school. This model also is based on the

266 HANDBOOK OF VOCATIONAL SPECIAL NEEDS EDUCATION

awareness, exploration, preparation, and placement/follow-up stages of career development.

· Career education curriculum content can be taught through separate programming. Separate career programming offers the student the opportunity to focus specific attention on learning information and skills related to competencies that are directly associated with the various stages of career development. For special needs students, it may be necessary to teach some aspects of the career education curriculum through separate programming similar to those programs provided in elementary education. For example, Cook has developed curriculum programming that is designed to instruct the student in the understanding and use of money.[21] Even though this content could be taught as a part of a math class, it is delivered by specifically focusing on the fundamentals of money. The major objective is to "effectively use official currency and coins of the United States."[22] Over a nine week period, the student is to learn the values of different coins and currency through a variety of activities. In addition, the student then is provided with opportunities to use real money and thus apply the knowledge learned. This method of instruction takes the special needs student away from the regular curriculum and directs the instructional activity of the teacher to a specific area of career education.

Experience-Based Career Education

Separate career education programming can offer special needs students the opportunity to relate practical experiences explicitly to knowledge learned in class. Some special needs students may be better served by this method of career instruction; however, educators must consider the level of disability and the particular needs of the student when considering the appropriate method of instruction.

One method of separate career education programming was developed through a cooperative effort of the Appalachian Educational Laboratory, Far West Laboratory for Educational Research and Development, Northwest Regional Educational Laboratory, and Research for Better Schools. This method of programming is called experience-based career education (EBCE).[23] The EBCE model uses the cooperative education model as its base, but differs in that it utilizes a number of different community sites to provide the student with exposure to a variety of occupations. The cooperative education model usually limits the student to one or two training sites.

The Appalachian Educational Laboratory, Iowa Central Community College, Iowa Arrowhead Education Agency, and the Iowa Department of Public Instruction collaborated to modify the EBCE model for use with special needs students. The modified EBCE model of career instruction involves five major changes.

The first change involves using the community as the base of the training provided. Community sites are used as a direct extension of the special education classroom. An individualized schedule is developed by the instructor and the student. This schedule becomes a part of the student's individualized educational plan (IEP). Participation by the student and the employer is voluntary and neither party receives any pay. Since EBCE is an exploratory experience, students may perform some work purely as a way for them to obtain a concrete understanding of the work required by the occupation. Students will change sites as determined by their specific interests and needs. Finally, in-school instruction is directly related to the different activities at each community site.

One of the major components of EBCE is the extensive assessment of student interests, needs, and attitudes. Based on this assessment information, the student is placed at sites that would be of interest and in occupations that the student is likely to demonstrate an aptitude for. Program models such as the EBCE model have allowed career education instruction to be practical and relevant to special needs students. The separate program focus, however, requires school personnel to change the traditional method of offering career education content.

Practical Arts

Some traditional school course offerings do permit students to explore different occupations. Practical arts courses, such as industrial arts, business education, and home economics, provide students with the opportunity to explore and prepare for occupations on a limited basis, which may lead to the development of an occupational choice.

Industrial arts courses, for example, afford students experiences in areas like mechanical drawing, which may lead to a career in engineering or architecture. Students have the experience of working with various types of materials, e.g., wood, metal, and plastics. In addition to working with these materials, students learn how to plan, organize, and develop projects. They apply basic reading and math skills to complete their projects. Although many parents, teachers, and students may not realize it, industrial arts courses give students exploratory experiences for possible careers during the secondary school years.

For special needs students, practical arts courses may be the only opportunity for them to obtain the type of experiences necessary to explore various career options. It is important for professionals to remember not to exclude special needs students from participating in these courses.

Practical arts courses, while providing exploratory experiences, also constitute one of the first steps toward vocational training. The next steps involve moving from the exploratory stage to the preparation stage. Moving from career exploration in the secondary schools can be accomplished by a variety of different methods. Some methods include the cooperative work-experience programs, such as distributive education, trade and industry, and multi-occupations. Methods like mentorship and apprenticeship are not often utilized, but they can be feasible career development options, especially for special needs students.

The Mentor Model

Mentor is a term frequently used to describe someone from whom a student has learned a great deal. Learning from a mentor may be achieved through the mentor's coaching, teaching, encouraging, or doing a combination of these. Farren, Gray, and Kaye have advocated the use of the mentor system in business through formal and informal programs.[24] These authors assert that mentors fulfill a number of roles. Mentors may act as sponsors, teachers, coaches, and devil's advocates, depending on the nature of the relationship with the student and the environment in which the work is performed.

Although Farren, Gray, and Kaye advocate the use of mentors in business and industry, the mentor system is utilized in the public schools more frequently than educators may be aware. Students often act as or perform duties as teacher assistants, particularly in laboratory settings. Teacher assistant–student relationships in many cases develop informally and can span all of a student's secondary school years. In other instances, the mentor relationship may last for shorter periods of time, e.g., a semester or a year.

For some special needs students, the mentor system may assist in making informed career choices based on the experiences, advice, and coaching provided by the mentor. Additionally, mentoring may facilitate the transition from career exploration to preparation.

Arranging the mentor model can be done both formally and informally. Formal mentor arrangements can be made if a teacher knows of an individual in the community who would be interested in serving as a mentor. The teacher could then determine the interests of the student and match them with the expertise of the mentor. In this case, the teacher serves as the coordinator of the mentor system.

An informal mentor system may involve the student locating his or her own mentor. Through informal contact with different persons, the student may find that he or she has a common interest with an adult who is working in a particular occupation. It is not unusual for an adult to take an interest in a student who is curious about the adult's occupation or vocation.

In general, the goal of the mentor model is to provide a student with learning experiences relating to a specific occupation through advice and coaching. The student, assisted by the mentor, would have opportunities to learn some of the specific skills and kinds of knowledge associated with an occupation. In most circumstances, the mentor would permit the student to try to learn and practice skills needed to function in the occupation.

Specific objectives could be designed so that the student would be responsible for demonstrating a skill or skills or for reporting what knowledge had been learned. Regardless of what objectives might be developed for the mentor system, the student would be able to explore one or more occupations through the assistance of an interested adult willing to serve as an advisor or coach.

The goal of the mentor model is to permit the student to acquire occupational experiences that might not otherwise be available through regular school programs. In addition, the student would have individual instruction from the mentor. Experiences obtained by participating in a mentor program could lead to the student's making more informed career choices. A major advantage of the mentor model for use with special needs students is that it provides the student with highly individualized experiences.

Apprenticeship   The final step in career education is preparation. Thus, this step interfaces with vocational education. Perhaps the oldest method of delivering vocational education is through an apprenticeship.

Apprenticeship dates back at least to the ancient Greeks and Romans. American familiarity with apprenticeship as a form of vocational training probably begins in the colonial period. American social studies textbooks often provide at least a brief account of apprenticeship, which has usually been discussed in terms of involuntary apprenticeship or indentures of apprenticeship. Indentures of apprenticeship have often been referred to negatively because of the reported abuse of apprentices by some masters.

According to Barlow, apprenticeships during colonial times had five purposes, namely, the provision of apprentices with (1) food, clothing, and shelter, (2) instruction in reading and writing, (3) religious instruction, (4) instruction in a trade, and (5) instruction in the secrets of a trade (usually the science and mathematics needed for the trade).[25] Barlow has also suggested that most of vocational training institutions and programs had their beginnings in the institution of apprenticeship.

Contemporary vocational training programs are not viewed as apprenticeships, but they share elements. The evolution of American society has eliminated the need for masters and the provision of food, shelter, clothing, religious instruction, and basic instruction. These functions have been taken on by other institutions and organizations. Vocational training, however, can be provided through the utilization of apprenticeships.

Perhaps apprenticeship, in its most primitive form, can be characterized as learning by doing. The basic goal of an apprenticeship is to teach the apprentice a specific trade. A person skilled in a trade is responsible for ensuring that the apprentice learns the trade sufficiently well to practice independently and competently.

Objectives related to apprenticeship training for disadvantaged students include teaching particular skills that are involved in a trade. If an individual is attempting to learn to be a home builder through the apprenticeship method, the individual observes the builder and then performs the observed tasks. The apprentice would continue to perform the tasks involved in home building until the learned skills could be performed independently and competently as determined by the trades person. Some labor unions have adopted the concept of apprenticeship by requiring an individual to work as an apprentice for a specified period of time. After the individual has reached the desired competency level and functioned as an apprentice for the required period of time, the union leadership usually bestows the title of journeyman on that individual.

During the time that a person is serving as an apprentice, the employer usually pays a wage less than that of a journeyman. In many instances, the union governs the wages of the apprentice. If the employer is nonunion, wage arrangements are usually agreed upon by the parties involved.

The use of the apprenticeship method can be effective in delivering vocational training to special needs students. Arranging an apprenticeship training opportunity should be done systematically by matching a student's needs with an employer interested in assuming the responsibility for training. To achieve the desired outcome of apprenticeship training, the trainee probably should already have received basic academic instruction prior to the apprenticeship. Furthermore, the apprentice should receive on-the-job training while receiving at least a minimum wage. Training provided in this way allows the trainee to receive training and learn a variety of skills in a wide range of environments.

Most contemporary vocational training models use modified versions of the apprenticeship method. Most training models now incorporate related classroom instruction and do not necessarily require the student to be paid.

Cooperative Programs

According to Barlow, cooperative work-experience programs have been developed as an outgrowth of the apprenticeship model.[26] Public school adoption of the work-experience model has popularized such programs and made them formal and systematic. Work-experience programs have also been modified to meet the educational and vocational needs of special needs students. A complete discussion of work-experience programs is provided in Chapter 7.

The benefits of contemporary career education for disadvantaged and mildly handicapped youth are evident; however, the benefits for severely impaired persons are less apparent. For career education to be viable for severely mentally handicapped youths, curriculum modifications and specific programs are required. It is difficult to conceive how to apply current career education models to students with severe mental handicaps, although most program efforts for such individuals would logically fall into the preparation/placement and follow-up stage. Focusing on specific prevocational and vocational training, professionals have utilized several different types of programs to serve the varying needs and abilities of the severely handicapped.

Programs for severely mentally handicapped include work activity centers, sheltered workshops, enclaves in business and industry, and, more recently, competitive employment. These programs have different but related training purposes and should be viewed as a continuum of options for severely handicapped persons.

Work Activity

Of the different program models designed for the severely impaired, work activity programs have been specifically created for the purpose of providing therapeutic activities.

Some present-day work activity centers, however, are now providing vocational assessment services and prevocational training to their clients. Vocational assessment services can include psychomotor assessment and assessment of manual dexterity, sorting, on-task behavior, visual discrimination, and social skills. Other prevocational skills include self-care, community functioning, and domestic skills. Training special needs clients in such skill areas would provide the opportunity to move to more advanced vocational skills for those who are able. Thus, work activity centers could become a part of a continuum of vocational training services that could contribute to more successful community-based training.[27]

Sheltered Work

Contemporary sheltered workshops have assumed three major roles. The first of these is an evaluative role, the second involves providing training for competitive employment, and the third involves providing employment for those who are unable to meet competitive employment standards (e.g., productivity rates and social skills). The most commonly recognized role of sheltered workshops is to provide long-term employment for those who are unable to meet competitive employability standards. Individuals employed long-term are paid on the basis of their ability to produce. Workshops frequently contract with business and industry to do work that would be too time consuming for employees or that would be too costly.

Sheltered workshops have been criticized for being ineffective environments in which to train severely mentally impaired individuals. Some of the major criticisms have been that (1) work skills are often not required or developed, (2) little emphasis is put on instruction, (3) deviant behavior is too often tolerated, (4) few opportunities to interact with nonhandicapped workers are available, and (5) exclusions, waiting lists, and rejections are frequent.[28]

Sheltered Work in Industry

One of the variations of sheltered work is the enclave. Based on normalization principles, enclaves provide severely handicapped persons the opportunity to work in industrial settings under supervision. One example of the sheltered work in industry was implemented by the Eastern Nebraska Community Office of Retardation (ENCOR). The ENCOR staff develop sheltered workshop enclaves within industries located in Omaha. Enclaves allowed special vocational needs clients to work in a normalized setting with nondisabled individuals. Clients work in small groups for training purposes or under supervision for extended employment.

Since clients perform their job skills in industrial settings, generalizing these skills is less difficult for those capable of moving to more independent jobs; this is because the environment remains the same. Methods of training thus concentrate more heavily on job performance, e.g:, production rates and social skills.

Supported Work Model

In recent years, the cooperative work-experience model has been modified to meet the needs of moderately and severely mentally disabled students. The supported work model differs from the work-experience model in that supported work is expressly intended to train moderately and severely mentally disabled individuals to work in the jobs in which they are trained, with support provided as needed.

With the advent of the supported work model, individuals with mental disabilities are now beginning to realize the benefits that can occur from working in competitive employment situations. Wehman has pointed out the benefits that occur from having severely handicapped persons work in competitive employment situations. Among these benefits are that various types of insurance coverage and retirement plans can be offered to the nonhandicapped worker.

The economic benefits derived from competitive employment are obvious, but other benefits occur as well. Wehman suggests that these benefits include (1) integration with nonhandicapped persons, (2) normalization, (3) greater opportunity for advancement, (4) improved perceptions by family and friends, (5) improved perceptions by employers, and (6) improved perceptions by legislators.[29]

Bringing about competitive employment benefits to severely handicapped individuals requires that trainers institute a systematic method of providing training. One such model has been proposed by Wehman and McLaughlin. This model, described below, involves a systematic step-by-step approach to community-based training of the severely handicapped.[30]

In order to determine the availability of jobs, a community assessment must be conducted. Community assessments are conducted by contacting a variety of sources, such as the Chamber of Commerce, local consumers, advocacy and parent groups, state employment offices, and local offices that administer state or federal employment service programs.

The second component in the model involves assessment of the client. This assessment may include evaluating the client with respect to a wide variety of the skills and abilities related to work, community functioning, and independent living.

Developing work adjustment objectives is the third component and usually involves determining possible occupations that would be suitable to the client. Work adjustment could include areas like custodial, horticultural, and hotel/motel services.

The fourth component requires that contact be made with the employer to enlist support and commitment to provide a site for the client. After the employer makes a commitment, a job analysis is conducted to ensure all elements of the job have been identified for training purposes.

The client is then matched with a specific job. This is the fifth component and requires more than just a passable match. The job should be matched as closely as possible to the client's interests and skill level. Matching the job and individual is important, since it may reduce the time needed for training and may enhance the client's employment longevity.

Training of the client is the sixth component. The initial training is used to develop new skills or refine existing skills on the job.

The seventh component involves placing the handicapped individual on the job for a short period of time and with very close supervision. Close supervision allows the trainer to observe the client's work and provides an opportunity to make necessary adjustments.

Trainers can make a decision to extend the length of the client's placement if the client has responded well to training and is performing in an independent manner. The eighth component should find the trainer reducing supervision of the client. If the client does not demonstrate sufficient independent work behavior, other job training sites may need to be identified.

The final component of the model is the evaluation of the program.

SUMMARY

Professional educators should understand that career education is not just for special needs youth, but is important for every child. Children who are handicapped or disadvantaged, however, may require that greater attention be paid to career development because their educational needs differ from those of other children. Failure to recognize the needs of special needs youth may well have major implications for America's already overburdened social service system. In an attempt to address the growing need for appropriate career education programming, this chapter has focused on the basic elements of career education for special needs youth.

Clearly, while definitions of career education may vary, it is broad-based and pervasive throughout educational curricula and is for students of all ages and ability levels. In addition, career education can be delivered through different content curricula and through a variety of methods. Much career education content can be taught by infusing it into regular content areas, but it may be necessary to provide special career education for students with special needs. Of course, the method of delivery and the nature of the content will be dictated by the needs of the individual student.

An attempt was made in this chapter to show the relationship between developmental theory and career development. Career development theory was offered as a basis for understanding career development models that drive and support the career education curriculum in the public schools for special needs youth. Along with the curriculum models, the relationship between career and vocational education was also explained. While vocational education has a clear emphasis on training for occupational skills and competencies, it is largely associated with the later stages of career education.

Finally, career education for the severely handicapped student is no less important than it is for other special needs students. Therefore, career education for the severely handicapped was dealt with and new and emerging activities for training them for competitive and semisheltered employment were described. Although the methods and strategies may be different for this group, the objective nevertheless is the same as it is for other special needs individuals.

NOTES

1. Kenneth B. Hoyt, *An Introduction to Career Education: A Policy Paper of the U.S. Office of Education* (Washington, D.C.: GPO, 1975), 3.

2. Charles Kokaska and Donn E. Brolin, *Career Education for Handicapped Individuals*, 2d ed. (Columbus, Ohio: Charles E. Merrill, 1985), 43.

3. Hoyt, *An Introduction to Career Education*, 3.

4. Kokaska and Brolin, *Career Education from Handicapped Individuals*, 43.

5. Lee E. Isaacson, *Career Information in Counseling and Career Development*, 4th ed. (Boston, Mass.: Allyn and Bacon, 1986), 37.

6. Ibid., 39–43.

7. Ibid., 43.

8. Ibid., 43–48.

9. Ibid., 45–46.

10. Ibid., 50–56.

11. Ibid., 53.

12. Ibid., 57–58.

13. Ibid., 57.

14. Kokaska and Brolin, *Career Education for Handicapped Individuals*, 53–58.

15. *Assessing and Evaluating the Career Development of Special Education Students* (Des Moines, Iowa: Iowa Department of Public Instruction, n.d.), 10.

16. Gary M. Clark and Warren J. White, *Career Education for the Handicapped: Current Perspectives for Teachers* (Boothwyn, Pa.: Educational Resources Center, 1980), 7–11.

17. Ibid., 8.

18. Ibid., 8.

19. Donn E. Brolin, *Vocational Preparation of Persons with Handicaps*, 2d ed. (Columbus, Ohio: Charles E. Merrill, 1982), 27.

20. Donn E. Brolin, *Life Centered Career Education: A Competency Based Approach* (Reston, Va.: Council for Exceptional Children, 1978), 7–13.

21. Iva D. Cook, *Curriculum Methods and Materials for Handicapped Learners in Career and Vocational Education: Module 4—Developing Learning Activities* (West Virginia: College of Graduate Studies, 1979), 17–22.

22. Ibid., 17.

23. *Experience Based Career Education: Basic Procedures Manual* (Fort Dodge, Iowa: Iowa Central Community College, 1976), 1–170.

24. Carla Farren, Janet D. Gray, and Beverly Kaye, "Mentoring: A Boon to Career Development," *Personnel* 61 (1984): 20–24.

25. Melvin L. Barlow, ed., *The Philosophy for Quality Vocational Education Programs* (Washington, D.C.: The American Vocational Association, 1974), 15–19.

26. Ibid., 16.

27. Brolin, *Vocational Preparation*, 13.

28. Lou Brown et al., "Teaching Severely Handicapped Students to Perform Meaningful Work in Nonsheltered Vocational Environments," in *Special Education: Research and Trends*, ed. R.J. Morris and B. Blatt (New York: Pergamon Press, 1986), 135.

29. Paul Wehman, *Competitive Employment: New Horizons for Severely Disabled Individuals* (Baltimore, Md.: Paul H. Brookes, 1981), 3–5.

30. Paul Wehman and Phillip J. McLaughlin, *Program Development in Special Education* (New York: McGraw-Hill, 1981), 361–89.

Chapter 11

Generalizable Skills Instruction

James P. Greenan, Ph.D.

Providing occupationally and job-related technical skills instruction and services to students has been a tradition in vocational programs. However, several national commissions, reports,[1] legislative initiatives, state education agencies, and local education agencies have recognized there is an increased need for basic or academic skills instruction for all students. This need results from the impact of high technology, greater occupational mobility, changing consumer needs, and the higher expectations of employers. Employment and training-related programs such as vocational education have therefore begun to examine their curricula with the aim of providing more basic skills instruction.

Research in vocational education has identified the concept of generalizable skills. A generalizable skill, operationally defined, is a cognitive, affective, or psychomotor trait (skill or skill area) that is basic to, necessary for success in, and transferable (or common) within and among vocational programs and occupations.[2] Therefore, generalizable skills are the basic skills in employment-related programs and occupations, and they constitute an integral rather than an additional component in vocational programs. Acquisition of these skills is important because they facilitate vocational program completion, job entry and maintenance, transition into postsecondary education, and occupational change and advancement.

Special needs learners sometimes lack the generalizable skills necessary for them to succeed in their vocational programs, and thus effective generalizable skills instructional services are particularly important for them. If special needs learners possess sufficient proficiency in generalizable skills, their employable and marketable skills will be enhanced for different occupations and jobs.

This chapter will focus on generalizable skills instruction relating to special needs learners. It is organized around three major areas: (1) curriculum, (2) implementation, and (3) evaluation. Practical strategies and procedures are offered. Vocational special needs education personnel must become involved in generalizable skills instructional activities to assist special needs learners in the transition through vocational programs and into postsecondary education or the world of work.

CURRICULUM   Research has identified four generalizable skill areas: (1) mathematics, (2) communications, (3) interpersonal relations, and (4) reasoning skills.[3] Generalizable skills clearly tend to focus in the cognitive and affective domains. In vocational programs and occupations, psychomotor or technical skills tend to be occupation- and job-specific. Psychomotor skills appear more generalizable in areas such as eye-hand coordination, fine motor dexterity, and gross motor dexterity. The cognitive, affective, and psychomotor domains, however, should be explicit components of a vocational curriculum. In many instances, certain levels of cognitive and affective skills may be prerequisites to, or required concurrently with, psychomotor or technical skills. A curriculum of identified and validated generalized skills is presented in Exhibit 11-1. The curriculum contains the following kinds of skills:

1. Mathematics (28 skills):

   - whole numbers (5 skills)
   - fractions (4 skills)
   - decimals (6 skills)
   - percent (2 skills)
   - mixed operations (4 skills)
   - measurement and calculation (6 skills)
   - estimation (1 skill)

2. Communications (27 skills):

   - words and meanings (9 skills)
   - reading (8 skills)
   - writing (3 skills)
   - speaking (3 skills)
   - listening (4 skills)

3. Interpersonal Relations (20 skills):

   - work behaviors (10 skills)
   - instructional and supervisory conversations (6 skills)
   - social conversations (4 skills)

4. Reasoning (40 skills):

- verbal reasoning (16 skills)
- problem solving (10 skills)
- planning (14 skills)

The skill areas and skills presented in Exhibit 11-1 are generalizable within and across vocational programs in agriculture, in business, marketing, and management, in health, in home economics, and in industrial education. Vocational teachers should examine and revise their existing curricula or develop curricula to include the necessary generalizable skills. For example, local vocational personnel could survey their programs and local employers to further identify and validate generalizable skills for their programs. Vocational educators should involve special educators in these initial activities. Special educators may thus become more aware of the total vocational curriculum and provide input into the writing of appropriate program goals and behavioral objectives. In addition, such communication could initiate and enhance collaboration in subsequent instructional activities such as assessment and planning. Vocational personnel should regularly re-evaluate and update their generalizable skills curriculum to ensure its relevancy to vocational programs and occupations.

IMPLEMEN-TATION

Implementation of generalizable skills instructional activities (following curriculum development and revision) involves assessment, planning, support services, resources, and instructional strategies. Communication and collaboration among vocational, special education, and other related personnel is critical to serve the special needs learner successfully. Each implementation activity is discussed below and strategies for collaboration are presented.

Assessment

Assessment of generalizable skills is important in helping to establish the present levels of performance of special needs learners in vocational programs. Practical assessment strategies and procedures that directly involve students and vocational teachers are most beneficial. Research has identified three major functional assessment strategies potentially useful for measuring the generalizable mathematics, communications, interpersonal relations, and reasoning skills of students in vocational programs. The strategies are (1) student self-ratings, (2) teacher ratings, and (3) performance measures. Each strategy is described below in terms of its purpose, reliability, validity, administration, uses, and resources.

Student Self-Ratings

The purpose of student self-rating assessments is to assess how well students can perceive or estimate their own generalizable skills. The format for student self-ratings may include Likert-type scales or open-ended items. These procedures have been found to possess a relatively high degree of content and face validity for students, teachers, and employers. A sample student self-rating assessment form is presented in Exhibit 11-2.

Exhibit 11-1 Generalizable Skills Curriculum

| | Agricultural Occs. | Business, Marketing and Management Occs. | Health Occupations |

KEY

- High Generalizability ($\bar{x}$ = 5.01 - 7.00)
- Medium Generalizability ($\bar{x}$ = 3.00 - 5.00)
- Low Generalizability ($\bar{x}$ = 1.00 - 2.99)

Column headers (Agricultural Occs.): Agricultural Mechanics; Ornamental Horticulture; Agricultural Cooperative Education; Conservation; Cooperative Work Training (CWT); **All Agricultural Occupations Programs**

Column headers (Business, Marketing and Management Occs.): Advertising Services; General Merchandise (Sales); Personal Services (Sales); Marketing Cooperative (D.E.); Accounting and Computing Occupations; Business Data Processing Systems; Computer Programming; Filing, Office Machines; General Office Clerking; Executive Secretary Science; Secretarial; Office Occupations Cooperative Education; Cooperative Work Training (CWT); Word Processing; Hospitality (Travel and Travel Service); Clerical Occupations; Office Occupations; **All Bus., Market. and Mgmt. Occupations Programs**

Column headers (Health Occupations): Dental Assisting; Practical Nursing; Nurse Aide; Health Care Aide; Medical Assisting; Health Aide; Medical Records; Medical Aide; Health Occupations Cooperative Education; Cooperative Work Training (CWT); Health Occupations; **All Health Occupations Programs**

Mathematics Skills

Whole Numbers
1. Read, write, and count single and multiple digit whole numbers
2. Add and subtract single and multiple digit whole numbers
3. Multiply and divide single and multiple digit whole numbers
4. Use addition, subtraction, multiplication, and division to solve word problems with single and multiple digit whole numbers
5. Round off single and multiple digit whole numbers

Fractions
6. Read and write common fractions
7. Add and subtract common fractions
8. Multiply and divide common fractions
9. Solve word problems with common fractions

Decimals
10. Carry out arithmetic computations involving dollars and cents
11. Read and write decimals in one and more places
12. Round off decimals to one or more places
13. Multiply and divide decimals in one or more places
14. Add and subtract decimals in one or more places
15. Solve word problems with decimals in one or more places

Percent
16. Read and write percents
17. Compute percents

Mixed Operations
18. Convert fractions to decimals, percents to fractions, fractions to percents, percents to decimals, decimals to percents, common fractions or mixed numbers to decimal fractions, and decimal fractions to common fractions or mixed numbers
19. Solve word problems by selecting and using correct order of operations
20. Perform written calculations quickly
21. Compute averages

Measurement and Calculation
22. Read numbers or symbols from time, weight, distance, and volume measuring scales
23. Use a measuring device to determine an object's weight, distance, or volume in standard (English) units
24. Use a measuring device to determine an object's weight, distance, or volume in metric units
25. Perform basic metric conversions involving weight, distance, and volume
26. Solve problems involving time, weight, distance, and volume
27. Use a calculator to perform basic arithmetic operations to solve problems

Estimation
28. Determine if a solution to a mathematical problem is reasonable

Communications Skills

Words and Meanings
1. Use plural words appropriately in writing and speaking
2. Use appropriate contractions and shortened forms of words by using an apostrophe in writing and speaking
3. Use appropriate abbreviations of words in writing and speaking
4. Use words appropriately which mean the same as other words but are spelled differently
5. Use words correctly which sound the same as other words but that have different meanings and spellings
6. Use words appropriately which are opposite of one another
7. Use appropriate word choices in writing and speaking
8. Add appropriate beginnings and endings to words to change their meaning
9. Punctuate one's own correspondence, directives, or reports

Reading
10. Read, understand, and find information or gather data from books, manuals, directories, or other documents
11. Restate or paraphrase a reading passage to confirm one's own understanding of what was read
12. Read and understand forms
13. Read and understand short notes, memos, and letters
14. Read and understand graphs, charts, and tables to obtain factual information
15. Understand the meanings of words in sentences
16. Use a standard dictionary to obtain the meaning, pronunciation, and spelling of words
17. Use the telephone and look up names, telephone numbers, and other information in a telephone directory to make local and long distance calls

Writing
18. Review and edit other's correspondence, directives, or reports
19. Compose logical and understandable written correspondence, directives, memos, short notes, or reports
20. Write logical and understandable statements, phrases, or sentences to accurately fill out forms

Speaking
21. Speak fluently with individuals or groups
22. Pronounce words correctly
23. Speak effectively using appropriate behaviors such as eye contact, posture, and gestures

Listening
24. Restate or paraphrase a conversation to confirm one's own understanding of what was said
25. Ask appropriate questions to clarify another's written or oral communications
26. Attend to nonverbal cues such as eye contact, posture, and gestures for meanings in other's conversations
27. Take accurate notes which summarize the material presented from spoken conversations

Home Economics Occs.	Industrial Occupations	ALL VOCATIONAL TRAINING AREAS AND PROGRAMS
Child Care; Clothing Management, Production, and Service; Food Management, Production, and Service; Home Economics Cooperative Education; Interior Decorating; Child Development; Cooperative Work Training (CWT); All Home Economics Occupations Programs	Air Conditioning; Heating; Appliance Repair; Automotive Services; Body and Fender Repair; Auto Mechanic; Aircraft Maintenance; Commercial Art; Construction and Building Trades; Carpentry; Industrial Maintenance; Diesel Mechanic; Drafting; Electrical Occupations; Industrial Electrician; Electronic Occupations; Radio/Television Repair; Graphic Arts; Machine Shop; Combine Metal Trades; Welding; Tool and Die Making; Cosmetology; Refrigeration; Small Engine Repair; Millwork and Cabinet Making; Industrial Cooperative Education; Cooperative Work Training (CWT); Truck Driving; Warehousing; Home Remodeling and Renovation; Custodial Maintenance; Communications and Media Specialist; All Industrial Occupations Programs	

KEY

- High Generalizability ($\bar{x}$ = 5.01 - 7.00)
- Medium Generalizability ($\bar{x}$ = 3.00 - 5.00)
- Low Generalizability ($\bar{x}$ = 1.00 - 2.99)

Column groups: Agricultural Occs. | Business, Marketing and Management Occs. | Health Occupations

Agricultural Occs. columns: Agricultural Mechanics; Ornamental Horticulture; Agricultural Cooperative Education; Conservation; Cooperative Work Training (CWT); All Agricultural Occupations Programs

Business, Marketing and Management Occs. columns: Advertising Services; General Merchandise (Sales); Personal Services (Sales); Marketing Cooperation (D.E.); Accounting and Computing Occupations; Business Data Processing Systems; Computer Programming; Filing, Office Machines; General Office Clerking; Executive Secretarial; Secretarial; Office Occupations Cooperative Education; Cooperative Work Training (CWT); Word Processing; Hospitality (Travel and Travel Service); Clerical Occupations; Office Occupations; All Bus., Market. and Mgmt. Occupations Programs

Health Occupations columns: Dental Assisting; Practical Nursing; Nurse Aide; Health Care Aide; Medical Assisting; Health Aide; Medical Records; Health Occupations Cooperative Education; Cooperative Work Training (CWT); Health Occupations (CWT); All Health Occupations Programs

Interpersonal Relations Skills

Work Behaviors

1. Work effectively under different kinds of supervision
2. Work without the need for close supervision
3. Work cooperatively as a member of a team
4. Get along and work effectively with people of different personalities
5. Show up regularly and on time for activities and appointments
6. Work effectively when time, tension, or pressure, are critical factors for successful performance
7. See things from another's point of view
8. Engage appropriately in social interaction and situations
9. Take responsibility and be accountable for the effects of one's own judgments, decisions, and actions
10. Plan, carry out, and complete activities at one's own initiation

Instructional and Supervisory Conversations

11. Instruct or direct someone in the performance of a specific task
12. Follow instructions or directions in the performance of a specific task
13. Demonstrate to someone how to perform a specific task
14. Assign others to carry out specific tasks
15. Speak with others in a relaxed and self-confident manner
16. Compliment and provide constructive feedback to others at appropriate times

Conversations

17. Be able to handle criticism, disagreement, or disappointment during a conversation
18. Initiate and maintain task focused or friendly conversations with another individual
19. Initiate, maintain, and draw others into task focused or friendly group conversations
20. Join in task focused or friendly group conversations

Reasoning Skills

Verbal Reasoning

1. Generate or conceive of new or innovative ideas
2. Try out or consciously attempt to use previously learned knowledge and skills in a new situation
3. Understand and explain the main idea in another's written or oral communication
4. Recall ideas, facts, theories, principles, and other information accurately from memory
5. Organize ideas and put them into words rapidly in oral and written conversations
6. Interpret feelings, ideas, or facts in terms of one's own personal viewpoint or values
7. State one's point of view, opinion, or position in written or oral communication
8. Defend one's point of view, opinion, or position in written or oral communication
9. Distinguish between fact and opinion in one's own and in other's written and oral communication
10. Identify the conclusions in other's written or oral communication
11. Identify the reasons offered by another and evaluate their relevance and strength of support for a conclusion
12. Compile one's own notes taken on several written sources into a single report
13. Compile ideas, notes, and materials supplied by others into a single report
14. Carry out correctly written or oral instructions given by another
15. Observe another's performance of a task to identify whether the performance is satisfactory or needs to be improved
16. Ask questions about another's performance of a task to identify whether the performance is satisfactory or needs to be improved

Problem Solving

17. Recognize or identify the existence of a problem given a specific set of facts
18. Ask appropriate questions to identify or verify the existence of a problem
19. Enumerate the possible causes of a problem
20. Use efficient methods for eliminating the causes of a problem
21. Judge the credibility of a source of information
22. Identify important information needed to solve a problem
23. Identify other's and one's own assumptions relating to a problem
24. Generate or conceive of possible alternative solutions to a problem
25. Describe the application and likely consequences of possible alternative problem solutions
26. Compare the application and likely consequences of alternative problem solutions and select a solution that represents the best course of action to pursue

Planning

27. Sort objects according to similar physical characteristics including shape, color, and size
28. Estimate weight of various objects of different shapes, sizes and makeup
29. Estimate length, width, height, and distance between objects
30. Use the senses of touch, sight, smell, taste, and hearing
31. Set priorities or the order in which several tasks will be accomplished
32. Set the goals or standards for accomplishing a specific task
33. Enumerate a set of possible activities needed to accomplish a task
34. Determine how specific activities will assist in accomplishing a task
35. Select activities to accomplish a specific task
36. Determine the order of the activities or step-by-step process by which a specific task can be accomplished
37. Estimate the time required to perform activities needed to accomplish a specific task
38. Locate information about duties, methods, and procedures to perform the activities needed to accomplish a specific task
39. Locate information and select the materials, tools, equipment, or other resources to perform the activities needed to accomplish a specific task
40. Revise or update periodically plans and activities for accomplishing a specific task

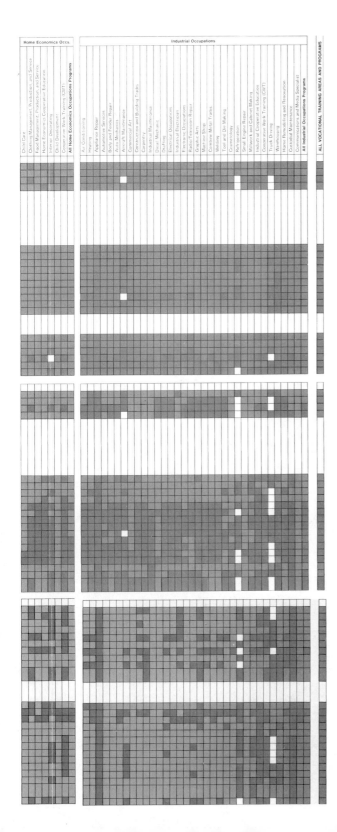

Exhibit 11-2 Sample Student Self-Ratings Form

GENERALIZABLE MATHEMATICS SKILLS ASSESSMENT

Student Self-Ratings

Directions: In the spaces provided, write your name, write your teacher's name, write the name of your school, check (✔) your vocational program area, and write the name of your vocational program.

Student Name: _____
Teacher Name: _____
School: _____

Vocational Program Area/Program:
_____ Agricultural Occupations: _____
_____ Business, Marketing, and Management Occupations: _____
_____ Health Occupations: _____
_____ Home Economics Occupations: _____
_____ Industrial Occupations: _____

Directions: Indicate, by circling the appropriate number, how well you believe you can do each of the following mathematics skills.

Example:

Mathematics Skill	**Degree of Skill**			
	Cannot Do	Cannot Do Too Well	Can Do Fairly Well	Can Do Well
Read and write common fractions	1	2	③	4

Mathematics Skills	**Degree of Skill**			
	Cannot Do	Cannot Do Too Well	Can Do Fairly Well	Can Do Well
Whole Numbers				
1. Read, write, and count whole numbers Examples: 6, six 54, fifty-four 375, three hundred seventy-five 4,128; four thousand one hundred twenty-eight	1	2	3	4

2. Add and subtract whole numbers

   Examples:

     Add: Subtract:

$$8 \quad 15,821 \qquad\qquad 76 \quad 12,872$$
$$+3 \quad\ \ 3,147 \qquad\qquad -23 \quad -\ \ 983$$
$$+\ \ \ 195$$

                         1   2   3   4

3. Multiply and divide whole numbers

   Examples:

     Multiply: Divide:

$$80 \quad 543 \qquad\qquad 7\overline{)147} \quad 125\overline{)34,318}$$
$$\times 3 \quad \times 81$$

                         1   2   3   4

4. Add, subtract, multiply, and divide whole numbers to solve word problems.   1   2   3   4

5. Round off whole numbers   1   2   3   4

In the following spaces, you may write comments about your mathematics skills:

_____

_____

_____

_____

_____

_____

_____

_____

_____

_____

Student self-rating assessment strategies have been shown to possess a relatively high degree of reliability. For example, internal consistency estimates are commonly above .90, and test-retest estimates are frequently above .60 for vocational program areas and programs, exploration and preparation programs, male and female students, low-, average-, and high-achievement students, and for identified special needs learners. However, an individual student's self-ratings may or may not agree with his or her actual generalizable skills (as measured by a criterion measure). For example, a student may over- or underestimate his or her skills. In some instances, student self-ratings may be assessing, not what they were intended to assess (e.g., generalizable mathematics skills), but some other variables (e.g., self-concept or the handicapping or disadvantaging condition). Vocational personnel need to be aware of this possibility so that they may modify assessment procedures, provide necessary guidance and counseling, become more aware of their students' functional learning abilities and problems, and use effectively the assessment information obtained to prescribe appropriate instructional interventions.

Student self-rating assessments should be conducted as often as is necessary for an individual student. For example, all or portions of the ratings could be administered at the beginning of a course or program, then daily or weekly thereafter (formative assessment), and also at the end of the course or program (summative assessment). Skill profiles developed from student self-rating assessments can assist the teacher in analyzing and summarizing information collected.

Student self-rating assessment strategies also have several potential uses in the implementation of generalizable skills instruction:

- to enhance student and teacher awareness of the generalizable skills requirements of their vocational programs

- to permit students and teachers to become actively involved in the assessment process

- to provide formative and summative assessment information about a student's functional learning strengths and learning problems

- to assist a student in becoming self-directed in the learning and decisionmaking processes

- to aid in instructional planning, curriculum development, instructional delivery, and evaluation activities

- to provide information useful for developing individualized vocational/career programs[4]

Specific and detailed instructional resources pertaining to generalizable skills student self-rating assessment instruments and skills profiles, reliability and validity data and information, administration and scoring procedures, and adaptation and modification procedures for use with special needs learners are available for vocational and special education personnel.[5]

Teacher Ratings

The purpose of teacher rating assessments is to assess how well teachers can perceive or estimate their students' generalizable skills. The formats used in teacher ratings are usually similar to those used with student self-ratings. Teacher ratings also have been found to possess a relatively high degree of content and face validity for students, teachers, and employers. A sample teacher rating assessment form is presented in Exhibit 11-3.

Teacher rating assessment strategies also have been shown to possess a relatively high degree of reliability. An individual teacher's ratings, however, may or may not accurately portray his or her student's actual generalizable skills; the teacher may over- or underestimate them. This may be due to prior information, teacher bias, the "Pygmalion effect," or some other variables. Teachers need to be aware of the potential for obtaining inaccurate information.

Teacher ratings, like student self-ratings, should be administered as frequently as is necessary. Skill profiles developed from teacher rating assessments can assist the teacher in analyzing and summarizing the information collected. In addition, teacher ratings have uses similar to those of student self-ratings.

Performance Measures

The major purpose of performance measures is to assess how well students can actually perform generalizable skills. Performance measures may contain closed response (e.g., multiple choice) or open-ended types of items. A sample performance measure assessment test is presented in Exhibit 11-4.

Performance measures of generalizable skills have been found to possess a moderate to a high degree of reliability. Internal consistency estimates are typically above .90 and standard errors of measurement are commonly low. Test-retest reliability and interrater reliability estimates frequently are reported to be greater than $r = .60$.

Performance measures should be administered as frequently as is necessary for individual students. Skill profiles can assist the teacher in interpreting information gathered from performance measures. Performance measures have uses similar to those of student self-ratings and teacher ratings. The instructional resources referred to in the notes for the student self-ratings and teacher ratings sections also contain useful information concerning performance measures.

Planning

Collaboration between vocational and special education personnel is essential in long- and short-range planning for special needs learners. The individualized education plan (IEP) is a total service plan and a management tool designed to guide in decisionmaking, selecting the appropriate placement, developing an appropriate

Exhibit 11-3 Sample Teacher Ratings Form

GENERALIZABLE MATHEMATICS SKILLS ASSESSMENT

Teacher Ratings

Directions: In the spaces provided, write your name, write your teacher's name, write the name of your school, check (✔) your vocational program area, and write the name of your vocational program.

Student Name: _____
Teacher Name: _____
School: _____

Vocational Program Area/Program:
___ Agricultural Occupations: _____
___ Business, Marketing, and Management Occupations: _____
___ Health Occupations: _____
___ Home Economics Occupations: _____
___ Industrial Occupations: _____

Directions: Indicate, by circling the number, how well you believe the student named on the cover sheet can do each of the following mathematics skills.

Example:

Mathematics Skill	Degree of Skill		
	Cannot Do	Cannot Do Too Well	Can Do Fairly Well	Can Do Well
Read and write common fractions	1	2	③	4

Mathematics Skills	Degree of Skill		
	Cannot Do	Cannot Do Too Well	Can Do Fairly Well	Can Do Well

Whole Numbers
1. Read, write, and count whole numbers
   Examples:
   6, six
   54, fifty-four
   375, three hundred seventy-five
   4,128; four thousand one hundred twenty-eight

| | 1 | 2 | 3 | 4 |

2. Add and subtract whole numbers

   Examples:

   Add: Subtract:

$$\begin{array}{ccc} 8 & 15{,}821 & 76 \\ +3 & 3{,}147 & -23 \\ & +\ \ 195 & \end{array} \qquad \begin{array}{c} 12{,}872 \\ -\ \ 983 \end{array}$$

                                                  1   2   3   4

3. Multiply and divide whole numbers

   Examples:

   Multiply: Divide:

$$\begin{array}{cc} 80 & 543 \\ \times 3 & \times 81 \end{array} \qquad \begin{array}{cc} 7/147 & 125/34{,}318 \end{array}$$

                                                  1   2   3   4

4. Add, subtract, multiply, and divide whole numbers to solve word problems   1   2   3   4

5. Round off whole numbers   1   2   3   4

In the following spaces, you may write comments about this student's mathematics skills:

_____

_____

_____

_____

_____

_____

_____

_____

_____

Exhibit 11-4 Sample Performance Test

GENERALIZABLE MATHEMATICS SKILLS ASSESSMENT

Performance Test

Directions: In the spaces provided, write your name, write your teacher's name, write the name of your school, check (✔) your vocational program area, and write the name of your vocational program.

Student Name: _____
Teacher Name: _____
School: _____

Vocational Program Area/Program:
_____ Agricultural Occupations: _____
_____ Business, Marketing, and Management Occupations: _____
_____ Health Occupations: _____
_____ Home Economics Occupations: _____
_____ Industrial Occupations: _____

Directions: Do each of the following problems by circling the correct answer. Please use the scratch paper provided to work out your answers.

Example:

Add: 8
       +7

(a) 6   (b) 25   (c) 15   (d) 5

Whole Numbers

1. 97 is written as:

(a) nine hundred seven
(b) nine thousand seventy
(c) ninety-seven
(d) seventy-nine

2. 4,132 is written as:

(a) four thousand one hundred thirty-two
(b) forty-one thousand thirty-two
(c) forty-one hundred thirty
(d) four hundred thirty-two

3. Eight is represented by which number?

    (a) 8   (b) 6   (c) 800   (d) 80

4. Five thousand nine hundred nineteen is represented by which number?

    (a) 519   (b) 59   (c) 591   (d) 5,919

5. How many screws are there in the following diagram?

    (a) 10   (b) 30   (c) 8   (d) 5

6. How many nails are there in the following diagram?

    (a) 791   (b) 792   (c) 691   (d) none of these

7. Add: 9
        +7

    (a) 13   (b) 22   (c) 15   (d) 32

8. Add: 302
         431
        +58

    (a) 26   (b) 2   (c) 16   (d) 17

9. Add: 12,031
         1,224
         8,341
      + 489

    (a) 22,985   (b) 22,085   (c) 21,085   (d) 22,075

10. Subtract: 98
            −27

    (a) 61   (b) 81   (c) 125   (d) 71

11. Subtract: 926
           −336

    (a) 590   (b) 690   (c) 592   (d) 692

12. Subtract: 13,104
          − 785

    (a) 13,319   (b) 13,621   (c) 12,329   (d) none of these

13. Multiply: 37
          × 8

    (a) 276   (b) 296   (c) 306   (d) 302

Exhibit 11-4 continued

14. Multiply: 40
                ×29

    (a) 1,160   (b) 1,189   (c) 1,260   (d) 1,060

15. Multiply: 789
                ×46

    (a) 35,294   (b) 37,284   (c) 7,890   (d) 36,294

16. Divide:

    8/224

    (a) 30   (b) 26   (c) 28   (d) 27

17. Divide:

    27/3,321

    (a) 13   (b) 132   (c) 1,230   (d) none of these

18. Divide:

    326/44,018

    (a) 135   (c) 105 R = 148
    (b) 135 R = 8   (d) 135 R = 80

19. Mr. Jones has 9 acres of farm land. He intends to buy 6 acres in the spring, 15 in the summer, and 48 in the fall. How many acres will he have at the beginning of next winter?

    (a) 30   (b) 68   (c) 58   (d) 78

20. Ms. Smith typed 126 pages on Wednesday. On Thursday she typed 58 pages. How many more pages did Ms. Smith type on Wednesday than on Thursday?

    (a) 68   (b) 184   (c) 78   (d) 168

21. Sixteen ounces of flour were called for in a recipe. If the recipe were doubled, how many ounces of flour would be needed?

    (a) 16   (b) 28   (c) 32   (d) none of these

22. How many 3-feet square sections can be cut from a piece of sheet metal 3-feet wide by 30 feet long?

    (a) 90   (b) 10   (c) 33   (d) 8

23. 64 rounded off to the nearest tens place is:

    (a) 60   (b) 70   (c) 65   (d) 80

24. 1,553 rounded off to the nearest hundreds place is:

    (a) 1,500   (b) 1,550   (c) 1,600   (d) 2,000

25. 23,974 rounded off to the nearest thousands place is:

    (a) 23,900   (b) 23,000   (c) 24,900   (d) 24,000

comprehensive program, and identifying appropriate special education services for special needs learners, especially handicapped learners. The IEP aids personnel in organizing, implementing, and evaluating the instruction and support services necessary for special needs learners to succeed. The individualized vocational education plan (IVEP) is one of several individual implementation plans contained within the IEP.

The IVEP of each special needs learner's IEP should include

- statements of present levels of educational performance
- statements of annual goals and short-term instructional objectives in generalizable skills and vocational skills
- special education and related services required for the student to participate in vocational education (including career counseling and counseling for transition)
- the extent of participation in regular educational programs
- dates of initiation and duration of services
- appropriate objective evaluation procedures and criteria for measuring student attainment of objectives[6]

Vocational educators must work collaboratively with special educators, regular educators, administrators, support personnel, and others in writing vocational goals and behavioral objectives for individual students. Vocational teachers should provide direct input into the IEP/IVEP using the generalizable skills assessment data and information collected. Vocational teachers should also provide input regarding needed support services, resources, teaching strategies, and evaluation methods for individual students. Sarkees and Scott[7] describe specific roles for vocational educators in collaborating with special educators in the IEP process.

The following case study shows how an IVEP that integrates generalizable skills can be developed as part of the IEP process.

Case Study

Chris is a 16-year-old high school sophomore who expressed an interest in becoming an automotive mechanic. Chris has been identified as learning disabled since sixth grade and has taken special classes in reading and mathematics during this time. Results of interest and aptitude assessments have indicated that auto mechanics is an appropriate placement. Chris should not have any problems with the "hands-on" component of the class, as attending, listening, and physical skills have always been his strengths. There is some concern about the reading and mathematics required in the program. Chris will work in the resource room on skills such as using manuals and critical vocabulary. Although Chris can perform basic arithmetic computations with a calculator, it is now necessary to learn the skills for success in auto mechanics. To assist with this, an individualized mathematics program is designed.

Chris and the instructor of the small engines course in which Chris is currently enrolled complete the three components of the Generalizable Mathematics Skills Assessment (see Exhibits 11-5, 11-6, and 11-7). A summary of these results follows.

The Student Self-Ratings has a total score of 3.6, which is in the high range. Scales range from 3.0 to 4.0, and individual skill ratings are all 3s and 4s. All of these ratings are in the high range. This indicates that the student believes he is able to perform all of the skills listed on the instrument fairly well. The Teacher Ratings has a total score of 1.7, which is considered low. Scale scores range from 1.0 to 2.8, and skill ratings range from 1 to 4. These ratings suggest strengths in some areas and a need for learning prescriptions/support services in others. The Performance Test has a total score of 43, which is in the low range. The whole numbers scale is high, while all other scales are low. A close examination of the skill assessment indicates that decisions based completely upon this information may be misleading. It is important to examine at the individual skill level. Using Exhibit 11-8, skill levels may be designated as low, average, or high. Examining the whole numbers scale this way illustrates that Chris is lacking one skill in this scale—solving word problems using whole numbers, which is an important skill for auto mechanics. This example demonstrates the need for skill assessment at the individual skill level.

Comparison of the three instruments in this example indicates that the student's skills are overestimated on the Student Self-Ratings in most areas. The Teacher Ratings are accurate, except for an overestimation regarding reading and writing decimals. The vocational special needs teacher states that Chris's overestimation could be caused by difficulty in reading and understanding some of the words. Chris had the option of doing the Student Self-Ratings orally, but chose not to. When Chris is shown the results of the Student Self-Ratings compared to the results of the Performance Test, he admits having difficulty with some of the words, but says that the examples seemed like content that had been studied previously.

At the time of Chris's scheduled IEP meeting, a staffing is held to set up the individualized mathematics program. This meeting includes Chris, his parents, the vocational special needs teacher, the auto mechanics teacher, and the mathematics teacher. After reviewing the results of the Generalizable Mathematics Skills Assessment, the group decides to compare Chris's Performance Test results with the skills indicated as highly generalizable for auto mechanics. A review of the generalizable skills chart (see Exhibit 11-1) shows that skills 1, 2, 3, 4, 6, 7, 10, 11, 12, 13, 14, 16, 17, 18, 22, 23, and 24 possess high generalizability. This list is compared to the Performance Test results to determine which of the required skills were identified to be difficult for Chris. The result of this comparison shows that Chris needs to work on skills 4, 7, 10, 12, 13, 14, 17, 18, 23, and 24. It is decided that the moderately generalizable skills will not be emphasized at this time, since there is a considerable amount to be done with the highly generalizable skills. It is also possible that some of the former skills will improve as a result of the emphasis on the highly generalizable skills.

The next step involves writing the IEP. The skills identified as highly generalizable to auto mechanics but which were low on the Performance Test become the short-term goals. The readministration of and score on the Generalizable Mathematics Skills Assessment constitute the evaluation method and skill level respectively. This process can be most clearly seen by reviewing the sample IEP prepared for Chris (see Exhibit 11-9).[8]

Exhibit 11-5 Student Self-Ratings Skill Profile

GENERALIZABLE VOCATIONAL MATHEMATICS SKILLS ASSESSMENT
STUDENT SELF-RATINGS
SKILL PROFILE

Scales/Skills	*Item Number*		*Student Self-Rating*	
Whole Numbers				
Read, write, and count	1		4	
Add and subtract	2		4	
Multiply and divide	3		4	
Solve word problems	4		4	
Round off	5		4	
		Total	20	
Fractions		Average(/5)	4	high
Read and write	6		3	
Add and subtract	7		3	
Multiply and divide	8		3	
Solve word problems	9		3	
		Total	12	
Decimals		Average(/4)	3	high
Read and write	10		3	
Add and subtract	11		3	
Multiply and divide	12		3	
Solve word problems	13		3	
Solve dollars and cents problems	14		4	
Round off	15		4	
		Total	20	
Percent		Average(/6)	3.3	high
Read and write	16		3	
Solve problems	17		3	
		Total	6	
Mixed Operations		Average(/2)	3	high
Change fractions, decimals, percents, mixed numbers, and decimal fractions	18		3	
Solve word problems	19		3	
Find averages	20		4	
Do written calculations quickly	21		4	
		Total	14	
Measurement and Calculation		Average(/4)	3.5	high
Read time, weight, distance, and volume scales	22		4	
Use standard weight, distance, and volume scales	23		4	
Use metric weight, distance, and volume scales	24		4	
Do basic metric weight, distance, and volume conversions	25		4	
Solve time, weight, distance, and volume word problems	26		4	
Use a calculator to solve addition, subtraction, multiplication, and division problems	27		4	

Exhibit 11-5 continued

Scales/Skills	Item Number	Student Self-Rating		
		Total	24	
Estimation		Average(/6)	4	high
Determine if a solution or answer to a mathematics problem is reasonable	28	Total	4	
		TOTAL	100	
		AVERAGE(/28)	3.6	high

Comments: _____

_____

_____

_____

_____

_____

_____

_____

_____

_____

_____

_____

_____

_____

_____

_____

_____

_____

_____

_____

_____

_____

_____

_____

_____

_____

_____

_____

_____

_____

_____

_____

_____

_____

_____

_____

_____

Exhibit 11-6 Teacher Ratings Skill Profile

GENERALIZABLE VOCATIONAL MATHEMATICS SKILLS ASSESSMENT
TEACHER RATINGS
SKILL PROFILE

Scales/Skills	*Item Number*	*Teacher Rating*	
Whole Numbers			
Read, write, and count	1	4	
Add and subtract	2	4	
Multiply and divide	3	4	
Solve word problems	4	1	
Round off	5	1	
	Total	14	
Fractions	Average(/5)	2.8	ave.
Read and write	6	4	
Add and subtract	7	1	
Multiply and divide	8	1	
Solve word problems	9	1	
	Total	7	
Decimals	Average(/4)	1.75	low
Read and write	10	4	
Add and subtract	11	1	
Multiply and divide	12	1	
Solve word problems	13	1	
Solve dollars and cents problems	14	1	
Round off	15	1	
	Total	9	
Percent	Average(/6)	1.5	low
Read and write	16	1	
Solve problems	17	1	
	Total	2	
Mixed Operations	Average(/2)	1	low
Change fractions, decimals, percents,			
mixed numbers, and decimal fractions	18	1	
Solve word problems	19	1	
Find averages	20	1	
Do written calculations quickly	21	1	
	Total	4	
Measurement and Calculation	Average(/4)	1	low
Read time, weight, distance, and volume			
scales	22	4	
Use standard weight, distance, and			
volume scales	23	2	
Use metric weight, distance, and volume			
scales	24	1	
Do basic metric weight, distance, and			
volume conversions	25	1	
Solve time, weight, distance, and volume			
word problems	26	1	
Use a calculator to solve addition,			
subtraction, multiplication, and division			
problems	27	4	

Exhibit 11-6 continued

Scales/Skills	Item Number	Teacher Rating	
		Total	13
Estimation		Average(/6)	2.17 ave.
Determine if a solution or answer to a			
mathematics problem is reasonable	28	Total	1
		TOTAL	48
		AVERAGE(/28)	1.7 low

Comments: _____

_____

_____

_____

_____

_____

_____

_____

_____

_____

_____

_____

_____

_____

_____

_____

_____

_____

_____

_____

_____

_____

_____

_____

_____

_____

_____

_____

_____

_____

_____

_____

_____

_____

_____

_____

_____

_____

_____

Exhibit 11-7 Performance Test Skill Profile

GENERALIZABLE VOCATIONAL MATHEMATICS SKILLS ASSESSMENT
PERFORMANCE TEST
SKILL PROFILE

Scales/Skills	Item Number	Number Correct	
Whole Numbers			
Read, write, and count	1–6		6 H
Add and subtract	7–12		6 H
Multiply and divide	13–18		6 H
Solve word problems	19–22		0 L
Round off	23–25		1 L
		Total	19 H
Fractions			
Read and write	26–31		5 H
Add and subtract	32–43		0 L
Multiply and divide	44–55		0 L
Solve word problems	56–59		0 L
		Total	5 L
Decimals			
Read and write	60–63		1 L
Add and subtract	64–75		6 A
Multiply and divide	76–87		2 L
Solve word problems	88–91		0 L
Solve dollars and cents problems	92–99		2 L
Round off	100–102		0 L
		Total	11 L
Percent			
Read and write	103–108		3 A
Solve problems	109–111		0 L
		Total	3 L
Mixed Operations			
Fractions to decimals to percents, mixed numbers, and decimal fractions	112–120		0 L
Solve word problems	121–123		0 L
Find averages	124–126		1 L
		Total	1 L
Measurement and Calculation			
Read time, weight, distance, and volume scales	127–133		4 A
Do metric weight, distance, and volume conversions	134–139		0 L
Solve time, weight, distance, and volume word problems	140–146		0 L
		Total	4 L
Estimation			
Determine if a solution or answer to a mathematics problem is reasonable	147–150		0 L
		Total	0 L
		TOTAL Score	43 L

Exhibit 11-7 continued

Comments: _____

_____

_____

_____

_____

_____

_____

_____

_____

_____

_____

_____

_____

_____

_____

_____

_____

_____

_____

_____

_____

_____

_____

_____

_____

_____

_____

_____

_____

_____

_____

_____

_____

Support Services

Providing support services in generalizable skills to special needs learners requires collaboration among vocational education, special education, rehabilitation, employment and training programs (e.g., Job Training Partnership Act [JTPA]), the private sector (e.g., business and industry), and related agencies. Sitlington states that it is important to identify the agency personnel who will deliver support services and to use the most effective procedures for selecting necessary support services based on learner needs and availability.[9] Several models of support services delivery have been identified.[10] These models describe the contexts and environments in which instruction may be provided. In general, to serve the needs of an individual student, the learning environment (i.e., curriculum, facilities, equipment, materials) may be

Exhibit 11-8 Relationship of the Skills Listed on the Student Self-Ratings and Teacher Ratings with the Items Included on the Performance Test

Student Self-Ratings and Teacher Ratings Skills (Range of Responses)	Performance Test Items (Range of Responses)	
4—"Can Do Well" (High)	"Correct Items"	
3—"Can Do Fairly Well" (Average)	"Incorrect Items"	
2—"Cannot Do Too Well" (Average)		
1—"Cannot Do" (Low)		
Whole Numbers		
1. Read, write, and count whole numbers	1–6	(High: 5–6) (Average: 3–4) (Low: 1–2)
2. Add and subtract whole numbers	7–12	(High: 5–6) (Average: 3–4) (Low: 1–2)
3. Multiply and divide whole numbers	13–18	(High: 5–6) (Average: 3–4) (Low: 1–2)
4. Add, subtract, multiply, and divide whole numbers to solve word problems	19–22	(High: 4) (Average: 2–3) (Low: 1)
5. Round off whole numbers	23–25	(High: 3) (Average: 2) (Low: 1)
(High: 3–4.00) (Average: 2–2.99) (Low: 1–1.99)	(High: 18–25) (Average: 9–17) (n = 25 items) (Low: 1–8)	
Fractions		
6. Read and write common fractions	26–31	(High: 5–6) (Average: 3–4) (Low: 1–2)
7. Add and subtract common fractions	32–43	(High: 9–12) (Average: 5–8) (Low: 1–4)
8. Multiply and divide common fractions	44–55	(High: 9–12) (Average: 5–8) (Low: 1–4)
9. Add, subtract, multiply, and divide common fractions to solve word problems	56–59	(High: 4) (Average: 2–3) (Low: 1)

Exhibit 11-8 continued

(High: 3–4.00)		(High: 24–34)
(Average: 2–2.99)		(Average: 13–23) (n = 34 items)
(Low: 1–1.99)		(Low: 1–12)

Decimals

10. Read and write decimals   60–63   (High: 4)
                                                (Average: 2–3)
                                                (Low: 1)

11. Add and subtract decimals   64–75   (High: 9–12)
                                                  (Average: 5–8)
                                                (Low: 1–4)

12. Multiply and divide decimals   76–87   (High: 9–12)
                                                  (Average: 5–8)
                                                (Low: 1–4)

13. Add, subtract, multiply, and divide
    common decimals to solve word
    problems   88–91   (High: 4)
                                                  (Average: 2–3)
                                                  (Low: 1)

14. Solve problems involving dollars and
    cents   92–99   (High: 6–8)
                                                   (Average: 3–5)
                                                  (Low: 1–2)

15. Round off decimals   100–102   (High: 3)
                                                  (Average: 2)
                                                  (Low: 1)

(High: 3–4.00)		(High: 30–43)
(Average: 2–2.99)		(Average: 16–29) (n = 43 items)
(Low: 1–1.99)		(Low: 1–15)

Percent

16. Read and write percents   103–108   (High: 5–6)
                                                  (Average: 3–4)
                                                  (Low: 1–2)

17. Solve word problems involving
    percents   109–111   (High: 3)
                                                  (Average: 2)
                                                  (Low: 1)

(High: 3–4.00)		(High: 7–9)
(Average: 2–2.99)		(Average: 4–6) (n = 9 items)
(Low: 1–1.99)		(Low: 1–3)

Mixed Operations

18. Change fractions to decimals, percents
    to fractions, fractions to percents,
    percents to decimals, decimals to

Exhibit 11-8 continued

percents, fractions or mixed numbers to decimal fractions, decimal fractions to fractions or mixed numbers	112–120	(High: 7–9) (Average: 4–6) (Low: 1–3)
19. Solve word problems by selecting and using the correct order of addition, subtraction, multiplication, and division for whole numbers, fractions, decimals, and percents	121–123	(High: 3) (Average: 2) (Low: 1)
20. Find averages (means)	124–126	(High: 3) (Average: 2) (Low: 1)
21. Do written calculations quickly	N/A	

(High: 3–4.00) (Average: 2–2.99) (Low: 1–1.99)	(High: 11–15) (Average: 6–10) (n = 15 items) (Low: 1–5)

Measurement and Calculation

22. Read numbers or symbols from time, weight, distance, and volume measuring scales	127–133	(High: 6–7) (Average: 3–5) (Low: 1–2)
23. Use measuring scales to determine an object's weight, distance, and volume in standard (English) units	N/A	
24. Use measuring scales to determine an object's weight, distance, and volume in metric units	N/A	
25. Do basic metric conversions involving weight, distance, and volume	134–139	(High: 5–6) (Average: 3–4) (Low: 1–2)
26. Solve problems involving time, weight, distance, and volume	140–146	(High: 6–7) (Average: 3–5) (Low: 1–2)
27. Use a calculator to solve problems involving addition, subtraction, multiplication, and division	N/A	

(High: 3–4.00) (Average: 2–2.99) (Low: 1–1.99)	(High: 15–20) (Average: 8–14) (n = 20 items) (Low: 1–7)

Exhibit 11-8 continued

Estimation
28. Determine if a solution or answer to a
    mathematics problem is reasonable   147–150   (High: 4)
                                                         (Average: 2–3)
                                                         (Low: 1)

(High: 3–4.00)	(High: 4)
(Average: 2–2.99)	(Average: 2–3) (n = 4 items)
(Low: 1–1.99)	(Low: 1)

TOTAL INSTRUMENT

(High: 3–4.00)	(High: 101–150)
(Average: 2–2.99)	(Average: 51–100) (n = 150 items)
(Low: 1–1.99)	(Low: 0–50)

modified or adapted, supplementary or remedial services may be provided, or instruction and related services may be provided in a separate program.

The Special Education Cascade Model[11] can serve as a framework for determining which, where, when, and how support services will be delivered (see Figure 11-1). The model, applied to generalizable skills, suggests that instruction can occur in regular vocational education programs with or without in-class assistance from special educators, special needs personnel, remedial personnel, regular content-related specialists (e.g., mathematics teachers), aides, tutors, consultants, or other support personnel. Students may also receive generalizable skills instruction or assistance in resource rooms, supplementing their instruction in the regular vocational program. A "separate" class (e.g., in generalizable mathematics skills) could also be an alternative. A separate class need not necessarily be a nonmainstreamed class. For most special needs learners, the least desirable option, in terms of the least restrictive environment, would be separate programs in vocational or generalizable skills. The ultimate determination of the most appropriate program, placement, and necessary support services is based on each student's individual learning needs.

Resources

Identifying, evaluating, selecting, and using instructional resource materials for teaching generalizable skills are important activities. Information gathered from the curriculum development-revision, assessment, and planning phases should assist the teacher in choosing appropriate resources for groups of students as well as individual students. Materials may have to be adapted or modified, at least to some extent, for each special needs student (e.g., with regard to reading level).

Exhibit 11-9 Sample Individualized Education Program Plan

INDIVIDUALIZED EDUCATION PROGRAM PLAN

Student's Name: Chris Brown

Birth Date: May 8, 1971

Present Date: May 30, 1987

Grade/Program: 11th—Mainstream

School: Jones/White

School: Local Community High

Primary Assignment(s):	Date Started	Expected Duration of Service
Auto Mechanics	Sept. 1987	June 1988
Resource Room Supervision	Sept. 1987	as needed

Special Media or Materials

Present material auditorily as much as possible. Assistance available in resource room for reinforcing class material, and providing alternative materials and taking tests orally.

Present levels of functioning: Chris completed the GMSA on April 12, 1987. The Student Self-Ratings indicated overestimation of skills when compared with the Performance Test (PT). This could be partially due to difficulty understanding some terms. Chris had the option of having the test read, but did not want this. Results of the PT indicate strengths in performing basic functions with whole numbers and decimals. Chris was allowed to use a calculator during this assessment. Areas of difficulty were all operations with word problems (some of these were tried orally and Chris didn't appear to have knowledge of the concepts necessary), operations with fractions and decimals, converting fractions, decimals and percents, metric conversions, and estimation. The Skills Profile of the PT (see Exhibit 11-7) is attached for more complete information. These skills have been identified as critical to Auto Mechanics classes and employment, and so they will become the focus of Chris's mathematics program.

Services:

Resource room supervision	Sept. 1987	June, 1988
for auto mechanics		
Individualized mathematics	Sept. 1987	June, 1988

Dates for review and/or revision of the Individualized Education Program Plan:

Nov. 1987

May 1988

Person(s) responsible for the maintenance and implementation of the Plan:

Mary Smith

William Jones

Exhibit 11-9 continued

IEP INSTRUCTIONAL OBJECTIVES

Student Chris Brown
ID # 123-456-789
IEP Case Manager

Annual Goal To develop the mathematics skills required to succeed in the Automotive Mechanics Program.

School Year 1987–88
Evaluation Period: From April 8, 1987 To April 12, 1987
IEP Implementer Mary Smith
Title Special Education Teacher

Short-Term Objectives	Methods & Materials	Evaluation	Date Objective Mastered
After instruction and practice in the mathematics skills necessary for success in auto mechanics, and with the use of a calculator, Chris will:	At the beginning of each new unit, Chris will confer with the auto mechanics instructor to determine how mathematics concepts relate to auto mechanics. Chris will explain what he has learned to the mathematics teacher.	1. At least 3 problems correct out of problems 19–22 on the GMSA Performance Test.	
1. Use addition, subtraction, multiplication, and division to solve word problems with single and multiple digit whole numbers.		2. At least 8 problems correct out of problems 32–43 on the GMSA.	
2. Add and subtract common fractions	Books such as "Mathematics for Auto Mechanics" and the "Number Power" series will be used to reinforce skills.	3. At least 5 problems correct out of problems 92–99 on the GMSA.	
3. Carry out arithmetic computations involving dollars and cents		4. At least 2 problems correct out of problems 100–102 on the GMSA.	
4. Round off decimals to one or more places	Once a week, Chris will practice the current concept on the microcomputer. He may also do so during his free time, if he chooses.	5. At least 8 problems correct out of problems 64–75 on the GMSA.	
5. Add and subtract decimals in one or more places		6. At least 8 problems correct out of problems 76–87 on the GMSA.	
6. Multiply and divide decimals in one or more places		7. At least 2 problems correct out of problems 109–111 on the GMSA.	
7. Compute percents		8. At least 6 problems correct out of problems 112–120 on the GMSA.	
8. Convert fractions to decimals, percents to fractions, fractions to percents, percents to decimals, decimals to percents, common fractions or mixed numbers to decimal fractions, and decimal fractions to common fractions or mixed numbers		9. Given 10 objects (for each category), Chris will determine the weight, distance, or volume in standard units correctly for all 10.	
9. Use measuring devices to determine object's weight, distance, or volume in standard units		10. Given 10 objects (for each category), Chris will determine the weight, distance, or volume in metric units correctly for all 10.	
10. Use measuring devices to determine object's weight, distance, or volume in metric units.			

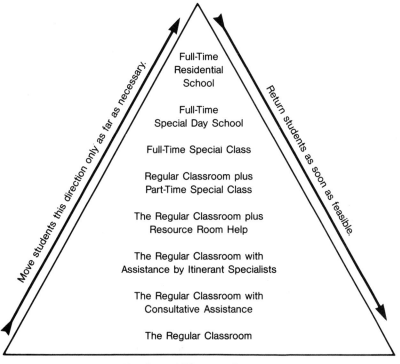

The Special Education Cascade

Figure 11-1 The Special Education Cascade *Source:* Reprinted from *Teaching Exceptional Children in All America's Schools* by M.C. Reynolds and J.W. Birch, p. 32, with permission of Council for Exceptional Children, © 1977.

Commercial as well as noncommercial resource materials are available for teacher use. Richard[12] and Parrish and Colby[13] reviewed and presented several materials potentially useful when providing instruction in the generalizable skills areas of mathematics, communications, interpersonal relations, and reasoning. In addition, there are several generalizable skills resource directories.[14] These directories provide comprehensive, but not necessarily exhaustive, lists of resources and are useful to personnel when selecting teaching materials in generalizable skills. The resource directories include, among other things, user guides, content-related resource materials, teacher resource materials, and lists of publishers. The resources sections include titles, authors, sources, descriptions, and costs. Teachers and other users should continually update their generalizable skills resource materials for their programs, and they are provided with suggestions in the resource directories on how to do this.

Instructional Strategies

The identification, selection, implementation, and evaluation of effective instructional strategies are essential in the delivery of generalizable skills instruction. The process involves identifying students' learning styles, selecting instructional materials, prescribing necessary modifications or adaptations, and selecting appropriate teaching strategies. These activities are not mutually exclusive and therefore they should be coordinated.

Generalizable skills instruction involves the visual, auditory, and tactile senses. Thus, teachers should identify special needs students' learning styles relative to their functional learning abilities and problems. Hartley and Lehmann[15] suggest that teachers should identify the modes or learning styles (i.e., visual, auditory, kinesthetic) through which students learn most effectively.

Obtaining and reviewing information regarding an individual student's special needs and identifying optimum learning styles assist personnel in selecting appropriate instructional facilities, materials, and equipment. Learning styles and alternative instructional methods are illustrated in Table 11-1.

Effective teaching strategies are critical in providing generalizable skills instruction to special needs learners. Teachers should analyze their existing teaching strategies and modify or adapt them for individuals or groups of students. Exhibit 11-10 presents several teaching strategies potentially useful with individual special needs learners. Teachers should continue to develop creative and innovative strategies as they need them. In many instances, teachers and support personnel are likely to use several strategies in combination, or use the most effective features of particular strategies. It is especially important, however, that vocational and special education personnel continue to collaborate during the selection, implementation, and evaluation of instructional delivery.

Another instructional consideration is the selection or modification and adaptation of curriculum and of instructional materials, equipment, and facilities. Modifications or adaptations must relate to the generalizable skills curriculum, obtained assessment information, optimum modes or learning styles identified for individual special needs

Table 11-1 Learning Styles and Appropriate Instructional Methods

Instructional Methods	Learning Styles		
	Visual	Auditory	Kinesthetic
Printed materials (books, texts, etc.)	X		
Verbal lecture materials		X	
Workbook sheets	X		X
Audio-visual materials (records, puzzles, films, filmstrip, slide/tape, TV, overhead transparencies with lecture)	X	X	
Demonstration using vocational tools, equipment, and concrete materials	X	X	X

Source: Reprinted from The Journal for Vocational Special Needs Education, Vol. 9, No. 1, p. 32, with permission of National Association of Vocational Special Needs Personnel, © 1986.

Exhibit 11-10 General Teaching Strategies

Demonstration	Field trip
Problem solving	Peer tutoring
Audio-visual	Simulation
Individualized instruction	Mastery learning
Manipulative (hands-on) activities	Conference
Reading	Experimentation
Contracting	Field (work) experience
Differentiated staffing	Seminar
Lecture	Homework
Discussion	Laboratory experience
Role playing	Observation
Skill practice	Modeling and imitation
Team teaching	Drill
Resource person	Programmed instruction
Recreation	Project

learners, and features or characteristics of the existing learning environment. As in other activities, vocational education, special education, and other related personnel should work collaboratively in suggesting modifications and adaptations of the generalizable skills curriculum and of instruction for individual students. Exhibit 11-11 presents several potential modifications or adaptations of instruction for special needs learners. Exhibit 11-12 presents several specific potential modifications for use when teaching generalizable skills.

EVALUATION

Evaluation of generalizable skills instruction with respect to its adequacy, quality, and effect is essential to improving vocational services for special needs learners. Several program evaluation models have been suggested to improve educational programs.[20] For example, Stufflebeam's program evaluation model focuses on context, input, process, and product.[21] Albright's model emphasizes program needs assessment, program planning, process, and outcomes.[22] Several pertinent evaluation questions are suggested for each phase in these models.

Generalizable skills program evaluation should focus on each instructional component, including curriculum, assessment, planning, support services, resources, and teaching strategies. Relevant evaluation questions that should be addressed when evaluating vocational programs regarding generalizable skills instruction include the following:

- Is the generalizable skills curriculum relevant to vocational program goals and occupational requirements?
- Are the generalizable skills of special needs learners being adequately assessed?

Exhibit 11-11 Possible Modifications That Can Make Vocational Materials More Effective for Special Needs Students

1. Taped versions of written material[a]
2. Written versions of taped material[a]
3. Regular materials in braille[b]
4. Large print versions of regular material[b]
5. Language at appropriate reading level using simplified versions of regular material[c]
6. Vocabulary list of essential vocational terms used in regular material[a]
7. Use of an interpreter for deaf students[b]
8. Use of a notetaker[b]
9. Use of a peer tutor[b]
10. Outlines of class lectures[b]
11. Oral tests and/or reports (could also be taped)[b]
12. Use of a person who serves as a reader (volunteer or paid)[b]
13. Self-instructional materials (at appropriate reading level)[b]
14. Captioned films/television[b]
15. Overhead transparencies, charts, and other visual materials[b]
16. Modified facilities and equipment[b]
17. Marginal gloss: Questions, tasks, and/or statements are written in the right margin of the text and refer to the important concepts within the narrative[d]
18. Highlighting: Underlining important or key facts in the narrative using a colored marking pen[d]
19. Boxing: Drawing a box around directions or critical paragraphs[d]
20. Grouping: Grouping problems requiring the same functions[d]
21. Sequence cards: Developing sequence cards which identify the steps to be followed in completing a task[d]
22. Masking: Placing a sheet of paper or cardboard cut to the width of the text to cover portions of the narrative[d]

[a]Alfest, Hartley, and Rocco[16]
[b]Hartley and Lehmann[17]
[c]Phelps[18]
[d]Johnson[19]

Source: Reprinted from *The Journal for Vocational Special Needs Education*, Vol. 9, No. 1, p. 33, with permission of National Association of Vocational Special Needs Personnel, © 1986.

- Are the generalizable skills assessment strategies and procedures useful and effective?
- Are the results and information obtained from assessment activities communicated among vocational education, special education, and other related agency personnel?
- Is generalizable skills assessment information described effectively in the IEP?
- Are relevant generalizable skills goals and objectives written in the IEP?
- Are students receiving adequate and effective support services necessary to enhance their generalizable skills?

Exhibit 11-12 Potential Useful Modifications in Generalizable Skills Instruction

---

Modifications for Academic Deficits:

- tape parts of the instruments which require reading
- have someone read the instruments and explain as needed
- preview critical vocabulary
- give directions in small increments
- have the student repeat directions
- review through one or more examples with the student, until you are certain that the directions are understood
- provide a "translation" sheet which uses the student's vocabulary—for example, "subtraction" may be understood as "take away"
- allow the student to ask questions about vocabulary while completing the instruments
- encourage the use of a marker to maintain place

Modifications for Behavioral Deficits:

- clearly state the purpose of the assessment, emphasizing how it will be used and the relatedness with the student's vocational program
- focus on the positive—let the student know that you want to find out what he/she is good at and how to best help him/her to succeed in a vocational program
- reassure the student that honest effort is important and that mistakes can be helpful when analyzed
- present the assessment in components small enough to enable the student to remain on task; clearly state the amount of time which he/she is expected to work; a timer may be useful for this; a contract may be established indicating some reward when the goals are met
- reinforce appropriate behavior
- provide encouragement
- structure the environment and minimize distractions
- set clear rules and a routine to be followed
- use planned ignoring, signal interference, proximity control, and humor to alleviate inappropriate behavior
- recognize the fact that some students may not perform consistently day to day

Modifications for Motor Deficits:

- remind the student that this is not a timed test
- allow verbal responses
- provide a book holder
- have someone turn pages
- set up the instruments on a computer and have student type in responses
- allow the student to type answers; some hints when using the typewriter for math are:

    —avoid line change; use 3x/y, rather than $\frac{3x}{y}$

    —avoid switching from upper to lower case; the student should develop his/her own code system and give it to the teacher; this could involve things such as, using ";" for division, rather than ":"; this is a time saver

Exhibit 11-12 continued

- modifications for measurement

  —use a ruler with a cork backing

  —use a press board; this is a plexiglass ruler supported above a board by spring bolts at each end; the student moves the object to be measured into place under the ruler and presses the ruler down; this holds the object in place

Modifications for Auditory Deficits:

- provide all directions in writing; if using the chalkboard, do not speak when turned towards the board
- use an interpreter for signing
- seat the student to facilitate lipreading; lipreading is difficult beyond 8–10 feet; do not stand in front of a window or bright light; remain in one place while speaking

Modifications for Visual Deficits:

- present all directions orally
- avoid such abstract terms as "over there" or "this"
- limit background noise
- provide a Braille or large print version of the instruments
- tape record the instruments
- provide a reader

Source: Reprinted from *Generalizable Mathematics Skills Assessment: User Manual* by J.P. Greenan and J. Richard, Office of Career Development for Special Populations, Champaign, Illinois, © 1985.

- Are generalizable skills being taught explicitly in vocational programs?
- How available and sufficient are existing instructional resources?
- What is the effect of implemented teaching strategies for individual special needs learners?
- Are the generalizable skills of students evaluated formatively and summatively?
- Do students, parents, and appropriate agency personnel receive periodic feedback regarding students' progress in obtaining desired levels of generalizable skills?
- How effective are vocational education, special education, and appropriate related agencies in working collaboratively in the delivery of generalizable skills instruction?
- Are generalizable skills instructional activities and outcomes articulated effectively?
- How and to what degree do generalizable skills instructional activities assist special needs learners in the transition from vocational programs to the world of work or continuing education?
- Are effective student follow-up activities planned and implemented?

These evaluation questions suggest several activities that personnel should engage in for the purpose of program evaluation. These questions can be expanded upon, and additional questions and activities can be generated based on the local context. Various evaluation strategies and procedures should be used to gather data and information regarding the adequacy, quality, and effectiveness of generalizable skills instruction in vocational programs. Results of program evaluations should be used in subsequent program planning and improvement activities.

SUMMARY

Generalizable skills are important for students if they are to succeed in vocational programs and to make the transition to employment or postsecondary education. Special needs learners may have functional learning problems in mathematics, communications, interpersonal relations, or reasoning skills. Instruction and necessary support services are therefore particularly important for special needs learners in vocational programs.

This chapter provided vocational education, special education, and related personnel with strategies and procedures regarding the components of generalizable skills instruction. Curriculum, implementation, assessment, planning, support services, resources, teaching strategies, and evaluation information and activities were presented. The need for collaboration among agencies was a theme throughout the chapter.

Vocational and special education teachers must work together in all phases of generalizable skills instruction. They should also participate actively in evaluation activities. It is essential that personnel use evaluation results and information regularly to improve instruction and services.

NOTES

1. E. Boyer, *High School: A Report on Secondary Education in America* (Washington, D.C.: Carnegie Foundation for the Advancement of Learning, 1983); The National Commission on Excellence in Education, *A Nation at Risk: The Imperative for Educational Reform* (Washington, D.C.: Department of Education, 1983); The National Commission on Secondary Vocational Education, *The Unfinished Agenda: The Role of Vocational Education in the High School* (Washington, D.C.: Department of Education, 1984); The Holmes Group, Tomorrow's Teachers: A Report of the Holmes Group (East Lansing, Mich.: Author, 1986).

2. J.P. Greenan, "Identification and Validation of Generalizable Skills in Vocational Programs," *Journal of Vocational Education Research* 8, no. 3 (1983): 46–71; J.P. Greenan, *Identification of Generalizable Skills in Secondary Vocational Programs: Executive Summary* (Springfield Ill.: Illinois State Board of Education, Department of Adult, Vocational, and Technical Education, 1983).

3. Greenan, "Identification and Validation of Generalizable Skills"; Greenan, *Identification of Generalizable Skills.*

4. J.P. Greenan and P. Richard, *Generalizable Mathematics Skills Assessment: User Manual*, 2d ed. (Champaign, Ill.: Office of Career Development for Special Populations, 1985).

5. J.P. Greenan, *Generalizable Mathematics Skills Assessment: User Manual* (Springfield, Ill.: Illinois State Board of Education, Department of Adult, Vocational, and Technical Education, 1984); J.P. Greenan, P. Marton, and J. Powell, *Generalizable Communications Skills Assessment: Resource Directory* (Springfield, Ill.: Illinois State Board of Education, Department of Adult, Vocational, and Technical Education, 1985); J.P. Greenan and C. McCabe, *Generalizable Interpersonal Relations Skills Assessment: Resource Directory* (Springfield, Ill.: Illinois State Board of Education, Department of Adult, Vocational and Technical Education, 1986); J.P. Greenan and C. McCabe, *Generalizable Reasoning Skills*

Assessment: User Manual (Springfield, Ill.: Illinois State Board of Education, Department of Adult, Vocational, and Technical Education, 1987); J.P. Greenan and J. Powell, *Generalizable Mathematics Skills Assessment: Resource Directory* (Springfield, Ill.: Illinois State Board of Education, Department of Adult, Vocational, and Technical Education, 1984); J.P. Greenan and J. Powell, *Generalizable Communications Skills Assessment: User Manual* (Springfield, Ill.: Illinois State Board of Education, Department of Adult, Vocational, and Technical Education, 1985); J.P. Greenan, J. Powell, and J.K. Dunham, *Generalizable Communications Skills Assessment: User Manual,* 2d ed. (West Lafayette, Ind.: Purdue University, School of Humanities, Social Science, and Education, 1986); J.P. Greenan and P. Richard, *Generalizable Mathematics Skills Assessment: User Manual,* 2d ed. (Champaign, Ill.: Office of Career Development for Special Populations, 1985); J.P. Greenan and M. Winters, *Generalizable Interpersonal Relations Skills Assessment: User Manual* (Springfield, Ill.: Illinois State Board of Education, Department of Adult, Vocational, and Technical Education, 1986).

6. R.A. Stodden and R. Boone, "Generalizable Skills in Individualized Vocational Program Planning for Special Needs Students," *The Journal for Vocational Special Needs Education* 9, no. 1 (1986): 11–15.

7. M.D. Sarkees and J.L. Scott, *Vocational Special Needs* (Alsip, Ill.: American Technical Publishers, 1985).

8. Greenan and Richard, *Generalizable Mathematics Skills Assessment: User Manual.*

9. P.L. Sitlington, "Support Services Related to Generalizable Skills Instruction," *The Journal for Vocational Special Needs Education* 9, no. 1 (1986): 16–19.

10. C.J. Johnson, *Preparing Handicapped Students for Work: Alternatives to Secondary Programming* (Reston, Va.: Council for Exceptional Children, 1980); G.D. Meers, "An Introduction to Special Vocational Needs Education," in *Handbook of Special Vocational Needs Education,* ed. G.D. Meers (Rockville, Md.: Aspen Publishers, 1980); M.C. Reynolds and J.W. Birch, *Teaching Exceptional Children in All America's Schools* (Reston, Va.: Council for Exceptional Children, 1977); Sitlington, "Support Services"; L. Wiederholt and B. McEntire, "Educational Options for Handicapped Adolescents," *Exceptional Education Quarterly* 1, no. 2 (1980): 1–10.

11. Reynolds and Birch, *Teaching Exceptional Children.*

12. P.A. Richard, "Resources for Teaching Generalizable Skills," *The Journal for Vocational Special Needs Education* 9, no. 1 (1986): 20–28.

13. L.H. Parrish and C.R. Colby, "Personnel Preparation Is Generalizable Skills Instruction," *The Journal for Vocational Special Needs Education* 9, no. 1 (1986): 34–37.

14. Greenan and Powell, *Generalizable Mathematics Skills Assessment: Resource Directory;* Greenan, Marton, and Powell, *Generalizable Communications Skills Assessment: Resource Directory;* Greenan and McCabe, *Generalizable Interpersonal Relations Skills Assessment: Resource Directory;* J.P. Greenan and D. Jefferson, *Generalizable Reasoning Skills Assessment: Resource Directory* (Springfield, Ill.: Illinois State Board of Education, Department of Adult, Vocational, and Technical Education, 1987).

15. N. Hartley and J.P. Lehmann, "Teaching Generalizable Skills," *The Journal for Vocational Special Needs Education* 9, no. 1 (1986): 29–33.

16. M. Alfest, N. Hartley, and R. Rocco, *Vocational Education for Students with Special Needs: A Teacher's Handbook* (Fort Collins, Colo.: Colorado State University, Department of Vocational Education, 1975).

17. Hartley and Lehmann, "Teaching Generalizable Skills."

18. L.A. Phelps, *Career Exploration and Preparation for the Special Needs Learner* (Boston: Allyn and Bacon, 1977).

19. C.J. Johnson, *Expanding Work Options for Exceptional Children: A Self-instructional Manual* (Reston, Va.: Council for Exceptional Children, 1979).

20. L.O. Albright, "Program Evaluation and Generalizable Skills Instruction," *The Journal for Vocational Special Needs Education* 9, no. 1 (1986): 39–41; R.O. Brinkerhoff, "Evaluation of Inservice Programs," *Teacher Education and Special Education* 3, no. 3 (1980): 27–28; D.L. Stufflebeam, "The CIPP Model for Program Evaluation," in *Evaluation Models: Viewpoints on Educational and Human Services,* ed. G.F. Madaus, M. Scriven, and D.L. Stufflebeam (Boston: Kluwer-Nijhoff Publishing,

1986); T.L. Wentling, *Evaluating Occupational Education and Training Programs* (Boston: Allyn and Bacon, 1980).

21. Stufflebeam, ''The CIPP Model for Program Evaluation.''

22. Albright, ''Program Evaluation and Generalizable Skills Instruction.''

Chapter 12

Transition from School to Work and Community

Ronald J. Anderson, Ph.D.
Marlene I. Strathe, Ph.D.

In recent years professionals working in special education and rehabilitation have been increasingly concerned with the lack of employment opportunities for individuals with disabilities who have graduated or left school. According to the United States Civil Rights Commission, the unemployment rate among persons with disabilities is estimated to be 50 to 75 percent, as compared to the current 7 percent rate for nondisabled persons.[1] Furthermore, Will has estimated that over 250,000 individuals with disabilities leave special education programs and enter adult life each year. These data indicate that many individuals with handicaps are entering,the job market with little chance of becoming employed.[2] As a result of concern over the lack of employment opportunities and the apparent problems that persons with disabilities are experiencing when they leave school and move into their communities as adults, Will and her colleagues developed a model to facilitate the adjustment process.[3] This model, now known as Transition, is one of the highest priorities of the Office of Special Education and Rehabilitation Services (OSERS) of the U.S. Department of Education.

In this chapter, the OSERS transition model will be discussed and contrasted with subsequent models offered by other experts. Organizational support by public schools and human service agencies will be addressed in relation to personnel needs and service delivery methods, and public school and human service agency responsibilities will be discussed in relation to training and services provided. The interfacing relationship of schools and human service agencies in transition activities will also be addressed.

Organizational and administrative considerations will be discussed in relation to similarities and differences of the educational and human service system. Assumptions, goals, realities, needed changes in the current systems, and outcomes will be delineated. Finally, the future of transitioning will be discussed in relation to funding and the administrative and service delivery elements of the model.

TRANSITION MODELS

The term *transition* may have different meanings for various professionals, depending on the perceived importance of services needed to accomplish intended goals. For some, transition may mean making adjustments from one residential setting to another or from secondary to postsecondary programs. For others, it may mean making adjustments necessary to move from sheltered employment to competitive employment. For still others, it may mean moving from a school setting to a work environment. The latter is perhaps the most widely accepted definition of transition, and the original intent of transition models was to move students from school to work.

The OSERS Model

The OSERS transition model uses a bridging concept to illustrate service methods to facilitate movement and adjustment from school to work. One or more of three service bridges can be utilized to facilitate the special needs student's transition from school to work. These service bridges are (1) no special services, (2) time-limited services, and (3) ongoing services. According to Halpern, no special services means that the student would only receive services available to anyone in the community.[4] Time-limited services are specialized services normally required as a result of an individual's disability. Ongoing services are those services that are uniquely designed and are not widely available in the service system. In the OSERS transition model (shown in Figure 5-1, p. 130), ongoing services, given the model's employment thrust, are exemplified by supported work.

It is clear that employment is the emphasis of the OSERS model. Halpern has suggested that while other services are important in relation to adult adjustment, the OSERS transition model appears to consider these services only as they apply to employment.[5] Halpern argues that the OSERS model can be challenged from both a philosophical and empirical perspective.[6] Furthermore, Halpern suggests that there are other elements of adjustment to community life that must be considered. These elements include the residential environment as well as social and interpersonal networks.

The Halpern Transition Model

The Halpern Transition Model utilizes the three service bridges of the OSERS model, but community adjustment is supported by three pillars, including residential environment, employment, and social and interpersonal networks. The primary focus of the Halpern model is clearly on employment, with the other pillars as contributors to community adjustment.[7]

The Vocational Transition Model

In each of the two models described above, employment is the dominant focus, with the Halpern model supporting employment with other aspects of community adjustment.

Wehman and his colleagues[8] have offered another transition model that deals almost exclusively with employment. This transition model is known as the Three Stage Vocational Transition Model for Handicapped Youth. The three stages of this vocational transition model are: (1) input and foundation, (2) process, and (3) employment outcome.

In the input and foundation stage, the student is in a secondary special education program characterized by a functional curriculum, integrated school environment, and community-based service delivery. During the input and foundation stage, parent and student input is acquired, along with interagency cooperation among agencies such as the school, rehabilitation, adult day programs, and (possibly) a vocational-technical center.

After consumer input and interagency cooperation has been achieved, the second stage involves the process of program planning. During the second (process) stage, an individualized program plan is developed and formalized. Wehman and his associates recommend initiating this planning process as soon as possible.

The final stage of the transition model focuses on employment outcome. Employment outcomes include a variety of work options, such as competitive employment, work crews, sheltered enclaves, or any other sheltered work option. Subsequent to placement in one of the identified employment options, the vocational model calls for a one- to two-year follow-up of the special needs individual.

The three transition models differ in their focus and assumptions. The OSERS and vocational models, for example, focus specifically on a vocational outcome, in particular, employment. The OSERS model utilizes a bridging concept and has few details concerning services needed to accomplish transition; it implies that other aspects of community adjustment are less important than employment. Although the OSERS bridging model provides three service bridges (no special services, time-limited services, and ongoing services),[9] it does not take account of individuals who might, at some point in time, no longer need certain services as a result of reaching an acceptable competency in a particular area of work or achieving successful community adjustment. (The OSERS model, as interpreted by both Halpern and Wehman, does imply that both short- and long-term ongoing services are limited by time.)

The Halpern transition model by contrast does not assume that community adjustment is only a function of employment.[10] This model broadens the base within which community adjustment must occur. Since the Halpern model is a modification of the OSERS model, it also lacks competency-limited services as one of necessary bridges in the provision of services.

The vocational transition model proposed by Wehman and his colleagues is primarily a school-based model that focuses on employment as the outcome. This model attempts to encourage transition planning at the earliest possible opportunity. Although the vocational transition model is designed for planning, it suffers from the exclusion of the residential component of community adjustment in the process and outcome stages.[11] The model assumes that appropriate curriculum, school integration, and community-based service delivery will be in place through the remaining stages of the planning process.

Each transition model makes a contribution in its own way to a better understanding of the transition process. It may be some time before a model is designed that encompasses all elements of community adjustment and facilitates the planning necessary to make transition of handicapped youths from school to work as smooth as possible. Smooth and effective transition of the handicapped student from school to work or to the community would seem to be aided by, if not demand, detailing the organizational support necessary to accomplish the transition.

ORGANIZA-TIONAL SUPPORT

Transitioning students from school to their communities, with the goal of employment, has been promoted largely through the development of conceptual models that lack details about the type of organizational support of the various organizations involved. In general, public schools and a wide variety of human service agencies will need to be involved to ensure that transitioning will work.

The assumption of current transition models is that the transition process begins in the schools. Transition usually begins with community-based vocational training, social skills training reinforced by integration, and appropriate transition planning. Undoubtedly, transitioning of special needs students will require considerable support from school officials. This support may include having a professional who provides vocational training to special needs students in the community through on-the-job experience. Community training includes on-the-job vocational training and training in vocationally relevant social skills and community mobility skills.[12] Such training requires the community trainer to be in the community much of the school day, arranging for new training sites or checking on students who are at a job site.

Community training demands that the trainer and classroom teachers maintain a strong line of communication in order to provide the student with appropriate vocational training. In addition, scheduling flexibility must be maintained, and sometimes transportation of the student to the job site may need to be coordinated by the school. Lastly, preparing the special needs student to leave school to enter supported work programs or to enter competitive employment necessitates that school personnel and parents be knowledgeable about the student's abilities and potential and about the services that are available in the community to help the student function at maximum potential.

School support requires that instructional personnel adopt the philosophical tenets of transitioning and that they work cooperatively to move the student to the most appropriate setting after leaving school. Furthermore, transitioning requires that at least one professional assume the responsibility for the student's transition plan. This person may be a counselor, teacher, community trainer, or consultant.

Although the support of personnel directly involved with the student's program is important, administrative support is also needed to make transitioning effective. Nietupski et al. have identified several areas where administrative support is important for community-based vocational training for special needs students.[13] A number of these areas affect transitioning as well. For example, providing leadership to parents and staff is important not only for community-based training but also for transitioning. Similarly, administrative support for transitioning in the area of staff hiring, resource allocation, and teaming is not significantly different from that needed for community-based training.

While the current transition models place the initial responsibility for transitioning students on the schools, human service agencies must become involved to support individual students as they move into the community. Community agency support can be provided in many forms, e.g., transportation, case management, and residential, medical, and social services. Community support services require adequately trained personnel to act as advocates, program monitors, and service providers.

Unlike the public schools, community service agencies have many and various types of services, eligibility requirements, funding patterns, and organizational structure (e.g., public or private). These factors have a direct impact on the nature of support that individuals with disabilities can expect to receive. Other factors, e.g., the size of the community, may also determine whether or not individuals can remain in their home community. Thus, community and human service support can significantly affect the quality and effectiveness of the transitioning of students with special needs from school into communities.

Each of the transition models discussed previously places considerable responsibility for the transitioning of students on the public schools. Only the vocational transition model, however, delineates the specific responsibilities of the school. (It should be noted that this model focuses on the severely handicapped student.. However, transitioning should be done with all students having disabilities that create special needs. If a student's needs so dictate, the responsibility for transitioning may be transferred to an organization or agency other than the school.)

In general, a school's responsibility for transitioning may vary with each student. For example, a student with a physical handicap who has the academic ability to benefit from attending a four-year college may need only to be referred to vocational rehabilitation through the school counselor. The rehabilitation counselor would then assume the responsibility for transitioning the student from the school to a college or university.

In another instance, where a student has a disability that makes attending a college or university inappropriate, a school program may need to be designed to provide at least introductory instruction in vocational education (e.g., auto mechanics or welding). The school counselor and the student's vocational instructor, along with the student, should develop a transition plan that involves additional training at a technical school. The school counselor would likely assume the responsibility of assisting the student in making decisions about what schools to apply to and in making contact with admissions personnel. Any special needs that the student may have should be described to counselors at the technical school or to the office of handicapped student services (if available). The transition is accomplished by the public school counselor communicating the student's needs to the technical school personnel and transferring responsibility for the student to a rehabilitation counselor after graduation. Follow-up and placement services would be provided by the technical school.

The transition process for students with moderate to severe disabilities is more complex. Transition planning should include determining the nature of the training

SCHOOL RESPONSIBILITIES FOR TRANSITION

that the school should provide. Such training might involve work experience or supported work. Additional training might include social skills training and training in basic functional academic skills and community mobility skills. Concurrently, counseling should be provided to both the student and parents to ensure that each party understands the nature of the training and services that may be required after the student leaves school. Furthermore, school personnel will need to determine what, if any, community services will be needed by the student. At this point, contact with appropriate service agencies should be made for referral purposes. Procedures for follow-up after job placement should be determined as well.[14]

The purpose of the transition process in each of the examples discussed above is to assist the student to become employed and to obtain the services needed to accomplish this goal. More specifically, each student is provided necessary information and assistance to make the transition as smooth as possible by transferring responsibility to the appropriate persons in each of the organizations involved. A major purpose of any transition process is to provide the opportunity for school personnel and human service agency personnel to interface for the common goal of ensuring that students with special needs are not left with inadequate support in their communities. Interfacing between the two types of personnel also provides educators and service providers with a better understanding of how best to meet the individual student's needs.

COMMUNITY AGENCY RESPON-SIBILITIES

Community agency responsibilities vary depending on the nature of the services provided by specific agencies. Some agencies, for example, offer a wide variety of services, while others provide only one or two specific services. In some cases, agencies may duplicate services, causing problems for service users in trying to determine which service agencies would provide the most appropriate services.

It is a service agency's responsibility to provide special needs individuals with services deemed appropriate by parents, guardians, advocates, service providers, and the individuals themselves. These services may include recreational and residential services, guardianship, transportation, work activity, sheltered work, and case management.

Often professionals working in human service agencies are unaware of the other services that may be available in the community. In planning for the transitioning of handicapped students, the agency responsible for carrying out the transition plan should be aware of the different services that are available. If service providers are unaware of the available services, a resource assessment should be conducted.

Case Management

Perhaps one of the most important services needed by many handicapped persons is case management. A case manager is a professional who assumes responsibility for a group of clients who are in need of support services but who lack the knowledge or skill to access and utilize services independently. The case manager may, for example, assist the person with a disability to obtain supplemental Social Security Income (SSI) or make residential arrangements. The manager may need to determine whether the person is capable of living independently or semi-independently as well as how much supervision will be required.

The case manager may also assist the disabled person with the acquisition of equipment or support through Title XIX of Public Law 92-323. Case managers must clearly understand the terminology used in any application for services. Clients are sometimes denied services because they do not understand the appropriate language used by people who determine the need for services or equipment.

Another service that can be provided by community service agencies is service coordination. The importance of service coordination cannot be overstated, since some services (e.g., transportation) are very scarce while others (e.g., evaluation services) are common. Effective service coordination frequently requires interagency cooperation that can be accomplished through the development of interagency agreements. Interagency agreements afford case managers, service coordinators, and service agencies an opportunity to better coordinate the services needed by persons with disabilities.

Interagency Agreements

Even though interagency agreements could assist in coordinating needed services, many problems still pervade the human service system. Variances in terminology, eligibility requirements, and the attitudes and political views held by administrators are common barriers to interagency cooperation. Concluding an interagency agreement is often difficult to accomplish because of "turf" issues and fear of the loss of funding and community support.[15]

Interagency agreements between different service agencies are especially important for maintenance or support of individuals with disabilities after they leave school. No less important is an agreement between a school and the service agency that assumes responsibility for a handicapped person after he or she leaves school. To ensure that the transition from school to community is made in a systematic manner, one state legislature (Massachusetts) has passed legislation requiring a transition plan be written and in place prior to the time that a handicapped student leaves school.

Regardless of the method used to accomplish transitioning of handicapped students from school to work or to the community, the purpose of the transition process is to ensure that students with disabilities increase their opportunities for employment, utilize community services, and become involved in community activities. The ultimate goal of transitioning is to allow a handicapped person to become as productive as the specific disability will allow.

ORGANI-ZATIONAL AND ADMIN-ISTRATIVE CONSIDERA-TIONS

The purpose of transitioning students with disabilities is clear. What remains unclear, however, is how two significantly different systems (education and human service) interface and collaborate. The organizational differences between these two systems have implications for the administration of transition efforts. They include differences in mission, organizational structure, funding, method of service delivery, and assumptions.[16]

Differences in the organizational structures of the public schools and human service agencies are too numerous to detail here. However, some of the major differences are discussed to provide an understanding of the issues that must be addressed to create successful transition programs. It is important to recognize from the beginning that the public schools operate from a mandate of inclusion. That is, all children regardless of sex, socioeconomic status, race, or disability have a right to a public education. This right is guaranteed by law and only under extraordinary circumstances are children denied public education.

On the other hand, human service agencies are operated on the basis of exclusion. Human service agencies, public or private, are not mandated by law to provide services to all persons. Generally, socioeconomic status and disability type and levels are the salient variables used to determine if an individual is eligible to receive services. There is considerable variability in eligibility criteria (related to severity of disability and socioeconomic status) among different service agencies.

A second difference is in administrative organization. In many communities, for example, public schools are organized around a single administrative unit that includes an elected school board and a single administrator employed by the board. In contrast, human service agencies operate independently of any other agency, usually with their own board and chief executive officer. Thus, in a community with a single school organization, there could be a number of different human service organizations.

Another major difference between public schools and the human service system is that the services provided by public schools are defined relatively well, perhaps because these services are time limited and are delivered within the confines of the school. Unlike those of public schools, services provided by human service agencies are often diverse and may not be limited by time. Additionally, services may be offered by more than one agency or be provided by combinations of two or more agencies. For example, one service organization may provide residential services in combination with transportation, while another agency may provide only residential services.

Perhaps the most significant difference between public schools and human service agencies involves the funding streams that support the organizations. By and large, public schools are supported by taxes. Human service agencies are supported by a number of sources, e.g., client fees, United Way, taxes, and donations. Public schools and human service agencies both are vulnerable to shifts in the economic conditions of their localities. Human service agencies, however, appear to be more susceptible to the ups and downs of the economy because of their varied sources of funding.

The differences between human service agencies and public schools delineated above create some impediments to transitioning students with handicaps from school to the community. Some of these impediments may involve the assumptions of school personnel and human service professionals. For the most part, school officials generally assume that they have met their responsibilities when students leave school. It seems that it is further assumed that students with handicaps leaving school will automatically receive the services they need. Assumptions such as these appear not to be true.[17]

The School

Special education programs in the public schools provide a variety of educational services that are assumed to assist students with handicaps to function independently as adults. The data from available follow-up studies of handicapped students who have left school suggest that this assumption may not be true. Such students apparently experience considerable difficulty entering the work force.[18] In view of this difficulty, it seems that more emphasis should be placed on vocational programming and transition services for students with special needs.

To see that there is a need for greater emphasis on vocational programming, it is important to examine the placement options now available and in use in special education programs. For some time, regular classroom placement, supplemented with part-time resource room placement, has been the primary method of providing educational services to mildly disabled students. At the elementary level, the focus of the curriculum is on basic skills, including reading, spelling, writing, and so on. At the secondary level, the emphasis is on the application of basic skills in more complex and abstract academic subjects, such as algebra, biology, English, foreign languages, and social studies. In many cases, the resource room has been used to provide handicapped secondary students with tutoring to ''get through'' the curriculum. Based on the information from current follow-up studies, the ''get through'' approach does not seem to be appropriate for students needing special education services.

It appears that the most appropriate curriculum for many handicapped students consists of vocational programs ranging from work experience to supported work. Furthermore, it appears that special education personnel and public school professionals will need to become more familiar with the human service system in order to introduce their students to the appropriate services needed after leaving school. The assumption that handicapped students will generally be employed and independent after leaving school will continue to be false until special education educators come to grips with the functional needs of the students for which they are responsible.

The Human Service System

The human service system consists of a variety of agencies and organizations that offer services ranging from counseling through residential, recreational, transportation, respite, medical, and evaluation and diagnostic services to vocational services. Vocational services include rehabilitation, job placement, sheltered work, and supported work. Human service agencies and organizations offer different types of services, and the requirements are often different for each.

More often than not, persons with disabilities find themselves not knowing what services are provided by what agency. Referrals are frequently hit or miss and it is difficult to find an appropriate agency providing the needed service. Because service agencies sometimes duplicate services, it is possible for a disabled individual to be referred to two or more agencies for a given service. In efforts to obtain services, parents and consumers sometimes find themselves frustrated and confused because the services offered are not necessarily needed or the eligibility requirements exclude individuals needing the service.

If a handicapped person is provided services, sometimes these services only marginally meet his or her needs. In essence, the handicapped individual does not or cannot benefit fully from the services that are provided. In addition, it is not uncommon that one agency lacks knowledge of another agency's ability to provide more appropriate services or of other needed services that might be available. Competition and the lack of communication among agencies may significantly affect the appropriateness and the quality of the services provided.[19]

INTERFACE BETWEEN EDUCATION AND HUMAN SERVICE

If the transitioning of handicapped students from school to work or to the community is to become a reality, it will require that the public schools, in particular, special education personnel, become more aware of the services provided by community, state, and federal service agencies, both public and private. Similarly, human service personnel will need to become more informed about what types of vocational programs are in place in special education programs.[20]

Although expanding the knowledge base of personnel working in special education and human services will do a great deal to facilitate transition efforts, it will not solve all the problems of transitioning handicapped students. The knowledge base of professionals who work with handicapped persons must include information on normalization, on community training, and on the functional limitations of different disabilities (from mild to severe). The expanded knowledge base must also include more information about the human service system (in the case of special educators) and about special education programs (in the case of human service personnel).

Second, philosophically the notion of transition makes perfect sense; however, it requires professionals to think clearly about the methods and systems that are needed to implement transition programs. One issue that must be dealt with immediately is this: At what point must special education and community services interface? Wehman and his colleagues suggest that it is the school's responsibility to follow handicapped students for at least two years.[21] School officials, at the same time, could argue that it is the obligation of a community service agency to assume responsibility for the handicapped student after leaving school. Regardless of when the change in responsibility occurs, it must be planned.

Planning for transition should include identifying the responsible school personnel and their counterparts in the human service agency. Special education personnel will also need to establish when planning should begin. Much of the transition planning could be accomplished through individual education plan (IEP) development. Thus, it could begin when handicapped students start their secondary school years. Three to four years should be enough time to allow special educators to assess the vocational potential and provide sufficient vocational training and experiences to match student needs with services after leaving school. This planning time would also permit school personnel to make contacts with appropriate individuals and service agencies to assure that transitioning will take place.

School administrators should also be prepared to enter into agreements with the agencies that provide services to the handicapped. Care must be taken to avoid the tendency to look to one agency for provision of all the services needed by a handicapped student. For example, public schools that operate segregated programs for the moderately and severely handicapped may be more likely to seek out agencies that provide work activity or sheltered work programs rather than agencies that have supported work programs. Thus, it is important for special education personnel to identify agencies that provide services that are consistent with societal normalization principles.

There are, of course, limitations to what schools can do in the transition process. Schools cannot ensure that former students are getting every service needed. They cannot control changes in the eligibility requirements or the funding sources of service programs. Finally, schools cannot control shifts in service philosophy and delivery methods. Conversely, human service agencies have limited influence on the programs that are offered in special education programs in the schools. Nor can service agencies ensure that special education programs adequately plan for the transitioning of handicapped students.

However, if adequate planning and communication between public school special education programs and human service organizations occur, students can be transitioned with a minimum number of problems. Paramount is that special education personnel realize that they will need to better understand the human service system. Furthermore, while special education personnel and the public schools may not need to follow students two years after their leaving school, there is little doubt that special education personnel will need to initiate transition planning.

INTERFACE ISSUES

Interfacing with the schools provides the human service system with the opportunity to develop case management methods of providing services. Having a single port of entry to the schools also provides a single port of exit. The single port of exit appears to be ideal for the promotion of a single port of entry into the community service system.

Creating and promoting a single port of entry to the human service system gives rise to some interesting concerns. First, it seems that in order for case management to work, one community service agency must take responsibility for a given handicapped individual. As indicated previously, vocational rehabilitation is an example of this type of case management. Other agencies, however, can achieve the same type of management by being involved in early transition planning with the school. Of course, case management does not mean that a case worker would need to take the student by the hand as he or she leaves school. Rather, meeting the student at the door merely means that pertinent school records be forwarded to the agency that will be responsible for the student.

Second, communication lines would need to be established between the community service agency and the school. That is, persons within each system would need to be introduced and have knowledge of the responsibilities and duties of the persons within the other system.

Third, specific responsibility for follow-up would need to be negotiated. Wehman and his colleagues have recommended that schools be responsible for at least a two-year follow-up of the student.[22] While there are very good reasons for schools to conduct follow-up studies of their graduates, legitimate questions can certainly be raised about the feasibility of such studies. Of particular concern is determining administrative responsibility. If a service agency is coordinating services beyond the school years, then it would be appropriate for the agency to be responsible for follow-up. Similarly, the school would take responsibility for follow-up if there are good reasons for it to do so.

Fourth, even though federal legislation has encouraged cooperation and collaboration among federally funded programs,[23] the reality is that this activity has not yet produced the desired results. All too often, persons with disabilities are left with little support after the specified period of time during which one or more agencies were to provide services. Therefore, the schools and community service agencies will need to agree when and how responsibility for the handicapped student will be given up or assumed.

PERSONNEL

Transitioning of disabled students will also require a fundamental change in the manner in which the schools and community service agencies relate to each other and interact. Interactions and school-agency relationships could be enhanced by the creation of transition advisory committees. Membership of such committees should include school and agency administrators, community trainers, special education teachers, case managers, employers, parents, and disabled persons.

Second, school personnel must become more familiar with community services and organizations. At the same time, service agency personnel must become familiar with what the students are being taught and trained to do in school. For example, it would be meaningless to provide a mentally retarded student with successful community-based training during his or her school years and then have this person placed in a sheltered workshop.

Finally, institutions preparing personnel to work with handicapped individuals must address the transition effort by implementing curriculum that facilitates school-agency interaction, collaboration, and cooperation. Preservice teachers should be given information on available community resources, on how to initiate and maintain communication with service providers, and on methods for transition planning and implementation.

Students who are training to work in human service agencies should also be instructed about new developments and methods regarding the vocational training of handicapped persons. They should become familiar with the range of vocational training options and the methods used for each option. Additionally, these preprofessionals should be instructed on how methods of service delivery differ between the school and the community.

OUTCOMES

The goal of transitioning handicapped students is to provide them with the opportunity to become as productive as their abilities allow. To most professionals, productivity requires becoming employed, either competitively or through a form of sheltered employment. The disabled person, through employment, should be able to maintain an independent lifestyle to the greatest extent possible.

The future of transitioning is questionable at this juncture. There is definitely a need for it, given the number of unemployed handicapped individuals throughout the United States. If transition programs are to be effective, models will need to be tested and modified, schools will need to place greater emphasis on vocational programs, focus will need to be on instruction that takes place beyond the school walls, and educators and administrators alike will need to become more knowledgeable of the human service system.

More important, the public schools and human service agencies will need to interact and collaborate.[24] Neither system can function in isolation and merely hope that transitioning will occur by waiting for "the other guy" to act. Simultaneous action will be needed by those working in both education and human services. Planning and negotiating responsibility will need to be taken seriously to ensure that handicapped persons are provided the necessary support as they approach vocational training and entrance into the community.

One major problem that will need to be addressed in the future is funding for transitioning handicapped individuals. School administrators will need to devote some resources to transitioning handicapped students. These resources may be in the form of staff assignments, funds for off-campus vocational training, and time for school staff to meet with human service personnel. If the responsibility for follow-up of handicapped students is assumed by the school, administrators will need to be aware of the time and resources necessary to conduct this activity.

Finally, administration of special education programs is becoming more and more complex, and as a result school administrators will need to become more sophisticated in the way they attempt to administer these programs. Unfortunately, the nature and extent of the training that administrators receive in special education does not seem to be keeping pace with the need.[25] Administrators will have to adopt the philosophy that the process of education must be redefined for handicapped students. The heavy emphasis on academics at the secondary level is, in most cases, inappropriate for handicapped students. In addition, attempts to provide vocational training within the confines of the school walls may not be effective for many students who require vocational training.

SUMMARY

Currently the concept of transitioning is receiving a great deal of attention, mainly because of the thrust of federal initiatives. There is little doubt that the need for transitioning exists, especially in light of high unemployment rates among special needs students. As with any new concept, many issues remain to be addressed. The work of a number of noted professionals in special education, vocational education, and human service has provided a conceptual base from which transitioning may be viewed. Yet much needs to be accomplished in regard to further refinement of conceptual and planning models. Additionally, other critical elements of transitioning, e.g., school and service agency responsibility, coordination of services, and personnel preparation, will need to be addressed in the future.

Since a great deal of the transition process occurs within the schools, the future of transitioning remains unclear. The problem of scarce resources for supporting public school programs looms as one of the major impediments to transitioning students with special needs. The problem of fragmentation in the human service system is also critical, because the success of transition programs will, in all likelihood, depend heavily on well-coordinated services.

Finally, but most important, successful transitioning of special needs students will require the work of dedicated professionals in education and human services. Such professionals must be willing to set aside turf and territoriality issues and either make existing programs function efficiently or create new effective programs. It is imperative that professionals be willing to communicate, negotiate, and collaborate to meet the common goal of successfully transitioning special needs students.

NOTES

1. U.S. Commission on Civil Rights, *Accommodating the Spectrum of Individual Abilities* (Washington, D.C.: Clearinghouse Publications, September 18, 1983), 29.

2. Clearinghouse on Handicapped, "Youth with Disabilities: The Transition Years Highlights of a Conference," in *Programs for the Handicapped* (Washington, D.C.: Department of Education and Rehabilitative Services, 1984), 1.

3. Madeleine Will, "Let Us Pause and Reflect—But Not Too Long," *Exceptional Children* 51 (1984): 15.

4. Andrew Halpern, "Transition: A Look at the Foundations," *Exceptional Children* 51 (1985): 480.

5. Ibid., 480.

6. Ibid., 480.

7. Ibid., 481.

8. Paul Wehman, John Kregel, and J. Michael Barcus, "From School to Work: A Vocational Transition Model for Handicapped Students," *Exceptional Children* 52 (1985): 28.

9. Halpern, "Transition," 480.

10. Ibid., 481.

11. Wehman, Kregel, and Barcus, *From School to Work*, 29.

12. John Nietupski, et al., "Establishing and Maintaining Vocational Training Sites for Moderately and Severely Handicapped Students: Strategies for Community Trainers," *Education and Training of the Mentally Retarded* 3 (1983): 169–75.

13. John Nietupski, et al.: "Proactive Administrative Strategies for Implementing Community Based Programs for Students with Moderate and Severe Handicaps," (Manuscript in review).

14. Paul Wehman, Sherril M. Moon, and Pat McCarthy, "Transition from School to Adulthood for Youth with Severe Handicaps," *Focus on Exceptional Children* 18 (1986): 1–12.

15. Wehman, Kregel, and Barcus, *From School to Work*, 31.

16. Daniel Anderson, "Planning Comprehensive Community Based Services," in *Integrating Moderately and Severely Handicapped Learners*, eds. M.P. Brady and P.L. Gunter (Springfield, Ill.: Charles C Thomas, 1985), 47–62.

17. Dennis Mithaug, Chisjo Horiuchi, and Peter Fanning, "A Report on the Colorado Statewide Follow-up Survey of Special Education Students," *Exceptional Children* 51 (1985): 397–404.

18. Susan Hasazi, Lawrence Gordon, and Cheryl Roe, "Factors Associated with the Employment Status of Handicapped Youth Exiting High School from 1979 to 1983," *Exceptional Children* 51 (1985): 455–69.

19. Wehman, Kregel, and Barcus, *From School to Work*, 31.

20. Frank Rusch, Dennis Mithaug, and Robert Flexer, ''Obstacles to Competitive Employment and Traditional Program Options for Overcoming Them,'' in *Competitive Employment Issues and Strategies*, ed. F.R. Rusch (Baltimore, Md.: Paul H. Brookes, 1986), 11.

21. Wehman, Kregel, and Barcus, *From School to Work*, 35–36.

22. Ibid.

23. Edna Szymanski and Marita Danek, ''School-to-Work for Students with Disabilities: Historical, Current, and Conceptual Issues,'' *Rehabilitation Counseling Bulletin* 29 (1985): 83.

24. Donna Owens, Kevin Arnold, and Caroline Coston, ''Issues Related to Administrative Planning: Supporting Transition to Postsecondary Vocational Training Programs,'' *Journal of Vocational Special Needs Education* 7 (1985): 26.

25. Stephan Stile, Sandra Abernathy, and Timothy Pettibone, ''Training and Certification of Special Education Administrators: A 5-Year Follow-Up Study,'' *Exceptional Children* 53 (1986): 210–12.

Postsecondary Institutions and Support Systems for Special Needs Learners in Vocational Education Programs

James M. Brown, Ph.D.
Paul M. Retish, Ph.D.

America's vocational education system consists of many divergent programs operating in widely varying state systems, which are each in turn responding to divergent state, national, and local issues and demands. But in spite of the fact that vocational education programs exist in many forms and at several levels, these programs tend to have numerous common threads of purpose, organization, methodology, and instructional content that suggest the extent of these programs' uniformity, cohesiveness, and common goals.[1]

Although the provision of vocational education is voluntary, all states have elected to provide vocational programs at the secondary or postsecondary levels. The commitment of many states to such programs has been made evident by the continued spending (by numerous states) of more than $10 of state funds for vocational education programs for every federal dollar of vocational education funding that they receive.

Efforts to expand the range of support provided to special needs learners in postsecondary vocational education programs have been accompanied, in the past decade, by proportionally greater enrollment of special needs learners. Concurrent with these trends, Congress has continued to strengthen the focus of federal legislation on efforts to better educate nontraditional students, special needs learners, and racial or ethnic minorities. These efforts were designed to bring these persons into the educational mainstream of employment activities and to reduce disparities between the wages of workers in these categories and the wages of many other workers. Beginning with Public Law 94-142, the Education for All Handicapped Children Act, Congress sought to influence, in a positive but indirect way, changes in the labor market through the impact of vocational education programs.[2] In addition, the Carl D. Perkins Vocational Education Act of 1984 extended the federal mandate that vocational education programs must provide meaningful services to a broad array of persons, including those who have handicaps or disadvantaging (special needs) learner characteristics.

About 55 percent of all workers employed in January 1983 needed specific training to qualify for their jobs. Of those persons employed, 35 percent had previously received additional vocational training to improve their job skills. College programs that are at least four years in length were the source of *job-qualifying skills* for 17 percent of America's workers in 1983, junior colleges and vocational-technical institute programs were the source for 5 percent, high school vocational programs for 5 percent, and private post–high school vocational programs for 2 percent. Surprisingly, few workers had been enrolled in programs in more than one of these categories. In terms of *skill improvement*, college programs impacted 6 percent of all workers; junior colleges and vocational-technical institutes, 3 percent; private post–high school vocational programs, 0.8 percent; and high school vocational programs, 0.4 percent.[3]

SECONDARY VOCATIONAL EDUCATION PROGRAMS

Although this chapter focuses on postsecondary issues, a brief examination of secondary vocational programs is necessary for comparison purposes. Taylor[4] reported in 1982 that almost two-thirds of the 27,753 institutions offering vocational education programs functioned at the secondary level. Taylor also noted that secondary programs contained 65.1 percent of the 19,563,175 persons enrolled in vocational education programs and that 55 percent of the secondary vocational students were in 11th and 12th grade programs focused on specific occupations.

Secondary vocational programs are typically housed in one of three types of institutions: (1) comprehensive high schools that offer college preparatory, general education, and vocational programs, (2) vocational high schools that offer full-time programs incorporating both academic and vocational components, and (3) area vocational centers that use cooperative agreements among multiple high schools to pool resources and students in order to provide programs that would otherwise be impractical or impossible to operate. Students in area vocational centers usually spend part of their school day in a general high school and the rest of their day in the vocational center.

INSTITUTIONS OFFERING POST-SECONDARY VOCATIONAL EDUCATION PROGRAMS

The system of postsecondary institutions that provides vocational programs is considerably more complex than its secondary counterpart. Institutions that offer postsecondary level vocational programs can be categorized as either public or private, and the programs can last from a few weeks to four years. It should be noted, however, that postsecondary vocational programs, as defined formally by federal legislation, offer less than a baccalaureate degree. Thus, most vocational educators view postsecondary vocational education programs as lasting two years or less. These programs enroll about one-third of the more than 19 million vocational students each year. In addition, over 90 percent of the students in these programs (including adult and continuing education students) receive occupationally specific training.[5]

Public and private noncollegiate postsecondary institutions (which contain most of the commonly recognized vocational programs) are representative of the widely varying vocational institutions that do not grant degrees recognized by regional collegiate accrediting commissions. These institutions typically provide instruction and preparation focused on specific occupations. In addition, this group of institutions includes publicly funded area vocational-technical institutes (the specific title for these institutions varies somewhat from state to state), public or private business schools, cosmetology and barber schools, correspondence schools, flight-related training schools, and a variety of others.

While two- and four-year institutions of higher education annually enroll about five million students in vocational programs, private noncollegiate postsecondary schools compose the second largest group of postsecondary institutions. This latter group of schools collectively serves about one million vocational students each year. There are almost 7000 of these noncollegiate postsecondary schools, the majority of which have enrollments of less than 100 students per school. It is important to note that none of these schools received federal vocational funding authorized by P.L. 94-482 (Vocational Education Amendments to Vocational Education Act of 1963), and since 1974 the number of such institutions has dropped by approximately 13 percent.[6]

Approximately 800 public noncollegiate postsecondary institutions offer vocational programs to about 750,000 students. The vast majority of these students (approximately 80 percent) are enrolled in programs that receive funds authorized by the Carl D. Perkins Act.[7]

Private correspondence schools provide postsecondary vocational programs for more than 300,000 students per year. However, none of these programs receives federal vocational funding. One final group of postsecondary vocational programs consists of the more than 500 state correctional facilities serving approximately 34,000 incarcerated adults each year. The National Center for Educational Statistics (NCES) has estimated that about 30 percent of the incarcerated adults were enrolled in programs receiving federal vocational funds.

Bottoms and Copa[8] describe the array of institutions that offer vocational programs at all levels. Table 13-1 presents brief descriptions of the major types of institutions offering vocational programs.

Recent Trends

In recent years there have been significant increases in the numbers of special needs learners enrolled in vocational programs. For example, between 1973 and 1980 the number of handicapped youths in vocational programs increased from 222,713 to 400,575—an increase of 89.9 percent. In that same period, the enrollment of disadvantaged students increased by 64.5 percent. In addition, increasing numbers of adults with special learning needs have been enrolling in postsecondary vocational programs. More than 15 percent of the students enrolled in vocational programs in 1980 were identified as having special needs and 70 percent of these special needs students were receiving support services. Those services typically included resource room teacher assistance, paraprofessional aides, modified or special instructional materials, modified equipment, extended class sessions, remedial services, and vocational assessment services. Special support services are often provided as components of comprehensive educational experiences tailored to meet each student's particular vocational education needs.[9]

Table 13-1 Types of Institutions Offering Vocational Education

Institutional Type	Characteristics
Comprehensive high school	A general school offering programs in a variety of different vocational subjects (although the majority of students are not enrolled in vocational education programs)
Vocational high school	A specialized secondary school offering a full-time program that combines vocational subjects; all or a majority of the students are enrolled in vocational education programs
Area vocational center, secondary	A shared-time facility that provides only vocational education instruction to students from throughout a school system or region; these students study academic courses in their regular high schools or in other institutions
Area vocational school, postsecondary	A non-degree-granting institution (or an institution offering a degree that is not recognized by the regional accrediting commission for higher education) that offers instruction only in vocational and technical subjects and whose educational programs are terminal
Community college or institution	A two-year, postsecondary, degree-granting technical institution (that may also award certificates and licenses) that offers a comprehensive instructional program in both general (often only in the community college) and vocational/technical education and a transfer program to institutions of higher education
Specialized postsecondary	Usually offers specialized preparation in one occupational area
Four-year institution, with two-year programs	A four-year college or university offering two-year programs in vocational or technical areas

Source: Adapted from *Phi Delta Kappan*, Vol. 30, No. 3, p. 350, with permission of Phi Delta Kappa, Inc., © January 1983.

Contextual Issues

Vocational education is probably less well understood than any other kind of education in the United States. It is as complex as any other kind and has changed more than any other during the past 25 years. The dramatic growth of vocational education saw participation increase from 1 in 37 Americans in 1965 to 1 in 17 by 1980. Given that vocational enrollments in many programs have doubled or tripled since 1960 and many totally new vocational program areas (e.g., microcomputer repair, robotics) have emerged, it is easy to understand why many people fail to realize the nature and comprehensiveness of vocational programs.[10]

Bottoms and Copa suggest that vocational programs can be logically classified into two broad categories: general and occupationally specific.[11] The general programs provide basic information for career decisions, assistance in the development of the prerequisite skills for mastering an occupational area, and training in general skills that are useful both in work and in everyday life. Bottoms and Copa identify five typical forms of general vocational education programs that seem particularly relevant to the unique educational needs of special needs learners:

1. consumer homemaking programs that focus on the improvement of family life through improved decisionmaking, interpersonal, and technical skills
2. prevocational programs designed to introduce postsecondary vocational students to the broad array of vocational areas and to the tools, materials, and processes used in each
3. prevocational basic skills programs that provide the skills needed to be qualified to enter occupationally specific training programs
4. related instruction programs that offer training related both to occupational content and to the science, mathematics, and communication skills required for specific jobs or occupational areas
5. employability skills programs that are designed to cooperatively teach on-the-job behaviors/discipline and broad skills related to effective interpersonal relations and communications

Bottoms and Copa also identify occupationally specific vocational programs where the primary focus is on instruction related to the knowledge and skills needed for employment in specific jobs or occupational areas. The following four types of categories represent distinct types of occupationally specific postsecondary vocational programs:

1. occupational-cluster programs (commonly found in comprehensive high schools) that are broad enough to focus on clusters of occupations, such as agribusiness, the metal trades, or office work
2. occupationally specific programs that are designed to prepare students for employment in a particular occupational area, such as auto mechanics or practical nursing
3. job-specific programs that are designed to prepare students for entry into particular closely defined jobs, such as lathe operator or typist
4. employer-specific programs that prepare participants for a particular job with predetermined employers (these programs usually enroll persons who are already employed, and the number of such programs is likely to increase substantially because of the impact of rapidly developing technology within our society and the workplace)

The past decade has seen a dramatic change in the age and educational needs of persons enrolled in postsecondary vocational programs. For example, 45 percent of the enrollment in Minnesota's Area Vocational-Technical Institutes (AVTIs) in 1975 was composed of persons who were just out of high school; by 1985 this group comprised only 27 percent of the enrollment. During that same period, the proportion of students over 26 years of age increased from 11 percent to 28 percent. In addition, thousands of Southeast Asians settled in Minnesota, many of whom sought to obtain job-related training in the AVTIs. Finally, the farm economy has deteriorated drastically since the early 1970s, and many businesses and industries have disappeared or automated, greatly reducing the numbers of employees needed in some occupational categories and in many geographic regions.[12]

These trends, as well as increasingly stronger federal legislative mandates to educate special needs populations, have encouraged vocational educators throughout the nation, as well as potential vocational students, to re-examine postsecondary vocational programs as potentially viable mechanisms to train or retrain people for success and productive working careers.

After analyzing its needs and resources, the following assumptions were identified by Minnesota's State Board of Vocational-Technical Education:[13]

1. The needs of students will continue to change.
2. Stable or decreasing resources will be available to the public sector.
3. Increased program flexibility is necessary to meet the changing needs of students.
4. Changing technologies in business, industry, and agriculture will require updated instructional equipment and the retraining and upgrading of AVTI staff in order to meet evolving educational needs and services requirements.

It has become apparent that the need for vocational programs and services for special needs learners greatly exceeds the currently available services and resources. The social benefits, however, of providing appropriate, effective opportunities in the AVTIs for special needs learners will far exceed the costs of providing such services.[14]

As a result of these crucial unmet learner needs and the potential benefits of addressing those needs, a wide array of services has emerged (or is currently being developed in many postsecondary vocational institutional settings). The services in the following list are arranged in order of severity of the learning needs for which the services are designed (the services listed later are specifically for more severe needs):[15]

1. equitable recruitment and access for special needs students to postsecondary institutions and those institutions' vocational programs
2. assessment of students' interests, abilities, and special learning needs
3. cooperative planning with special educators and support service personnel
4. specific special needs support services:

    • guidance, counseling, and career development activities
    • remedial communications

- remedial computations
- technical tutoring
- transitional services

5. special needs student tracking and information system
6. monitoring of students identified as having special needs
7. observation of student functions
8. student follow-up activities and related data analysis
9. special instructional materials
10. lower reading level curricular materials
11. curricular materials tailored for learning styles
12. instructional materials in Braille
13. large print materials
14. printed substitutes for verbal instruction
15. adjusted time schedules for skills mastery
16. modified instructional materials:

- sound for visual materials
- visuals for sound materials
- special safety devices
- sensory devices
- sound amplification devices
- note-taking systems
- teletypewriters
- wheelchair-adapted desks and workstations
- adaptation of equipment controls

17. inservice training for instructors and support service staff
18. analysis of curricula to identify relationships with employment opportunities
19. placement and follow-up designed specifically for special needs learners
20. cooperative agreement with other key service providers (e.g., vocational re-habilitation, Job Training Partnership Act programs, special education)
21. competency-based programs tailored to special needs learning styles
22. interagency agreements for long-term support services
23. job placement and development staff
24. highly specialized remedial and counseling staff
25. multi-institutional services via collaborative agreements and programs
26. housing services
27. transportation services
28. health care services
29. year-round prevocational services:

- designation of specific staff to manage coordination with other community agencies

- staff trained in diagnosis of special needs characteristics
- staff trained in vocational evaluation
- staff skilled in work adjustment issues
- structured avenues of access to vocational programs
- facilities, equipment, and materials for prevocational activities
- periodic consultation with regular vocational staff

30. continuing education for job-placed completers
31. media centers adapted to special needs learners
32. organized adapted recreational activities

SUPPORT SERVICES AND SERVICE PROVIDERS

Sanger,[16] Farber,[17] and Retish, Hitching, and Hitching[18] all indicate that support services—their availability and their accessibility—are important in efforts to enhance the success of special needs learners. Though their research primarily concerns how disabled individuals attain success, it is possible to speculate on what the results suggest about special needs individuals in general.

The research findings indicate that support services that assist special needs individuals to find and maintain jobs are vital to their success. Furthermore, the openness of facilities and the ease of taking advantage of services are vitally important to the success of special needs individuals. The success or failure of such individuals in the community is based on three primary factors: (1) whether services are physically close to where the clients are located, (2) whether services are easily available, and (3) whether the professionals who provide the services are accessible and willing to help individuals to become eligible for their services. Furthermore, what particular service a provider is trying to provide does not seem to be as important as the fact that the service is there and that people who are in need of assistance can be helped.

For students in postsecondary facilities, these services are located both on and off the campuses. Each set of services can be related to a variety of support activities necessary to enable special needs individuals to accomplish their goals. The most used and most frequently available services on campus or in the community are briefly described below. The list of services is not intended to be exhaustive, but it is designed to give readers an idea of the wealth of services that are often available.

On-Campus Services

This section describes the array of services often provided on campuses to assist students while they attend a postsecondary institution.

Counseling Services

The purpose of counseling is to assist students (1) to make effective vocational program-related decisions, (2) to gain information on other directions to take, both in coursework and outside of school, and (3) to provide various levels of support for personal needs. This support is sometimes limited by the level of sophistication of the counselors and by the type of problems individuals are encountering. Counselors are also professionally obligated to become aware of other appropriate support services that may provide students with the specific assistance that they need.

Most institutions have on-campus medical and psychological services that are available to students. Among other things, these facilities provide assistance for physical pain and birth control and make referrals to medical specialists.

Health Services

For students who qualify for scholarships or who are in need of financial support, a financial support agency acts as a clearinghouse for information and applications and it helps students obtain financial assistance. Financially related services can provide information on scholarships and application forms and may have access to additional information about work sites where individuals can earn money while in school.

Financial Support Services

Associated closely with the goals of financial aid offices, work-study programs provide assistance to eligible students regarding part-time jobs that are available and information on how to best seek out and keep employment.

Work-Study Programs

Both of these on-campus agencies are specifically designed for targeted populations, provide support programs, and, where necessary, work with students who need special adaptation of courses, tutoring services, and other special services.

Office of the Handicapped and Office of Minority Concerns

This office assists students who are undecided or confused about their career preferences or what vocational choices are available to them. Very often, career consultations can assist students, by means of standardized measures and counseling, to explore areas that might be of interest to them.

Career Placement Office

For many special needs students, this is the best source of personal or financial support. Once individuals are clients of Vocational Rehabilitation, they are provided whatever services are deemed to be necessary and feasible to assist them to become productive workers.

Vocational Rehabilitation

A wide variety of additional service-providing agencies and organizations are usually available at postsecondary institution campuses. Such organizations provide services to individuals and are usually concerned with each individual's extracurricular life, ethnicity, religion, or social needs. All of these needs should be explored by support service personnel when they provide the services needed to help special needs individuals to function effectively within society.

For most people, especially special needs individuals in vocational training programs, the use of support services consists of a combination of on- and off-campus agencies. Services not connected with educational institutions focus on a wide range of issues, including day-to-day existence, information, advocacy, leisure, and many other facets of special needs individuals' lives.

Off-Campus Services

This section examines a sample of agencies, starting with those most frequently used, and it analyzes other options that can be pursued if other needs arise that are not adequately met by the agencies listed. Note that when financial and political climates change, the available resources tend to diminish at the local level. Agencies may disappear, change their priorities, or run out of funds. Service providers and their special needs clients should be prepared for such events and seek access to an array of resources that they can use when support is needed. Persons seeking access to government programs, therefore, should be prepared to fill out form after form, experience long waits, and answer questions that seem to confuse issues rather than assist them with their problems. If individuals need and want the services to be provided, they will have to cope with the mandatory administrative procedures for service eligibility.

Vocational Rehabilitation

This is a federally sponsored agency that distributes funds to states and to local community service providers. This agency is charged with assisting qualified clients to become more employable. The first step is to determine if a person is eligible to become a client and then to make sure that he or she matches the priorities of the agency. Almost all special needs individuals, as defined for this chapter, are qualified clients of Vocational Rehabilitation, but at times less emphasis is given to some types of needs than others. This agency can provide diagnosis, prosthetics, personal and career counseling, financial support for job-related training, wheelchairs (and other adaptive devices and equipment), and vocational training. All of this support should be targeted at assisting individuals to become more employable.

Social Services

These are state-supported agencies with numerous local offices that can be of substantial assistance in daily routines, can provide support personnel, and can establish linkages with other agencies and personnel. Counseling services that stress personal needs are also available. Unfortunately, many social workers have very high client-to-staff ratios and therefore cannot offer their clients as much time and attention as would be ideal.

State Employment Agencies

These service agencies list available jobs in local areas and regions. They can also evaluate the qualifications of candidates and try to match up qualified individuals with available jobs. They tend to be very cautious and protective of employers to whom they send job applicants. Therefore, special needs individuals should be aware of how these agencies view the world of work and should act accordingly.

Mental Health Units

These local facilities are available for those individuals who need psychological support. There is little or minimal cost associated with many of the services. Mental health units are often somewhat crowded and the time available to assist individual clients is constrained by staff and funding limitations.

Job Training and Partnership Act (JTPA)

This is an agency formed by the U.S. Department of Labor for the purpose of assisting people to become more employable. As with other agencies, individuals must meet certain qualifying criteria and be prepared to complete application forms before being declared eligible for JTPA services.

Learning Centers

The term *learning center* is intended to describe all of the various facilities that help individuals to get GEDs or that provide assistance in particular areas, such as English, reading, or specific vocational skills.

This is not an exhaustive list of the agencies that are available to assist postsecondary individuals in their transition to additional education, work, or daily living. Also, it should be remembered that everyone is not automatically eligible for these services, so determination of eligibility is of primary concern. Yet it may be better to allow agencies to determine the eligibility of potential clients rather than to permit individuals to inappropriately seek the services of agencies on their own.

Most of the above agencies are available to postsecondary special needs learners, whether on postsecondary campuses or as a result of collaboration among various in-school or community agencies. Although it is difficult at times to believe these agencies exist for the sole purpose of assisting their clients, special needs individuals must be carefully coached to accept that this is indeed the underlying purpose and be encouraged to be assertive as they seek services that are sometimes denied to them.

The ability to gain access to these services is a skill that special needs individuals frequently must be taught. Furthermore, those coaching these individuals should attempt to teach them appropriate skills regarding how to find and use the correct service agencies. Time limitations and lack of professional assistance sometimes cause less assertive special needs individuals to experience difficulties obtaining the services they are potentially eligible to receive. Retish, Hitching, and Hitching clearly indicate that accessibility to services is the key to effectively assisting special needs individuals through the morass that they must face outside of public schools.[18] Furthermore, they maintain that too often the service providers tend to distribute their commodities (services) based on what they know rather than what clients need. Special needs individuals usually require (but seldom receive) specific training to use the support systems that were designed to meet their needs.

ADAPTING TO FUTURE CHANGES

Obviously, we cannot allow ourselves to be totally satisfied with the postsecondary programs and support services that currently exist. Personnel in all postsecondary systems should already be attempting to adapt to the changing needs of the times. With the advent of computer literacy and the need to apply computer-related skills in an increasingly automated workplace, postsecondary vocational training may soon be delivered to students directly in their homes. The students will become computer literate and learn how to apply computers to specific job situations.

Another strategy to assist students in their preparation for employment is the use of ''guaranteed jobs.'' In such arrangements, secondary schools make contracts with students, who are guaranteed postsecondary training or job placement if they attend classes, pass minimum competency tests, and graduate. Similarly, some schools make contracts with students such that students are permitted to preselect rewards (tangible, work-related, or postsecondary experience) that they receive if they meet all conditions specified in the contracts. (Note: Some high schools are now experimenting with the use of ''letters'' for high academic performance similar to the letters given for excellence in athletic programs.)

There are basic changes in the complex industrial environment in the United States, including a movement away from large ''smokestack industries'' toward employment opportunities where ideas are the most valued commodities. Therefore, computers, with their ability to instantly transport ideas across large distances and to communicate and process information, may constitute the principal industry of the near future. Personnel in postsecondary vocational programs should begin to recognize these changes are occurring and make the appropriate modifications in their programs and support services.

For learners who have skill deficits, such as mental retardation or learning disabilities, the changing employment pattern could be disastrous. What they have to offer—such as a strong work ethic, unskilled labor, or limited information processing skills—will not often be needed. Many of these individuals may be unemployed, but not unemployable. Postsecondary institutions should offer strategies to retrain them and provide them with desired work skills. However, these institutions should also begin to assist special needs learners to develop daily living skills so that they can cope with the various problems associated with being unemployed for extended periods of time.

REVIEW

Having discussed the institutional environments in which most postsecondary vocational programs exist, as well as many of the support services and service-providing agencies, this chapter will end with a discussion of four special needs learners. A series of questions will require a review of the previously presented information about service providers and the nature of the services they provide. This final component of the chapter is intended to present situations that many vocational educators encounter when adapting or developing individualized programs to maximize students' abilities to achieve their vocational objectives.

Case # 1

Kathy is a 19-year-old female student who for the last six years has been in special education and is now graduating from high school. Her vocational counselor's report indicates that she reads at the fifth-grade level, has some difficulties in fine motor skills, and has limited physical endurance. She is highly motivated to work and has talked about trying to develop sufficient skills to work somewhere in a hospital. She is quite familiar with the public transportation system and her parents are supportive of her goal to obtain postsecondary vocational training.

Questions

1. What agencies would you contact and refer Kathy to so that the needed information can be accessed?
2. What postsecondary programs would you investigate to determine their appropriateness for Kathy?
3. What timeline would you propose in order to prepare her for getting a job?

Case #2

Harley is a 27-year-old male student entering an area vocational-technical institute. One year ago, Harley suffered a stroke that paralyzed his right arm (he is right-handed). He is now single, lives alone, has a modest income from his part-time job, and is a client of the local office of Vocational Rehabilitation. Harley insists on staying in the two-year gunsmithing program, which he has been attending for three weeks.

1. What types of information would you seek in order to identify Harley's specific learning needs and to develop a plan to help him become a gunsmith, if that is in fact feasible?
2. Who would you contact to seek assistance in order to analyze his medical and educational needs?
3. What types of problems do you expect Harley will encounter during vocational training and when seeking employment?

Clarence is a 20-year-old male who dropped out of high school at age 16 and who now works for a grocery store as a sweeper-stocker. His family is on welfare and they count on Clarence's paycheck to get them through each week. Two years ago Clarence got his GED through night school and has started to think of his future. He was twice arrested and convicted for breaking and entering while he was a juvenile, but has had no contact with the police for the last four years. He has no idea what he wants to do, but knows he does not want to continue what he is doing at the grocery store. When asked what his main goals were, he answered, "To make more money so I can live better."

Clarence has a car, but it behaves erratically; whenever the weather gets cold, the car will not start. Clarence's girlfriend is pregnant and they are discussing long-term plans. His mother is quite upset because she is afraid he may move out and take his earnings with him.

1. As the person he has contacted, what agencies would you encourage *him* to get in touch with? List the agencies and prioritize them according to the degree of his need for them.
2. What agencies would *you* contact to assist Clarence and his girlfriend?
3. What agencies would you suggest contacting to assist the *family* regarding income, independence, and future strategies?
4. What postsecondary programs could be explored with Clarence?

Darlene has just graduated from college with a teaching degree in secondary history and special education. In her junior year at college, she started to get terrible headaches and noticed that she was having difficulty in seeing writing on chalkboards. A little while later she had trouble reading books. She went to the college infirmary and it was discovered that she had a genetic disorder that would cause her to lose all her vision.

Darlene now has tunnel vision and knows that she will lose all of her vision in six months. She has already begun to categorize all of her clothing. She is now deciding when she should give up her driver's license and if she should enroll in a program that would teach her mobility skills using a cane.

Darlene has applied for a number of teaching jobs, but she has not been hired. Upon examining her file from college, you find she is a better-than-average student (g.p.a. 3.25), has good recommendations, and did a better-than-average job when student teaching.

She wants suggestions regarding whether she should continue to look for a teaching position, go to graduate school and get additional skills, or concentrate her energies in a different career area.

Questions

1. What sources of information could you use to assist Darlene?
2. Does she need to see a lawyer regarding her employment difficulties?
3. What aspects of her private life should she put in order while she has some vision, e.g., driver's license, clothing, mobility skills?
4. What other jobs are available given her teaching license and background?

NOTES

1. R. Taylor, "Vocational Education," in *Encyclopedia of Educational Research*, 5th ed., ed. H. Mitzel (New York: American Educational Research Association, 1982), 2002–12.

2. H. David, *The Vocational Education Study: The Interim Report*, ERIC Documentation Service no. ED 195 743.

3. U.S. Department of Labor, *How Workers Get Their Training*, Bulletin no. 2226 (Washington, D.C.: GPO, 1985).

4. Taylor, "Vocational Education."

5. Ibid.

6. Ibid.

7. Ibid.

8. G. Bottoms and P. Copa, "A Perspective on Vocational Education Today," *Phi Delta Kappan* 30, no. 3 (1983): 348–54.

9. American Vocational Association, *Fact Sheet: Serving Special Needs Populations in Vocational Education* (Arlington, Va.: Author, 1982).

10. Bottoms and Copa, "A Perspective on Vocational Education Today."

11. Ibid.

12. M. Jacobson, *Developing a Delivery Mechanism for Prevocational Services: A Final Report* (St. Paul, Minn.: Minnesota State Board of Vocational-Technical Education, 1986).

13. Ibid.

14. Ibid.

15. Ibid.

16. G. Sanger, *The Adjustment of Retarded Adults in the Community* (New York: International Department of Health Resources Board, 1957).

17. B. Farber, *Effects of a Severely Retarded Child on Family Integration*, Monograph no. 24, Series no. 7 (Albany, New York: Society for Research in Child Development, 1959).

18. P. Retish, B. Hitching, and S. Hitching, "Parents' Perspective of Vocational Service for Moderately Retarded Individuals," *Journal of Career Development* 13, no. 4 (Spring 1987), 56–62.

Chapter 14

The Role of Parents in the Education of Vocational Special Needs Youth

Stanley F. Vasa, Ed.D.
Allen L. Steckelberg, M.Ed.

Within the past two decades, the perceived relationship between the home and the school has undergone a major transformation. Whereas, in the past, parents were not regarded as particularly useful in contributing to the educational process, their more extensive involvement in the school is now increasingly viewed by educators as essential. This change in attitude about parent involvement has been brought about by several factors: (1) passage of legislation (specifically Public Law 94-142 and Public Law 94-482) that delegates certain responsibilities to parents in their children's education, (2) the increasing realization that parents play a key role in the education of their children, and (3) the realization that parents also play an important role in the vocational choices of their children.

Increased interest has focused on transitional programming for students with handicapping conditions who are about to leave school programs. One of the critical factors in transition planning for handicapped students is the parents' role in this process. Feldman[1] reported adolescents received a majority of their career-related information from parents and only secondarily from classroom teachers. Counselors were cited less frequently as individuals who assisted in career decisionmaking. Halpern found that one-third of the parents had very vague expectations about whether or not their child would be working in any type of setting after leaving school.[2] One-fourth of the parents were unclear about the degree of independence their child would be able to have as an adult. In short, Halpern found that parents had limited knowledge of their child's capabilities and the type and availability of services that they might need to ensure their child's success in postschool settings.

The effectiveness of parent involvement in vocational programs is determined by the ability of the school and, more specifically, of the vocational educator to coordinate communication between the home and the school. The effectiveness of the parent-school relationship rests to a great extent on the planning and implementing of a meaningful parent education program. In this chapter, we examine some assumptions regarding the role of parents in education, the purposes of parent education programs, program delivery models, and the importance of program evaluation.

ASSUMPTIONS ABOUT PARENTS

Three well-founded assumptions about parents and their role in education serve both as a basis and a rationale for the development of parent-school communications:

1. Parents care more about their children than the school does.
2. Parents have the right to know about and be involved in their child's educational programs.
3. Parents can be effective teachers.

The first assumption is simply that parents have a greater personal and emotional interest in their child than the school has. This assumption is often misunderstood by educators, who conclude that parents' nonparticipation in school-related activities is tantamount to their not caring about their child's education. In reality, parents may choose noninvolvement for any number of reasons, such as fear of inadequacy in discussions with educators, irrelevance of past contacts with the school, and failure to understand the role the school expects of them.

That parents have a right to know is documented in the laws governing the education of the handicapped. For example, parents are afforded the right of access to school records as stipulated in the rules and regulations governing Public Law 94-142:

> The public school shall permit parents to inspect and review any education records relating to their children which are collected, maintained, or used by the agency . . . The agency shall comply with a request without unnecessary delay and before any meeting regarding the individualized educational program or hearing relating to the identification, evaluation, or placement of the child, and in no case more than 45 days after the request has been made.[3]

Parents play a key role in three segments of the handicapped child's vocational education. First, they participate in and approve their child's placement; second, they participate in the development of the individual educational program (IEP); third, they monitor their child's progress and the school's performance of services outlined in the IEP. The Family Educational Rights and Privacy Act further documents the right of parents to access and to monitor the individual student's records maintained by the school.

The literature supports the contention that parents are effective teachers.[4] We must also recognize that parents of exceptional children have probably invested more of their personal time in the education of their children than have parents of students enrolled in regular education. Parents can and do play a key role in the education of their children; it is impossible for them to delegate totally the teaching responsibility to the school. Indeed, parents have universally assumed the responsibility of teaching their children basic self-care skills, such as dressing and speaking.

Parents are thus effective support personnel in the education of their children. For example, in the transition to employment, parents are regarded as key individuals in the choosing of occupations by students. Handicapped students are likely to receive considerable support from their parents in making such choices. Parents are in a particularly advantageous position to use outside opportunities to expand their children's education. Vasa and Steckelberg have pointed out that "with the aid of good teaching skills, such as establishing behavioral goals, utilizing systematic reinforcement and identifying successful and unsuccessful teaching techniques, parents can provide home and community experiences which contribute to their child's learning."[5] Parents also provide continuing support to handicapped individuals both outside of school and during employment. Parents can help to compensate for deficiencies in skills and abilities in daily living and community adjustment.

PURPOSES OF PARENT EDUCATIONAL PROGRAMS

Specific Goals

The first step in establishing a meaningful parent education program is to determine the specific purpose of the program. It can be assumed that improved parent-school communications will be helpful in the establishment of strong vocational educational programs in the community. However, to rest the importance of parent education programs solely on the vague concept of communications can be potentially disastrous. Meaningless communication and disorganized conferences can quickly alienate an otherwise interested parent. To avoid the pitfall of purposeless and meaningless parent interaction with the school, vocational educators must quickly assess what should the potential goals of communication be—both for the parent and for the education of the handicapped student. For the parents of handicapped students, the potential goals of parent education programs include a better understanding of

- what to expect from the school vocational program
- the scope of the vocational education program
- the program's safety standards and provisions
- the ways that parents can support the acquisition of specific skills
- the grading and evaluation procedures utilized by the school system
- the content and rationale of the career education program
- the acquisition of skills by their children
- the needs of the vocational program for future growth and development
- the performance of their children in the vocational program
- community placement options
- postschool services available in the community

But parents are not the only beneficiaries of parent-school communication. Vocational educators can also benefit by

- obtaining information about an individual student's progress
- obtaining information about the students' experiences and expectations from the perspective of their parents
- increasing the opportunities for individual students by involving parents in the educational process
- transmitting information about parents' rights and responsibilities under the law
- obtaining support from groups of parents for the expansion and alteration of present vocational programs to better accommodate the handicapped
- obtaining information about other services being provided to the student

Needs Assessment

The needs assessment is the second essential component of a viable parent education program. This assessment should help the vocational educator define more precisely the program's priorities. Priorities may be based on the need for information in particular areas where knowledge is lacking or the need to explore topics identified by either the parents or the vocational educator. Parent education programs commonly attempt to provide information about the parents' goals for their children, about experiences outside the school, about the purposes of the school program, and about the expectations of the school.

The needs assessment can be conducted in a variety of ways. Parents can be polled by telephone, written questionnaire, or personally. The major consideration for the teacher is to make sure that the choices offered to the parents are those that the teacher can reasonably deliver in a parent education program. In addition to obtaining information about what the parents want to learn, the needs assessment instrument can be used to determine how the parents wish to receive the information (e.g., through individual conferences or large group orientation sessions). Only through careful analysis and use of the information from a needs assessment can a successful parent education program be planned and implemented.

PROGRAM DELIVERY MODELS

Vocational educators must be aware of the many ways of communicating with parents and the many forms of parent education programs. Some of the modes of communication available to vocational educators are

- individual parent conferences
- telephone conferences with parents
- correspondence with parents by mail or as transmitted through students
- small group parent meetings
- large group parent orientation meetings
- home visits

Each of these means of interacting with parents is designed for a specific purpose. But all parent contacts are potentially valuable for the education of the student. The harvesting of the resulting information is the responsibility of the teacher.

One of the most important communication delivery systems available is the parent conference. This is the single most commonly used mode of transmitting information to and receiving information from the parents. An interesting phenomenon is apparent in parent education programs: parent participation in conferences tends to decrease as the age of the student increases. The cause for this appears to be twofold: (1) parents have become turned off by parent conferences for a variety of reasons, and (2) as students mature in age and development, parents become more and more removed from direct participation in their lives.

Individual Parent Conferences

The first cause is often avoidable if sufficient replanning and attention is given to the conduct of the conference. The educator is responsible for establishing a purpose for each conference and expressing this purpose to the parent, either prior to or at the beginning of the conference. Conversely, parents who want a conference with the educator should declare their purpose prior to the meeting. The declaration of purpose should allow both the parent and the teacher time to prepare for the conference and to determine the issues to be discussed. In Exhibit 14-1, a set of guidelines is presented as a checklist—and as a gentle reminder to the vocational teacher of the importance of preparing for parent-teacher conferences.

It is important that the teacher be acquainted with both the potential values and the dangers of telephone conferences. On the one hand, telephone conversations are valuable as a means of relaying information to the parents and announcing the availability of other forms of communication. On the phone, teachers can give positive feedback to the parents about a student and also information about the general needs of the student. The disadvantage of the telephone conversations lies in the inability to guarantee the confidentiality of the message. The content of the conversation must be of such a nature that potentially sensitive information cannot be obtained by an unwanted listener. The best policy is to use the telephone judiciously in conversing with parents. When it is utilized, teachers should try to follow up on sensitive issues through an individual conference.

Telephone Conferences

When mailed correspondence is used to communicate with parents, the composition of the letter requires careful consideration. The correspondence must be monitored to ensure that the parent does not misinterpret the content and that factual information is provided. Accuracy of written communications is important in maintaining good parent-teacher relations and demonstrates professionalism on the part of the teacher.

Correspondence

A written communication is most frequently used to do one or more of the following:

Exhibit 14-1 A Checklist of Parent Conference Guidelines for Educators

Educators should:

- plan for all student conferences in advance
- have a clear purpose in mind for each conference, for example, to report student progress
- inform parents of the purpose of the conference
- have all student records available for review prior to the conference
- consider the parent conference as an important event and not merely routine
- allow enough time to discuss the issues thoroughly; the parent should not feel rushed during the conference
- conduct the conference privately in a place free from distractions and interruptions
- have prior knowledge of the conference for purposes of self-briefing
- invite others to the conference only if they will contribute to resolving an issue or problem
- invite the student to attend, unless the conference covers emotionally laden subjects that might adversely affect the student
- hold the conference at a time convenient to the parent
- be aware of parent transportation needs and child care needs
- deal honestly with parents
- listen to the parents and respect their confidence
- avoid using educational jargon in conversing with the parent
- try to put themselves in the parents' role during the conference
- not jump to conclusions based on statements made by parents
- back the school administration and other teachers during the conference
- be cautious of the content of written communications
- keep a record of the conference
- keep the parent informed of change following the conference
- establish a means of communication between the parent and teacher
- evaluate the effectiveness of the conference
- attempt to answer all questions raised by the parent
- realize that the responsibility for the success of the conference lies with the teacher
- not argue with the parent
- avoid giving direct advice to the parents on parenting

- announce a parent meeting or conference
- announce a meeting or conference that may be of interest to parents
- provide descriptive information about the vocational program
- solicit parents' involvement in the evaluation or development of the vocational program
- provide parents with positive feedback on the achievements of their children
- solicit parents' approval for student involvement in field trips and other activities
- provide parents with evaluation data about each student's achievement in the program

Small group meetings are frequently used to transmit information or to seek support from parents who have common interests. Such meetings are generally limited to no more than ten parents. The small number is necessary to permit maximum interaction and to guarantee commonality of concerns. The meetings could be conducted for the purpose of discussing a specific problem or to solicit parent input on the organization of a specific component of the vocational training program.

Small Group Meetings

Small group meetings offer the advantages of being more intimate and personal. They permit a more careful delineation of specific topics for discussion based on the interest of the group. The disadvantages of such meetings are the time-consuming burdens they impose on both the vocational educator and the parents.

In planning a small group meeting, a number of considerations should be kept in mind:

- Each session should last no longer than two hours.
- The educator and the parents should not meet more often than once a week.
- The time between meetings should be less than ten weeks.
- The meeting group should be no larger than ten persons.
- Parents should play an active role in determining meeting content.

Largely overlooked at the secondary level of vocational education is the large group orientation meeting. This type of meeting has the advantage of allowing the vocational educators to present information needed by a large number of parents in a relatively short period of time and in one session. Such meetings can be used for providing a summary of the curriculum of the program or information about the amount and degree of involvement requested of parents and the unique or specific requirements of the course of study. Parents often prefer to attend a few large sessions when learning about the vocational program rather than receive this general information at individual conferences. Vocational teachers can save considerable instructional and personal time by clearly delineating the most frequently requested information from parents and developing a general orientation session to provide such information.

Large Group Orientation Meetings

The success of an orientation session depends on the accuracy of the vocational educator in assessing the parents' need for information. The parents' satisfaction with the session will depend on the accuracy of the information announcing the purpose of the session and their comfort level in receiving the information.

Exhibit 14-2 lists certain points about parents that are important to remember in the planning of parent education programs. This checklist should be reviewed prior to developing the content of any group activity with parents. The points listed underscore the fact that parents are adults who have their own interests and priorities. Giving careful attention to this checklist will enhance the probability of success for group education programs for parents.

Exhibit 14-2 Important Points to Remember about Parents in Planning Parent Education Programs

Parents:

- are individuals who have pride
- have other interests and responsibilities besides their children and the school
- have creative ideas and a wealth of experience
- have established child-rearing philosophies
- have a limited amount of free time for school programs
- can assimilate a limited amount of information that is contrary to their individual philosophies and beliefs
- are individuals who have developed behavior patterns consistent with their values, attitudes, and beliefs
- have decisions to make and problems to solve
- have, if parents of handicapped children, developed a certain amount of resistance to suggestions from specialists and school personnel
- are often bewildered and confused by all of the options available to them
- have frustrations and concerns about the services previously rendered to their children
- are suspicious of the school and its functions
- are secretly afraid of failing in the rearing of their children
- do not like to be talked down to or belittled for their failures
- can *change*

Home Visits

Home visits have been an important part of a number of vocational programs, especially in the area of vocational agriculture, where instructors often monitor the progress of students in the establishment and maintenance of projects in conjunction with their school programs. Home visits can provide important information to the vocational educator about the family environment of the student and economic conditions under which the student lives. However, this information may also prejudice the educator's expectations for the students.

A home visit should be made only when a specific reason for it has been ascertained. Having the parents visit the school program is potentially more valuable than having the educator visit the home. Parents should be encouraged to visit and participate in the educational program for their children. Generally, home visits provide the parent with little usable information about the school.

Following are four guidelines for home visits:

1. Home visits should be made only at the request of the parent or when the parent refuses to visit the school.
2. Home visits should be made when a specific tangible benefit for the student's educational program can be anticipated from the visit.
3. Home visits should be made only with the approval of the student or at the student's request unless mitigating circumstances exist.

4. Home visits should occur only when parents are informed of their time and purpose in advance.

Home visits are potentially valuable if utilized properly. If used indiscriminately, however, they can add on the burden of extended working hours for the teacher, invade the privacy of the parents, and possibly humiliate the student.

Program evaluation is the final component of a successful parent education program. Evaluation is undertaken for two reasons. First, it can determine the effectiveness of the program in meeting stated objectives. Second, the information obtained through the evaluation can provide helpful information for future planning decisions.

PROGRAM EVALUATION

The goal of any educational program is to bring about a positive change in the parents' knowledge, attitudes, or behavior (e.g., concerning school or child rearing). The evaluation, therefore, must be designed to determine the effectiveness of the program in changing

- the parents' attitudes
- the parents' knowledge

Table 14-1 Evaluation of the Parent Education Program

Parameters	Dependent Measures	Data-Gathering Techniques
Parent increase in knowledge	Attainment of knowledge objectives, e.g., what is covered, parents' school relationships, parents' role in the home, etc.	Pre/post assessments Observations Self-assessment scales Interviews Questionnaires
Parents' change in attitudes	Change in attitudes toward child rearing; change in attitude toward career; change in attitude toward school, etc.	Questionnaires Opinionnaires Rating scales Interviews
Parents' behavior	Involvement in the education process, e.g., cooperation with the school, parent/child involvement	Attendance rosters Teacher observations Interaction analyses Anecdotal records Records of parents School contacts
Child's behavior	Increase in knowledge or performance in related areas, e.g., career options, values, attitudes, habits, decisionmaking, etc.	School attendance Test data IEP objectives Sociometrics Observations Teacher records

- the parents' behavior
- the students' behavior

A wide variety of dependent measures and measurement devices can be used in collecting such information. Table 14-1 lists a number of alternatives for data gathering in each of the four areas listed above. Selection of a specific means of collecting information should be based on several factors, including cost, the feasibility of carrying out the procedures, and the value of the data collected.

NOTES

1. S. Feldman, *Readings in Career and Vocational Education for the Handicapped* (Guilford, Conn.: Special Learning Corporation, 1979).

2. A.S. Halpern, "Transition: A Look at the Foundations," *Exceptional Children* 51, no. 6 (1985):479–86.

3. U.S., *Federal Register* 42, August 23, 1977, 42498.

4. B.P. Berkowitz and A.M. Graziano, "Training Parents as Behavior Therapists: A Review," *Behavior Research and Therapy* 10 (1972):297–317; E. Denhoff, "The Impact of Parents on the Growth of Exceptional Children," *Exceptional Children*, January 26, 1960, 271–74; E. Kelly, "Parental Roles in Special Education Programming: A Brief for Involvement," *Journal of Special Education* 7 (Winter 1973):357–64; D. MacDonald, "Parents: A New Resource," *Teaching Exceptional Children* 3 (1971):81; W.O. Walder et al., "Teaching Behavioral Principles to Parents of Disturbed Children," in *Behavior Therapy with Children*, ed. M. Graziano (Chicago: Aldine-Atherton, 1971).

5. S.F. Vasa and A.L. Steckelberg, "Career Education, Parents' Roles, and the Choices for the Handicapped," in *Proceedings of the Barkley Memorial Conference* (Lincoln, Nebr.: University of Nebraska-Lincoln, 1979).

Chapter 15

The Administrator's Role in Vocational Special Needs Programs

Rosemary F. Kolde, Ed.D.

The major responsibility for an effective vocational special needs program lies with the building administrator. The administrator is the acknowledged educational leader of the school, and thus it could be said that "as the administrator goes, so goes the school." Effective administrators demonstrate good leadership by developing cooperative working relationships and by participating in cooperative ventures and seeing them to a successful completion. Good leadership is not just a matter of possessing a certain combination of traits.

If we briefly examine a few of the characteristics of a leader, we will immediately perceive why the administrator is responsible for making a program effective. A leader

- acts toward others in a positive way
- has more influence than any other member of the organization
- has the greatest effect on setting and achieving the goals of the organization[1]

Once an individual has accepted an appointment to a position of leadership (i.e., as an administrator), the individual is required to accept the responsibility that goes with such a leadership role.

THE ROLE OF THE ADMINISTRATOR

What can administrators do to provide a quality vocational special needs program? They can take charge! They can take control! They can make things happen! The role of the administrator begins with the creation of a positive attitude within the building. Attitudes do not necessarily need to be communicated through words; they can be communicated through actions. A positive attitude toward the vocational special needs program by the administrator will spread among both the staff and the student body. Such an attitude increases the probability that handicapped and disadvantaged students will achieve success in their vocational and academic programs.

Attention to details affecting the special needs program is another important aspect of the administrator's role. The Education for All Handicapped Children Act of 1976 (Public Law 94-142) requires schools to educate the handicapped in the least restrictive environment appropriate to their needs. Individually prescribed support services enable many students with mild to moderate physical and learning handicaps to succeed in regular vocational education programs. Although the mainstream model has been extremely successful, it does require a great deal of commitment by the administrator to ensure that a positive learning atmosphere exists.

Communication channels must be kept open between all staff members who have responsibility for a handicapped or disadvantaged student. Coordinators, counselors, and instructional and support staff should function together as a team in establishing and providing the components necessary for a student's individual education plan (IEP). The administrator can assist in keeping the communication channels open by providing active and participatory leadership.

There are many activities through which administrators can demonstrate a positive attitude. They can

- provide quality instruction that meets the needs of all students, both academically and socially
- ensure that the facility design is barrier free
- provide appropriate equipment to meet the needs of the handicapping conditions of the students
- assign an adequate number of staff to meet the needs of the handicapped and disadvantaged students
- plan for future improvements and expansion of the programs, i.e., numbers, space, equipment, staff
- monitor and review all program components on an ongoing basis
- maintain quality programs which meet the needs of both the labor market and the individual student
- promote the benefits of mainstreaming and the special vocational needs program through public relations efforts[2]

There is a real challenge in bringing special and regular students together in a vocational classroom. The administrator needs to be cognizant of the fact that to be successful in this endeavor several elements must be incorporated:

- planning
- careful classroom management
- a comfortable classroom atmosphere
- a support network

The planning responsibility for special vocational education should be a team effort, with the administrator serving as the recognized leader of the team.

The school district of residence is ultimately responsible for providing handicapped children with a free and appropriate education. It should be the school district's goal to provide quality vocational special needs programming for any handicapped or disadvantaged student who can benefit from such an educational program. Such programming may be provided through a comprehensive high school or through an area vocational school. **PHILOSOPHY AND POLICY**

Area schools, as a vocational delivery system, have grown in popularity in recent years. The area school, serving as an extension of the affiliate school districts, should offer vocational training as one of the educational alternatives provided to special needs students by each of the participating local school districts.

Policies developed for a vocational special needs program must be in harmony with both Public Law 94-142 and the policies of the participating schools. A comprehensive high school will be concerned only with its own district's policies and the federal law.

Because of the complexities of administrative coordination for a program with several school districts participating, the balance of this chapter will be concerned with the area school perspective. The content is pertinent and transferable to comprehensive systems, the only difference being one of complexity.

Students who are eligible for services under Public Law 94-142 and have an IEP should qualify for the services provided through a vocational special needs program. The IEP serves as a guide to facilitate proper placement and programming for handicapped students. Disadvantaged youths are often in need of many of the same services as handicapped youths. They frequently have difficulty with reading, communication, and other skills. Often they are below grade level in school achievement, primarily in their conceptual and reasoning abilities. The administrator should strive to establish a comprehensive program that will provide the special needs students with the following services: **PROVISION OF SERVICES**

- assistance in selecting an appropriate vocational program from available alternatives
- support assistance to ensure successful performance in a regular vocational program
- assistance in job placement at the appropriate time

A comprehensive program will include the following four components:

1. *Assessment:* Vocational assessment is the key to determining the selection of an appropriate vocational program. The occupational areas in which a student is

most likely to be successful can be identified through the evaluation of academic abilities and the assessment of work-related aptitudes and career interest.

2. *Vocational Training:* Students are mainstreamed into the appropriate vocational program with the support of a vocational special education (VOSE) coordinator. The VOSE coordinator, with the vocational instructor, develops the necessary program adaptations. It is the administrator's responsibility to support and encourage this essential communication between the coordinator and the vocational instructors and to provide the means for any and all program adaptations.

   The VOSE coordinator also provides the following services, when appropriate:
   - modification of the vocational program, teaching techniques, and instructional materials
   - individual and small group instruction for both vocational and academic classes
   - coordination with participating schools, agencies, and other in-school support programs, (e.g., nurses, math and reading coordinators, guidance counselors, and administrators)
   - assistance with job placement
   - individual counseling[3]

3. *Support Services:* To allow both the instructor and student to function successfully, support services are a top priority. The administrator should arrange for such services to be provided on a continuing basis. These services should be responsive to rapidly changing situations and conditions, both in school and on the job. Services that should be considered for inclusion by the administrator are of the following types:
   - Instructional support services

     —assistance for instructor in modifying materials or strategies
     —monitoring of programs
     —assistance in identifying and solving problems
     —direct one-on-one instructional support for student
     —assistance for instructor with setting objectives and evaluating progress
   - Counseling support services

     —initial contact with student
     —referral to counselor for regular ongoing contact
     —assistance for counselor with problem solving
     —facilitation of transition from school to employment
     —assistance with liaison to participating school district
   - Job placement services

     —assistance for instructor with job placement activities

—assistance with liaison between instructor and participating school work study coordinator

4. *Successful Employment:* Job placement is the ultimate goal for the vocational special needs student. A special needs job placement coordinator works to combine effectively all of the efforts of the vocational instructor, the VOSE coordinator, and the student to reach that goal.

The administrator's role in the total process is one of encourager, facilitator, manager, and supervisor. Keeping communication channels open cannot be emphasized enough as the key to a successful program.

PARTICIPATING SCHOOL DISTRICT RELATIONSHIPS AND RESPONSIBILITIES

An effective administrator ensures that proper procedures are in place to identify, evaluate, and enroll handicapped students. If the vocational training is to take place at an area vocational school, the administrator should foster communications between all schools involved and should facilitate the establishment of policies regarding standards for due process and of procedural safeguards for handicapped students applying for enrollment in vocational programs.

Identification of Handicapped Students

Identification activities designed to locate handicapped students are normally the responsibility of the participating school district prior to the students' enrollment in a vocational program at the area vocational school.

Evaluation of Handicapped Students

Evaluation is generally also considered the responsibility of the participating school district. Area vocational schools often will provide limited evaluation to aid in the decisionmaking process and to help a student determine the vocational choices and training alternatives. Such evaluation should be multifactored and include measurement of basic skills, general vocational aptitudes, and interests, as well as including work sampling/situational assessment. The evaluation process *must* be explained to the student's parents (or guardians), and the parents *must* give written consent for the evaluation to take place.

Enrollment and the Individualized Education Plan

Initial enrollment of a handicapped student into a vocational program should be through the regular established enrollment procedures. The prevocational evaluation report should be used to help make decisions concerning the student's vocational program or possible modifications of that program. A member of the vocational special needs program should attend the review at the school district of residence and assist in the preparation of the student's IEP. This assistance should include identification of the following:

- annual goals for the vocational program
- short-term instructional objectives
- an implementation plan, including the services to be provided by the vocational special needs staff and the area vocational school
- the appropriate evaluation procedures and the schedule for program review

The written course of study for the vocational program and the student's current level of performance as identified in the prevocational evaluation can be used as the basis for the development of the long-term goals and short-term instructional objectives. Any further modifications needed after the student's attendance in the program should be reviewed by a case conference team that might consist of the following:

- a VOSE coordinator or administrator
- a vocational counselor
- a vocational instructor
- a participating school counselor or administrator

Recommendations of the case conference team are referred to the participating school for appropriate review with the parents and school representatives.

The administrator ensures that a review of the appropriateness of the handicapped student's IEP is made at the end of each school year, or more frequently if necessary. This action will require both communication with the participating school district to establish the time and place of the review and notification of the student's parents at least fifteen days prior to the meeting.

Handicapped Student Records   The administrator is responsible for assuring the confidentiality of any personal data. Within an identified length of time after personal data are no longer needed to provide an educational program or services to the student, such data should be returned to the participating school district and that district's policies and procedures for notifying parents and destroying data should be implemented. The area vocational school should maintain the following data on the student:

- name, address, and phone number
- birthdate
- grades and classes attended
- attendance record
- grade level completed and year completed[4]

QUALITY PRO-GRAMMING   As indicated earlier, the administrator is the educational leader of the school. The administrator's expectations will determine the quality of the programs within the building. Maintaining high program quality is one of the most important duties of an administrator. Instruction must be comprehensive and up-to-date. Vocational programs must keep in tune with the needs of both the student and the labor market. Adapting education to the individual differences of each student is a vital ingredient of quality programming. Curriculum methods must be utilized that are best suited to each student. The administrator's support (both moral and financial) and encouragement are absolutely necessary.

The technological society that exists today is complex, and the needs of business and industry are constantly changing. One area of rapid change is equipment. To maintain an up-to-date vocational program, the administrator must assume responsibility for appropriately equipping the vocational laboratory and seeing that the necessary adaptations and modifications are made for the handicapped student.

Instructors must also be kept up-to-date on the changes being made in the industrial setting. The administrator should strive to make opportunities available for instructors to gain this information by periodic work sessions in industrial settings and by on-the-job training. On-the-job training is essential for instructors with handicapped students; it provides an opportunity for them to observe positions within the industry that would be appropriate for job placement of their students.

High-quality vocational programs that allow mainstreaming require assistance to be given to special needs students in several critical areas, and the administrator must be aware of these. Students with special needs should have available to them

- diagnostic assessment and career guidance
- supplementary and remedial instruction in basic skills
- vocational student organization activities, including leadership development
- supervised on-the-job learning opportunities
- counseling and assistance during the school-to-employment transition[5]

The involvement of vocational special needs students in vocational student organizations provides an important means for them to achieve a higher self-image. Poor self-image is often evident in a handicapped or disadvantaged student. This poor self-image can be more of a disadvantage to them than their actual handicapping condition. Vocational student organizations are vehicles that the administrator can utilize for confidence building. The students have an opportunity to take an active part in the student organization by being contributing members, leaders, and regional or state winners in skill competition.[6]

The vocational special needs student's success in the vocational program is the primary goal of both the administrator and the instructor. Harold Howe II, former U.S. Commissioner of Education and co-chairman of the National Board of Inquiry into Schools, has noted that "children at risk" are growing in numbers and proportion in our schools.[7] The current education reform movement has placed an emphasis on higher standards. Administrators must be aware that these higher standards may increase the risk for many low-achieving minority and disadvantaged students of being mistakenly labeled as handicapped. It is the responsibility of the administrator to provide a supportive and cooperative atmosphere within the school to ensure the attainment of higher standards while avoiding that risk. The administrator must be supportive of the program and of the instructors. Administrative responsibility includes ascertaining that the instructors have the necessary flexibility to meet the needs of the special students. The instructors should have ample time and resources to develop instructional activities that will motivate the students as they progress through the program. Instructors should be aware of any problems that might arise or any stumbling blocks that could hinder a student's chance for success. The student's interest and ability should be well matched to the vocational program.

Deterrents to the student's success must also be monitored by the administrator. Disadvantaged youths often have difficulty with reading, communication, and other conceptual and reasoning skills. They also suffer from feelings of isolation, helplessness, and dependency. Poor attendance patterns, pregnancy, substance abuse, discipline problems, apathy, failure by choice, game playing, poor reading skills, and refusal of assistance are only a few of the "alert" signs for which an administrator must watch.

Administrators need to provide various means to help special needs students to overcome their feelings of alienation from the educational system. Consideration should be given to offering

- prevocational and career exploration modules to disadvantaged and handicapped students
- an assessment system to identify each special needs student's skills and abilities
- a program to increase disadvantaged and handicapped students' math, reading, writing, and oral communication skills

JOB PLACEMENT

Appropriate job placement for students is a fundamental concern of both the administrator and the instructor. The administrator should search for effective ways to make the job placement process less difficult. It is imperative that a job placement for a disadvantaged or handicapped student provides room for growth and advancement and that the student's potential is considered and not ignored.

Having a job placement coordinator for the vocational special needs students (school size and budget permitting) should ease the process for both students and instructors. The coordinator can assist with job development, job readiness, the transition process, individual job counseling, and follow-up services. Working closely with the VOSE coordinator(s), instructors, counselors, students and parents, the job placement coordinator can greatly contribute to the achievement of job placement goals for each handicapped student.

If a job placement coordinator cannot be employed, the administrator, with the instructors, should develop appropriate guidelines for job placement. These should include guidelines for

- preparing students for interviews

    —interview role playing

—job leads or possibilities for students

—interview appointments

—stressing competencies (e.g., good attendance, skills, ability to follow directions, good team worker)

- follow-up and evaluation of students

    —interview experiences

    —adjustment to work site[8]

Also, the administrator should provide any additional information to the instructional staff that would make the placement process easier for the student.

Employability skills should be greatly stressed. It is a recognized fact that the majority of employees do not lose jobs because of a lack of skills but because of a failure to follow rules, a poor attitude, or an inability to get along with others. All students need training and practice in the employability skills of filling out job applications, writing resumes, and interviewing, as well as in basic social skills. Additional emphasis on these skills for the handicapped or disadvantaged student will enable them to feel more comfortable when job seeking.

Other Placement Concerns

A primary role of the administrator in the placement procedure is to keep instructors informed concerning federal legislation, including new changes that might occur. Instructors should be aware that current federal legislation prohibits discrimination against the handicapped in the following areas:

- recruitment
- hiring
- layoffs or firing
- job assignments
- promotion
- transfers
- training opportunities
- leave of absence
- sick leave
- rates of pay
- fringe benefits
- employer-sponsored activities[9]

COMMUNITY RESOURCES

By combining the efforts and resources of community agencies and the school, a cost-effective, comprehensive program for vocational special needs students can be established. The administrator should be familiar with the community agencies that work with the handicapped and disadvantaged and should strive to create a cooperative relationship between them and the school.

Many community agencies and organizations can provide support services to students that may not be available, or feasible, through the school. These may include financial, psychological, and medical services, as well as employment opportunities for the students. The administrator should have a working relationship with

- social agencies
- clubs
- civic groups
- churches
- professional organizations
- fraternal organizations
- the Bureau of Vocational Rehabilitation

The Handbook on Mainstreaming, sponsored by the Ohio Advisory Council for Vocational Education, states that it is also important to be familiar with the policies and procedures governing assistance from the Social Security Administration, Bureau of Employment Services, and other state and federal agencies.

The most comprehensive source of assistance and direct services to the handicapped student is the Bureau of Vocational Rehabilitation (BVR). Through the BVR, a student may receive all types of evaluation services, therapeutic services, tools, equipment, counseling, transportation, job placement, and many other additional services.[10] The BVR is an important agency and a school should consider using it as a component of the school's overall vocational special needs program.

SUMMARY

The administrator has an important, leading role in the success or failure of a vocational special needs program within a school. Where successful programs currently exist, an administrator saw the need for such a program, felt a professional commitment toward establishing or perpetuating such a program, gave support and encouragement to the instructional staff as the program was initiated and progressed, and ensured that there were sufficient resources—both financial and human—to provide and maintain a quality program.

The role of the administrator includes creating a positive attitude toward the vocational special needs program within the school, attending to the myriad details affecting the special needs program, and establishing and maintaining open communication channels between all staff members involved with handicapped students.

Eligible students under Public Law 94-142 who have IEPs should qualify for support services. A comprehensive program should be established by the administrator that includes vocational assessment, quality vocational training and support services, and successful employment.

Vocational special needs programming requires the efforts of a team—a team comprising the administrator, instructors, and support service staff. Such programming requires innovation, perseverance, care, concern, and the ability to dream. Many of the students served, or to be served, have lived through years of disappointment and failure. A unique challenge faces administrators: to provide opportunities for success as these special students participate in and complete a vocational program. It is an opportunity for administrators to be a significant influence in the life of each of these students.

Administrators can make things happen. They can be the catalyst within the school for providing an additional opportunity for success for handicapped and disadvantaged students. Perhaps, like Robert Schuller, they should have the philosophy "If it's going to be, it's up to me!"[11]

NOTES

1. Ohio Department of Education, *Leadership Practices for Directors of Vocational Education* (Columbus, Ohio: Author, 1979).

2. Gary D. Meers, *Handbook of Special Vocational Needs* (Rockville, Md.: Aspen Publishers, 1980), 284.

3. Great Oaks Joint Vocational School District, *Your Vocational Education Department and Your Occupational Development Program* (Cincinnati, Ohio: Author, 1981), 17.

4. Ibid., 5.

5. L. Allen Phelps, "Issues and Options for Special Populations," *VocEd* 59, no. 1 (January-February 1984): 34.

6. Berger Anderson et al., "Training Handicapped Youth through Teamwork," *VocEd*, 61, no. 1 (January-February 1986): 33–35.

7. Jose Cardenas and Joan McCarty First, "Children at Risk," *Educational Leadership* (September 1985): 7.

8. Ohio Advisory Council for Vocational Education, *Handbook on Mainstreaming* (Columbus, Ohio: Author, 1983), 24.

9. Ibid., 26.

10. Ibid., 21.

11. Robert H. Schuller, *Tough Times Never Last, But Tough People Do!* (Nashville, Tennessee: Thomas Nelson, Publisher, 1983), 59.

BIBLIOGRAPHY

Brolin, D., and Associates. *Mainstreaming (Handicapped) Students in Vocational Education: A Resource Guide for Vocational Educators*. Jefferson City, Mo.: Missouri State Department of Elementary and Secondary Education, 1978.

Cobb, R. Brian, and David E. Kingsbury. "The Special Needs Provision of the Perkins Act." *VocEd* 60, no. 4 (May 1985): 33.

Cardenas, Jose, and Joan McCarty First. "Children at Risk." *Educational Leadership* (Alexandria, Va., Association for Supervision and Curriculum Development) (September 1985): 4–8.

Dahl, Peter R., Judith A. Appleby, and Dewey Lipe. *Mainstreaming Guidebook for Vocational Educators*. Salt Lake City, Utah: Olympus Publishing Company, 1978.

Handbook on Mainstreaming. Columbus, Ohio: Ohio Advisory Council for Vocational Education, 1983.

Harrington, Thomas F. *Handbook for Career Planning for Special Needs Students*. Rockville, Md.: Aspen Publishers, 1982.

Hoellein, R., Jr. *Vocational Administrator's Guidebook: Mainstreaming Special Needs Students in Vocational Education*. Indiana, Pa.: Indiana University of Pennsylvania, 1979.

Least Restrictive Environment. Columbus, Ohio: Ohio Department of Education, 1982.

Meers, Gary D. *Handbook of Special Vocational Needs Education*. Rockville, Md.: Aspen Publishers, 1980.

Morse, D., C. Minugh, L. Buck, and J. Connell. *Policy and Procedures Manual: Career Planning and Vocational Programming for Handicapped Youth.* Columbus, Ohio: Ohio State University, 1981.

Phelps, L. Allen. "Issues and Options for Special Populations." *VocEd* 59, no. 1 (January-February 1984): 33.

Rules for the Education of Handicapped Children. Columbus, Ohio: Ohio Department of Education, 1982.

Special Education Administrative Policies Manual (SEAP). Reston, Va.: Council for Exceptional Children.

Weisgerber, R. *Vocational Education: Teaching the Handicapped in Regular Classes.* Reston, Va.: Council for Exceptional Children, 1978.

Appendix A

Additional Special Needs Resources

The following resources will assist the reader in securing additional information and assistance in programming for special needs students. The list is in no way meant to be inclusive; the books and films included are, however, representative of the many resources currently available.

BOOKS

Altfest, Myra. *Vocational Education for Students with Special Needs: A Teacher's Handbook.* Fort Collins, Colo.: Department of Vocational Education, Colorado State University, 1975.

Bailey, L.J., and R.W. Stadt. *Career Education: New Approaches to Human Development.* Bloomington, Ill.: McKnight Publishing Company, 1973.

Barlow, M.L. *History of Industrial Education in the United States.* Peoria, Ill.: Chas. A. Bennett Company, 1967.

Bowe, Frank. *Handicapping America.* New York: Harper & Row, 1978.

Brolin, Donn. *Vocational Preparation of Retarded Citizens.* Columbus, Ohio: Merrill, 1976.

Cook, J., and E. Earlley. *Remediating Reading Disabilities.* Rockville, Md.: Aspen Publishers, 1979.

Cruickshank, W.M., and G.O. Johnson, eds. *Education of Exceptional Children and Youth,* 2d ed. Englewood Cliffs, N.J.: Prentice-Hall, 1967.

Dahl, Peter, Judith A. Appleby, and Dewey Lipe. *Mainstreaming Guidebook for Vocational Educators: Teaching the Handicapped.* St. Lake City, Utah: Olympus Publishing Company, 1978.

Frierson, E.C., and W.B. Barbe, eds. *Educating Children with Learning Disabilities: Selected Readings.* New York: Appleton-Century-Crofts, 1967.

Gagne, R.M. *Learning and Individual Differences: A Symposium of the Learning and Research and Development Center, University of Pittsburgh.* Columbus, Ohio: Merrill, 1967.

Gardner, David C., and Sue Allen Warren. *Careers and Disabilities.* Stamford, Conn.: Greylock Publishers, 1978.

Gearheart, B.R. *Teaching the Learning Disabled: A Combined Task-Process Approach.* St. Louis, Mo.: Mosby, 1976.

Hammill, D.D., and P.L. Myers. *Methods for Learning Disorders.* New York: John Wiley & Sons, 1976.

Haring, N.G., and R.L. Schiefelbusch. *Teaching Special Children.* New York: McGraw-Hill, 1976.

Harkness, C.A. *Career Counseling.* Springfield, Ill.: Charles C Thomas, 1976.

Industry-Labor Council of the White House Conference on Handicapped Individuals. *Steps: Handicapped Workers and Today's Labor Market.* Washington, D.C.: Industry-Labor Council, 1977.

Kirk, S.A. *Educating Exceptional Children.* Boston: Houghton Mifflin, 1972.

Kolstoe, O.P. *Teaching Educable Mentally Retarded Children,* 2d ed. New York: Holt, Rinehart and Winston, 1976.

Lieberman, L. *Preventing Special Education for Those Who Don't Need It.* Weston, Mass.: GloWorm Publications, 1984.

Lieberman, L. *Special Educator's Guide to Regular Education.* Weston, Mass.: GloWorm Publications, 1986.

Meyan, E.L., G.A. Vergason, and R.J. Whelan. *Alternatives for Teaching Exceptional Children: Essays from Focus on Exceptional Children.* Denver, Colo.: Love Publishing Company, 1975.

Payne, J.S., E.A. Polloway, J.E. Smith, and R.A. Payne. *Strategies for Teaching the Mentally Retarded.* Columbus, Ohio: Merrill, 1977.

Phelps, L.A., and R. Lutz. *Career Exploration and Preparation for the Special Needs Learner.* Boston: Allyn & Bacon, 1977.

Pophan, W.J., and E.L. Baker. *Establishing Instructional Goals.* Engelwood Cliffs, N.J.: Prentice-Hall, 1970.

Pruitt, W. *Vocational Work Evaluation.* Menomonie, Wis.: Walt Pruitt Associates, 1977.

Pruitt, W. *Work Adjustment.* Menomonie, Wis.: Walt Pruitt Associates, 1983.

Rosenberg, M.B. *Diagnostic Teaching.* Seattle, Wash.: Special Child Publications, 1968.

Stellern, J., S.F. Vasa, and J. Little. *Introduction to Diagnostic-Prescriptive Teaching and Programming.* Glenn Ridge, N.J.: Exceptional Press, 1976.

Stephens, T.M. *Directive Teaching of Children with Learning and Behavior Handicaps,* 2d ed. Columbus, Ohio: Merrill, 1976.

Towenbraun, S., and J.Q. Affleck. *Teaching Mildly Handicapped Children in Regular Classes.* Columbus, Ohio: Merrill, 1976.

U.S., Department of Health, Education, and Welfare, Office of Education. *A Primer for Career Education*. Washington, D.C.: GPO.

Weisenstein, G., and R. Pelz. *Administrator's Desk Reference on Special Education*. Rockville, Md.: Aspen Publishers, 1986.

Weisgerber, Robert, ed. *Vocational Education: Teaching the Handicapped in Regular Classes*. Reston, Va.: Council for Exceptional Children, 1979.

Wircenski, Jerry. *Employability Skills for the Special Needs Learner*. Rockville, Md.: Aspen Publishers, 1982.

U.S., Department of Health, Education, and Welfare, Office of Education. *Improving Occupational Programs for the Handicapped*. Washington, D.C.: GPO.

(for information write to address listed) **FILMS**

A Different Approach
South Bay Mayor's Committee for the Employment of the Handicapped
2409 North Sepulveda
Suite 202
Manhattan Beach, CA 90266

Cipher in the Snow
BYLL Press
Brigham Young Univ.
170 W. Stadium
Provo, UT 84602

Count Me In
Stamfield House
12381 Wilshire
Suite 203
Los Angeles, CA 90025

Differences
A.C.I. Films, Inc.
Distribution Center
P.O. Box 1898
12 Jules Lane
New Brunswick, NJ 08902

Getting It Together
FMS Films
1040 North Los Palmas
Los Angeles, CA 90038

If a Boy Can't Learn
Lawren Productions
P.O. Box 1542
Burlingame, CA 94010

Not Without Sight

American Foundation for the Blind
15 West 16th Street
New York, NY 10011

The Reluctant Delinquent

Lawren Productions, Inc.
P.O. Box 666
Mendocino, CA 95460

To Live as Equals

London Films
52 Undercliff Terrace South
West Orange, NJ 07502

Glossary of Special Needs Terms

This glossary was developed with the assistance of Stanley F. Vasa, Professor of Special Education, University of Nebraska, Lincoln, Nebraska, and Judith Johnson, Assistant Superintendent of Public Instruction, Helena, Montana.

Academic Aptitude: The combination of native and acquired abilities that is needed for school work; likelihood of success in mastering academic work, as estimated from measures of the necessary abilities. (Also called *scholastic aptitude*.)

Acoustics: The science of sound, including the origin, transmission, and effects of mechanical vibrations in any medium, whether audible or not.

Acting-Out: Behavioral discharge of tension in response to a present situation or stimulus as if it were the stimulus that was originally associated with the tension. Often a chronic and habitual pattern of response to frustration and conflict.

Adaptive Behavior: That behavior that is considered appropriate for a given individual in a specific context. This term usually refers to behavior that is judged acceptable by authorities, such as teachers, and not in need of modification. These authorities are guided by developmental and societal norms in making such judgments.

Adjustment: The relation between the individual, his inner self, and his environment.

Adventitiously Deaf: Those who become deaf from accident or disease after birth or lose hearing after acquisition of language.

Advisory Committee: A group of persons, usually outside the educational profession, selected for the purpose of offering advice and counsel to the school regarding the vocational program. Members are representatives of the people who are interested in the activities with which the vocational program is concerned.

Affect: Emotional feeling tone or mood.

Affective Disorder: Disorder of mood or feeling with resulting thought and behavioral disturbances.

Agriculture/Agribusiness Education: An occupation in agriculture/agribusiness is defined as an employment opportunity requiring competencies in one or more of the areas of plant science, animal science, soil science, management, mechanization, conservation, environmental quality, human relations, and leadership development needed to satisfactorily fulfill the employment needs in one or more of the functions of producing, processing, and/or distributing products and services related thereto.

Ambidextrous: Able to use either hand effectively.

Ambivalence: Simultaneous existence of conflicting feelings or attitudes toward an object or person. May be conscious or unconscious.

Ambulation: The art of walking without assistance from others. It may include the use of crutches, canes, or other mechanical aids.

Amnesia: A disorder characterized by partial or total inability to recall or to identify past experiences; lack or loss of memory.

Amplitude: Largeness; wideness; breadth of range or extent; the distance through space a vibrating body moves; directly related to intensity of sound and sometimes used synonymously with intensity and volume.

Anomaly: A structure or function that deviates from the normal.

Anoxia: Deficient amount of oxygen in the tissues of a part of the body or in the blood stream supplying such a part.

Anxiety Reaction: A neurotic reaction with diffuse anxiety and physiological anxiety indicators, such as sweating and palpitation based on an exaggerated state of fear or tension.

Apathy: Lack of feeling or response.

Aphasia: Loss or impairment of the ability to use or understand oral language. It is usually associated with an injury or abnormality of the speech centers of the brain. Several classifications are used, including expressive and receptive, congenital, and acquired aphasia.

Aptitude: A combination of abilities and other characteristics, whether native or acquired, known or believed to be indicative of an individual's ability to learn in some particular area. Thus, *musical aptitude* would refer broadly to that combination of physical and mental characteristics, motivational factors, and conceivably other characteristics, that is conducive to acquiring proficiency in the musical field.

Articulation: The enunciation of words and sentences. Also, the coordinated movement of special needs students or clients from one human service agency to another.

Assimilation: The reception and correct interpretation of sensory impressions.

Ataxia: Condition in which there is no paralysis, but the motor activity cannot be coordinated normally. Seen as impulsive, jerky movements and tremors with disruptions in balance.

Athetoid Cerebral Palsy: Characterized by difficulty with voluntary movements, especially in controlling those movements in the desired direction (demonstrated by extra or purposeless movements).

Athetosis: A form of cerebral palsy marked by slow, recurring, weaving movement of the limbs.

Atrophy: A wasting away or diminution in the size of cell, tissue, organ, or part.

Attention Span: The length of time a person can concentrate on a single activity before losing interest.

Audiogram: A graphic summary of the measurements of hearing loss, showing the number of decibels loss at each frequency tested.

Audiologist: A professional person who is engaged in the study of the hearing function; responsible for the evaluation of persons with hearing problems and for the planning of education programs for people with hearing impairments.

Auditory Discrimination: Ability to discriminate between sounds of different frequency, intensity, and pressure-pattern components; ability to distinguish one speech sound from another.

Aura: Premonitory sensations or hallucinations that may warn of an impending epileptic seizure.

Aural: Pertaining to the ear or to the sensation of hearing. Same as *auditory*.

Autism: A childhood disorder in which the child, responding to unknown inner stimuli, is rendered noncommunicative and withdrawn. Characterized by extreme withdrawal and inability to relate to other persons.

Baseline: Beginning observations prior to intervention; level of functioning established or measured without any active intervention from the observer.

Behavior Modification: A technique of changing human behavior based on the theory of operant behavior and conditioning. Careful observation of events preceding and following the behavior in question is required. The environment is manipulated to reinforce the desired responses, thereby bringing about the desired change in behavior.

Bilateral: Pertaining to the use of both sides of the body in a simultaneous and parallel fashion.

Bilingual: Using or able to use two languages.

Blind (Legally) (see also Visually Handicapped): Having central visual acuity of 20/200 or less in the better eye after correction, or visual acuity of more than 20/200 if there is a field defect in which the widest diameter of the visual field subtends an angle distance no greater than 20°.

Body Image: The concept and awareness of one's own body as it relates to orientation, movement, and other behavior.

Brain-Injured Child: A child who before, during, or after birth has received an injury to or suffered an infection of the brain. As a result of such organic impairments, there are disturbances that prevent or impede the normal learning process.

Business and Office Education: Business and office education is designated to meet the needs of persons enrolled in secondary, postsecondary, and adult programs and has as its purpose initial preparation, the refreshing and/or upgrading of individuals' skills leading to employment and advancement in business and office occupations.

Career Education: The totality of experiences through which one learns about and prepares to engage in work as part of a way of life.

Central Nervous System (CNS): That portion of the nervous system to which the sensory impulses are delivered and from which the motor impulses pass out; in vertebrates, the spinal cord and brain.

Cerebral Dominance: The state in which one hemisphere of the brain is more involved in the mediation of various functions than the other hemisphere; a theory, expostulated largely by Orton, Delacato, and Travis, that one hemisphere is a dominant controller; right-hemisphere-dominant and ambidextrous people show mixed dominance.

Cerebral Palsy: Any one of a group of conditions in which motor control is affected because of lesions in various parts of the brain.

Channels of Communication: The sensory-motor pathways through which language is transmitted, e.g., auditory-vocal, visual-motor, and other possible combinations.

Cloze Procedure: A technique used in testing, teaching of reading comprehension, and determination of readability. Involves deletion of words from the text and leaving blank spaces.

Conceptual Disorders: Disturbances in the thinking process and in cognitive activities, or disturbances in the ability to formulate concepts.

Concrete Mode: One of the styles of cognitive functioning that describes the child's approach to problem-solving at a simple, elementary level. Also, the use of tangible objects in instruction, as opposed to purely verbal instruction.

Conductive Hearing Loss: A condition that reduces the intensity of the sound vibrations reaching the auditory nerve in the inner ear.

Congenital: Present at birth; usually a defect of either familial or exogenous origin that exists at the time of birth.

Consumer and Homemaking Education Programs: Education programs designed to help individuals and families improve home environments and the quality of personal and family life; includes instruction in food and nutrition, child development, textiles and clothing, housing, family relations, and management of resources, with emphasis on selection, use, and care of goods and services and on budgeting and other consumer responsibilities. Such programs are designed to meet the needs of persons who have entered or are preparing to enter useful employment in the home and are enrolled in secondary, postsecondary, or adult programs.

Continuum of Services: A full spectrum of services that are tailored to the individual needs of each student at any given time during the student's educational career.

Cooperative Vocational Education: A program of vocational education for persons who, through a cooperative arrangement between the school and employers, receive instruction, including required academic courses and related vocational instruction, by alternation of study in school with a job in any occupational field. The two experiences must be planned and supervised by the school and employers so that each contributes to the student's education and employability. Work periods and school attendance may be on alternate half-days, full-days, weeks, or other period of time in fulfilling the cooperative work-study (vocational education) program.

Coordinating Teacher (Teacher-Coordinator): A member of the school staff who teaches the related and technical subject matter involved in work experience programs and coordinates classroom instruction with on-the-job training.

Coordinator (Cooperative Education): A member of the school staff responsible for administering the school program and resolving all problems that arise between the school regulations and the on-the-job activities of the employed student. The coordinator acts as liaison between the school and employers in programs of cooperative education or other part-time job training.

Crisis or Helping Teacher: A teacher who provides temporary support and control to troubled students when they are unable or unwilling to cope with the demands of the regular classroom.

Cross-Modal: Including more than one sensory modality.

Curriculum: The organized content of a particular discipline with established parameters for instruction.

dB: Decibel.

Deaf: The child is impaired in processing linguistic information through hearing, with or without amplification, which adversely affects educational performance.

Deaf-Blind: Concomitant hearing and visual impairments which cause severe communication and other developmental and educational problems that cannot be accommodated in special education programs solely for deaf or blind children.

Deafened: Pertaining to adventitious loss of all usable hearing.

Decibel: A unit of hearing or audition. One decibel is approximately equal to the smallest difference in loudness that the human ear can detect.

Desensitization: A therapeutic technique, based on learning theory, in which a client is first trained in muscle relaxation and then imagines a series of increasingly anxiety-provoking situations, until the person no longer experiences anxiety while thinking about the stimuli. The learning principle involved is reciprocal inhibition, according to which two incompatible responses cannot be made simultaneously by a person.

Directionality: Awareness of the up-and-down axis (verticality) and of the relative position of one side of the body versus the other (laterality).

Disadvantaged: Persons (other than handicapped) who have academic or economic handicaps or have limited English-speaking abilities and who require special services and assistance in order for them to be able to succeed in regular vocational education programs.

- Academic handicaps are determined by (1) instructor's records that indicate that the student cannot succeed in vocational education programs without special support services or (2) information obtained from tests that indicates that the student needs help in one or more academic areas in order to be able to succeed in regular vocational education programs.

- Economic handicaps are determined on the basis of the family income-level standards established by the United States Department of Commerce and/or the United States Department of Agriculture for the issuance of free and reduced price meals, provided that the economic handicap is impairing the student's success in regular vocational education programs.

- Limited English-speaking ability. Persons who demonstrate minimal ability or lack the ability to express fundamental needs or thoughts lucidly, are unable to follow directions or react appropriately, and exhibit unnatural reticence in communicating with classmates may be considered to lack a functional command of the English language.

Distributive Education: Education that identifies a program of instruction designed to meet the needs of persons enrolled in secondary, postsecondary, and adult programs by

- introducing and orienting each individual to the field of distribution
- providing educational experiences that will enable the student to achieve career-level employment

- creating an occupational learning environment that will contribute to an increased awareness of career opportunities, advancement, and educational patterns for continued achievement

Diversified Occupations Education Program: A program that provides an opportunity for schools in small communities to make available vocational education with supervised work experience in a variety of occupations. It can be utilized in communities that are not large enough to provide part-time jobs in sufficient quantity to support an occupational experience program in a particular area (e.g., agriculture, distribution, business, home economics, health, or trades and industries). If a program related to their vocational objectives is offered in the school, diversified occupations students should be enrolled in or have completed course work in this program. If it is not offered, the students could go directly into the diversified occupational education program in their senior year.

Due Process: The process through which the child and parents or surrogate parents are informed of the pending educational placement and either agree in writing or appeal the placement based upon their rights in Public Law 94-142 Subpart E.

Dyscalculia: Loss of ability to calculate, to manipulate number symbols, or to do simple arithmetic.

Dysgraphia: Impairment in spontaneous writing, the ability to copy being intact.

Dyslexia: A disorder of children who, despite conventional classroom experience, fail to learn to read. The term is most frequently used when neurological dysfunction is suspected as a cause of the reading disability.

Echolalia: Automatic reiteration of words or phrases, usually those which have just been heard.

Educable Mentally Retarded: Education terms used to describe retarded who can profit from academic education; mildly retarded—I.Q. generally from 50 to 75.

EEG: Electroencephalograph.

Electroencephalograph: An instrument for graphically recording electrical currents developed in the cerebral cortex during brain function; often abbreviated EEG.

Electronic Mobility Devices: Devices to enhance hearing efficiency, detect obstacles, enable individuals to walk in a straight line, or reveal specific location of obstacles in the environment.

Epilepsy: A disturbance in the electrochemical activity of the discharging cells of the brain that is produced by a variety of neurological disorders. The causes are not clear. The electrochemical disturbances usually result in a seizure of some degree, i.e., in one of the following:

- petit mal: a mild seizure in which dizziness or staring into space takes place
- grand mal: a seizure in which there are severe convulsions and loss of consciousness or a coma
- Jacksonian: spasms limited mainly to one side of the body and often to one group of muscles
- psychomotor: motor acts that the patient cannot remember performing

Expressive Language: The ability to express or communicate verbal, written, or symbolic language.

Familial: Occurring in members of the same family; a familial disease.

Finger Spelling: The use of the manual alphabet to spell out words for the deaf.

Free Appropriate Public Education (FAPE): Special education and related services that are provided at public expense, including preschool, elementary school, or secondary school education.

General Education: Education that is concerned with the needs that are common to all members of society and that enable individuals to live with others, in order that they may be active in the social and democratic phases of life. Such education focuses upon knowledge, skills, and attitudes that are held useful for successful living, without reference or application to any particular vocation. General education fits people for life in general and acquaints them with the means of sustaining life.

Genetic: Pertaining to inherited factors.

Glaucoma: The intraocular pressure of the eye increases to such a level that the eye becomes damaged and sight is impaired.

Grand Mal Seizure: A type of epilepsy characterized by considerable neural discharge and usually lasting about five minutes. It begins with a severe contraction of the muscles and proceeds to rhythmic movements and tremors.

Handicap: A physical or mental impairment that substantially limits one or more major life activities.

Haptic: Pertaining to the sense of touch.

Hard-of-Hearing: A hearing impairment, either permanent or fluctuating, that adversely affects educational performance but is not included under the definition of *deaf*.

Health Occupations Education: Education designed for persons who are preparing to enter one of the health occupations and for persons who are, or have been, employed in such occupations in hospitals or institutions or establishments other than hospitals that provide patients with medical services.

Hearing Loss Degrees:

- Mild (27–40 dB): The person will have difficulty with faint or distant speech, may need favorable seating, and may benefit from speech reading, vocabulary, and/or language instruction or may need speech therapy.
- Moderate (41–55 dB): The person can understand conversational speech at a distance of three to five feet; probably will need a hearing aid, auditory training, speech reading, favorable seating, speech conversation, or speech therapy.
- Moderately severe (56–70 dB): Conversation must be loud to be understood; speech will probably be defective; may have limited vocabulary; may have trouble in classroom discussions; services used are at moderate level, but specific assistance from the resource/itinerant teachers in the language area may be needed.
- Severe (71–90 dB): The person may hear loud voices at one foot; may have difficulty with vowel sounds but not necessarily consonants; will need all services mentioned and require many techniques used with the deaf.
- Profound (91 + dB): The person may hear some sounds, but hearing is not the primary learning channel; needs all mentioned services with emphasis on speech, auditory training, and language; may be in regular class part-time or attend classes that do not require language skills.

Home Economics Related Occupations Programs: Vocational education designed to meet the needs of persons (enrolled in secondary, postsecondary, or adult programs) who have entered or who are preparing to enter gainful employment in an occupation involving knowledge and skills of home economics subjects.

Human Services: Consists of specialized assistance to individuals for the purpose of fulfilling their needs. These services are diverse in nature and deal with people-oriented projects that will realistically aid individuals who are unable to help themselves.

Hyperactivity (Hyperkinesis): A personality disorder of childhood or adolescence characterized by overactivity, restlessness, distractibility, and limited attention span.

Hypokinesis: Absence of normal amount of bodily movement and motor activity.

IEP Planning Meeting: A group meeting in which the students and teachers develop the individual education plan.

Individual Educational Program (IEP): The IEP is a written statement for a handicapped child that includes the present level of educational performance, a statement of annual goals, short-term objectives, specific and related services to be provided, projected dates for initiation of services, deliverers of the services, and the evaluation procedures to be used.

Inner Language: The process of internalizing and organizing experiences without the use of linguistic symbols.

Intelligence: A term used to describe a person's mental capacity; generally related to such things as problem-solving ability, ability to adapt to environment, or memory for learned material.

I.Q.: A numerical score used to indicate a person's relative standing on an intelligence test.

Itinerant Teacher: A teacher who travels from school to school helping children with special needs and acting as a consultant to the regular teacher.

Jacksonian Epilepsy: A form of epilepsy in which the seizure manifests no loss of awareness but involves a definite series of convulsions affecting a limited region of the body.

Lateral Dominance: The preferential use, in voluntary motor acts, of ipsilateral members of the different paired organs, such as the right ear, eye, hand, and leg, or the left ear, eye, hand, and leg.

Least Restrictive Environment: The environment in which handicapped students are educated with nonhandicapped students in public or private schools or care facilities to the maximum extent possible and appropriate to the needs of the students.

Mental Age (MA): An expression of the level of performance obtained on a standardized test. Compared with the performance of the average person of a given chronological age (CA).

Mentally Retarded: Significantly subaverage general intelligence functioning, along with deficits in adaptive behavior, that is manifested during the developmental period and adversely affects a child's educational performance.

Microcephaly: Abnormal smallness of the head.

Minimal Brain Damage: Early term for designating children with neurogenic learning and adjustment problems. The term is unsatisfactory because brain dysfunction is not necessarily due to damage. The term is often used and applied inaccurately for that reason.

Mobility Aids:

- Sighted guide: a sighted person who takes the blind person to a destination
- Dog guide: a specifically trained dog used by a blind person to get to a destination
- Cane: a white or silver cane, often with a red tip, used for getting to and from a destination
- Electronic aids: aids that are usually more successful when used as a companion with the cane (two of the more acceptable ones are the Laser Cane and the Kaye Spectacles)

Modality: An avenue of acquiring sensation; the visual, auditory, tactile, kinesthetic, olfactory, and gustatory are the most common sense modalities.

Modeling: A procedure for learning in which the individual observes a model perform some task and then imitates the performance of the model. This form of learning accounts for much verbal and motor learning in young children.

MR: Mentally retarded.

Multihandicapped: Concomitant impairments (such as mentally retarded–blind, mentally retarded–orthopedically handicapped, etc.) that cause severe educational problems that cannot be accommodated in special education programs solely for one impairment. Does not include *deaf-blind*.

Multiple Sclerosis: A disease marked by hardening in sporadic patches throughout the brain or spinal cord, or both. Among its symptoms are weakness, incoordination, strong jerking movements of the legs and arms, abnormal mental exaltation, scanning speech, and nystagmus.

Multisensory: Generally applied to training procedures that simultaneously utilize more than one sense modality.

Muscular Dystrophy: One of the more common primary diseases of the muscles. It is characterized by weakness and atrophy of the skeletal muscles with increasing disability and deformity.

Neurological Lag: Neurological or nervous system development that is slower than other physical development.

Norm: An average, common, or standard performance under specified conditions, e.g., the average achievement test score of nine-year-old children or the average birth weight of male children.

Ocular: Pertaining to the eye.

On-the-Job Training: Instruction in the performance of a job given to an employed worker by the employer during the usual working hours of the occupation. Usually the minimum or beginning wage is paid.

Ontogeny: The developmental history of the individual.

Ophthalmologist: A trained person with a medical degree who specializes in identification and treatment of eye diseases and disorders.

Optometrist: A person who studies the measuring of visual acuity and grinds lenses for glasses, does not have a medical degree, and cannot prescribe medicines or treat eye diseases or disorders.

Oral Method: Method of teaching communication of language to deaf or hard-of-hearing patients by spoken words.

Orientation: An individual's use of relevant senses to establish a position and relationship to objects in the environment.

Orthopedically Impaired: Severe orthopedic impairment that adversely affects a child's educational performance. Includes impairments caused by congenital anomaly, disease, amputation, fractures, burns, and cerebral palsy.

Other Health Impaired: Limited strength, vitality, or alertness due to chronic or acute health problems such as heart condition, tuberculosis, rheumatic fever, asthma, sickle cell anemia, epilepsy, etc., which adversely affects a child's educational performance.

Otitis Media: Inflammation of the middle ear.

Pathology: The study of the nature of disease and its resulting structural and functional changes.

Perceptual-Motor: A term describing the interaction of the various channels of perception with motor activity. The channels of perception include visual, auditory, tactual, and kinesthetic.

Perinatal: Occurring at or pertaining to time of birth.

Perseveration: The tendency for one to persist in a specific act or behavior after it is no longer appropriate.

Petit Mal Seizure: A type of epilepsy that is characterized by short lapses of consciousness; commonly begins in early childhood.

Phobia: Pathological fear of some specific stimulus or situation.

Physical Therapy: Helps overcome neuromuscular disability through exercise, massage, heat, water, light, sound, or electricity.

Postnatal: Occurring after birth.

Practical Arts Education: A type of functional education predominantly manipulative in nature that provides learning experiences in leisure-time interests, consumer knowledge, creative expression, family living, manual skills, technological development, and similar outcomes of value.

Prenatal: Existing or occurring prior to birth.

Prosthesis: The replacement of a part of the body by an artificial substitute.

Psychiatry: That branch of medicine that deals with mental disorders.

Psychomotor Seizure: A type of epilepsy characterized by automatisms that range from the unconscious continuing of normal activity to bizarre, inappropriate, or obsessive behavior.

Psychopathology: The study of the causes and nature of mental disease.

Psychosis: A severe emotional illness in which there is a departure from normal patterns of thinking, feeling, and actions. Commonly characterized by loss of contact with reality, distortion of perception, regressive behavior and attitudes, diminished control of elementary impulses and desires, and abnormal mental content, including delusions and hallucinations.

Psychosomatic Disorder: An ailment with organic symptoms attributable to emotional and other psychological causes. The disorder is aggravated by or results from continuous states of anxiety, stress, and emotional conflict.

Readability Level: An indication of the difficulty of reading material in terms of the grade level at which it might be expected to be read successfully.

Reauditorization: A term used to denote the retrieval of auditory images.

Receptive Language: Language that is spoken or written by others and received by the individual. The receptive language skills are listening and reading.

Resource Teacher: A specialist who works with children with special learning needs and acts as a consultant to other teachers, providing materials and methods to help children who are having difficulty within the regular classroom. The resource teacher may work from a centralized resource room in a school where appropriate materials are housed.

Seizures: Occur when there are excessive electrical discharges released in some nerve cells of the brain. The brain loses control over muscles, consciousness, senses, and thoughts.

Self-Care Skill: The ability to care for oneself; usually refers to basic habits of dressing, eating, and so on.

Sensory Perception: Direct awareness or acquaintance through the senses.

Seriously Emotionally Disturbed: Child exhibits one or more of the following characteristics over a long period of time and to a degree that adversely affects educational performance: inability to learn which can't be explained by intellectual, sensory, or health factors; inability to build and maintain satisfactory interpersonal relationships; inappropriate behavior or feelings under normal circumstances; pervasive mood of unhappiness or depression, or a tendency to develop physical symptoms or fears associated with personal or school problems. Includes children who are schizophrenic or autistic. Not the socially maladjusted unless it is determined they are seriously emotionally disturbed.

Sheltered Workshop: A facility (usually in the community) that provides occupational training or protective employment of handicapped individuals.

Sign Language: A system of communication among the deaf through conventional hand or body movements that represent ideas, objects, and action; distinguished from finger spelling.

Special Class in a Regular School: Classes for students who receive their academic instruction from a special education teacher but may attend schoolwide activities, such as assemblies and concerts, or nonacademic classes, such as physical education or industrial arts, with their peers.

Special Day Schools: Schools designed for students who have a serious handicap or are multihandicapped and need comprehensive special education services for their entire school day.

Special Education: A subsystem of the total educational system responsible for the joint provision of specialized or adapted programs and services (or for assisting others to provide such services) for exceptional children and youths.

Special Educator: One who has had special training or preparation for teaching the handicapped; may also work cooperatively with the regular classroom teacher by sharing unique skills and competencies.

Specific Learning Disabilities: Disorder in one or more of the basic psychological processes involved in understanding or using language, spoken or written. Problems in listening, thinking, speaking, reading, writing, spelling, or minimal brain dysfunction, dyslexia, and developmental aphasia. Does not include problems which are a result of visual, hearing, or motor handicaps of mental retardation or of cultural, environmental, or economic disadvantage.

Speech Impaired: Communication disorder such as stuttering, impaired articulation, language impairment, or voice impairment that adversely affects educational performance.

State Plan: An agreement between a state board for vocational education and the U.S. Office of Education describing the vocational education program developed by the state to meet its own purposes and conditions and the conditions under which the state will use federal vocational education funds (such conditions must conform to the federal acts and the official policies of the U.S. Office of Education before programs may be reimbursed from federal funds).

Task Analysis: The technique of carefully examining a particular task to discover the elements it comprises and the processes required to perform it.

Technical Education: Shall be designed to train persons for employment as highly skilled technicians in recognized technical occupations requiring scientific knowledge. Technical education should be conducted primarily on the post–high school or adult level.

Trade and Industrial Education: Education to provide students with an understanding and the technical knowledge of our industrial society and to develop the necessary skills for employment in the skilled and semiskilled trades, crafts, or occupations that function directly in the designing, producing, processing, assembling, maintaining, servicing, or repairing of any manufactured product. Training in trade and industrial education enables young men and women to prepare for initial employment in trade, industrial, and technical operations. The basic principle of such education is learning by doing. The needs of the individual worker are the foundations upon which all instructional activity is based. Instructional objectives are tied to the skill or trade being pursued as a career.

Transition: A concept of developing a coordinated plan whereby handicapped students can move from school to adult community life. The transition plan involves support service personnel, parents, school officials, and the handicapped individuals in ongoing decisionmaking. All transition efforts focus on individual independence, integration, and productivity.

Trauma: Any experience that inflicts serious damage to the organism; may refer to psychological as well as physiological insult.

Vakt: A multisensory teaching method involving visual, auditory, kinesthetic, and tactile sense modalities, e.g., the Fernald ''hand-kinesthetic'' method.

Visually Handicapped: Visual impairment that adversely affects educational performance, even with correction. Both partially sighted and blind.

Vocational Education: Vocational or technical training or retraining that is given in schools or classes (including field or laboratory work and remedial or related academic and technical instruction incident thereto) under public supervision and control or under contract with a state board or local education agency. The training or retraining is conducted as part of a program designed to prepare individuals for gainful employment as semiskilled or skilled workers or technicians or subprofessionals in recognized occupations in advanced technical education programs, but excluding any program to prepare individuals for employment in occupations generally considered professional or which require a baccalaureate or higher degree.

Vocational Educator: Persons who have had training or occupational experience in their chosen area of specialization.

Vocational School: A school that is organized separately under a principal or director for the purpose of offering training in one or more skilled or semiskilled trades or occupations. It is designed to meet the needs of high school students preparing for employment and to provide upgrading or extension courses for those who are employed.

Vocational Special Needs Education: Vocational education for disadvantaged or handicapped persons supported with funds under the Vocational Education Act of 1976 (Public Law 94-482) to include special educational programs and services designed to enable disadvantaged or handicapped persons to achieve vocational education objectives that would otherwise be beyond their reach as a result of their handicapping condition. These programs and services may take the form of modification of regular programs or be vocational special education programs designed only for disadvantaged or handicapped persons. Examples of such special educational programs and services include the following: special remedial instruction; guidance, counseling and testing services; employability skills training; communications skills training; special transportation facilities and services; special educational equipment, services, and devices; and reader and interpreter services. Such education includes working with those individuals in need of vocational training who cannot succeed in a regular vocational program due to a handicapping condition or the effects of disadvantagement.

Vocational Subject: Any school subject designed to develop specific skills, knowledge, and information to enable the learner to prepare for or to be more efficient in a chosen trade or occupation.

Work-Study Program: A program designed to provide part-time employment for youths who need the earnings from such employment to commence or continue a vocational education program.

Index

A

Academic disadvantage, 54, 57
Administrator's role in vocational education
  community agencies' assistance, 363–364
  duties, 355–357
  establishment of policies, 359–362
  services provided, 357–359
Adult basic education, 37
Adult work experience programs, 37
Adventitiously deaf, 88
Advocacy training, 146
Agriculture Education (AgEd), 166
Aid to Dependent Children (ADC), 207
American Academy for Cerebral Palsy, 92
American Association for Vocational
  Instructional Materials (AAVIM), 116
American Association on Mental Deficiency,
  99
American National Standards Institute, 9
American Vocational Association (AVA), 19,
  21, 122–123
Amputation, 93
Appleby, J., 213
Apprenticeship, 10–12, 268–270
Area Redevelopment Act of 1961 (P.L. 87-27),
  36, 44
Area Vocational-Technical Institutes (AVTIs),
  336
Articulatory defects, 107
Assistive devices, 120
Asthma, 95

B

Bardon-LaFollette Act of 1943 (P.L. 113), 32
Barlow, Melvin L., 269–270
Basile, Joseph, 116
Batsche, Katherine, 149
Blank, William, 125
Blind
  educational and vocational needs of the,
  91–92
Blindness, 90
  See also Visually handicapped
Bloom, Benjamin, 50
Bottoms, G., 333, 335
Brantley, John C., 73
Brolin, Donn E., 259–260, 263, 265
Brown, James M., 136
Breulhide, Kenneth L., 146
Bucchioni, Eugene, 48
Bureau of Vocational Rehabilitation (BVR),
  364
Business and Office Education (BOE), 166

C

Career development, 188–189, 191–193
Career education for the special needs student
  curriculum, 264–271
  definition, 18–20, 259–260
  development models, 263–264
  economic benefit, 271–272
  theories, 260–263

Career-vocational preparation program, 201–204
Carl D. Perkins Vocational Act of 1984 (P.L. 98-524), 41, 44, 56–57, 60–61, 63, 158–159, 204
  affect on postsecondary education, 331, 333
  aspects of curriculum selection, 139–140
  mandates of, 116–122, 124, 134–135
  role in vocational assessment, 213–220, 230–233, 239, 242
Case management, 320–321
Cataracts, 90
Causal factor, 88
Center for Vocational Education, 116
Cerebral palsy, 92, 109
CETA, 14, 37–38, 44, 55
CETA Reauthorization Act of 1978 (P.L. 95-524), 38, 41
Circular method of curriculum. *See* Cyclical method of curriculum
C.T.T.E. learning styles instruments, 224–225
Civil Rights Act of 1964, 17
Civil rights of the handicapped, 42
Civilian Conservation Corps, 35
Clark, Gary, 263–264
Classroom instruction, 184, 188–189, 191, 193, 195–198
Cleft palate speech, 109
Cluster method of curriculum, 142
Cobb, R.B., 230
Commissioner of the Rehabilitation Services Administration, 34
Committee on Vocational Assessment of NAVESNP, 238
Community-based instruction, 129
Community service pilot programs, 34
Competency-based career curriculum model, 265
Competency-based education, 140
Competency-based instruction, 141, 144
Comprehensive Employment and Training Act (P.L. 93-203). *See* CETA
Conaway, Charlotte, 131
Conductive, 88
Congenital anomaly, 93
Congenitally deaf, 88
Consistency of instruction, 151
Conte, J.M., 49
Contractures, 93
Cooperative vocational education
  See also Vocational education
  barriers, 208–210
  characteristics and functions of, 168–169
  classroom instruction, 184–189, 191–196

coordination of instructional management, 196–197
  placement process, 177–181
  role of teacher, 169–172
  training process, 181–184
  training site, 172–177
  transition, 197–198
  types of, 165–168
Cooperative work-experience model, 271
Copa, P., 333, 335
Cordasco, Francesco, 48
Council for Exceptional Children (CEC), 122–123, 264–265
Counseling services, 338
Countercyclical Public Service Employment Programs, 38
Criminal offenders, 59–60
Criterion-referenced instruments, 223, 226–227
Curriculum development
  course syllabus, 126
  evaluation methods, 127, 134–135
  grading systems, 128
  training, 125
  transition efforts by personnel, 130–133
Curriculum mapping, 142
Curriculum modification
  content, 140–146
  framework of, 138–140
  target groups, 147–150
  tools and equipment, 146–147
Curriculum softening, 139, 141
Cyclical method of curriculum, 143–144

D

Dahl, T., 213
Deaf
  definition, 83, 87
  educational provisions for, 88–89
  training and employment of, 89–90
Deaf-blind, 83
Decade of implementation, 14
Deinstitutionalization, 14
Department of Education Organization Act of 1979 (P.L. 96-88), 41
Deutsch, Martin, 51
Diabetes, 97–98
Diabetic retinopathy, 90
Direct instruction, 152–153, 193–196
Disadvantaged
  characteristics of, 47–48
  classification of, 57–61
  definition of, 7–9
  environmental characteristics, 49–50

identification and assessment of, 62–73
learning traits, 48–49
needs of, 50–52
vocational education of the, 53–56
Disadvantaged Learner Referral Forms, 65–66
Disadvantaged students
criteria to identify, 216–217
Displaced homemakers, 60–61
Distributive and Marketing Education (DME), 166
Donaldson, Joy, 141
Dunham, Daniel, B., 73

E

Eastern Nebraska Community Office of
Retardation (ENCOR), 271
Economic Opportunity Act of 1964
(P.L. 88-452), 36–37, 53
Economically disadvantaged, 54, 57–58
Educatable, 100
Education for All Handicapped Children Act of
1975 (P.L. 94-142), 3–4, 9, 16, 20–21, 72,
81–82, 87, 92, 102, 104–105, 117, 122,
157–159, 214–215, 234, 331, 345–346,
356–357
Education for All Handicapped Amendments of
1977 (P.L. 95-49), 43
Education for All Handicapped Amendments of
1978 (P.L. 95-561), 43
Education for All Handicapped Amendments of
1980 (P.L. 96-341), 43
Education for All Handicapped Amendments of
1983 (P.L. 98-199), 43, 124, 217
Educational Amendments of 1972
(P.L. 92-318), 40
Eisenberg, Leon, 48, 50–51
Eisenson, J., 107
Elementary and Secondary Education Act of
1965, 42
Employment Act of 1946 (P.L. 304), 35
Englemann, Siegfried, 152
English, Fenwick, 142
English as a second language (ESL), 147
EPIC. *See* Experience programs in the
community
Epilepsy, 95–96
Experience programs in the community, 26
Experience-based career education (EBCE), 26,
266–267

F

Failure
stages of, 8–9

Fair, George W., 115
Family Educational Rights and Privacy Act,
346
Fantini, Mario D., 47, 50
Farber, B., 338
Farren, Carla, 267–268
Feck, Vincent, 50
Federal Board for Vocational Education, 13, 31
Finch, Curtis, 20
Formal assessment, 228–230
Formal instruments, 229
Functional curriculum, 128–129

G

General education, 18
Generalizable mathematics skills assessment,
289–298
Generalizable skills
assessment of, 280–288
curriculum, 276–279
evaluation of, 307–311
implementation of, 279–280
instructional strategies, 305–307
planning for, 288–292
resource materials for teaching, 302–305
support services, 298, 302
Gold, Marc W., 140, 148
Grand mal, 95–96
Gray, Janet D., 267–268
Grimes, G.H., 49
Guaranteed jobs, 341
Guliano, Daniel, F., 128

H

Hailstones, T.J., 36
Hallahan, D.P., 85
Halpern, Andres, 316, 345
Halpern Transition Model, 316
"Handbook on Mainstreaming," 364
Handicapped
conditions, 85–90
definition, 7, 82
identification, 82–85
physical and social barriers, 9–10
public agency requirements, 16
transition from school to life, 17
Hands-on training, 26
Hard of hearing, 83, 87
Harless, J., 193
Heart disease, 94
Hendricks-McCracken, K.A., 176
Hill, P., 213

Hitching, B., 338, 341
Hitching, S., 338–341
Holland's Vocational Choice Theory, 261
Home Economics Education (HE), 166
HOT. *See* Hands-on training
Howe, Harold, 361
Hoyt, Kenneth, B., 259–260
Human service agencies
    role in the transition process, 322–323
Hyde, Thomas E., 65–67

I

IDVEP. *See* Individually designed vocational
    education programs
IEP. *See* Individual educational plan
IEP/IVEP, 247–251
Independent living center (ILC), 207
Individual educational plan (IEP), 16–17,
    72–76, 126, 129–130, 158, 204, 210, 266,
    288, 346, 356–357
Individual transition plans (ITPs), 130, 210
Individual vocational education program
    (IVEP), 126, 129, 244, 247, 288
Individualized work rehabilitation plan (IWRP),
    206
Individually designed vocational education
    programs (IDVEP), 168
Industrial training guidelines, 193–196
Informal assessment, 220–227
Informal instruments, 227
Inner-city disadvantaged, 50
Instruction modification
    framework, 150–152
    paradigms, 155–157
    principles, 152–155
    program guidelines, 157–158
    role of administrator, 158–160
Instructional management schedule, 196–197
Integrated school services, 129
Intensive Technical English Language program,
    (ITEL), 147
Interactive teaching, 151–152
Interagency cooperation, 129
Interorganizational framework dimensions,
    208–210
Iowa Career Development Model, 263
Isaacson, Lee E., 260–261
IVEP. *See* Individual vocational education plan

J

Jacksonian, 96
Jensen, Arthur, R., 51
Job corps, 37

Job placement, 362–363
Job placement coordinator, 359
Job Training Partnership Act (P.L. 97-300),
    38, 44, 55, 58, 118, 139, 208, 214, 217, 340
Johnson, Samuel, 29
Jones, Barbara, 116
Jones, Reginald L., 149–150
Joyce, Bruce, 138
JTPA. *See* Job Training Partnership Act

K

Kaufman, J.M., 87
Kay, Evelyn R., 53–54
Kaye, Beverly, 267–268
Kemp, Barbara H., 53–54
Keogh, Barbara K., 149–150
Krajewski, Robert J., 138
Kokaska, Charles, 259–260, 263

L

Labor market growth, 6–7
Land Grant Act of 1862, 30
Lansing Community College, 147
Language impairment, 109
Learner analysis profile, 68–71
Learner educational plan, 77
Learning centers, 340
Learning disabled (LP), 105–107
Least restrictive environment, 16
Legislation
    See also entries for specific legislation
    effect on social attitudes, 35–39
    foundation of federal, 30
    vocational education, 29–30, 39–43
    vocational rehabilitation, 31–35
LEP. *See* Limited English Proficiency
Likert scale, 224
Limited English Proficiency (LEP), 57, 59, 147
Link, H.J., 91
Lipe, D., 213
Local educational agency (LEA)
    guidelines to obtain funds from state
    agencies, 132
Longitudinal educational assistance, 25–26
Lutz, Ronald J., 63

M

Macmillan, Donald L., 149–150
Macular degeneration, 90
Madden, John E., 50

Mainstreaming, 14–15
Manpower Development and Training Act of
    1962 (P.L. 87-415), 36–37, 44
Mastriana, F.V., 36
McNutt, G., 94
MDTA. *See* Manpower Development and
    Training Act
MDTA Amendments of 1963 (P.L. 88-214), 36
MDTA Amendments of 1966 (P.L. 88-792), 36
Mental retardation
    classification of, 100
    definition of, 83, 98–99
    education for the, 101–102
    identification criteria, 99
Mentor model, 267–268
Migrant children
    education of, 37
Mildly retarded, 100
Miller, Herman P., 50
Minnesota Department of Education, 169, 181
Moderately retarded, 100
Morril Act. *See* Land Grant of 1862
Multihandicapped, 83

N

"Nation at Risk," 137
National Association for Retarded Citizens
    (NARC), 176
National Association of Vocational Education
    Special Needs Personnel (NAVESNP),
    122–123, 219
National Census of the Deaf Population
    (NCDP), 88–89
National Center for Educational Statistics
    (NCES), 333
National Commission on Secondary Vocational
    Education, 203–204
National Council on the Handicapped, 34
National Institute of Handicapped Research, 34
National Rehabilitation Association (NRA),
    123
National Society for the Prevention of
    Blindness, 90
Neighborhood Youth Corps, 37
Nietupski, John, 318

O

Occupational Data Analysis System (ODAS),
    126–127
Office of Special Education and Rehabilitation
    Services (OSERS), 35, 41, 128–129, 315
Office of Vocational and Adult Education, 41

Ogilvie, M., 107
Ohio Enabling Act, 30
Ordinance of 1785, 30
Orthopedically handicapped, 92–98
Orthopedically impaired, 83
OSERS model, 316–317
Outcome dimension, 209

P

Paradigms, 155–157
Parental involvement, 129
Parents' role in vocational assessment, 238,
    242
Parents' role in vocational education
    assumptions about, 346–347
    communication modes, 348–353
    goals, 347–348
    program evaluation, 353–354
Peterson, Mike, 213, 218
Petit mal, 96
Pettigrew, Thomas F., 51
Phelps, L. Allen, 63, 67, 73
Placement process, 176–181
Positive learning environment, 119–120
Postsecondary vocational education
    definition, 332–333
    issues, 334–338
    personnel, 341–342
    support services, 338–341
    trends in, 333
Practical arts, 21–22, 267
Prep-human services, 142
Prep-tech, 142
Private Industry Council, 39, 44, 55
Process dimension, 209
Profoundly retarded, 100
Program development, 115–116
Psychomotor, 96
Public education objectives, 18
Public Law 58-171, 13
Public Law 64-347. *See* Smith Hughes Act
Public Law 87-27. *See* Area Redevelopment
    Act
Public Law 87-415. *See* Manpower and
    Development Training Act
Public Law 88-210. *See* Vocational Education
    Act of 1963
Public Law 88-214. *See* MDTA Amendments
Public Law 88-452. *See* Economic Opportunity
    Act
Public Law 88-792. *See* MDTA Amendments
Public Law 90-99, 32
Public Law 90-576. *See* Vocational Educational
    Act of 1968

Public Law 91-112. *See* Vocational Rehabilitation Act of 1973

Public Law 91-230, 14

Public Law 92-318. *See* Educational Amendment of 1972

Public Law 92-323. *See* Title XIX

Public Law 93-103, 38

Public Law 93-112. *See* Rehabilitation Act

Public Law 93-203. *See* CETA

Public Law 93-516. *See* Rehabilitation Act Amendments of 1974

Public Law 94-124, 14

Public Law 94-142. *See* Education for All Handicapped Children Act of 1975

Public Law 94-482. *See* Vocational Education Amendments of 1976

Public Law 95-49. *See* Education of the Handicapped Amendments of 1977

Public Law 95-93. *See* YEDPA

Public Law 95-524. *See* CETA Reauthorization Act of 1978

Public Law 95-561. *See* Education for All Handicapped Amendments of 1978

Public Law 95-602. *See* Rehabilitation, Comprehensive Services, and Development Disabilities Amendments of 1978

Public Law 96-88. *See* Department of Education Organization Act of 1979

Public Law 96-341. *See* Education for the Handicapped Amendments of 1980

Public Law 97-14. *See* Youth Employment Demonstration Program

Public Law 97-300. *See* Job Training Partnership Act

Public Law 98-199. *See* Education for All Handicapped Amendments of 1983

Public Law 98-221. *See* Rehabilitation Amendments of 1984

Public Law 98-524. *See* Carl D. Perkins Vocational Education Act of 1984

Public Law 113, 32

Public Law 179. *See* Smith-Sears Act

Public Law 236. *See* Vocational Rehabilitation Act of 1920

Public Law 304. *See* Employment Act of 1946

Public Law 565. *See* Vocational Rehabilitation Act of 1954

Public Works Administration, 35

Q

Quadraplegic, 93

R

Reciprocal curriculum infusion, 139–140

Referral identification process, 63

Rehabilitation Act (P.L. 93-112), 9, 14, 33, 81, 91, 118

Rehabilitation Act Amendments of 1974 (P.L. 93-516), 33

Rehabilitation Amendments of 1984 (P.L. 98-221), 34

Rehabilitation, Comprehensive Services and Development Disabilities Amendments of 1978 (P.L. 95-602), 34

Rehabilitation technology, 120

Research and Policy Committee of the Committee for Economic Development, 53

Retarded language development, 109

Retinitis pigmenfosa, 90

Retish, P., 338, 341

Ridini, Leonard M., 50

Riessman, Frank, 47

Rioux, J.W., 36

Rivers, L.H., 32

Roberts, C.L., 213

Roe's circular model, 260–261

Rogers, Will, 27

S

Sanger, G., 338

Sarkees, Michelle D., 117, 120, 127, 210

Saunders, Frances G., 53–54

School administrator role of, 158-160

School-based career education model, 263

Scott, John L., 117, 120, 127, 210

Scott, Keith G., 140, 148, 210

Secondary vocational education, 331–332

Seizures, 95–96

Seligman, Ben, 48

Senate Committee on Labor and Public Welfare, 61

Sensory-neural, 88

Seriously emotionally disturbed, 83, 102–104

Severely retarded, 100

Sheltered workshops, 270–271

Sheppard, N. Alan, 20

Signals, 154

Single parents, 60

Situational dimension, 209

Smith-Fess Act. *See* Vocational Rehabilitation Act

Smith-Hughes Act of 1917 (P.L. 64-347), 13, 30–31, 39
Smith-Sears Act of 1918 (P.L. 179), 31, 43
Snellen chart, 90
Special education. *See also* Vocational education, 20–21
Special education cascade model, 302, 305
Special needs students
  educational process, 27
  employment opportunities, 7
  society's expectations, 26
Special vocational needs, 29
Special wage certificates, 176
Specific learning disabilities, 84
Speech defects due to impaired hearing, 110
Speech impaired, 84, 107–110
Spina bifida, 93
Spinal cord injuries, 93
Steckelberg, A.L., 354
Strickland, Bonnie, 73
Strom, Robert D., 49
Structural dimension, 209
Student profile, 3–4
Student self-rating assessments, 280–285
Stufflebeam, D.L., 307
Stuttering, 107
Super, Donald, 261–262
Support services
  definition, 358
  from the community, 206–207
  postsecondary level, 207–208
  secondary level, 204–206
Supported work model, 271–272
Swanson, R., 193

T

Task analysis, 140–141
Task Force Report on Career Education, 19
Taylor, R., 332
Teacher attitudes toward handicap students, 15
Teacher-coordinator, 169–172
Teacher rating assessment, 285–288
Teachers
  demands of, 6
  guidance for vocational education, 224–227
  role in generalizable skills, 306–307
  role in vocational education, 251
Teaching approach, 4
Teaching with examples, 150, 151
Thabet, Nancy, 116
Three fundamental domains, 230–231

Three Stage Vocational Model for Handicapped Youth, 316
Title XIX, 321
Totten, Jan, 62
Trade and Industrial Education (T&I), 166
Trainable, 100
Training plans for business and industry, 195–196
Training process for cooperative work, 181–184
Training site selection, 172–177
Transition from school to work
  community responsibility, 320–321
  human service agency support, 322–323
  interaction between school and government agencies, 324–326
  models of, 316–318
  of the handicapped, 17, 197–198
  organizational support, 318–319
  school's responsibility, 319–320
Turnbull, Ann P., 73

U

Urban and Rural Community Action Programs, 37

V

Vasa, S.F., 354
Verbal cues, 154
Visually handicapped. *See also* Blindness
  definition, 84, 90
  education, 91–92
Vocal defects, 107
Vocational achievement, 231
Vocational aptitude, 230–231
Vocational assessment
  See also Vocational education
  benefits, 218–219
  decision making model, 238–240
  definition, 213–214, 357–358
  identification and referral, 241–243
  legislation, 214–217
  placement review, 243–252
  planning, 251–253
  purpose, 217–218
  types of, 219–232
Vocational assessment profile information, 221–222
Vocational education
  See also Cooperative vocational education

definition, 18, 22
goals for graduates, 165
personnel, 233–238
stigma of, 23
task of educators, 62–73
teachers, 21, 56
types of institutes offering, 334
Vocational Education Act of 1963
    (P.L. 88-210), 29, 34, 39, 42, 53
Vocational Education Act of 1968
    (P.L. 90-576), 40, 44
Vocational Education Amendments of 1968,
    40, 53
Vocational Education Amendments of 1974, 54
Vocational Education Amendments of 1976
    (P.L. 94-482), 8, 14, 40, 81, 333, 345
Vocational Evaluation and Work Adjustment
    Association (VEWAA), 123
Vocational interest, 230
Vocational occupations, 6–7
Vocational programs
    competencies of educators, 120–123
    curriculum development, 125–128
    evaluation of, 133–135
    journals associated with, 123–124
    long-range plans, 116
    philosophical assumptions, 119
    professional development, 120–125
    professional involvement, 118
    transition models, 128–133
Vocational rehabilitation, 251, 339–340
Vocational Rehabilitation Act of 1920
    (P.L. 236), 31
Vocational Rehabilitation Act of 1954
    (P.L. 565), 32
Vocational Rehabilitation Act of 1973
    (P.L. 91-112), 9, 14, 33–34, 214, 217
Vocational Rehabilitation Amendments
    (P.L. 90-99), 32–33
Vocational school psychologist, 205
Vocational special education (VOSE), 358, 362
Vocational special needs programs, 24–25

Vocational-Technical Education Consortium of
    States (V-Tecs), 127
Vocational training
    attitudes, 10
    definition, 358
    historical perspectives, 10–17

W

Walker, Robert W., 49
Walsh, John, 62
Wehman, Paul, 136, 316
Weil, Marsha, 138
Weinstein, Gerald, 47, 50
West, Lynda L., 132
White House Conference on Handicapped
    Individuals, 34
Whole boy philosophy, 13
Will, Madeleine, 129, 315
Wircenski, Jerry L., 63, 65, 67
Work Experience and Career Exploration
    Program (WECEP), 167
Work Experience Disadvantaged Programs
    (WED), 167
Work Experience Handicapped Programs
    (WEH), 167–168
Work activity programs, 270
Work study programs, 37, 339

Y

YEDPA, 14, 38
Young Adult Conservation Corps, 38
Youth Employment Demonstration Program
    (P.L. 97-14), 38
Youth Employment Demonstration Projects
    (P.L. 95-93). *See* YEDPA
Ysseldyke, J.C., 219

Z

Zahorik, John A., 151